Smart Development in Smart Communities

T0362270

The concept of smart cities has become one of the most significant new lines of thinking to emerge in the social sciences in recent years, both from the research and policy angles. To date, the focus in smart specialization has been on what regions as a whole can do to bring about innovation, but it hasn't necessarily addressed the role cities play within the field. This book aims to address that gap, drawing together a team of leading contributors, to illustrate this process with particular focus on cities.

Smart Development in Smart Communities discusses the cross-fertilization between smart specialization and cities in fostering smart development and its interactions with the macro-, micro- and meso-economic framework, from both a theoretical and applied perspective. Specific topics covered by the book include: human capital formation and utilization; centralized/decentralized industrial policies; innovation policies; collective learning; and the role of public utilities in sustaining smart development processes.

This book tackles some of the most important questions that must be faced when investigating how structural change and innovation processes are shaping local and global economic development. It will be of interest to academics and researchers in the area of Development Economics, Urban Studies and Public Management.

Gilberto Antonelli is Full Professor of Economics at the University of Bologna, Italy.

Giuseppe Cappiello is Assistant Professor of Management at the University of Bologna, Italy.

Routledge Advances in Regional Economics, Science and Policy

Smart Development in Smart Communities

Edited by Gilberto Antonelli
and Giuseppe Cappiello

Routledge
Taylor & Francis Group
LONDON AND NEW YORK

First published 2017
by Routledge

2 Park Square, Milton Park, Abingdon, Oxfordshire OX14 4RN
52 Vanderbilt Avenue, New York, NY 10017

Routledge is an imprint of the Taylor & Francis Group, an informa business

First issued in paperback 2019

British Library Cataloguing in Publication Data
A catalogue record for this book is available from the British Library

Library of Congress Cataloging-in-Publication Data
A catalog record for this book has been requested

ISBN: 978-1-138-18904-1 (hbk)
ISBN: 978-0-367-87460-5 (pbk)

Typeset in Times New Roman
by Apex CoVantage, LLC

Contents

Figures

Tables

Contributors

Gilberto Antonelli is Full Professor of Economics at the University of Bologna, Italy.

Marco Baccan works at Finlombarda SpA, financial company of Lombardy Region. Since 2013, he has been supporting the Directorate General of University, Research and Open Innovation in the development and implementation of the Smart Specialization Strategy (S3) of Lombardy Region. He got a degree in engineering from the Politecnico di Milano and after university attended a specialization course in innovation and technology transfer at the MIP – Business School of Politecnico di Milano. Recently, he attended a course at the European Foundation for Cluster Excellence (EFCE) in Cluster Management. He started his career as a researcher at Politecnico Innovazione – a consortium of Politecnico di Milano focused on technology transfer from university to small and medium enterprise (SME). He developed expertise in regional competitiveness development, SME growth, innovative SMEs and emerging industries, cluster development policy, technology transfer and intellectual property rights.

Silvano Bertini is Head of the Office for Economic Development, Industrial Research and Technological Innovation for the Emilia-Romagna Region. He graduated in Political Science in Bologna and attended a master in business and economic systems management in Ancona. He started his career as a researcher in industrial policy in Nomisma, a private company for economic research and consultancy. He developed expertise in regional economic development, small and medium enterprise (SME) growth and cluster development policy through projects in Italy and abroad. Since 1999, he has been working in a managing role in the Emilia-Romagna Region, and he is involved in competitiveness strategy and program elaboration, implementation of programs and projects concerning R&D, technology transfer and innovation, high tech start-ups, regional development, interregional co-operation and managing European Funds. He is also a Lecturer of Economics of Innovation at the University of Bologna.

Patrizio Bianchi is Full Professor of Applied Economics at the University of Ferrara and Regional Minister of Emilia-Romagna Region for the coordination of European development policies, Education, Training, University, Research and

Employment. He holds a Bachelor's in Political Science at the University of Bologna and a specialization at the London School of Economics and Political Science. He was the Rector of the University of Ferrara till 2010. He is an expert in economics and industrial policies. He has served both Italian and international institutions and the governments of several countries. He published more than 30 books and 200 scientific articles. For his academic activity, he has been inducted into the Order of Merit of the Italian Republic with the rank of Commendatore.

Alessandro Camilleri is Manager of Development, Training and Organisation at the Hera Group. He holds a degree in economics and business studies and a Master's in management accounting and corporate finance from the Faculty of Economics and Business Studies of Turin. He began his career as a junior controller at Martini & Rossi in 2000, working in the commercial area. In 2001, he joined the Fiat Group, taking part in the Fiat Grade project, a managerial development programme aimed at training and fast-tracking managers with very good inter-sectorial and international skills. In January 2008, he joined the Group Personnel and Organisation Department of Hera S.p.A., first of all as Organisation Manager and later as Head of Development and Organisation. In December 2010, he was appointed Head of Development, Training and Organisation. He is also a member of the Confindustria-Assoknowledge Scientific Committee and a lecturer in leadership, corporate organization and change management for various postgraduate Master's programmes.

Giancarlo Campri has been the Director of Personnel and Organisation at the Hera Group since 2002. He holds a degree in Political Science and a C.U.O.A. Master's earned in 1985. He has held an executive position since 1992. His outstanding experience in organizational development and personnel management has been garnered since 1985 through roles of increasing managerial responsibility at Praxi S.p.A., Magneti Marelli S.p.A., Compagnie De Saint Gobain, Ocean S.p.A. and at the Piaggio Group. He was also Director of Human Resources and Organisation at Seabo S.p.A. in Bologna while concurrently holding the post of Senior Executive Vice President of IT Systems and Head of the ERP project. Currently he is a member of di FederUtility's Federal Trade Commission, the C.C.N.L. gas-water-power Negotiation Delegation and the C.C.N.L. Federambiente Environmental Work Group. He was a member of the board of directors at Antoniana S.r.l (2006/2007), Famula On Line S.p.A. (2001/2003) and Fleet Service S.r.l. (2001/2003), as well as a member of the Province of La Spezia executive self-evaluation team (2001/2007).

Alina Candu works at Finlombarda SpA, financial company of Lombardy Region. Since 2013 she has been supporting the Directorate General of University, Research and Open Innovation in the development and implementation of the Smart Specialization Strategy (S3) of Lombardy Region. In the Republic of Moldova, she got two degrees in journalism and the science of communication and in law. In Italy, she got a degree in law at the LIUC University. She started her career as manager of Isimbardi Ltd, placed in Moldova, whose core activity was to support the foreign entrepreneurs launch start-ups in Moldova or to find new suppliers or clients (e.g. Vivienne Westwood, Benetton). Moving to Lombardy, she focused on internationalization and technological and scientific cooperation projects. She developed expertise in regional competitiveness development, internationalization, start-ups, cluster development policy, innovation and research themes.

Giuseppe Cappiello is Assistant Professor of Management at the University of Bologna, Italy.

Cosimo Casilli graduated in Law and Pharmacy. He was professor of political economy at the University of Salento and still gives lectures at other universities. He has held numerous public appointments at regional and national level (including Italian parliamentary republic, general manager of the province of Lecce, etc.). He has published a number of articles at national and international level about public sector and smart city.

Luca Cattani is an Adjunct Professor of Project Design, monitoring and evaluation at the Political Sciences Faculty of the University of Bologna. He holds a PhD in European Economics and Law at the University of Bologna, a Master's Degree with honours in Local and International Cooperation and Development from the University of Bologna, and a Bachelor's Degree in International Cooperation and Development from the University of Bologna. He was Visiting Research Student at the Institute for Employment Research (IER), University of Warwick. His major research areas are economic of education, inequality, labour economics and project planning.

Enza Cristofaro works in Regione Lombardia, since 2013, as the Directorate General of University, Research and Open Innovation. In particular, she follows the activities, development and implementation, concerning the Smart Specialization Strategy (S3). She got a degree in Territorial, Urban and Environmental Planning at the Politecnico di Milano and after university attended a Master course in Project Management of Public Works at the Politecnico di Milano. She started her career as Planner in the Municipality of Borgomanero. She developed also expertise in the Directorate General Territory, Urbanism and Soil Conservation in particular on Strategic Environmental Assessment. Since 2008, she has focused on activities concerning the Structural Funds, internationalization and technological and scientific cooperation initiatives. She developed expertise in research and innovation themes, regional competitiveness development, internationalization and cluster development policy.

Armando De Crinito is Deputy Director University, Research and Open Innovation and Head of the Unit Programming, Research, Innovation and University in Regione Lombardia since May 2013. He graduated in Law at the Università

Cattolica del Sacro Cuore in Milan and is a Lawyer (with Italian license to practice law). He has a vast experience in activities concerning research and innovation policy framework, technology transfer and internationalization. He has developed major know-how on setting up the management of large RTD projects and networks.

He has developed extensive governmental, European and industry networks and has been involved in technology transfer and technology funding. More recently, he has taken on the management of several projects relating to 'foresight and technology assessment' and to support the Lombardy region in starting a program of the evaluation system to reward and to strengthen the excellences, to assure the adequacy of the offer, to promote the continuous improvement of the Lombardy research system and to foster interactions between research organizations and industry.

Nicola De Liso is Full Professor of Economics at the University of Salento. He holds a degree cum laude in Political Science Major Economics from the University of Bologna. He has a Master's and a PhD in Economics from the University of Manchester. He has coordinated several research projects and is a former Dean of the Faculty of Law of the University of Salento and former Member of the Commission for Scientific Research of the Italian Society of Economists. He is also an expert evaluator for the European Commission. His major research areas are evolutionary economics, economics and knowledge and methodologies in economics.

Gianluca Di Pasquale is Senior Manager, Advisory Services, Mediterranean Region (Ernst & Young). He has about twenty years of experience at the intersection of business and technology focusing on the strategic management of innovation. He holds several international patents, some of which have re-established the principles and the economic models of modern telecommunication networks. With special attention to Smart Cities and the Sharing Economy, Gianluca has supported leading companies and public administrations to establish new business and operating model enabled by the Internet economy, in sectors such as Energy, Mobility, Government and Education. He is responsible for the EY Innovation Hub.

Giovanni Guidetti is Assistant Professor of Economics at the University of Bologna. He holds a Bachelor's in Political Science, Economics from the University of Bologna; a Master's of Science in Economics, Scottish Doctoral Programme from the University of Glasgow; and a PhD in Economic Structure and Behaviours from the University of Bologna. His major research areas are varieties of capitalisms, inequality, labour economics and institutional economics.

Riccardo Leoncini is full Professor of Economics at the University of Bologna; Senior Fellow at the Freiburg Institute for Advanced Studies (FRIAS) University of Freiburg; and Research Associate, IRCrES-CNR (National Research

Council) in Milan. He holds a PhD in Economics, Faculty of Economic and Social Studies, University of Manchester; an MA in Economics, Faculty of Economic and Social Studies, University of Manchester; and a BA in Political Science (major Economics), Faculty of Political Science, University of Florence. His major research areas are the following: firms as complex system of resources, capabilities and competences; variety of organizational designs; firm performance as a function of the capacity to develop idiosyncratic elements that mould differences in adaptation to change; firms as elements of larger agglomerations (Industrial Districts); and models of technological diffusion, focusing in particular on diffusion regimes characterized by different models of appropriations (e.g. proprietary vs. open source).

Dorel Nicolae Manitiu is a Project Manager at the International Relations Office and Projects of the AlmaLaurea Inter-University Consortium. He holds a Bachelor's in Law from the University of Craiova; a Master's of Business Administration (MBA) from the Faculty of Economic Sciences of Brasov; a Master's in Development Innovation and Change (MiDIC) from the University of Bologna; and a PhD in Law and Economics from the University of Bologna, Italy. He is also a Lecturer in Economics at the Faculty of Law of the University of Bologna. His major research areas are local development and project planning and evaluation.

Valentino Moretto graduated in management engineering. He is co-founder and member of the board of directors of beMINT, where he is also Head of the Research and Innovation unit. He is involved in the creation of innovative scenarios in the areas of smart cities and e-health, participating in national and international competitions. He has published a number of articles at the national and international levels about public sector, e-government, smart cities, process management and quality.

Andrea Paliani is Managing Partner, Advisory Services, Mediterranean Region (Ernst & Young). He is responsible of the business consulting practice for the EY Mediterranean Region, which includes Italy, Spain and Portugal. Andrea leads a team of about 1,700 professionals and about 45 active partners in the strategic and operational advice aimed at achieving complex transformations and growth strategies for industrial companies, service providers, infrastructure and public administration, including through the digital revolution under way. Formerly, he has been appointed as the Global Power & Utilities industry leader and the Western Europe Telecom, Media and Technology industry leader.

Giulio Pedrini, PhD in Law and Economics, is currently a Research Fellow of the Interuniversity Research Centre on Public Utilities (CRISP) – University of Milan-Bicocca and an adjunct Professor in Economics of Innovation at the University of Bologna. He holds a Bachelor's Degree in Economics and a Master's Degree in Law and Economics. He was Visiting Research Student at the Institute for Employment Research (IER), University of Warwick. His primary areas of research are labour economics, human capital development and local development. On these topics, he has published articles and working papers and has also participated at national and international conferences

Marco Ruffino is an Adjunct Professor of Analysis of Social Networks at the University of Bologna and a consultant. He has worked as a consultant for public institutions, Italian universities, large companies, local development agencies, National Bilateral Authorities, training inter-professional funds, national trade unions and employers' organizations and national and foreign research bodies. He has been scientific leader of European and national research projects. He has been teaching since the academic year 2001/2002 as senior lecturer in the universities of Camerino, Roma la Sapienza, Valle d'Aosta and Bologna. His major research areas include professional/training needs analysis, competencies certification systems development, organizational development and knowledge management and educational/vocational training and welfare systems.

Tomaso Tommasi di Vignano is the Executive Chairman of Hera S.p.A. since November 2002. He has a degree in Law. He began his career in the personnel sector at Sip S.p.A., where he went on to become Group Personnel Manager in 1989. From December 1992 to May 1994, he was Chief Executive Officer of Iritel S.p.A. From 1994 to 1997, he was General Manager of Telecom Italia, responsible for the International, Business Customer and Residential Customer Divisions. In 1997, as Chief Executive Officer of STET, he successfully completed the merger of the company with Telecom Italia, a group with 126,000 people and revenues of USD 24 billion. In 1997, he was appointed Chief Executive Officer of Telecom Italia and oversaw the Group's full privatization. From 1999 to 2002, he held the post of Chief Executive Officer of the multi-utility ACEGAS S.p.A. and managed its privatization through an initial public offering.

Stefano Venier, Chief Executive Officer of Hera S.p.A, has a degree in computer science and a Master's in energy management from the Enrico Mattei School in Milan. He began his career in May 1987 at Zanussi as an assistant to the head of production planning control in the laundry division. From 1989 to 1996, he worked at Eni – Enichem, rising through the ranks as strategic planning assistant, head of market analysis and then head of strategic projects. In 1996, he joined management consultancy firm A.T. Kearney, where he focused on the energy, utilities and telecom sectors. In 2002, he was named Vice President of Energy & Utilities. From 2004 to 2008, he was Head of Business Development and Strategic Planning at the Hera Group. From July 2008, he was Director of the Development and Marketing Department of the Hera Group.

Luca Zamparini is Associate Professor of Economics at the University of Salento. He holds a PhD in Economics and Institutions from the University of Bologna, a Master's of Science in Economics from the London School of Economics and Political Science, and a Degree in Law from the University of Bologna. He is also a Lecturer in Economics at the University of Bologna. His major research areas are transport economics and tourism economics.

Foreword

The 'smart' attribute is by now a popular leitmotiv that advocates innovativeness, participation, collaboration and coordination within a rationale of network-based and policy-defined spatiality. Despite some fuzziness in its scope and theoretical bases, the concept of smartness can be a valuable container for the discussions about regional and urban development models that try to reconcile the pursuit of competitiveness and sustainability of local communities within a 'smart development' agenda. Such a concept goes beyond the one of 'smart growth' and is driven by two interacting forces: 'smart specialization' and 'smart city'.

This book represents an attempt to provide an original approach in addressing the most important research questions arising from the pursuit of smart development through the creation of smart communities.

It draws from two background papers that have been prepared for two workshops held in 2013 in Modena[1] and in 2014 in Bologna,[2] respectively,[3] and from the discussion of the papers that have been presented in the same occasions. The first workshop was focused on the composite notions of smart specialization, smart development and industrial policy in a local and global perspective. The second workshop discussed the different meanings of the smart city concept in function of local development policies. Through these workshops, we addressed specific research questions dealing with the key role of human capital in driving the evolution of urban areas in a smartness perspective and the possible tasks of the different levels of government in promoting the development of smart cities and communities in accordance with Europe 2020 strategy for smart, sustainable and inclusive growth. The volume can thus be viewed as the intermediate goal of the research and debate launched with these two workshops and continued later with seminars, meetings and other initiatives involving research and discussion at national and international levels. After having extensively dealt with the relationships between smart specialization, smart city and local development, we now present a comprehensive study of the nature, causes and effects of 'smartness' in relation to economic development.

In line with this premises, the volume is divided in three parts. The first part is devoted to the conceptualization of the idea of 'smartness' as a blending of smart specialization and smart city within the 'smart development' paradigm. The second part is devoted to the measurement and application of the notion of smart development, mainly but not exclusively, to the Italian context. The third part is devoted to the assessment of the implications of the previous essays and contemporary debate on the role of multi-level governance in order to map the policy agenda of smart development in Italy and in Europe. Specific sections will concern transport planning and the public utilities sector in light of their crucial roles in shaping the supply side of the smart development paradigm.

Overall, there is a clear theoretical relevance of both strategic and operational issues addressed in this book. Both scholars and experts are paying more and more attention on these topics in the perspective of exploring new paths of economic development after the global crisis. Within this stream of research we need a clear idea of (1) the implications of the cross-fertilization between smart specialization and smart city in fostering smart development and of its interactions with the macro-, micro- and meso-economic framework; (2) what are the really important characteristics of labour markets functioning, human capital formation and utilization, human development and social capital strengthening as the key driver of smart development and structural reform policies; and (3) the really important features of industrial policy at the centralized/decentralized level as companion policies for smart development. This, in turn implies a clear definition of the relationships between investment policy, industrial policy and innovation policy and the respective fields of action. A first cornerstone is the relevance of the multidisciplinary approach to the topic. Different skills and types of knowledge are involved both in the analysis of the concept and in the prediction of the relevant applications. A second inference lies in the crucial role of people, and women in particular, as conscious actors in the processes of transformation of the urban economic structure, which interacts with the critical role of innovation. A third key point relates to the quality of services provided to citizens and to good governance requirements concerning their production and provision. The governance of smart development is required to promote accessibility to information, transparency, public involvement in the decision-making process, citizens' participation and social inclusion. This implies that governments effectively promote cooperation among stakeholders and that administrators are endowed with both relational and managerial skills. Moreover, there should be no restrictions on information flows and a sufficient coordination between different levels of government.

A pivotal role for the achievement of smart development is played by human capital (a part of the smart people dimension) and social capital. Firms' innovative and learning capabilities go beyond the presence of information and communication technology (ICT) infrastructures and extend to the production of knowledge, innovative and cultural/creative services. This generates positive effects in terms of demographic and economic growth through the attraction of additional human capital. However, progress or technical change may accelerate the obsolescence of knowledge and skills to an extent that penalizes low-qualified workers ('skill-biased technical change'). This generates the need to make educational agencies and firms' training departments adequate for increasing skill complexity and the intangible networks unfolding by the competitive environment. In particular, firms can support the activation of tailored entities that set in motion complex cognitive processes spreading and reshaping knowledge throughout the organization. They can also integrate internal labour markets in the processes of knowledge transmission and intersection of cultures, technology and innovation. This perspective would be particularly suitable at regional level where the relationship between firms and local community could support the creation of learning networks that contribute to the distinctive features of regional innovation paths.

In the Hera Group, the commitment to such a model matched with the choice of establishing a corporate university named HerAcademy. Provided that workplace training is no longer able by itself to cover all the work-based learning needs, the objective of HerAcademy is to integrate internal training practices with a wide variety of learning activities within and outside the organization. In this respect, the main role of HerAcademy is to improve the internal organization of knowledge while at the same time contributing to the enhancement of the external organization of knowledge and of social interactions with local communities. HerAcademy is also involved in the evaluation and monitoring of all staff training activities for employees of the group and concerning the upgrading of different strategic skills. In this framework, a corporate university can become a driver of the renewed economic organization of knowledge within the group by fruitfully interacting with the external organization of knowledge.[4]

Consistently with this approach, HerAcademy represents a space of reflection and discussion on the issues of knowledge sharing, innovation enhancement and skills development within the processes of human and social capital accumulation. Moreover, it facilitates the achievement of high standards of sustainability (economic, environmental and social) in local communities. HerAcademy therefore constitutes a 'meeting place' between the firms' strategies, instances and needs coming from the internal and external community of stakeholders and the scientific progress on skills' and human capital development. These three components are respectively represented by the governance model of HerAcademy (Figure 0.1).

Overall, HerAcademy can play the following potential roles in contributing to the creation of smart communities, both internal and external to Hera Group: (1) identifying new ways to store and share knowledge (including tacit ways), (2) implementing the pipelines of professional skills as they are redefined by organizational and institutional change, (3) improving skills assessment by promoting reflections about measuring skills and evaluating the performance of training initiatives and (4) serving as a vehicle for implementing partnerships and initiatives with local communities.

In line with its mission, HerAcademy promotes the academic and institutional discussion on topical issues that can generate relevant implications for both the activities of the Hera Group and of local communities. Once the topic has been identified, such discussion takes place in three phases. In a preliminary phase, a complete review of the state of the art in the scientific and grey literature is performed in cooperation with experts and academic institutions. This activity is

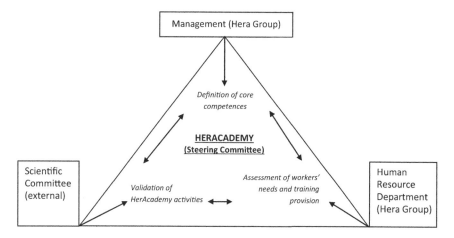

Figure 0.1 The governance of HerAcademy

undertaken in a comparative perspective and is necessarily grounded on a solid theoretical framework. This work leads to the preparation of the background paper to be used as basic reading by all the stakeholders.

The main lines of analysis of the background paper are then presented and discussed in dedicated workshops. This phase aims to promote an in-depth brainstorming on the theme aimed at identifying discussing the main associated challenges for organizations and policy makers, with a particular focus on the implications for human resources development policies. This phase is character-ized by the goal of broadening the debate by addressing the issues in both the local and the international context. Eventually, the background papers and the contribu-tions are bundled together in a scientific book or in a special issue that contribute to a more systematic understanding of the subject.

As for other themes and in line with its mission, HerAcademy has contributed to the scientific debate on smart development and smart community by organizing the workshops mentioned earlier and providing scientific and organizational sup-port to the publication of this book. Grounding on a solid theoretical framework, and with comprehensive and contemporary references and evidence supporting its propositions and implications, this volume provides insights from leading research on the links between smart development and smart communities in the European framework while shedding light on the implications for public policy from a multi-level governance approach.

The contribution of HerAcademy to the scientific debate on smart develop-ment will continue through future research on some of the liveliest issues related to smart development. In particular, the complementarity between human capital and innovation in stimulating sustainable development paths based on idiosyncratic structural change will be further discussed. The integration of education and training initiatives with knowledge-based production factors can be considered one important framing condition for balanced development patterns of urban and regional communities within. Specific issues will concern, for instance, the role of public utilities within public–private networks devoted to soft skills development in the field of energy use, transportation infrastructures and knowledge-intensive business services. These multidisciplinary topics are relevant to both business and policy in the ongoing debate about governance and policy instruments aimed at stimulating the formation of smart communities in innovation-based ecosystems.

Tomaso Tommasi di Vignano

Notes

1 HerAcademy, Smart Communities and Local Development: Objectives, Actors, Value Creation Workshop, 17th July 2013, Modena, Italy.
2 HerAcademy, Smart Communities and Local Development: The Cities of Tomorrow Workshop, 26th March 2014, Bologna, Italy.
3 Both workshops were organized by HerAcademy, the corporate university of the Hera Group, one of the largest utility companies in Italy.
4 For instance, HerAcademy contributes to training programs in partnership with educational agencies and to the organization of joint events (forums, seminars, workshops and conferences).

Introduction

Gilberto Antonelli and Giancarlo Campri

1 Premise

The pursuit of new paths for making real sustainable development, together with the innovation and change that this implies, is one of the main challenges for the economies of the global North and the global South, as well as for the European Union.

New and strong chances of growth are at stake when we are led even to envisage a fourth industrial revolution or to think about the development outlooks of the emerging powers. A European perspective would suggest new opportunities for a parallel recovery of our economies at the local, national and supranational level with an approach based on human development. This is why the smart specialization strategy (S3) and the smart city strategy (SCS) adopted by EU at the beginning of the present decade are important efforts in this direction.

At the same time, both at the local, national and supra-national level, the resistance against change is strong for several reasons. They range from the loss of confidence deriving from repeated crises and failures to the unwillingness to accept change and competition in groups, regions and countries starting from a high level of affluence, to the high economic and social costs of solidarity.

In our view, the effort to find new strategies of growth can be better rewarded and their successful application assisted if we engage in an attempt to deepen their scope and try to put them in relation to different local and national backgrounds. In this volume, we engage ourselves in this task, starting from the Italian experience. However, we deem that this analysis can be helpful also for other member countries of EU.

Our theoretical underpinning relies on the concept of smartness, which is a winning example of a semantic container that can be applied to many aspects of economic and social life and ends up in a variety of recipient applications. Moving from the need to reconcile competitiveness and sustainability in different contexts and perspectives, smartness is the origin of a multiplicity of multidimensional recipients and applications. Smart projects and policies can involve infrastructures, lifestyles, institutional processes, methods of analysis and so on.[1]

The concept of smartness can be converted into the more definite paradigm of smart development. In this way, it can be applied to both the demand and the supply sides of markets and to static and dynamic features of growth that allow us to detect some recurring and identifiable common elements. In particular, scrutiny of the paradigm of smart development identifies at least three common elements that underlie its different connotations: first, the centrality of technological innovation and, in particular, the growing potential of ICT; second, the role of networks, which connect the ICT infrastructure with those intangible assets related to knowledge innovative services (KIS), the organization of knowledge and cultural activities; and third, the importance of the economic organization of knowledge – in particular, of transferrable knowledge – and human capital – including soft skills – in fostering innovation. A fourth distinguishing characteristic of smart development concerns the bottom-up approach, which leverages the vocation of each individual component of the system and the communities involved. The need for a bottom-up process is linked especially to the centrality of the phases of listening, participation, co-design, dissemination and exchange of information and leads to collaboration between the different agents. This requirement is interlocked with the theme of government and governance, viewed as a system consisting of a plurality of multiple agents based on the effectiveness of the adjustment, the large degree of freedom granted to individuals, on accountability of the actors involved.

On such bases, we consider smart specialization and smart cities applications as the two basic pillars of the paradigm of smart development on the supply side and the demand side of the markets, respectively, and interlock these two ideas through their complementarity in fostering smart development in smart communities. In particular, we focus on the importance of the structure of labour markets,[2] human capital formation and utilization, human development and social capital strengthening in shaping smart development path and structural reform policies. On the other hand, two major recipients of the paradigm of smart development are represented by regional and urban systems. There, smartness underpins the need to reconcile competitiveness and sustainability (Herrschel, 2013) in interventions aimed at promoting innovation and knowledge in the perspective of an inclusive economic development. The attractiveness of the paradigm thus derives from the underlying interlocking between innovation and knowledge, on the one hand, and sustainability and local specificities, on the other hand. A prominent case is the European 2020 strategy that combines smartness with the typical attributes of a balanced development process: sustainable and inclusive. These goals can generate delicate trade-off. A proper balancing of these goals requires policy makers to explain smart development strategies also in relation to the evolution of knowledge and its organization in terms of poor access to education and training and of growing inequality in human capital. The focus on sustainability also implies the recognition of the crucial role of the local dimension, understood as a complex of socio-economic relations founded on relations among communities, private individuals and local authorities in policy development.

This introduction presents the meaning of the 'smartness' label and its applications in order to draw the foundations and the distinguishing elements of this symbolic representation in their different fields of applications. This analysis is not only theoretically rewarding but also practically helpful, since it contributes to avoid ambiguous and confounding uses of abstractions like, for instance, those of 'innovation sectors', 'territory' and 'talent', which are widely spread in contemporary pamphlets of smartness-related themes. In order to reach practical and effective recipes for each distinct topic, two levels of analysis are performed. First, as the allegory of smartness can be applied to both the demand and the supply sides of the markets, we clarify the relationships between smart specialization and smart city and emphasize their cross-fertilization for understanding the useful paradigm of smart development. Second, the paradigms of smart development and smart community, which express actors and objectives associated with smartness, are viewed as the relevant applications for building up a comprehensive synthesis of the concept of smartness.

This conceptual framework will be presented to the reader with the gradual composition of a puzzle that corresponds to the different parts of the volume.

The Foreword, Introduction and Conclusion are addressed to explain the general approach of the book and how it has been conceived and achieved by means of a strong interaction between academic and business culture. Moreover, suggestions about how its results can be practically useful and applied at a sectoral level will be offered.

Part I is devoted to the conceptualization of the idea of 'smartness' as a blending of smart specialization and smart city. The matching framework of analysis is found in the 'smart development' paradigm.

In Part I.1, we explore the origins of the 'smart specialization' notion both in the grey literature of high-level consultants as well as in the scientific literature. Apart from the main answers of innovation theory, significant benchmarks are identified in the scientific research on variety in capitalism models and variety in industrial policy.

Afterwards, in Part I.2, the origins of the 'smart city' notion are explored again both in the grey literature of high-level consultants as well as in the scientific literature. The main tenets of innovation theory are explored together with the interpretations of the scientific research on regional economics, human capital and the new geography of jobs.

The outcomes relevant within the paradigm of smart development are derived in Part I.3.

Part II is devoted to the measurement and application of the smart development paradigm mainly, but not exclusively, in the Italian context. Smartness indicators are discussed and employed in an in-depth empirical study focused on the European urban framework. Weaknesses and opportunities linked to Southern Italy, as a test for backward regional specificities and perspectives, but also to Central and Northern Italy are explored. Moreover, a wide and original international comparison is presented to point out the relevance of the public utilities sector in this domain.

Part III is devoted to assessing the implications of the previous essays and of the contemporary debate on the government of smart development. Government and governance at the different levels of administration are addressed to. Suggestions offered both by big private actors and public agencies and governing bodies are examined in order to map the policy agenda that is under implementation in Italy and Europe. Due to their particular relevance and the role played on the supply side of the smart development paradigm, a closer investigation is performed in the case of transport planning and with reference to the strategies of the public utilities sector

The remaining part of the Introduction can serve as a guide for the reader and is divided into six sections. Sections 2 and 3 concisely review notions of smart specialization and smart cities, respectively. Section 4 introduces the paradigm of smart development as an ideal interaction between smart city and smart specialization. This paradigm will be further discussed in the volume, and it can be considered a novel contribution. Section 5 stresses the role of human capital in smart development. Section 6 deals with how the role of human capital and social capital can be enhanced through government and governance in fostering the paradigm of smart community, another ideal type that will be further discussed in this volume and that can be considered another novel contribution. We provide concluding remarks in Section 7.

2 Smart specialization

Smart specialization (S2) refers to a spatial-based industrial development grounded on the exploitation of regional potential and the resulting sector diversification of the local economy based on their vocation in science and technology. From an industrial perspective, S2 requires both "an entrepreneurial process of discovery that can reveal what a country or region does best in terms of science and technology" and "a learning process of discovery of the research and innovation domains in which a region can hope to excel" (Foray et al., 2009, p. 2). Accordingly, the creation of an interregional competitive advantage in one or more industrial sectors relies on the generation of knowledge spillovers on a local basis. In this context, the application of ICTs can trigger the necessary productivity growth for the co-invention of applications and the diffusion of innovation across related sectors (Boschma, 2005; Boschma and Iammarino, 2009) through a process of diversification of existing specialization. From a regional perspective, McCann and Ortega-Argilés (2011) identify the following specific factors that contribute to specify S2: (1) embeddedness, (2) relatedness and (3) connectivity. Embeddedness refers to the need to develop these processes within a specific social and economic context, local labour markets, as well as a particular sectoral composition. Relatedness refers to the need to pursue differentiation strategies aimed at developing technologies that are relatively close to those existing in the regional context ('major local embedded industries') who already have a sufficient dimensional scale. Connectivity introduces the need to promote development processes that involve external areas related to the regional context, with the aim of exploiting knowledge spillovers to the outer economic systems. S2 thus strengthens the ability of learning and innovation thanks to the potential of the territorial context, enriched by internal and external economies. The underlying logic is to address the tangible and intangible resources available to the economic activities with a potential competitive advantage inter-regional and global as possible. This requires the achievement of a consistent matching between investments in human capital and knowledge, on the one hand, and the productive vocation of local economic systems (Camagni and Capello, 2013).

As S2 is grounded on the evolutionary approach, it is not so much the intensity of investments in science and technology (S&T) and research and development (R&D) that generate the domestic capabilities, but rather the cross-dissemination of research results and applications that permit large-scale implementation of 'general purpose technologies'. This is made possible by bottom-up processes that differentiate each regional system and the involved communities on the basis of their vocational and local specificities. In turn, the need for bottom-up processes entails the centrality of participation, co-design, dissemination, exchange of information, and collaboration between the agents. Hence, S2 requires a place-based approach that introduces criteria of differentiation between the different types of innovative regions depending on the economic and social context, such as embeddedness and relatedness. This implies, however, some potential contradictions with the evolutionary theory to the extent that S2 is applied to regional policy. First, it is not clear whether the policy maker enjoys some degree of freedom when paving the way for the development of formerly less-developed or backward regions. Second, it is difficult to *ex ante* specify a perfect process of institutional building that favour the process of smart development, in view of the different varieties of capitalism that still exist in Europe. Third, S2 implies the restructuring of the 'external' organization of knowledge in order to cope with the new 'knowledge needs' at local level as S2 requires the creation of new jobs and the availability of new cohorts of workers with the appropriate skills for both achieving incremental innovations and absorbing the new technologies introduced in the system.

In turn, the need for bottom-up processes entails the centrality of the phases of listening, participation, co-design, dissemination and exchange of information and collaboration between the involved agents. This brings us to the theme of government[3] and governance, which, however, lacks a satisfactory analysis in the literature that deals with the concept of smartness. In particular, the idea of institutional complementarity, which implies that the interaction between two or more institutions decisively influence the strategic choices of the agents, should be recognized as critical in shaping a suitable bundle of institutions for smart specialization. In any case, the paths of smart specialization are viewed as increasingly dependent on the need for investing in human capital and promoting access to education and training[4] that the demand for skills in the medium and long term entail. These insights reinforce the idea that the pursuit of S2 is not always addressable with interventions on a limited scale. On the contrary, it is sometimes necessary to introduce some kind of top-down action, based on substantial investments, coming from the higher levels of government for coordinating the different actors that are active at the local level.

This is especially true when taking into account the so-called 'fourth industrial revolution' and the emerging 'smart factories of Industry 4.0'. Indeed, the fourth industrial revolution is currently defined as a collective orientation to technologies and concepts concerning the organization of the value chain that combines cyber-physical systems, the internet of things and the internet of service (Kagermann et al., 2013; Hermann et al., 2015). Via the internet of things, cyber-physical systems would communicate and co-operate in real time with each other and with humans. Then, through the internet of service, both internal and inter-firm services are offered and used by all the participants to the value chain. Such an automated process is supposed to facilitate the set up and implementation of the smart factories where cyber-physical systems would monitor the physical processes and create a virtual copy of them. Eventually, this would facilitate decentralized decisions during the production process as in the S2 scheme.

3 Smart city

Despite the heterogeneity of the definitions proposed by the international scientific community, the policy makers and the major ICT international players, we can identify two different views of the application of the concept of 'smartness' to urban areas, i.e. the 'smart city' (SC). The first one focuses on innovation and ICT's as the main engines for making a city smart. It emphasizes an image of a city

> that monitors and integrates conditions of all of its critical infrastructures, including roads, bridges, tunnels, rails, subways, airports, seaports, communications, water, power, even major buildings, can better optimize its resources, plan its preventive maintenance activities, and monitor security aspects while maximizing services to its citizens.
>
> (Hall, 2000, p. 634)

This definition, centred on physical infrastructures, is influenced by other related concepts centred on ICT technology: wired city, technocity, digital city, creative city and knowledge-based city. All of them emphasize the novelty of the technological paradigm, considering the SC as a place that guarantees better quality of life for residents through the incorporation of ICT technologies and digital information into new products and/or their use in specific areas of intervention (e.g. Marsa-Maestre et al., 2008). The second approach refers instead to the effective implementation of innovative solutions in the perspective of improving the overall sustainability and 'liveability' of urban areas. Accordingly, the notion of sustainable urban development, primarily understood especially in environmental terms, is also related to social aspects through the inclusion of the objectives of inclusiveness, promotion of social capital and participatory governance and becomes one of the core conceptual components of the SC (Hollands, 2008; Toppeta, 2010; Nam and Pardo, 2010).

Under this second interpretation, which is inherently multidimensional, the SC label is attached to a broad spectrum of goals, themes and sectors. SC has been considered as an ecosystem formed by a complex infrastructure that combines together different 'soft' components among which we find the connections between cultural systems, social networks and communities and various forms of social inclusive principles (Zygiaris, 2013). SC thus requires the construction of networks that go beyond the technological element and extend to those intangible assets related to knowledge-intensive business services (KIBS), the organization of knowledge, and cultural activities. This second approach also underlies the existence of a positive relationship between human capital and cities' attractiveness and the endogenous characteristics of the transformation driven by innovation and creativity that the concept entails. All things considered, smart cities are required to combine together different visions of urban life in an integrated way. Sustainability can thus be seen as a cross-conceptual criterion to analyze the outcome of smart-oriented urban policies. It joins together different aspects and issues of urban life, while it is related to other SC dimensions via the objective of quality of life (Inoguchi et al., 1999; Satterthwaite, 1999; Polese and Stern, 2000) or liveability. Accordingly, the construction of the SC underpins a set of coordinated interventions able to interpret and revise the environmental, social and cultural needs of the relevant context.

However, several trade-off arises from the intrinsic nature of the challenge of "combining competitiveness and sustainable urban development simultaneously" (Giffinger et al., 2007, p. 5). The wide spectrum of objectives, themes and sectors causes fragmentation of the concept when projects are actually put into practice. In order to deal with the pursuit of such heterogeneous objectives, the SC has thus been conceived as a "framework for policies supporting technological and ecological urban transition . . . and fertilising national and local political agendas" (Vanolo, 2014, p. 894). Meanwhile, it calls for an original and complex set of indicators or providing additional evidence able to capture the multidimensionality of urban environment. Under such a theoretical and empirical background, actors and levels of government would be able to employ a plurality of tools in order to pursue their aims.

4 Stressing the interactions between smart specialization and smart city in fostering smart development and smart community

In trying to compare S2 and SC, and then to combine them in a broader notion of smartness, we consider how structural change and competitiveness bring about the need for a paradigm of smart development, which ties together the two notions while leaving to them a relative autonomy. The sequence goes (1) from high volume to high value, (2) from integrated processes to un-bundling and off-shoring, (3) from tangible to intangible assets and (4) from spatial agglomeration to international clusters and networks. Then we note how the driving forces of structural change (1) gave a crucial premium to knowledge proximity rather than to the geographic one, (2) made the boundaries between goods and services vanish and social goods become more and more important and (3) made the models of capitalism evolve both in space and over time. Finally, a theoretical model is proposed in which a parallel is drawn for smart specialization and smart city, respectively: (1) in the market place, the former works on the supply side, while the latter works on the demand side; (2) in the economic organization of knowledge, the former mainly makes use of the producer's learning, while the latter mainly employs the customer's one; (3) in the evaluation domain the former is mainly based on the producer's assessment, while the latter is mainly based on the customer's evaluation; (4) in the management sphere both government and governance play a critical role, even if subsidiarity could have more room for manoeuvre in the case of the latter.

Following these insights, like the 'smart development' paradigm can encompass both S2 and SC, 'smart community' can be the paradigm that encompass 'smart networks' and 'collective learning' and may be able to function in synergy with the former. The Intelligent Community Forum (2011) defines a wide set of potential communities: aggregations of small towns, cities, regions, nation states. Their common denominator is to be oriented to enhance the development of inclusive local systems starting from existing experiences jointly addressing social, environmental and technological aspects. They become smart when they seek to prepare the system to face the complex challenges attached to the pursuit of competitiveness and sustainability in a dynamic environment through solutions based on cooperation between different actors. In this context, the term community source from a local dimension requires the creation of social networks and emphasizes trust and relationship among its components. Active participation and internal cohesion help to build new ties that can lead to original recombination of knowledge. Accordingly, also smart community can be referred to S2 and SC to the extent that, at the regional level, the various players build a socio-economic community based on the existence of distinctive local knowledge, defined as "regional knowledge domain" (Cooke, 2009). The notion of social and cultural proximity is thus used in order to promote mechanisms of innovation-oriented knowledge transfer.

Smart community also implies adherence to institutional models based on the approach of non-formal bottom-up processes as preludes to new models of coordinated governance of policy tools oriented to the achievement of smart development. In this perspective the community affects the actual functioning of the institutions, by favouring the establishment of complementary relationships of the first with the second and the development of an economic system (Bowles and Gintis, 2002). The interaction between communities and institutions helps in balancing the incentives they provide, respectively, to economic agents (Farole et al., 2011). On the one hand, the community positively influences the construction of reputational mechanisms, the overcoming of information asymmetries, the reduction of transaction costs and the identification of the members in the system. Smart community does not therefore require communities to prevail over institutions but to interact effectively with them.

From smart community emerges a different configuration of community that refers to the social, cultural and value environment in which the community works, which, taken together, constitute that "sense of community" that helps to form the social capital in each region (Barca et al., 2012). This perspective is based on knowledge and local distinctive values in the region of reference. At the same time, smart community prevents the risks of degeneration of the "sense community" in "community confinement" (Barca et al., 2012) or "inertia of the community" (Cooke, 2009). Smart community is thus characterized by high heterogeneity, low social entry barriers and loose ties among people that can generate new forms of civic involvement under a shared vision of inclusive and harmonic development.

5 Stressing the role of human capital and social capital as key factors in smart development

A pivotal role for the success of smart development is played by human capital (a part of the smart people dimension). However, when using this concept in this context, we cannot confine ourselves to the tenets of human capital theory.[5] The complementarity of human capital and social capital in our framework is twofold. First, the distinction is fuzzy in several respects, and the notion of social capital can encompass that of human capital. Second, in our conceptual model, the synergy between smart development and smart community is crucial. Therefore, a pivotal role is played by both kinds of capital.

Firms' innovative and learning capabilities go beyond the presence of ICT infrastructures and extend to the production of knowledge, innovation and cultural/creative services. This generates positive effects in terms of demographic and economic growth through the attraction of additional human and social capital. In particular, the role played by urban areas in stimulating workers' and firms' productivity has been widely acknowledged by the literature, which shows the existence of a complementary role between the cultural consumption-oriented and the production-oriented city models. In other words, the model of the three Ts (technology, talent, tolerance) is interconnected with the one of the three Ss (skills, sun, sprawl). Not only can Marshall-Arrow-Romer (MAR) and Jacobs externalities generate this effect, but also other factors such as the presence of amenities or the existence of a suitable environment that is able to attract human capital. In this perspective, thick labour markets, hub infrastructure and access to markets, particularly in the service sector, all matter in the perspective of smart development. Such smart communities, characterized by high heterogeneity, low social entry barriers and loose ties among people can generate new forms of civic involvement and a shared vision of urban development. However, not only do they have to be exciting and safe places to live and visit (consumer cities), but also have to provide a great amount of job opportunities to both skilled and unskilled workers.

On the other hand, however, we observe an increasing dualism between progressively more dynamic areas and increasingly depressed ones that is attributed to the 'brain-gap', a particular type of path-dependence. Even cities characterized by a limited initial advantage in terms of high-skilled workers have been able to expand this gap throughout the years by enhancing their valuable human capital with increasing speed. Higher productivity attached to human capital fruitful complements with agglomeration effects associated with the urban dimension. The actual uneven distribution of human capital among the urban areas helps to determine a new 'geography of jobs'. Urban areas with concentrated innovative sectors get stronger and stronger, while the least dynamic cities lose jobs and population to an increasing extent. This geographic polarization, which parallels the employment polarization observed by Autor and Katz (2010) in several developed countries, can no longer be regarded as random, requiring, on the contrary, a careful reflection on the underlying causes of this phenomenon. Namely it is to be attributed to the structural change occurring in production methods and to the increasing openness of international trade.

This model has been mainly applied to the U.S. context.[6] However, it has been also referred to the European context in order to capture similar dynamics of agglomeration that occur in our continent, especially in Northern Europe. Narrowing the territorial scope of reference, however, we can see that similar patterns coexist within single countries, each of them including both highly innovative areas and depressed regions still relying on traditional products. There have been also attempts to adapt this model to the specific socio-cultural reality of European cities by combining the concentration of human capital with other idiosyncratic factors of European economic growth. The most important consequence is that, in the new geography of development, the strategic role of urban areas is increased, while economic sectors and development patterns of the future cities will be more and more connected to the relevant model of capitalism. Even the effectiveness and attractiveness of the local administration can be affected in a marked way.

Another important issue lies in the relationship between smartness and social sustainability, having been a long time since the European Commission addressed this issue at the institutional and policy level. The effects of smart communities on social sustainability are ambiguous. They can be either an opportunity for enhancing fairness or a threat that may lead to an undesirable growth of inequality, even within a city that can be otherwise considered as smart. In the second hypothesis, the boundary line depends on the long-term sustainability of urban areas at both individual and aggregate levels. A typical risk in this respect is represented by progress or technical change associated with smart city projects. Indeed, it may accelerate the obsolescence of knowledge and skills to an extent that penalizes low-qualified workers – 'skill-biased technical change'. This is likely to create social inequalities that may be hardly compatible with the other attributes of growth and development evoked by the concept of smartness as it has been outlined in the European context.

Overall, the possible relationships between agglomeration economies, jobs creation and the rate at which jobs are reallocated within the urban area, discriminating between inter-sectoral components (related to Jacobs's externalities) and intra-sectoral (associated with MAR externalities), could be the natural goal of an applied study that applies the smart development concept to urban areas.

6 Implications for government, governance and policy

From our analysis it emerges that the already substantial literature that deals with smartness still lacks a satisfactory examination of the institutional framework on which the policies of smart development should rest. Indeed, assuming that even in its phase as a knowledge-based economy, "capitalism is as much a system of distributed ignorance as it is a system of distributed knowing" (Metcalfe et al., 2012, p. 3), and we have to take into account that smartness is unfortunately designed for coexisting with failure.[7] This brings us to the discussion of the theme of government[8] and governance in relationship with the concept of smartness (Antonelli, 2012). Government, governance and policy are called to continuously reshape this concept and define its multidimensional nature and its evocative function in order to support the process of transformation that the notion of 'smartness' intrinsically entails. They have a role in fostering the capability of the system to generate changes, which gives well-thought and clever answers to complex issues. Smartness by itself is in fact insufficient to embrace the plurality of knowledge forms needed for developing innovative projects and to activate very complex institutional processes. In particular, the idea of institutional complementarity, which implies that the interaction between two or more institutions decisively influence the strategic choices of the agents, should be recognized as critical in shaping a suitable bundle of institutions for smart development and smart communities. In any case, the paths of smart specialization are viewed as increasingly dependent on the need for investing in human capital and promoting access to education and work-based learning that the demand for skills in the medium and long term entail. When we refer to smart communities, the goal in terms of government's action is well defined:

> [C]ities should be places of advanced social progress and environmental regeneration, as well as places of attraction and engines of economic growth based on a holistic integrated approach in which all aspects of sustainability are taken into account.
>
> (European Commission, 2012, p.3)

However, it becomes increasingly clear that the smart label covers many areas; most of them are correlated and sometimes overlapping. Each actor – European Union municipalities, businesses – contributes to shape cities and communities through. Once again the role of the public sector in providing a framework of opportunities and constraints in determining socio-economic development is a crucial issue.

On the other hand, concerning innovation, different skills and types of knowledge are involved both in the analysis of the topic and in the prediction of the relevant applications: knowledge of technological opportunities, scientific knowledge of the regulatory framework, creation of new knowledge. In this regard, there is room for the typical debate on the role of the public sector in providing incentives and disincentives. Finally, the creation and the use of different types of knowledge is a multi-dimensional aspect that covers all the domains we have referred to. In addition, knowledge is characterized by a series of interactions that embraces scientific, technological and economic fields. Meanwhile it is related to the demand for satisfying widespread social needs. Hence, we need to combine the smartness with the opportunities that emerge from new modes of knowledge production. This calls for the role of governance in promoting accessibility to information, transparency, public involvement in the decision-making process, citizens' participation and social inclusion.

7 Conclusion

Given the relevance of a multi-disciplinary approach to the concept of smartness, it can be viewed as a conduit for 'squaring the circle' between the quest for both competitiveness and sustainability in a spatial perspective. Getting deeper into the meaning of the basic notions of smart specialization and smart city throughout their comparison is not only theoretically rewarding but also practically helpful. On the one side, it helps to avoid ambiguous and confounding uses of abstractions widely spread in contemporary pamphlets on related themes. On the other side, it allows better interpretation of the impact of this innovation trajectory, which is still little dealt with in the literature. This complex framework, however, entails the risk of emphasizing the trade-offs attached to the pursuit of heterogeneous objectives by placing them under the same umbrella (i.e. the concept of smartness).

Moving from a multi-dimensional approach, the notion of smartness is viewed as an analytical framework for exploring the intersection between urban, regional, industrial and local development policies from both the demand and the supply side in the ultimate perspective of a harmonic and inclusive development process. From the demand side, the main application concerns the promotion of citizen-centred sustainable urban areas, i.e. the smart cities. Demand-side agents can be seen as conscious actors in the processes of transformation of the economic structure, which interacts with the critical role of innovation. A related objective concerns the quality of services provided to citizens and the good governance requirements for their production and provision. From the supply side, the notion of smart specialization reflects the potentials for a self-centred industrial development of local systems of production based on the exploitation of regional potential in terms of innovation and sector diversification grounding on their vocation in science and technology. Both smart city and smart specialization, however, can be viewed as normative notions to the extent that they imply that proper institutions are required for managing dispersed knowledge, reacting to multidimensional change and endogenously stimulating innovation processes that rely on bottom-up learning, production varieties and differentiation of needs and preferences.

This is interlocked with the theme of governance, viewed as a system consisting of a plurality of multiple agents based on the effectiveness of the adjustment, the large degree of freedom granted to individuals and on accountability of the actors involved. Governance is required to promote accessibility to information, transparency, public involvement in the decision-making processes, citizens' participation and social inclusion. The governance of smartness is based on the interaction between communities living in the urban area and the local system. This insight assumes that governments effectively promote the cooperation among stakeholders and promote co-creation of services and that officials are endowed with both relational and managerial skills. Moreover there should be no restrictions on information flows, and a sufficient coordination between different levels of government. This entails the participation in the institutional processes of a plurality of actors, also including, third sector operators.

Finally, we emphasize the role of labour markets functioning, human capital formation and utilization, human development and social capital strengthening as key drivers of smart development and structural reform policies. From this perspective of analysis, the concept of smartness can embrace both smart city and smart specialization and requires a thorough rethinking of the external organization of knowledge aimed at human capital development, both in terms of education and work-based learning, in order to cope with the new 'knowledge needs' on a local basis. Smart communities actually call for an inclusive process of construction, not only of a 'creative class', but also of a cohort of workers with the appropriate skills, among other things, to make possible the incremental innovation, as well as the maintenance of new technologies. Meanwhile, we stress some critical aspects related to the dynamics of skill-biased technical change that a boost to sector specialization may determine and the polarization of the demand for human capital, to the detriment of the professions medium, determined by innovative processes. Relevant policy implications deal with the elaboration of new institutional tools to identify and limit the mismatch between the demand for and the supply of knowledge and skills, both vertically and horizontally, and to promote access to education and training, depending on the long-term outcomes of the specialization paths.

Notes

1 The present introduction is based on the contents of the essays published in this volume, alongside with other works, presentations and teaching activities done in the last few years on the relationships between local development, smart development and smart communities. First of all, it rests on the insights of two background papers dealing with the concepts of smart specialization (Leoncini et al., 2013) and smart cities (De Liso et al., 2014). These papers have been presented at the two workshops organized by HerAcademy: the "Smart Communities and Local Development: Objectives, Actors and Creation of Value" workshop, held in Modena on the 17th of July 2013, and the "Smart Communities and Local Development: The Cities of the Future" workshop, held in Bologna, on the 26th of March 2014. Second, it is grounded on the papers prepared for the Emilia-Romagna Region seminars on "The Emilia-Romagna Region after the Crisis: Scenarios for Reflecting on Challenges and Facing Change" held in Bologna on the 10th of December 2012 and on "What Regional Strategy for Smart Specialization Is Needed? Innovation, Research and Smart Specialization of Territories" held in Bologna on the 14th of January 2013 and for the ERVET seminar on "Smart Specialization, Smart Cities, Local Development", held in Bologna on the 14th of July 2014. Third, an invaluable contribution comes from the teaching activities organized in the framework of Economics of Local Systems course for the Master's degree on Local and Global Development at the University of Bologna.
2 In particular, more attention should be paid to the labour demand side and the job creation/destruction processes.
3 Taking also into account how the different levels of government (supra-national, national, local, sectoral) in Europe have experienced complex bonds with industrial and innovation policies.
4 Or better work-based learning.

5 And especially in the Gary Becker version.
6 Moretti (2012) speaks of "Three Americas", while Robert Reich (1992) proposes the tripartite distinction between the three "jobs of the future".
7 For further considerations, see Antonelli (2011).
8 Taking also into account how the different levels of government (supra-national, national, local, sectoral) in Europe have experienced complex bonds with industrial policy and innovation policy.

Bibliography

Antonelli, G. (2011), Global economic crisis and systemic failure, *Economia Politica: Journal of Analytical and Institutional Economics*, XXVIII (3), 403–434.

Antonelli, G. (2012), Governo e governance dei servizi di pubblica utilità per lo sviluppo umano:un'introduzione, *Economia dei Servizi*, VII (2), 217–236.

Antonelli, G. (2014), *Smart specialization, smart cities, local development*, Department of Economics, University of Bologna, presented at the ERVET Seminar, Bologna, 14 July.

Autor D.H. and Katz L.F. (2010), *Grand challenges in the study of employment and technological change: A white paper prepared for the National Science Foundation*, Harvard University and NBER, September.

Barca, F., McCann, P. and Rodriguez-Pose, A. (2012), The case for regional development intervention: Place-based versus place-neutral approaches, *Journal of Regional Science*, 52 (1), 134–152.

Boschma, R. (2005), Proximity and innovation. A critical survey, *Regional Studies*, 39 (1), 61–74.

Boschma, R. and Iammarino, S. (2009), Related variety, trade linkages, and regional growth in Italy, *Economic Geography*, 85 (3), 289–311.

Bowles, S. and Gintis, H. (2002), Social capital and community governance, *Economic Journal*, 112, F419–36.

Camagni, R. and Capello, R. (2013), Regional innovation patterns and the EU Regional Policy reform: Towards smart innovation policies, *Growth and Change*, 44 (2), 355–389.

Cooke, P. (2009), The knowledge economy, spillovers, proximity and specialization, in D. Pontikakis, D. Kyriakou and R. van Bavel (eds.), *The question of R&D specialisation: Perspectives and policy implications*, Brussels, European Commission, Directoral General for Research, pp. 27–40.

De Liso, N., Cattani, L., Manitiu, D.N., Pedrini, G. and Zamparini, L. (2014), *Smart cities e sviluppo locale: stato dell'arte*, Bologna, HerAcademy, Background Paper 1.

European Commission. (2012), *Smart cities and communities*, Bruxelles, European Innovation Partnership, COM(2012) 4701.

Farole, T., Rodrıguez-Pose, A. and Storper, M. (2011), Cohesion policy in the European Union: Growth, geography, institutions, *Journal of Common Market Studies*, 49 (5), 1089–1111.

Foray, D., David, P.A. and Hall, B.H. (2009), Smart specialisation. The concept, *Knowledge Economists Policy Brief*, 9, available at http://ec.europa.eu/invest-in-research/pdf/download_en/kfg_policy_brief_no9.pdf.

Giffinger, R., Fertner, C., Kramar, H., Kalasek, R., Pichler-Milanović, N. and Meijers, E. (2007), *Smart cities: Ranking of European medium-sized cities*, Centre of Regional Science (SRF), Vienna University of Technology.

Hall, P. (2000), Creative cities and economic development, *Urban Studies*, 37 (4), 633–649.

Hermann, M., Pentek, T. and Otto, B. (2015), *Design principles for Industrie 4.0 scenarios: A literature review*, Technische Universitat Dortmund, Working Paper No. 1.

Herrschel, T. (2013), Competitiveness and sustainability: Can "Smart City Regionalism" square the circle?, *Urban Studies*, Special Issue, 1–17.

Hollands, R.G. (2008), Will the real smart city please stand up? Intelligent, progressive or entrepreneurial?, *City*, 12 (3), 303–320.

Inoguchi, T., Newman, E. and Paoletto, G. (1999), *Cities and environment: New approaches for the ecosociety*, New York, UN University Press.

Intelligent Community Forum. (2011*), Intelligent communities: Platforms for innovation*, available at http://www.intelligentcommunity.org/clientuploads/PDFs/WP-Platforms-for-Innovation.pdf, accessed on 17 June 2013.

Kagermann, H., Wahlster, W. and Helbig, J. (eds.) (2013), Recommendations for implementing the strategic initiative Industrie 4.0. Final report of the Industrie 4.0 Working Group, National Academy of Science and Engineering (ACATECH), April.

Leoncini, R., Cattani, L., Guidetti, G. and Pedrini, G. (2013), *Smart specialization e sviluppo locale: stato dell'arte*, Bologna, HerAcademy, Background Paper No. 1.

Marsa-Maestre, I., Lopez-Carmona, M.A., Velasco, J.R. and Navarro, A. (2008), Mobile agents for service personalization in smart environments, *Journal of Networks*, 3 (5), 30–41.

McCann, P. and Ortega-Argilés, R. (2011*), Smart specialisation, Regional growth and applications to EU cohesion policy*, Document de treball de l'IEB 2011/14, Institut d'Economia de Barcelona.

Metcalfe, S., Gagliardi, D., De Liso, N. and Ramlogan, R. (2012), *Innovation systems and innovation ecologies: Innovation policy and restless capitalism*, Openloc, Working Paper No. 3.

Moretti, E. (2012), *The new geography of jobs*, New York, Houghton Mifflin Harcourt.

Nam, T. and Pardo, T.A. (2010), Conceptualizing smart city with dimensions of technology, people, and institutions, in *The Proceedings of the 12th Annual International Conference on Digital Government Research*, 282–291.

Polese, M. and Stern, R. (2000), *The social sustainability of cities: Diversity and the management of change*, Toronto, University of Toronto Press.

Reich, R. (1992), *The Work of Nations*, New York, Vintage Books.

Satterthwaite, D. (1999), *Sustainable cities*, London, Earthscan.

Toppeta, D. (2010), *The smart city vision: How innovation and ICT can build smart, "livable", sustainable cities*, The Innovation Knowledge Foundation, Think! Report N. 005.

Vanolo, A. (2014), Smartmentality: The smart city as disciplinary strategy, *Urban Studies*, 51 (5), 883–898.

Zygiaris, S. (2013), Smart city reference model: Assisting planners to conceptualize the building of smart city innovative eco-systems, *Journal of the Knowledge Economy*, 4 (2), 217–231.

Part I

Conceptualizing the idea of smart development

I.1 Smart specialization

1 Issues and challenges for smart specialisation

Riccardo Leoncini

1 Introduction

The concept of *smart specialisation* is universally attributed to the Knowledge for Growth (K4G) Expert Group created in March 2005 by EU Commissioner for Research, Janez Potoc?nik. This group of scholars produced a vast array of contributions on the themes of innovation and knowledge, which constituted the theoretical and methodological base for the subsequent rich debate on the concept of smart specialisation strategy (S3 if we adopt the acronym proposed by the European Commission to refer to the smart specialisation strategy).[1]

The K4G Group produced a series of policy briefs on the themes of education, technology and research to help overcome the deficit that EU has with regard to the other world areas in fields such as R&D, education, training and lifelong learning strategies, university–industry links, processes of technological diffusion, and the globalisation of R&D.

According to the proponents, the concept of S3 can be defined as "an entrepreneurial process of discovery that can reveal what a country or region does best in terms of science and technology. That is, we are suggesting a learning process to discover the research and innovation domains in which a region can hope to excel" (Foray et al., 2009, p. 2).

The idea of S3 seems to emerge from a quite extended and well-known literature to which the proponents seem to 'naturally' refer, that is that of a process of development based on the evolutionary principles, self-centred, endogenous, and bottom-up. These characteristics should favour the growth of regions and/or countries that are not necessarily technological leaders. In particular, the bottom-up process is linked to the well-known concepts developed by the evolutionary/institutionalist approach, such as entrepreneurship, technological learning, and local and tacit knowledge. They seem to be useful to discover areas in which there exist technological opportunities for future specialisations that can be developed from the material and immaterial resources locally available.

More recently, in the framework of the studies on Cyber-Physical Systems, Big Data or Cloud Computing and of the debate on national industrial strategies,[2] also the notion of 'smart factory' has been introduced. This debate can be seen as one of the follow-ups[3] of S3.

The analysis of the concept of smartness allows for the individuation of some crucial elements such as, for instance, the centrality of technological innovation and, in particular, the increasing potentialities of the information and communication technologies (ICT), both in terms of the competitiveness of local economic systems and of the sustainability of their techno-economic development. In turn, from the technological domain, it is possible to thread some other connected elements such as the role of networks, so widely analysed by the literature, that transcend the material infrastructure (such as for instance, the ICT) to encompass the immaterial ones linked to knowledge-intensive business services (the so-called KIBS), to organisation of knowledge, to cultural activities.

Another element is the reference to the knowledge and its transferability: on the one side, S3 implies the generation of knowledge spillovers on a local/regional basis; on the other side, the urban environment is considered to be an ideal locus for the interactions among 'peers', such as those belonging to the creative class (Florida, 2002). Among the determinants of comparative (or absolute) advantages, some are particularly important, such as the attraction and the training of human capital. Human capital and highly skilled labour have thus a new role, as they are the main elements to be able to participate in innovative processes. The increasing role of professions with high cognitive content and their localisation all contribute to enhancing the spillover processes, that is they contribute to generate complementarities between demographic dimension of the urban area and productivity, specific competences of 'high-level' professionals, and new techniques of production. However, this creates a tension between two attributes ('smart' and 'inclusive') of the economic growth that the European Commission put forward because of the likely wage discriminations that this could produce to the disadvantage of less skilled workers. This implies the necessity of institutional solutions focused on a higher level of participation for all the economic actors in order to better guide the process.

Another element to underline is that according to this approach, it is not the intensity of investments in science and technology (S&T) to insure a competitive advantage, but rather the cross-fertilisation of the results of research efforts and the development of applications allowing adaptation on a large scale of the General Purpose Technologies (GPT). Hence, the emphasis is on the transversality of second-level applications rather than on the race for the first-level ones. The logical corollary is that applications must be regional (but possibly cross-national) and intersectoral and facilitate the diffusion/adoption of these technologies through the creation and/or the highlighting of complementarity and transversal elements (such as, but not only, ICT).

A final and fundamental characteristic of smart projects is their bottom-up nature.[4] This is why smart technologies can model themselves on the basis of the vocation of each single component of the system and of the community involved. The bottom-up approach is to be seen especially in its leaning on elements such as listening, participation, co-design, and diffusion and exchange of information. This leads to the effective collaboration of the agents involved and also decreases the strong competitive forces that otherwise the market would put on agents. This leads to the problem of governance, which in this case is to be meant as a multi-centric system made of a plurality of agents, based on efficacy of regulation, on high degrees of freedom for private agents, and on accountability. On these themes, however, the wide literature on smartness still lacks a satisfying analysis of the institutional framework that smart specialisation policies badly need.

2 Smart specialisation

Smart specialisation defines industrial growth as a self-centred process mainly based on innovation, on the utilisation of regional potentialities, and on the ensuing sectoral diversification of local economic systems, starting from their scientific and technological vocation. Within an evolutionary approach, this result is obtained through a dynamic process of entrepreneurial discovery (Foray et al., 2009), joined to the creation of local knowledge, which must be original and coherent to the so-called 'pertinent specialisations' of the region (David et al., 2013). In this way, the process of knowledge creation can exploit the existing capabilities and can generate complementarities with other regions, close either geographically and/or sectorally.

The process of discovery is delegated to the economic agents involved in the production and transfer of the knowledge and of the factors incorporating it (in both codified and tacit forms). Moreover, it assumes different characteristics depending on the fact that it can be in regions that can be either leader (or core) or follower (or adapter). In the former, investments are channelled towards the introduction of General Purpose Technologies (GPT), which are thus partially endogenous. In the latter, investments are more oriented towards the 'co-invention of applications', that is, sectoral applications of GPT in one or more areas of interests beneficiary of S3.

The diversification does not exclude traditional sectors (such as tourism, fishing, clothes, etc.) that can anyway embark in innovative and transformative trends, whenever prerequisites at the local level are found. In this way, firms in follower regions can redefine the markets within which they operate and re-locate themselves within them with an increased competitive capacity. Moreover, firms can increase the (private and social) returns of the inventions they use, in this way incentivising also the innovative activities of the leader regions.

For this purpose, S3 presupposes the generation of knowledge spillovers on a regional basis. In so doing, it outdoes the concept of national system of innovation and attributes to a properly defined set of actors (researchers, entrepreneurs, suppliers, users) the function of selecting the knowledge-intensive areas where smart strategies must focus. This happens through the recognition of technological and/ or market niches that can be exploited (McCann and Ortega-Argiles, 2011).

In this context, the applications of ICTs are relevant because they are susceptible to trigger the growth in productivity necessary for the process of co-invention of applications and to diffuse innovation to other sectors different from the originating one. This would increase the returns on innovative investments.

EU endorsed this approach; S3 strategies are defined as paths of specialisations aimed at favouring the strengthening of existing industries at the regional level and at favouring the diversification of the paths of innovation and growth on an intra-regional basis. To accomplish this task, the concept of related variety (Boschma, 2005) was adopted. According to this concept, the competitive advantage of a certain region comes from building a certain degree of variety into its industries. However, this must be correlated in terms of competences through a process of diversification of the exiting specialisations. On an inter-regional basis, it is necessary to enhance connectivity between leader regions, where industries operate in high-intensity knowledge sectors, and follower regions, specialised in sectors active in the co-invention of applications. Complementarities can thus be generated either within the same region or between different areas (Foray et al., 2012) depending on the spatial, cognitive, and sectoral proximity characterising them.

Smart specialised regions reinforce the capacity to apprehend and innovate, thanks to the potentialities of the peculiar territorial context, and they are enriched by both internal and external economies obtained by means of S3. The idea is that of channelling material and immaterial resources towards economic activities, showing a potential inter-regional and, whenever possible, global competitive advantage. This presupposes a coherent match between investments in knowledge and human capital, on the one side, and the production specialisation of the local economic systems, on the other (Camagni and Capello, 2012).

On the basis of the suggestions contained in the agenda for growth of the Europe 2020 Strategy, and of the classifications of innovative regions elaborated by OECD (2011), McCann and Ortega-Argiles (2011) highlight three particular factors contributing to the specification of the concept of S3: (1) embeddedness, (2) relatedness, and (3) connectivity.

The notion of *embeddedness* refers to the need to develop these processes of S3 within a specific socio-economic realm, characterised by a local labour market and a certain sectoral composition. As a consequence, smart processes of development need the presence of both sectors and co-invention of applications of relevant dimension and the presence of a sufficiently skilled labour force.

The notion of *relatedness* refers to the need to follow strategies of specialised differentiation, oriented towards the development of technologies that are relatively close to those already existing in that particular regional context ('major local embedded industries'). They have already a dimensional scale that is big enough to undertake such strategies. The aim of this strategy seems to be that of favouring, in a painless way in terms of jobs and consistency of the industrial structure, the absorption of idiosyncratic shocks that are external to the region.

The notion of *connectivity* introduces the need to promote growth processes that involve sectors connected to others external to the region, with the aim of exploiting knowledge spillovers and, more generally, all the transactions and flows between the regional economic context and the external economies.

This definition of smartness presupposes the empirical analysis of the quantitative and qualitative endowment of production factors of the region and its capacity to increase its knowledge stock. In turn, this involves the recognition of the main factors of competitiveness and of the bottlenecks, through a process of discovery. This allows concentrating resources and private and public investments on the fundamental priorities, avoiding uniformity and duplications of investments (in innovation), with respect to the neighbouring regions.

In this way, regions can value proximity in a model that builds relationships between innovative rates and economic growth with the indicators of related variety, thanks to the knowledge spillovers it induces (Cooke, 2009). In the EU, S3 strategies are one of the preconditions for an efficient use of European funds, to be defined and shared with citizens and firms, in order to channel European resources towards innovation policies and the mobilisation of private investments towards the chosen sectors of specialisation. This values complementarities between public and private sector and the knowledge distribution that can derive from it.

S3 however is distinct from the traditional regional policies for innovation, because of its outward orientation: it is indeed aimed at reinforcing the competitiveness of the entire EU and makes it more attractive to foreign investments in R&D.

3 Smart specialisation: some open questions

In this paragraph, some theoretical and methodological problems characterising the S3 debate will be discussed. Indeed, S3 is

> [s]uch a success story in such a short period of time is a perfect example of 'policy running ahead of theory': while smart specialisation seems to be already a policy hit and policy makers show some frenetic engagements towards smart specialisation, the concept is not tight in particular as an academic concept.
>
> (Foray et al., 2011, p. 1)

We will thus highlight some of the evolutionary elements of the concept of S3, in order to discuss the problems that emerge when this positive notion is used in a normative way.

3.1 The evolutionary background to the concept of smart specialisation

To discuss the evolutionary foundations of the concept of S3, it is preliminarily necessary to recall which are the main elements characterising evolutionary theory and how it evolved through the biological analogy.

In general terms, the concept of evolution refers to the self-transformation (i.e. the transformation from within) over time of a certain population (that can vary from a population of human beings to one of ideas). This self-transformation mainly follows stable and predictable paths, but since the transformation from within often results in novelty, the system might produce, besides stable trajectories, also less predictable jumps. Evolution is indeed an open process of which it is not possible to thoroughly predict the final outcome.

An evolutionary theory shows the following characteristics: it is inherently dynamic, it is historically based, it is able to produce from within the forces engendering the process of self-transformation, and it is focused on populations as units of analysis (rather than on single entities). In spite of the fact that these characteristics should be self-explanatory, some considerations are necessary to understand the implications for the concept of S3. First, the fact that an evolutionary theory is dynamic implies that the analysis focuses on processes, and thus, all the comparative statics apparatus on which the orthodox analysis is based is no longer valid. The fact that it is historically based implies concepts such as irreversibility and path-dependency. Moreover, for the sake of the argument, these elements represent constraints to the degrees of freedom of the process of change, and even when recurrent patterns can be observed, the processes never reproduce themselves identically through time. This happens because of the main characteristics of the evolutionary process, which is its capacity to transform from within. In particular, the analysis focuses on the way in which diversity in behaviour originates, as it produces the novelty necessary for the dynamics of the system to start. And then, how this diversity resolves in the process of change is through a diffusion process. The generation of novelty (of variety) in the system is therefore endogenous, and it is the mechanism itself that determines growth. Or better, change is produced exactly by the capacity of the system to produce novelty (variety). This mechanism of growth can be produced only within a population (as it cannot derive from the single agent), and it is thus the dispersion (the variance) of these characteristics that engenders growth.

On the basis of this very sketchy description, we will discuss the evolutionary content of the concept of S3, from both the positive and the normative side. In particular, as far as the latter is concerned, as S3 has been used largely as a policy tool, we will discuss also how exporting this concept outside of its domain has generated some problems with the elements upon which the theory itself has been built.

3.2 The positive side

The concept of S3 has been developed starting from the acknowledgment of the relative delay of EU with respect to US as far as R&D and innovative capacity at large is concerned. To this end, S3 aims at strengthening the weak (sometimes even absent) relationships between R&D and innovative activity, on the one side, and the sectoral structure of the economy, on the other. It must be noted, in fact, that S3 has been proposed initially as a sort of neutral sectoral policy, the purpose of which is to find a way to incentivise innovative activities within the European techno-economic system to close the gap with US. Thus, it must be recalled that S3 is a process that, by definition, since the word specialisation is used in relative terms, is not aimed at finding the 'best' combination of region/R&D/innovation in absolute terms. But rather, the best combination, in relative terms, of the initial endowment of a certain region or how to focus certain sectoral characteristics that are better fit towards innovative activities rather than others. In this way, for example, the classic notion of division of labour is rejected in favour of that of complementarity.

The 'entrepreneurial discovery process' is a crucial element for the functioning (for the mere existence, it could be said) of the S3 process. Indeed, it is only through a process of this type that, according to the proponents (Foray et al., 2011, p. 7), it is possible to find the 'right' patterns of development. The entrepreneurial discovery process is an element that reminds obviously to the logic of the evolutionary model: firms are the subjects of the discovery process through a typical mechanism of trial and error. Indeed,

> a successful smart specialisation strategy will not be found by reading the tables of contents of the most recent issue of Science or Nature but rather by observing the structures of the economy and supporting the processes of discovery undertaken by the firms and other organisations operating in this economy.
>
> (Foray et al., 2011, p. 4)

Hence, the discovery process is a sort of power-assisted process rather than guided by the public authority, which offers to entrepreneurs certain infrastructural resources, both material and immaterial.

The fundamental elements are thus the following. First, the entrepreneurial discovery is not necessarily linked to technological elements but rather more frequently to the discovery of new fields of specialisation. In this regard, the notion of Schumpeterian innovation is quite evidently called forth. Second, policies are not aimed at 'explaining the entrepreneurs what is right to do', but rather to accompanying the process, for example, by supplying the necessary public goods and the infrastructures (such as for example education and training). Third, the two preceding activities quite naturally imply that they do not build a 'simple' innovation, but by focusing on a particular domain, they build a techno-economic system. The interactions between these processes generate the potential for economies of scale, of scope, and for spillovers. Thus, new knowledge is produced on the future economic value of a possible structural change (Foray et al., 2011, p. 8).

These elements are intrinsically evolutionary, as in an evolutionary model the knowledge-generating process is a dispersed one, during which several units act in parallel. In this way, the possibilities to generate novelty in the system are maximised, and thus the system itself (but not the single units) maximises the likelihood of success. Moreover, as innovative activity at large is characterised by uncertainty, trial-and-error activities are the only ones able to furnish plausible answers to complex questions.

Such a system is created to operate in contexts characterised by high levels of information asymmetry. As the degree of novelty generated within the system determines its performance level, in order to generate novelty, agents need to behave the most idiosyncratic way possible. In fact, it is important that every agent behaves differently from others, from both the microeconomic (different behaviours will have higher possibilities to be positively selected from the selection environment) and the systemic point of view (the higher the degree of diversity, the higher the number of elements of the system that will likely survive the selection process and that will be able to transmit their idiosyncratic characteristic to the descendants, thus improving the aggregate performance). In this regard, it must be noted that evolutionary theory, since it is aimed at the performance of the whole system and not of single agents, finds in this type of dynamics those that maximise efficacy (with different agents that operate in parallel, the probability of finding a solution is presumably very high) but not efficiency (because of the level of redundancy that characterise this process). Furthermore, redundancy increases the resiliency of the system.

Finally, it is worth noting that the process of evolutionary development is intrinsically adaptive, in the sense that the research of the best performance in general is made in complex environments, and thus these mechanisms will likely lead towards local optima. From these local optima, it is also difficult and costly to move away to search for global maxima. In other words, the research algorithms of better solutions are typically local.

3.3 The normative side

If on the positive side it is fairly evident that the concept of S3 is firmly anchored to the evolutionary principles, from the normative point of view, although it still explicitly refers to the evolutionary theory, it is necessary to better detail the theoretical basis to frame the ensuing discussion. Indeed, while orthodox theory with its reference to the capacity of the market to reach maximum allocative efficiency can define normative criteria quite precisely and explicitly, evolutionary theory finds its fundamental element in the continuous capacity of innovative processes to elaborate knowledge and to produce change. The underlying notion of welfare is thus divergent with respect to the neoclassical one: from the evolutionary perspective the capitalist system is seen as an engine that incessantly generates growth and thus is seen as a mechanism that continuously generates structural change and disequilibrium. In this sense, the neoclassical stable equilibrium is de facto incompatible with the evolutionary process of growth and is also incompatible with the concept of efficient allocation and/or market failure. Therefore, the normative implications of the evolutionary viewpoint must take into consideration: (1) the impossibility to apply welfare analysis to intrinsically dynamic phenomena, that is to emergent phenomena; (2) the uncertainty (and not risk) governing the evolutionary dynamics. Therefore, states of equilibrium (whether they happens or not) are scarce or of no interest for dynamic analysis. And, since every state of the system is consequence of change, then the idea itself of equilibrium leaves room to that of order, meant as an objective of economic agents and thus with a procedural meaning.

From an evolutionary viewpoint, it is possible to see the normative implications, from both the standard and the systemic point of view. As an evolutionary system is intrinsically dynamic, it continuously produces structural change (i.e. creative destruction) that alters the distribution and for that reason needs compensative interventions. On the one side, the normative value of the concept of S3 should be connected to the capacity to manage what agents desire. This is possible if the actual structure of relationships and of possible targets of economic policy is held constant. On the other side, i.e. on the systemic point of view, the normative activity concerns the global functioning of the techno-economic system and originates from equivalence between welfare and concepts such as innovation or learning. From this perspective, it implies the capacity to understand which is the best institutional framework to elaborate the dispersed knowledge of the system. Through the endogenous generation of variety, processes of learning and thus of techno-economic change are generated in turn. This obviously implies a comparative institutional analysis based on the idea of multi-dimensional welfare. Hence, while from the individual point of view it is important to define criteria to evaluate how the different positions of the single agents have changed in the process, and thus if a normative intervention is necessary at all, from a systemic point of view, it is important to decide how to find, put at work, and remunerate the resources necessary to the growth of the system. The process is a complex one, as it involves the discovery of new possibilities for future specialisations for populations of agents. Therefore, from an evolutionary viewpoint, two important problems arise for the public authority: (1) how to know what is good for a population and (2) how to manage the problem of the lack of coordination. A way to satisfy the two most demanding requisites of the system is to make it to develop in time (through the generation and the working of new knowledge) and then to succeed in not marginalising the losers, trying to find a way to keep them within the (dynamic) system. And it is exactly to this problem that policy prescriptions refer.

A first important element emphasised by the proponents of the S3 concept is related to that of redundancy. Indeed, the trade-off between efficiency and effectiveness, at first sight, seems to be resolved in favour of the latter: "Technological evolution and application are non-deterministic and even what appears as duplication often creates diversity and distinctive capabilities and/or new opportunities" (Giannitsis, 2009, p. 6). In particular, since the beginning, it can be noted that the possible negative effects of, otherwise positive, policies to incentivise and accelerate technological change could be even stronger because of the techno-economic barriers, of the concentration of resources in certain areas, of the exclusion of certain types of actors, of the limitation of the windows of opportunities, etc.

A second element, also linked to the evolutionary nature of the S3 process, has to do with the problem of asymmetric information. Indeed, since asymmetric information is the engine of diversity production (and thus of the system's performance), it cannot be dealt with through the usual orthodox methods of market failure. In this regard, it is recommended to manage a portfolio of technological policies that favour variety and selection mechanisms. It is important to note that any policy option that declares its willingness to deal with market failures, systemic failures, or the like does not understand the evolutionary nature of the process and therefore does not understand the way in which the process itself feeds its own developmental dynamics.

Finally, the evolutionary focus on processes implies a vision according to which the continuous process of change produces the requisites for its stability through the transformation of its capacities from potential to effective. This can be done by means of a self-organisation process of the ecological niche that is built by differentiated institutions. The interactions are thus continuously created and re-created in unforeseeable ways (for the single agent) and have different nature from the kind of problems that generated them. A sort of division of labour is thus created, which allocate the generation of absorptive capacity to firms and the structure of interrelationships to institutions. The entrepreneurial capacities form better around opportunities than around weaknesses, and this is a fundamental element of policy-making. Moreover, knowledge is distributed within the system, and this makes no agent to have (and to reasonably pretend to have) a superior knowledge with respect to the others (also as social planner). Policies must thus be conceived in this way and must be functional to the transmission of knowledge in both directions.

4 Smart specialisation as a tool for regional policy

The regional topics emerging from the formulation of the themes of smart specialisation have immediately been subsumed as cornerstones of EU interventions. At his regard, the President of the European Commission José Manuel Barroso, in his introduction to the Communication of the Commission on Programme Europe 2020 writes:

> To achieve a sustainable future, we must already look beyond the short term. Europe needs to get back on track. Then it must stay on track. That is the purpose of Europe 2020. It's about more jobs and better lives. It shows how Europe has the capability to deliver smart, sustainable and inclusive growth, to find the path to create new jobs and to offer a sense of direction to our societies.

Since the first contributions, the proponents of the concept of S3 have highlighted its intrinsic potentialities to act as crucial element for regional/national policies (Foray et al., 2009). They thus highlighted a regional dimension that is not present in the usual readings of this concept, focused as they are more on the sectoral dimension: "[a] promising strategy appears to be to encourage investment in programs that will complement the country's other productive assets to create future domestic capability and interregional comparative advantage" (Foray et al., 2009, p. 1).

In this way, it becomes possible to link the process of entrepreneurial discovery to a learning process based on local competences. This should allow regions to excel in particular areas. Following this process, it is possible to overcome the problem of the lack of (or of insufficient) incentives through the creation of excellences that ensure absolute advantages, rather than comparative ones. Hence, effective policies of help focusing to increase the level of commitment can be based on them. These policies would be linked to a conscious redrafting of the interventions, which should be more (if not only) oriented towards the supply of infrastructures (both material and immaterial). In this way, the role of public intervention would be limited to the creation of connections and to their coordination to create and increase positive externalities.

The creation of complementarities has thus a fundamental role in the division between regions that invest in basic inventions and those that invest in specific co-inventions. Therefore, the concept of S3 needs a policy commitment markedly different, whose objectives are process-oriented (i.e. they are attempts to influence the result through indirect actions) and related to the creation of regional units, to the geographical concentration of resources, and to the enhancement of social externalities. This commitment needs a strong consensus (as its success is normally recognisable only ex-post, rather than the search for a social optimum) and a very high level of co-management (through the definition of minimum requisites and objectives of the processes), rather than detailed plans.

From this viewpoint, it appears 'normal' that regional economics attempted to intervene. For example, through policy interventions whose target is to subsidise weak regions (the followers) through the development of networks between researchers to spread their specialist knowledge throughout whole regions. This, of course, creates a problem of cognitive proximity, since on the one side geographical proximity makes it possible to transmit knowledge, but on the other side, this is not enough since these exchanges could result in asymmetric relationships between entities with different levels of competences and high cognitive distance. These situations could not work even with a very close level of competences, given the top-down nature of this kind of policy intervention.

The transition to a regional dimension has been made possible, on the one side, by the endorsement of place-based policies (rather than the spatial-neutral ones, typical of the sectoral approach of the S3 proponents), with particular reference to the EU cohesion policies. On the other side, the definition of different typologies of innovative regions was made possible by how the following three fundamental concepts of embeddedness, relatedness, and connectivity are combined (McCann and Ortega-Argilés, 2011).

The first concept refers to place-based interventions, which are differentiated from space-neutral ones, as the latter are focused, for instance, on maximising human capital mobility with respect to market signals. Relatedness constitutes an important element to geo-referencing S3 (Boschma, 2005; Frenken et al., 2007). Based on this concept, it is possible to produce relative diversification within a neighbourhood of the competences already developed and interrelated. In other words, the diversification can be neither too much (as it would engender advantages, presumably, at random), nor too little (as specialisation would make the technological and industrial structure of a region vulnerable to one single big shock). In order to build embeddedness and relatedness, agents need to be able to exchange information and knowledge among them (connectivity). Indeed, for an S3 policy to work in a regional context, policy interventions must necessarily focus on the creation of knowledge spillovers and of learning relationships, both intra- and inter-regional.

The regional transposition of the S3 concept, however, shows some problems. Here we will propose some discussion stressing not so much the methodological problems (such as, for instance, which are the best indicators to understand this kind of phenomenon), but rather the problematic elements related to the normative applications of this model, which must be remembered is evolutionary. First of all, moving the focus of S3 from sectors to regions implies moving from processes to structure and to results. This obviously must be done in accordance with the implications of the evolutionary model, according to which policy prescriptions must obey the well-specified requisites. Moreover, a regionalist approach implies that policy interventions are focused on historical evidence, on the attempts to fix realistic objectives and on avoiding resources dispersion (see, for instance, McCann and Ortega-Argilés, 2013).

Therefore, it must be noted that these typologies of evolutionary models are not very well suited to very precise and detailed policy prescriptions and to obtaining particular results. The idea itself of market failure, if seen from an evolutionary perspective, lends itself to creating a dynamic process of creative destruction through differential access to knowledge. And this seems not very well in line with policy prescriptions related to how to monitor and evaluate the results of policies aimed to correct distortions and/or dead losses of the market process. The policies for local growth cannot be produced and applied by a superior instance but must be the result of an interactive process in which the public side has a role of indirect animation and of sustaining innovative activities, rather than addressing and correcting deviations from the steady path. Also the idea that policies should avoid the dispersion of resources must be critically evaluated. Especially in the light of the fact that, since the unit of analysis of evolutionary theory is the population and not the singe agent, system performance is ensured by the duplication of resources. It is indeed redundancy, which from the perspective of efficiency should be eliminated, the factor determinant of the system's performance. From this point of view, policies should target efficacy rather than efficiency.

Another element that seems a bit problematic is the idea that, because of path-dependency, a policy option might be that of observing the past to understand the main strongholds of a system of relationships and hence trying to influence them. Also in this case, it is necessary to pay attention. Indeed, the temporal stability of the growth patterns is an epiphenomenon and not a cause. In practice, path-dependency is the result of a series of hypothesis on agents' behaviour, among which we find myopia, search processes, and local knowledge. In this sense, path-dependency acts as one of the stabilising elements of a potentially explosive and chaotic dynamics, which is generated by variety. Hence, to consider it as one of the key elements upon which policy-makers activity should focus, means stressing the static characteristics of the model and not the dynamic ones. Also it means stressing negative feedback (that smooth oscillations towards equilibrium) and not positive feedback. In this way, the capacity of the system of generating novelty results to be quite limited. Also the idea itself of related variety, if from the positive point of view constitutes a good ex-post predictor of regional performance, however it can with difficulty be considered as an ex-ante instrument (being based as it is on the already existent, past, techno-industrial structure) to understand where a qualitative change of the system will happen.

So, it seems quite evident that such policies could be more successful in so-called intermediate regions, where the presence of rural and urban areas can be a catalyser for S3 processes that can thus fix more realistic targets. Also in this case, however, some problems emerge, related to the necessity to define precisely what intermediate actually means. And, if it exists, how big is the threshold beyond which policies are ineffective. Also the idea of realistic targets is extremely slippery and can allow for quite big differences in the implementation of S3 policies.

Moreover, with reference to the evolutionary ideas, it is maybe possible to suggest a way to build policies (in general, but especially for S3) that take into account the two fundamental elements on which the model is based: the distribution of knowledge and the generation of novelty. In fact, as already said, it is possible to take the instrumental side of the intervention policies as possibilities of intervention in a given structure with a given mid-period aim. In this case, the policies can furnish guidelines to intervene in already formed ecological niches with precise characteristics, within which the policy interventions can highlight with reasonable accuracy (and, more importantly, participation) some realistic targets that could reasonably be reached. Another case is about the possibility of structural interventions in the long run. In this case, the role of the public should be 'limited' to the search of a shared strategic vision, upon which to base the entrepreneurial activities of the single firms. In both cases, the policy intervention should be conditioned from the capacities to start an effective exchange process (and thus of acquisition) of information and knowledge. These in turn, should be the basis for the construction of a shared global vision through partnerships with other institutions, leaving to single agents the definition of different ways with which to pursue the desired outcomes.

Finally, it must be noted that the definition of the various levels of intervention is highly dependent on the tension between top-down and bottom-up types of interventions. Indeed, a quite diffused emphasis on bottom-up approaches allows smart strategies to model themselves on the basis of the vocation of each single component of the system and the communities involved. The need for a bottom-up approach is linked mainly to the central role of the phases of listening, participation, co-design, diffusion, and exchange of information. This should lead to close collaboration between the different agents involved. As far as S3 is concerned, this implies a focus on the already available knowledge to start an effective process of diversification (Iacobucci, 2012). In particular, in its evolutionary version, S3 seems to be incompatible, at least in its early steps, with the imposition of sectoral specialisation through a top-down sort of bureaucratic process (Foray et al., 2009). It should be a duty of the agents acting in the territorial context, firms and universities overall, together with the communities of reference, to highlight the more promising settings for future specialisation areas. From them, a true regional system of innovation could be developed. The higher levels of governance should be limited to make the discovery process more effective by means of an appropriate system of incentives. The involvement of the local communities hence would also contribute also to S3 as a generator of variety, which is needed to favour a sectoral diversification of the local economic system and to ensure a competitive advantage in an environment characterised by increasingly complex value chain, especially in terms of the knowledge involved.

Different elements, however, lead to the necessity to adopt a bottom-up approach in relation to specific elements. The rigid contraposition between top-down and bottom-up approaches seems to refer to the EU policy-maker, that is to high-level interventions. But it is attenuated at lower levels of governance. When we instead refer to regions, for instance, it can be said that the definition of smart strategies and their specific related objectives all imply decisional processes of the top-down type, at least in their early phases (Iacobucci, 2012). A top-down intervention is furthermore requested in relation to processes of development of human capital, in terms of education, training, and work-based learning. This would allow facing the new 'knowledge needs' on local scale, based on the development of a cohort of workers with the necessary competences to make incremental innovations and the maintenance of the new technologies introduced in the region following the S3 strategies.

5 Conclusions

In the socio-economic transition that the contemporary society is undergoing, the concept of *smartness* is indeed a fashionable one, especially for its different dimensions according to which smartness can be deciphered (social, economic, institutional) and for the innovative elements it conjures up. However, as the concept, on the one side, is relatively newly developed and, on the other side, involves a wide plurality of reference models, some problematic issues emerge at both the theoretical and applied levels.

In this chapter, an attempt to frame the concept of S3 is made by advocating evolutionary theory, although some open questions still hold true.

First, some critical elements exist in the relationship between S3 and regional policies. S3 is indeed produced as a sort of neutral sectoral policy tool based on evolutionary theory. Its aim should be thus to incentivise innovative activities of the EU techno-economic system to catch up with that of USA. The ensuing regional transposition was made possible through a place-based translation. This emphasises, besides the geographical element, context-specific elements such as embeddedness and relatedness. This gives rise to potential contradictions as it shifts the focus from processes to structure and results and focuses on efficiency rather than efficacy, on static rather than dynamic elements, and on top-down decisional procedures.

Second, by focusing on institutional innovation, it highlights the role of elements such as institutional complementarities to favour the dynamics of institutional building and of institutional change functional to smart specialisation. The creation and the management of relationships become thus the centrepiece of this type of intervention.

Notes

1 For more information, see http://ec.europa.eu/invest-in-research/monitoring/knowledge_ en.htm, and the documents in which almost all the main contributions are summarised (EC, 2008 and EC, 2009).
2 On the side of business industry, this notion has been used in the framework of the so-called Industry 4.0. This term has been used for the first time in 2011 at the Hannover Fair. In October 2012, the Working Group on Industry 4.0, chaired by Siegfried Dais (Robert Bosch GmbH) and Henning Kagermann (Acatech) prepared a list of recommendations on industrial development for the German government. In April 2013, again at the Hannover Fair, the final report of the Working Group was issued.
3 Even the research projects conceived in the framework of the Horizon 2020 programme, launched by the EC in 2015, can be seen as another follow-up of this idea.
4

> [T]he idea of smart specialisation does not call for imposing specialisation through some form of top-down industrial policy that is directed in accord with a pre-conceived "grand plan". Nor should the search for smart specialisation involve a fore-sight exercise.
>
> (Foray et al., 2009, p. 2)

Bibliography

Boschma, R. (2005), Proximity and innovation. A critical survey, *Regional Studies*, 39 (1), 61–74.

Camagni, R. and Capello, R. (2012), *Regional innovation patterns and the EU Regional Policy reform: Towards smart innovation policies*, Paper presented at the 52° ERSA Conference in Bratislava, 21–24 August 2012.

Cooke, P. (2009), The knowledge economy, spillovers, proximity and specialization, in D. Pontikakis, D. Kyriakou and R. van Bavel (eds.), *The question of R&D specialisation: Perspectives and policy implications*, Brussels, European Commission, Directoral General for Research, pp. 27–40.

Crouch, C., Streeck, W., Boyer, R., Amable, B., Hall, P.A. and Jackson, G. (2005), Dialogue on institutional complementarity and political economy, *Socio-Economic Review*, 3 (2), 359–382.

David, P., Foray, D. and Hall, B. (2013), Measuring smart specialisation: The concept and the need for indicators, mimeo.

European Commission. (2008), *Knowledge for growth. European issues and policy challenges*, Bruxelles, Luxembourg, Office for Official Publications of the European Communities.

European Commission. (2009), *Knowledge for growth. Prospects for science, technology and innovation. Selected papers from Research Commissioner Janez Potoc?nik's Expert Group*, Bruxelles, available at http://ec.europa.eu/invest-in-research/pdf/download_en/ selected_papers_en.pdf.

Florida, R. (2002), *The rise of the creative class, and how it's transforming work, leisure, community and everyday life*, New York, Basic Books.

Foray, D., David, P. and Hall, B. (2009), Smart specialisation – The concept, *Knowledge Economists Policy Brief*, 9, available at http://ec.europa.eu/invest-in-research/pdf/down load_en/kfg_policy_brief_no9.pdf.

Foray, D., David, P. and Hall, B. (2011), *From academic idea to political instrument, the surprising career of a concept and the difficulties involved in its implementation*, MTEI-WP 2011–001, College of Management of Technology, Lausanne.

Foray, D., Goddard, J., Goenaga Beldarrain, X., Landabaso, M., McCann, P., Morgan, K., Nauwelaer, C. and Ortega-Argilés, R. (2012), *Guide to research and innovation strategies for smart specialisation (RIS 3)*, Smart Specialisation Platform, European Commission.

Frenken, K., Van Oort, F. and Verburg, T. (2007), Related variety, unrelated variety and regional economic growth, *Regional Studies*, 41 (5), 685–697.

Giannitsis, T. (2009), Technology and specialization: Strategies, options, risks, *Knowledge Economists Policy Brief*, 8, available at http://ec.europa.eu/invest-in-research/pdf/down load_en/kfg_policy_brief_no8.pdf?11111.

Iacobucci, D. (2012), *Developing and implementing a smart specialisation strategy at regional level: Some open questions*, c.MET Working papers No. 05.

McCann, P. and Ortega-Argilés, R. (2011), *Smart specialisation, regional growth and applications to EU cohesion policy*, Document de treball de l'IEB 2011/14, Institut d'Economia de Barcelona.

McCann, P. and Ortega-Argilés, R. (2013), Redesigning and reforming European regional policy: the reasons, the logic and the outcomes, *International Regional Science Review*, 36 (3), 424–445.

OECD. (2011), *Regions and innovation policy, OECD reviews of regional innovation*, Paris, OECD Publishing.

2 Smart specialization and models of capitalism

Luca Cattani and Giovanni Guidetti

1 Institutions for smart development

In these last fifteen years within the institutionalist approach to economic analysis, a group of scholars has focused the attention on models of capitalism. Through a set of rather heterogeneous contributions (Aoki, 2001; Hall and Soskice, 2001; Amable, 2003) this literature has set up a conceptual framework of analysis to interpret the complex network of relations that link the institutions of an economic system to the agents operating in it. The basic idea of this strand of the economic literature is that the institutional architecture plays a pivotal role in defining the objective functions of economic agents and in modelling and constraining their interactions and expectations. Before discussing what this approach can suggest for the analysis of smart development, it is useful to summarize the notion of institution that can be found in this approach.

Despite not being the first economist who defined institution (see, among the others Commons, 1934 and Veblen, 1899), North (1990) defines institutions as

> [T]he humanly devised constraints that structure politic, economic and social interaction. They consist of both informal constraints (sanctions, taboos, customs, traditions and codes of conduct), and formal rules (constitutions, laws, property rights). Throughout history, institutions have been devised by human beings to create order and reduce uncertainty in exchange. Together with the standard constraints of economics they define the choice set and therefore determine transaction and production costs and hence the profitability and feasibility of engaging in economic activity. They evolve incrementally, connecting the past with the present and the future; history in consequence is largely a story of institutional evolution in which the historical performance of economies can only be understood as a part of a sequential story. Institutions provide the incentive structure of an economy; as that structure evolves, it shapes the direction of economic change towards growth, stagnation, or decline.

The greater part of interpretations of North's definition emphasizes that organizations should not be conceived as institutions but as special economic agents submitted to the rules of behaviour set by institutions. As claimed by Hodgson (2006), according to North (1994),

> [T]he interaction between institutions and organizations . . . shapes the institutional evolution of an economy. If institutions are the rules of the game, organizations and their entrepreneurs are the players. Organizations are made up of groups of individuals bound together by some common purpose to achieve certain objectives.

However, Hodgson points out that institutions cannot be conceived as undifferentiated monoliths but rather as complex structures in which agents with possibly contrasting objectives coexist and operate. The British economist, consistently with North's approach, maintain that institutions "are systems of established and embedded social rules that structure social interactions" but also that organizations "are special institutions that involve (1) criteria to establish their boundaries and to distinguish their members from non members, (2) principles of sovereignty concerning who is in charge, and (3) chains of command delineating responsibilities within the organization." Conclusively, following Hodgson's approach, one can state that organizations can be considered as an array of formal and informal rules that regulate the interactions among agents operating within the organizations themselves and whose objectives might well be conflicting. Additionally, in the organization, the agents' behaviour is bound by the hierarchical structure, which defines the chain of command and defines decisional responsibilities.

2 Models of capitalism

In the aforementioned literature on the models of capitalism, a conception of organization à la Hodgson prevails. In fact, organizations such as firms, unions, political parties, and public agencies are always envisaged as complex and non-monolithic units in which heterogeneous agents operate. This heterogeneity of agents is a key factor of the analysis, which is focused on income distribution and on the institutional regulation of the distributional conflict between profits and wages. As a matter of fact, the way the institutions confront and manage the distributional conflict can be defined as model of capitalism.

Hall and Soskice's (2001) approach to the analysis of models of capitalism is definitely the most useful to the analysis of the idea of smart development, because the firm and the interactions occurring in it among the diverse economic agents are the core of their analysis. This framework of analysis identifies two distinct ideal-types of capitalism: (1) liberal market economies, i.e. Anglo-American economic systems, and (2) coordinated market economies, which are generally linked to the German economic model. According to this approach, the firm is a complex system in which five sub-systems interact and influence each other through a set of feed-back mechanisms. The diversity between the German and the American ideal-types is based on a comparison among the five sub-systems, which define the firm as an institution. Inside the firm, each sub-system identifies one or more institutions that interact and influence each other. This complex set of relations and feed-back dynamics among institutions define each sub-system and how the sub-systems interact. These five sub-systems and their interactions specify how firms manage and solve the problem of coordinating among both the agents operating inside the firm and the other public and private organizations with which the firms are related. The five sub-systems are the following: (1) the sub-system of industrial relations (2) the sub-system of training of employees, considered especially in relation to the school system; (3) the sub-system of corporate governance; (4) the sub-system of relations with other firms; and (5) the sub-system that defines how the firm searches, finds and develops the employees' skills.

(1) *The sub-system of industrial relations* refers to the mechanism of bargaining among workers and employers and/or their representatives. Basically, this sub-system defines how relationships among workers and employers are coordinated with respect to variables, which are generally bargained among workers and employers such as wages and working conditions (working time, work shifts). (2) *The sub-system of training and skill development* defines how firms solve their problems in the formation and development of human capital, setting a level of investment for this key variable for the competitiveness of the economic system. (3) *The sub-system of corporate governance* identifies how the firm solves its problems in finding financing means. Furthermore, this sub-system points out how investors strive to keep the profitability of their investments through some form of management control aimed at reaching the economic equilibrium in a well-defined lapse of time. (4) *The sub-system of relations among firms* refers to the coordination of relationships among the firm, its suppliers, and its customers: relations with suppliers and buyers of raw materials and semi-finished products, relations with public and private suppliers and buyers of technology. (5) As for *the coordination of the relations* among the firm and the workers, this sub-system particularly takes into account the problems of both work organization and development and diffusion of skills and competences inside the firm.

What is really important to underscore is that, in order to understand the role played by institutions in the determination of the performance of the economic systems, one has to analyze the structuring of these sub-systems and their interactions. The institutionalist literature (Aoki, 2001; Hall and Soskice, 2001; Amable, 2003; Crouch et al., 2005; Hopner, 2005) has emphasized three different typologies of relations, which can connect two or more institutions: (1) coherence, (2) hierarchical relations and (3) complementarity. These prototypes of relation define how institutions arise, interact and work.

1   Following Hopner (2005), each institution has been built on the basis of specific principles that model the operation and the governance of the institution. One can state that there is coherence among two or more institutions when the principles adopted for the construction of the institutions and the deriving styles of operation and governance are the same.

2   According to Amable (2003), an institution is hierarchically superior to another one if the subordinate institution's behaviour is a direct effect of the

operation and the working of the dominant institution. Basically, that means that the functioning of the hierarchically subordinated institution is the result of what happens in the dominating institution. These hierarchical relationships are always the outcome of a precise choice operated by the institutional builder.

3　The greatest efforts of analysis of relations among institutions have been devoted by both economists and political scientist to the analysis of complementarity relations. Following Hopner (2005), the definition of institutional complementarity among institutions requires not only a reference to the functional characteristics of the institutions but also some measure of the performance of the function carried out. One can claim that two or more institutions are in complementary relation when the functional outcome performed by an institution depends on the existence and the operation of one or more other institutions. In order to differentiate complementarity from hierarchical relations, one has to state that a complementarity relationship is always symmetrical; the operations of institutions in complementary relations affect each other.

From this complex conceptual framework, two interesting results arise: (1) efficient and effective institutional change cannot be focused on the transformation of a single institution but must take into account the network of relations established among institutions and (2) as proved by Aoki (2001) using a game-theoretical approach, the prevailing of institutional complementarities can give rise to non-Pareto efficient but stable equilibria. Aoki demonstrates that the transition towards a Pareto-efficient equilibrium can imply a too costly change as it involves a large and indefinite amount of institutions.

One can state that a model of capitalism can be defined as a set of institutions, classified according to the five sub-systems outlined in the previous paragraphs and whose interactions occur on the basis of the three typologies of relations just described. Table 2.1 outlines the two main models of capitalism, pointing out the features of the five sub-systems. For our purpose, it can be useful to discuss how these institutional settings that characterize each model of capitalism influence the capability to create and diffuse technological innovations (see, among others, Amable, 2003; Hall and Soskice, 2001). According to Hall and Soskice (2001) the German model favours the introduction of incremental technological innovations because of the great propensity of both workers and employers in investing in the development of firm-specific skills. Besides, in this economic system, the employers exhibit a greater propensity to introduce product differentiation policies rather than devising radical innovations of product. Conversely, the Anglo-American model of capitalism seems to have a greater inclination to introduce radical innovation due to a higher propensity of workers to develop general skills by investing massively in tertiary education. In addition to that, this attitude is strengthened by a financial market with fewer restrictions than the German one and by a poor degree of cooperation among firms.

Table 2.1 The models of capitalism

	German model	Anglo-American model
Industrial relations	Centralized bargaining. Strong role of both workers' and employers' unions.	Decentralized bargaining.
System of vocational training and education	School system and vocational training favour investment in human capital by both workers and employers. Dual education system.	School system and vocational training favour investment in general human capital. Low propensity for on-the-job training.
Corporate governance	Firms' governance favour capital profitability in the medium-to-long run. Protection from hostile takeover.	Firms' governance favour capital profitability in the short run. Possibility of hostile takeover.
Relations among firms	The system provides incentives for long-term relations among firms through different forms of cooperation and technological transfers.	Harsh competition among firms. Technological transfers through market exchanges.
Finding and managing workers and skills. Monitoring the labour market, hiring of workers and finding the suitable skills.	Long-term employment relations and development of firm-specific skills. Low incidence of stock options in the remuneration of the management	Labour demand follows the business cycle. High incidence of stock options in the remuneration of the management.

3 Institutions and smart specialization

The recent economic literature on smart development focuses on industrial policies and technological transfer. However, these analyses do not take into due account the institutional setting suitable for these policies. As maintained by Hall (2005), the emphasis on institutional complementarities does not imply that the establishment of certain institutions give rise to other complementary institutions. The processes of institutional creation and change are the results of political options and choices and not the outcome of economic efficiency and effectiveness. Institutions are often the aftermath of compromises among different and sometimes contrasting social, political and economic groups. Additionally, the process of institutional change is so complex and the network of potential complementary relations so close that it is barely possible for an ex-ante determination of the optimal institutional setting. In a context of limited rationality, the processes of institutional change follow paths of procedural rationality à la Simon in which incremental institutional innovations in indefinite lapses of time prevail. For this reason, defining ex ante a process of institutional building favouring smart development is quite problematic. However, it can be useful to discuss the properties that the institutions of smart development should have on the basis of the three typologies of relations, which can connect two or more institutions.

Consistent with McCann and Ortega-Argiles (2011) approach, one can single out four distinct kinds of institution and the relations that can be established among them. The institutions are the following:

1   Institutions providing the incentives to start the processes of entrepreneurial discovery. Even though smart development is inherently a bottom-up process, one needs to design a set of institutions that favour the process of introduction of innovative applications. Basically, these institutions should provide incentives to entrepreneurs for the development of applications to either newly created firms or start-ups in industrial sectors already well established in the local area. Furthermore, one can conceive tools to stimulate neo-entrepreneurships such as spin-offs and business incubators in cooperation with organizations and agencies existing in the local area (universities, chambers of commerce).

2   Institutions related to embeddedness. In this case, one refers to those institutions aimed at fostering the creation and the development of human capital. Particularly, it is important to devise institutions for the creation and the finding of workers with the proper skills, without falling in the so-called Krugman shadow effect. These processes of skill creation and development will occur inside the firms and, therefore, will give rise to firm-specific skills and not to general skills. As mentioned previously, with reference to the German model, investment in specific skills needs long-run employment relations. Besides, skill specificity requires some form of coordination among the firms, the industrial sectors involved in smart development and the school and the vocational training systems. The dual education system combining apprenticeships in a firm and vocational education might well be a solution to these problems of coordination.

3   Institutions of relatedness. In this case, one refers to institutions that complement those introduced under (1) and (2) in order to push firms in developing general purpose technologies (GPT) applications and, more generally, incremental technological innovations. This kind of institution requires firms with corporate governance supporting the cooperation among firms in R&D activities and in technological transfer.

4   Institutions related to connectivity. These institutions advance the connections among different regions with common strategic interests. These institutions have to regulate workers' mobility and exchanges of goods, services, knowledge and technology among regions.

Definitely, these processes of institutional building can create remarkable problems among these newly founded institutions and also with pre-existing local institutions. As a matter of fact, one can observe difficulties in coherence, hierarchy and complementarity as far as the relations among institutions (institutional network) are concerned. These problems can be quite difficult to address and can hinder the functioning of the new institutional architecture. The existence of hierarchical relations among institutions can prevent the efficient functioning of an institution if the latter is incoherent with another hierarchically superior institution. For instance, this can be the case when a new law aimed at fostering start-ups breaks EU legislation. Or perverse complementary relations can arise such that the operation of an institution hampers the working of another one. However, as mentioned in previous paragraphs, the requirement to set up complementary relations among institutions is a key point in the processes of institution building as complementarity can influence not only the efficiency and the effectiveness of institutions but also their dynamics. For a single institution, the establishment of complementary relations with either new or already existing institutions can bring about also a significant strengthening/weakening of its efficiency. In this respect, it is very important to find as many complementary relations as possible with the target of augmenting the level of productivity of the institutions involved. Conclusively, in the process of institutional building, not only do single new institutions need introducing, but also a network of coherent and complementary institutions has to be founded and has to be taken into careful consideration, if one wants to avoid the occurring of institutional dysfunctions whose source is not the nature of the single institution but the web of badly (poorly) devised links.

4 Human capital and the smart development approach

Human capital investments and the attraction of highly qualified/skilled labour are increasingly considered among the most important drivers of comparative advantage for modern economies, thus coming to represent much more than simple production factors. On the one hand, the localization and specialization of economic activities in a given, often urban, area is still regarded as desirable as a standard positive externality since it provides a pool of skilled and specialized labour, thereby minimizing transition, training and scouting costs. On the other hand, the smart development approach adopts a systemic point of view on technological flow borrowing from the literature on Regional Systems of Innovation (RSI) and stressing the importance of bottom-up processes led by multiple agents set up as building blocks and the need to re-consider human capital as a main source of knowledge production and dissemination/transmission. In this perspective, the localization of cultural and educational organizations such as universities and research centres allows the exploitation of complementarities thus favouring technical progress via the increased absorptive capacity of firms (Malerba, 1996; Smith, 1997). A second key aspect of the spatial concentration of human capital and highly skilled labour is represented by the increased capability of cross-pollinating scientific discoveries and innovations, which may take place either in basic and applied research and in terms of both development and design. At the institutional level, it may be needed in some cases for a rethinking of the territorial governance marked by pluralism, multi-dimensionality and behavioural additionality of public policies in order to ensure efficient training/attraction of highly qualified human resources, which are crucial in order to exploit either local sectorial/technological and interregional/global complementarities (Chaminade et al., 2009). For this purpose, the spillover effect potential of such interactions can be triggered to some extent by a certain degree of sectorial variety, thus avoiding both technological and commercial lock-ins (Smith, 1997), or by acting directly on the variety/selection trade-off and trying to foster a productive heterogeneity within a few related cognitive fields, thus introducing the concept of related variety (Boschma and Iammarino, 2009; Basile et al., 2012; Camagni and Capello, 2013). A well-established example of such related variety is represented by all those economic activities taking place in the Italian region of Emilia-Romagna that employ mechatronic knowledge, method and tools.

4.1 Specialization, education and training

From a theoretical point of view, investing in and attracting human capital in a smart development perspective should raise concerns related either to the specific complementarity between development paradigms, and the relative in-place availability of related skills, and the necessity to contaminate these dimensions with the Europe 2020 agenda priorities: social cohesion (inclusive growth) and environmental sustainability (sustainable growth).

While the latter priority does not seem to raise major problems, the former has already led to the identification of a couple of issues at both the theoretical and the practical levels. First, a big emphasis on specialization strategies is suitable to exacerbate and/or accelerate skills obsolescence following a *skill-biased technical change*[1] path and thus crowding out many workers employed in other sectors. Second, labour forces census data show a non-linear development path in advanced economies, Italy included (1991, 2001, 2011). Particularly, there is no evidence of an upgrading of medium-skilled professions into highly skilled ones while, quite the contrary, a dangerous polarization is actually taking place with a steep increase in both highly skilled professions (+128% between 1991 and 2001) and poorly skilled professions.[2]

This polarization, along with segmentations occurred in local labour markets, imply at least two priorities in the political agenda at the various levels of territorial government, which are suitable to represent an exception to the bottom-up approach typically associated with S3. On the one hand, skills obsolescence requires new tools to identify and limit the mismatch between demand and supply of knowledge and skills, both vertically and horizontally. On the other hand, the required consistency among territorial education and training policies implies a pivotal role for the highest levels of government, at both the national level and EU level. A regional S3 strategy should thus be based onto the skills demanded to undertake the desired specialization path in the long run. Different government levels hence need to address the formation, attraction and composition of human capital consistently with the local skill needs identified by the S3 strategy (Foray, 2009) by promoting access to education and training, either directly or through subsidies to businesses, workers and training agencies.

The evolution of knowledge and its organization in a smartness perspective brings additional risks in terms of inequality: between regions that can be labelled as leaders and followers, between creative cities and not creative ones, or within the same region or city. Capitalism, even in its knowledge-based version, continues to be a "system of distributed ignorance" (Metcalfe et al., 2012, p. 3) in which the lack of access to education and training leads to growing inequality based on different human capital endowments. Hence, smartness requires a transformation of the economic organization of knowledge intended to lead to greater structuring of the smartness itself and an upgrading of human resources in response to new forms of division of labour, even if taking the move from the existing organizational and technological complementarities. Consistently, the European Union, while pursuing intelligent growth, fosters research and innovation jointly with special policies to encourage people to learn, study and update their skills. Moreover, in a space-neutral approach, for increasing levels of human capital, the propensity to migrate from follower regions may thus increase displacing policies for education and training at a regional level. However, this phenomenon is mitigated by the existence of idiosyncratic skills on a local basis.

Firms themselves are required to rethink their knowledge organization. Sector-related competences and skills, intangible networks, an increasingly open and global society, along with the necessity to localize working performances in a well-defined geographical area, altogether require firms to build an internal training system that allows staff to cope with the misalignment generated between the output of the institutional education and training systems and the input of knowledge, skills and competencies that this growing demand expresses, both in terms of current and prospective needs. In addition, the complementarity between general (as provided by the education system) and specific training (Acemoglu and Pischke, 1999) attributes to the firm an increasing role in the delivery of the first as well. It is hence crucial for companies to learn how to build, consolidate and accumulate knowledge in efficient forms in order to achieve a sustainable competitive advantage based on the productivity of physical capital and *knowledge workers*.

5 The "creative class"

Human capital and highly skilled labour deliver to workers a new active role in the innovation and technical progress processes resulting in an endogenization, from a theoretical point of view, of the processes themselves. The idea of an emerging "creative class" has gained some consensus and has opened a florid debate, thus leading to an abundant and heterogeneous niche in the economic literature since the seminal work of Florida (2002, 2005). The growing shares on the total labour forces of highly demanding professions and their territorial localization (stickiness) jointly and directly contribute to either increase workers' productivity and create and transmit knowledge, partially contradicting the idea that analytical and coded knowledge could not enjoy territorial spillovers as tacit knowledge does.

The focus is therefore shifted from businesses and industries to creative individuals capable of generating spillovers in urban and regional contexts (as in Almeida and Kogut, 1999), thus reversing the traditional setting of agglomeration externalities (Gleaser et al., 1992). The concept of creative class is still compatible with other perspectives, like endogenous growth theories, which can be described as less systemic and more rigidly formal, to the extent that they recognize social interactions and/or complementarities between human and physical capital as vehicles of technological progress (Lucas, 1988; Acemoglu, 1996). The novelty in Florida's view relies in the focus on ecological factors, some of which are not necessarily of economic nature: these ecological factors help boost the attraction of creative individuals, and ultimately urban and regional development, resulting in an important attempt to explore the socio-cultural dimensions of economic growth, where an open, tolerant and culturally vibrant environment constitutes an important economic opportunity. At first sight, this might seem a simple extension of pre-existing models and theories that includes non-economic drivers. However, in the "creative" approach, the interaction between demand and supply of highly skilled (or "creative") labour is at odds with the traditional representations of the labour market: here, professions and job opportunities follow creative individuals and not the other way around. In this new approach, size and sector do not determine the allocation/attraction of human capital, which is dictated solely by the nature of the places. It is a real entrance of geography in economic discourse. Hence, a mapping of labour forces capable of taking into account the territorial distribution of talent is needed, measuring the presence of graduates and highly skilled professions.[3] Florida's approach articulates the analysis of the creative class and puts it in relation to the "three Ts" (talent, technology and tolerance), preparing a set of indicators capable of measuring these factors of smart and inclusive development.

5.1 Measuring creativity

The multi-dimensional nature of the concept of creativity not only requires the establishment of new measures but imposes an original interpretation of measurements capable of taking into account the dynamic and systemic context in which the phenomena of interest are inserted. On the one hand, it will be thus impossible to get sufficient information about a given local context focusing only on the share of "creative professions" on its total labour force without making reference to structural elements such as the economic and production structure. On the other hand, there will be room to take into account also ecological factors not necessarily economic in nature, capable of favouring the concentration of the creative class and the exploitation of its capacities.

A particularly eloquent example of such multi-dimensional measurement is provided the case of the Italian Creativity Index calculated for all the provincial capitals by Padula and Tinagli (2005). Taking into account only the quantitative data concerning professions identified as "creative", the picture delivered from censuses and from ISTAT's Labour Force Survey (RCFL) sees all the major cities at the top of the ranking, including those ones in the South, which are generally little innovative and competitive but highly bureaucratized. In this first exercise, all medium-sized cities, characterized by strong traditional industrial vocations and widespread entrepreneurship appear to be penalized. However, the picture changes considerably once results are controlled for indexes built on the three Ts.

1   When the talent index (built on the percentage of graduates and researchers on the total labour force) is included into the estimates, Creative Italy seems to be located in the North and Centre of the country and based on medium-sized cities (Bologna, Florence, Genoa, Milan). Interestingly, some medium-sized industrial cities (e.g. Modena, Reggio Emilia and Bergamo) appear at the bottom of the ranking, indicating a vocation to traditional productions, which are little innovative, as confirmed also by the technological indexes. Further food for thought is brought by the mismatch, observable for many cities, between the index of talent and that of the creative class, where excellent and creative professions are not accompanied by adequate levels of human capital, indicating a delay in the development of a managerial class with formal and appropriate skills.

2   The technology index, which captures the weight of high-tech industries, the number of patents and connectivity, confirms the primacy of the North also recovering some Emilian cities (such as Modena and Reggio Emilia) that failed to meet high concentrations of capital human. Particularly significant for this latter case is the gap between the components of the index where a strong innovative capacity-patent is not accompanied by a significant proportion of high-technology sectors.

3   The tolerance index, built on indicators of the presence of foreigners, their integration (mixed marriages, education of children, etc.) and tolerance towards the gay population, indicates the true value added by the ecosystemic approach of the Creative Class signalling open and welcoming environments and their relationship with the best economic performances. Despite the greater attractiveness of foreign human capital, large metropolitan cities show levels of tolerance and integration that are significantly lower than the averages of the medium-sized cities located in the Centre-North, where the cities of Emilia-Romagna (Rimini, Modena and Ravenna above all) are placed systematically in the leading positions concerning mixed marriages, education and tolerance towards gays.

5.2 Criticism and possible further developments of the "creative class"

This new approach is not immune to problems and weaknesses. For example, the idea that tolerance and social inclusion can bring about the innovativeness of local businesses through the creation/attraction of human capital and knowledge, while supported by some empirical studies (Marlet and van Woerkens, 2007; McGranahan and Wojan, 2007; Florida et al., 2008), failed to meet acceptable robustness checks through different operational definitions, and some studies (Glaeser, 2005; Boschma and Fritsch, 2009) actually question the statistical significance of these effects when controlled for measures of school performance and titles of study. These environmental drivers should be therefore interpreted, according to these authors, as nothing more than a useful proxy to measure the contribution of human capital in the economic growth of an urban area, driven primarily by complementarity between human capital itself and technologies. In addition, the definition provided by Florida of the creative class is built at levels that are too aggregated ("major groups" in the Standard Occupational Classification, "major occupational groups" in the Italian Classification, the CP2011), and this would lead to a systematic overestimation of the size of the phenomenon by including professional units and job titles that are certainly not characterized by creativity or creative tasks but still included in these groups (Markusen, 2006). However, there remains room for further analysis at the level of individual professional units and job titles, along the lines of the work carried out by Purcell and colleagues (2012) with their new classification named SOC(HE)-2010. Another useful investigation can be carried out by referencing national occupational classifications to the European Qualification Framework (EQF) taxonomy, as done by ISTAT and ISFOL (2007); finally, it may be useful to apply the concept of creative class to analyses, such as those of Cedefop (2013), by taking into account the field of study and the horizontal dimension of the educational mismatch.

Notes

1 Skill-biased technical change (SBTC) occurs when a change in production techniques favours more skilled workers at the expense of others, increasing their productivity and therefore their relative demand for labour and their wages. This hypothesis is based on a postulated complementarity between new technologies and the skills of the advantaged workers. On the contrary, there is substitutability between these technologies and unskilled labour. Similar dynamics can discriminate also highly skilled workers in the event that the new techniques are not complementary to their actual skills. For a complete formalization and analysis, please refer to Acemoglu (2002).
2 In Italy, there was a serious decrease between 1991 and 2001 of medium-skilled occupations such as employees (−18%), skilled workers and artisans (−35%) and plant workers (−40%). Data and stylized facts about Italy come from the censuses in 1991, 2001 and 2011 as processed by Padula and Tinagli (2005), following the methodology set out later in this same paragraph.
3 There are several operational definitions of the creative class that are suitable for measurement, the most utilised of which (Florida, 2005) usually include entrepreneurs, public and private managers, managers, researchers, practitioners and technical occupations and artistic high specialization, grouped and labelled as creative core, creative professionals and bohemians, respectively.

Bibliography

Acemoglu, D.K. (1996), A microfoundation for social increasing returns in human capital accumulation, *Quarterly Journal of Economics*, 111 (3), 779–803.

Acemoglu, D.K. (2002), Technical change, inequality and the labor market, *Journal of Economic Literature*, XL (March), 7–72.

Acemoglu, D.K., and Pischke, J.S. (1999). Beyond Baker: Training in imperfect labour markets, *Economic Journal*, 109, F112–F142.

Almeida, P. and Kogut, B. (1999), Localization of knowledge and the mobility of engineers in regional networks, *Management Science*, 45, 905–917.

Amable, B. (2003), *The diversity of modern capitalism*, Oxford, Oxford University Press.

Aoki, M. (2001), *Toward a comparative institutional analysis*, Cambridge, MA, MIT Press.

Basile, R.G., Capello, R. and Caragliu, A. (2012), Technological interdependence and regional growth in Europe: Proximity and synergy in knowledge spillovers, *Papers in Regional Science*, 91 (4), 697–722.

Boschma, R. (2005), Proximity and innovation. A critical survey, *Regional Studies*, 39 (1), 61–74.

Boschma, R. and Iammarino, S. (2009), Related variety, trade linkages, and regional growth in Italy, *Economic Geography*, 85 (3), 289–311.

Boschma, R.A. and Fritsch, M. (2009), Creative class and regional growth: Empirical evidence from seven European Countries, *Economic Geography*, 84 (4), 391–423.

Camagni, R. and Capello, R. (2013), Regional innovation patterns and the EU Regional Policy reform: Towards smart innovation policies, *Growth and Change*, 44 (2), 355–389.

Cedefop. (2013), *The skills mismatch challenge in Europe*, in Staff Working Document SWD(2013) 2, Volume VIII/IX.

Chaminade, C., Cummings, A. and Szogs, A. (2009), *Building systems of innovation in less developed countries: The role of intermediate organizations*, Lund University CIRCLE Electronic Working Papers 1/2009.

Commons, J.R. (1934), *Institutional economics. Its place in political economy*, New York, Macmillan.

Crouch, C., Streeck, W., Boyer, R., Amable, B., Hall, P.A. and Jackson, G. (2005), Dialogue on Institutional complementarity and political economy, *Socio-Economic Review*, 3 (3), 359–382.

Florida, R. (2002), *The rise of the creative class, and how it's transforming work, leisure, community and everyday life*, New York, Basic Books.

Florida, R. (2005), *Cities and the creative class*, London, Routledge.

Florida, R., Mellender, C. and Stolarick, K. (2008), Inside the black box of regional development – Human capital, the creative class and tolerance, *Journal of Economic Geography*, 8, 615–649.

Foray, D. (2009), Understanding smart specialisation, in D. Pontikakis, D. Kyriakou and R. van Bavel (eds.), *The question of R&D specialisation*, Brussels, JRC, European commission, Directoral General for Research, 19–28.

Glaeser, E.L. (2005), Review of Richard Florida's the rise of the creative class, *Regional Science and Urban Economics*, 35, 593–596.

Gleaser, E., Kallal, H.D., Schinkmann, J.A. and Shleifer, A. (1992), Growth in cities, *Journal of Political Economy*, 100, 1126–1152.

Hall, P. (2005), Institutional complementarity: Causes and effect, *Socio Economic Review*, 3 (2), 373–377.

Hall, P.A. and Soskice, D. (eds.) (2001), *Varieties of capitalism: The institutional foundations of comparative advantage*, Oxford, Oxford University Press.

Hodgson, G.M. (2006), What are institutions?, *Journal of Economic Issues*, XL (1), 1–25.

Hopner, M. (2005), What connects industrial relations and corporate governance? Explaining institutional complementarity, *Socio-Economic Review*, 3, 331–358.

Lucas, R. (1988), On the mechanics of economic development, *Journal of Monetary Economics*, 22, 3–42.

Malerba, F. (1996), Public policy in industrial dynamics: An evolutionary perspective, TSER-ISE Workshop, mimeo.

Markusen, A. (2006), Urban development and the politics of a creative class: evidence from a study of artists, *Environment and Planning*, 38 (10), 1921–1940.

Marlet, G. and van Woerkens, C. (2007), The Dutch creative class and how it fosters urban employment growth, *Urban Studies*, 44, 2605–2626.

McCann, P. and Ortega-Argilés, R. (2011), Smart specialisation, regional growth and applications to EU cohesion policy, *Economic Geography Working Paper*, Faculty of Spatial Sciences, University of Groningen.

McGranahan, D. and Wojan, T. (2007), Recasting the creative class to examine growth processes in rural and urban counties, *Regional Studies*, 41, 197–216.

Metcalfe, S., Gagliardi, D., De Liso, N. and Ramlogan, R. (2012), *Innovation systems and innovation ecologies: Innovation policy and restless capitalism*, WP 3/2012, Openloc WP Series.

North, D.C. (1990), *Institutions, institutional change, and economic performance*, Cambridge, Cambridge University Press.

North, D.C. (1994), Economic performance through time, *American Economic Review*, 84 (3), 359–367.

Padula, G. and Tinagli, I. (2005), *L'Italia nell'Era Creativa*, Report, Creativity Group Italia.

Purcell, K., Elias, P., Atfield, G., Behle, H., Ellison, R., Luchinskaya, D., Snape, J., Conaghan, L. and Tzanakou, C. (2012), *Futuretrack stage 4: Transitions into employment, further study and other outcomes*, Manchester, HECSU. Summary report.

Smith, K. (1997), Systems approaches to innovation: Some policy issues, TSER-ISE Workshop, mimeo.

Veblen, T.B. (1899), *The theory of the leisure class: An economic study in the evolution of institutions*, New York, Macmillan.

3 Smart specialization and supply-side outcomes in an industrial policy perspective

Patrizio Bianchi and Silvano Bertini

1 Introduction

The *Smart Specialization Strategy* represents the most relevant innovation introduced in the new phase of structural policies of the European Union. This conditionality imposed by the Commission requires a very complex conceptual effort to the regions, but at the same time, it also implies the recognition of a role of full responsibility and autonomy for regional authorities in designing specific development and innovation pathways, a role not simply limited to designing general policy schemes, but also in individuating specific knowledge themes and trajectories in which concentrating innovation efforts and actions for competitiveness and in which research organizations and innovative firms can work in synergy.

Paradoxically, this requirement of greater responsibility, awareness and strong commitment to the regions for development policies happens in a period in which the governance of the European Union seems to privilege a confederal, intergovernmental approach that reduces the centrality of regions in the perspective of creating a large integrated economic space under a real European leadership.

As we will try to show in this short contribution, the potential innovation of the Smart Specialization Strategy approach can lead to a number of effective innovation strategies, but they risk remaining separated and fragmented if not included in an integrated and open perspective, which is not favored by such an institutional context in the Union. And it can represent a risk for European integration and for regional cohesion.

2 Smart specialization and regional innovation systems in the framework of European strategies

In the new global economic scenario, characterized by an increasing level of openness of markets, countries and regions can limit the effects of price competition to their internal equilibrium by developing an intense capacity to generate high-added-value products and services. High technology in itself is not a sufficient condition to face this challenge, since technologies are also difficult to protect and investment decisions by multinationals can lead to investment decisions worldwide, according to the type of advantages they look for. It appears that competitive regions need to develop efficient and dynamic innovation ecosystems characterized by high levels of knowledge circulation, generation of ideas, projects and business decisions; they need to combine science, production expertise, entrepreneurial attitudes, creativity and the capacity to understand social evolution and social needs, in order to generate innovation through interdisciplinary and multidimensional mechanisms.

Promoting such knowledge ecosystems implies a complex rethinking of regional development policies. Smart Specialization is an attempt to develop a new approach to regional policies for competitiveness. It can be considered not a new theory, but the convergence of several policy research and analysis traditions and different points of view for regional development policies.

The relevance of the regional and local dimension of industrial development and of industrial policies was initially put in evidence in the '70s, with the discovery of the power of bottom-up phenomena, local networks and clusters ("industrial districts") able to evolve into competitive systems of firms and has continued with the more recent contributions on regional innovation systems and knowledge economies.

In detail, in the Smart Specialization Strategy approach the following visions and/or methodologies converge:

- the tradition of literature on regional development focused on local production systems and on the recovery of the Marshallian concept of industrial district, emphasizing local endogenous development factors, individuated in shared community values, civic traditions, trust, production networks and coalitions to react to external competitive pressures and to provide collective answers (Sabel, Piore, Beccattini, Brusco and others);
- the approach of the analysis of competitive advantage at the regional or national level, based both on economic and management instruments, which analyzes factors of competitiveness and methodologies for building internationally competitive clusters, not as a simple local reaction to external pressure, but as a specific policy strategy aiming at developing synergy, and complementarities along the value chains for system competitiveness (Porter and others);
- the vision focused on the analysis of knowledge circulation and accumulation at the system or community level, mapping the different actors of the regional innovation systems, their reciprocal relationships, mechanisms and even cognitive processes in order to create virtuous circles for generating knowledge and innovation (Lundvall and others); and
- finally, the contributions related to policy methodologies at the regional level in an open economic context, dealing the complicated problem of activating bottom-up sustainable development processes for obtaining at the same time competitiveness and social equilibrium for the local communities (Bianchi and others).

All these different contributions have one element in common, that one of individuating the local forces and the territorial context as the ground where to create competitive advantages and development, by networking, complementarities, core competencies. They must anyway face two important questions:

- First, how to activate bottom-up development processes in those contexts poor in endogenous resources and lacking critical mass in terms of knowledge accumulation and entrepreneurship
- Second, how to avoid the risk of hyper-specialization and crowding out of existing clusters and to address the need of activating processes of diversification and cross-contamination to activate new trajectories and new advantages

The Smart Specialization Strategy approach is not a conclusive answer to these challenges but tries to contribute to them by increasing the emphasis on R&D activity and through the introduction of the "entrepreneurial discovery" process at the regional level, a participative process aimed at individuating strategic issues, highest potential assets and even hidden resources to unlock for development.

The emergence of this approach in the European policies, as a conditionality for research and innovation policies within operational programs of structural funds, is not casual. The achievement of the Lisbon goals is still hard to obtain for 2020, after several years of policies with limited impact and lack of coordination between them. In the last few years, it has increased awareness of the importance of the regional dimension of knowledge and innovation policies and the need to find adequate roles for them in coordination with other policies for science and technology at the European and national levels.

In the '90s, the great perspective of creating a large integrated market and a unique competitive environment, through the reduction of barriers to trade and the progressive introduction of common standards, was balanced by structural, regionally based policies aimed at reducing development gaps and activating local development factors, especially in weaker and disadvantaged regions. Some experimental attempts to reinforce regional innovation systems were made through the support of the so-called Regional Innovation and Technology Transfer Strategies (RITTS) programs, but with very limited resources.

After the Lisbon Council of 2000, which established a new great objective for the European Union, that of creating the greatest knowledge- and innovation-based economy in the world, European policies should have undertaken a new strategic perspective and should have been re-oriented towards this objective. But such a reaction, in practice, was very slow. The regulation for Structural Funds for the 2000–2006 period had been already approved, and they were coherent with previous planning periods: strategic objectives and criteria for resource allocation were based, as before, on the reduction of development gaps in quantitative terms. Knowledge was not yet individuated as a key word and as a strategic objective. Even in the more developed regions, Objective 2 sub-areas were individuated by complex territorial delimitations, sometimes even established at the level of street addresses. Just a little part of the global European Regional Development Fund (ERDF) (0.4%) was dedicated to the so-called Innovative Actions Programs, developed on a regional scale; it was, indeed, a sort of experimental action for those regions more sensitive to innovation.

In parallel to Structural Funds, the Sixth Framework Program for Research, not yet funded as much as Horizon 2020, followed a problem-solving approach very oriented to applied research and to developing concrete results of economic and social relevance and less attentive to knowledge and scientific progress.

In the second half of the first decade of the new millennium, it was clear that the Lisbon strategy indicators were would still be difficult to achieve in time for 2010, and in addition to this, the gap between regions in terms of innovation capacity tended to increase. Structural Funds had limited impact on the reinforcement of regional innovation systems. Only regions that developed their own strategies with national funds could improve their position. But, the macroeconomic constraints due to the monetary integration, step by step, reduced the possibilities of autonomously funded policies.

The Sixth Framework Program, on the other side, for its methodological orientation, did not contribute to the improvement of the European position in the international technology competition; in particular, it didn't help Europe play an important role in breakthrough technologies advancement or in the capacity of opening new technological trajectories, in contrast to the United States.

As a consequence of this situation, in the following period (2007–2013) some changes were introduced.

The new Structural Funds regulation abolished the so-called "Objective 2" sub-regional areas. The policy approach became at the whole regional level both in disadvantaged regions, now defined as "Convergence" regions and, in the more advanced regions, now "Competitiveness and Employment" regions. Industrial research and technology transfer became strategic objectives, especially in "Competitiveness" regions, in order to build a new European cohesion on a competitive base, through the development of knowledge and innovation systems at the regional level. The funds invited regions to concentrate measures on the "demand side", that is especially on R&D activity of firms and on territorial initiatives for technology transfer and promotion of innovative firms. Actually, efficient regional innovation systems could play a significant role to multiply the impact of research expenditure, especially towards SMEs.

On the other side, the Seventh Framework Program followed a different approach and gave more emphasis to science and technology in order to recover the competitiveness of the European scientific system at the global level.

It can be said that the level of complementarity between the two programs, despite some attempts, remained very low: high scientific level on one side, fragmented, isolated strategies, without a shared methodology and integration but with excess of emphasis on business R&D, on the other side.

Again, results are not satisfactory. Of course, some parts of Europe, namely several Northern regions in the German, Scandinavian, British and French areas were very close to the achievement of Lisbon goals, and sometimes they exceeded them. Even in these countries, in any case, there were areas of relative weakness. In Southern Europe, there were some groups of regions with good industrial performance but also weak innovation systems, still far away from Lisbon goals.

The weakness and contradictory aspect of the European strategy was that of concentrating Structural Funds policies excessively on the demand side, while the resource allocation was only determined by income and employment gaps indicators; as a consequence, regions with higher firm density had very little resources to spend, especially in Southern Europe. In these regions, such limited resources, together with the increasing fiscal restraints, concretely limited the possibilities of fostering adaptation to higher European standards and of leading the other weaker neighboring regions in undertaking the same process.

Actually, in the allocation of resources, it should have been considered, at least, the presence of a relevant number of innovative SMEs, to be driven into knowledge economy, typical of several regions of Southern Europe, but also in the rest of Europe.

It must be considered that the Northern regions, already reaching Lisbon goals, obtained these results mainly thanks to important national efforts (Finland) and/or consolidated research and innovation institutions (Germany, Sweden, Holland), not so much to Structural Funds.

The Funds had limited additional impact for two opposite reasons on regional innovation systems in the "Competitiveness" and in "Convergence" regions. In the former, Structural Funds were used in substitution (in the best cases) for decreasing national funds, and it led regions to use them not according to clearly finalized objectives. They tried to keep vital their regional innovation systems with all innovative companies and productive systems, without concentrating enough on selected qualified strategic scopes.

In "Convergence" regions, at the same time, there was an excess of resources dedicated to research and innovation, in relation to the number of innovative enterprises able to absorb advanced knowledge. This led, in several cases, to waste and dispersed resources and to overfunding knowledge organizations, with little possibilities of generating impact on the regional economic system and, at the same time, to become competitive in the international technology competition.

In a few words, the use of funds was quite generic and poorly targeted at specific objectives of structural reinforcement from a technological point of view, of developing strategic and competitive clusters or innovation systems within or across regions.

The Commission, thanks to various evaluation analyses, was aware of this criticism. And, right on the base of this consideration, in the new programs that started in 2014 and that will end in 2020, some new elements were introduced. The elaboration and approval of a Smart Specialization Strategy at the regional (eventually, at the national) level, as an ex-ante conditionality for research and innovation measures, tries to give an answer to this criticism. The objective of the S3 approach is that of individuating key innovative assets within the regional technology and productive system and to specialize programs in these areas.

In some way, it is possible to say that the more interactive formulation of the so-called "Triple Helix" is proposed. Regions, as government bodies, are not simply facilitators and proposers of general schemes, but participate in, or even coordinate, the individuation of specific thematic areas where to orient strategic choices and concentrate measures and resources. Universities and research organizations must individuate the concrete fields of application of their technology assets in the regional economic system and society (as a starting point) and develop the capacity to provide solutions but also to propose anticipatory results and demonstrators. Firms, as major final users of results, must make explicit their specific technology needs and potential for their present businesses, but they should also individuate possible diversification perspectives on the base of their consolidated competences and their dialogue with research units.

Thanks to the approach, it is possible to expect that regions can develop key specific areas of real competitive advantage and technology knowledge, by activating both measures to support R&D activity, innovation and competitiveness (ERDF), and measures for advanced education, training and human resources (European Social Funds [ESF]). In this way, it could be easier to generate critical mass and synergy between Structural Funds and the new framework program, Horizon 2020.

Horizon 2020, on the basis of lessons from the previous programs and also thanks to a relevant increase of resources, has established a more integrated strategy combining S&T and R&D especially by supporting strategic projects with a complete value chain from research to market and by selecting three major horizontal priorities: S&T excellence, industrial leadership and social challenges. All of these three priorities match, at the same time, the technology priorities individuated in the program, basically centered on the so-called Key Enabling Technologies, and the various types of policy measures.

The effort of the Union is relevant. The possibility to create bridges between these two different types of funding in terms of complementarity of instruments and co-evolution or connection of technology items and results is more suitable than in past periods.

It is still too soon to see the effectiveness of this new strategy (Europe 2020) and how it will combine competitiveness, technology advancement and regional cohesion. There are still some criticisms in the global design; we will point these out in the rest of the chapter.

3 Smart specialization strategies and regional patterns

According to the concept of regional innovation ecosystems (or regional innovation systems) of high competitiveness and highly attractive for investments and talents, four interconnected elements are necessary:

1 Science, technology and research (presence of scientific infrastructure of national and European relevance, centers of competence and applied research organizations, technology transfer structures)
2 Leading industrial and service clusters (complex clusters including high-tech and high-value-added activities, strong control of the value chain, exports and international presence, good level of technical knowledge)
3 Talent and innovative start-ups (graduates, diplomates, experienced workers, innovative and creative firms and professionals)
4 Territory and urban quality (broadband, transport and logistic infrastructure; welfare services; sustainable development; well-organized, qualified and cultured cities)

Regions must work on these four elements, in parallel starting from different conditions. But the Smart Specialization Strategy needs to work for improving these elements of the ecosystem not simply with horizontal and/or institutional policies, but with a higher detail of objectives and fields of action, including also vertical elements.

As just mentioned, the Smart Specialization Strategy is a complex task for regional authorities. The Commission made available methodological guidelines and established a Joint Learning Platform open to all regions, managed by the Institute for Prospective Technological Studies (IPTS) of Seville, in order to share good practices, providing data, case studies and specific tools, networking groups of regions by common features or by technology and innovation tools.

It is clear that we are not in the sphere of pure bottom-up policies. At the same time, we are not in the world of industrial policies by sector, like in the '60s and '70s. It appears clear that industrial policy in the knowledge economy needs active leadership by policy makers, not limited to enabling factors but able to indicate specific perspectives on the base of local resources.

It is not possible, in a knowledge-based economy, to address innovation policies to specific sectors simply identified on the base of statistical codes. There are several other variables: mix of technologies; position in the value chain; range of possible applications; inter-industry contamination; functional design; post-production services to be embodied; stakeholders involved and answers to transversal drivers (sustainability, health, equal opportunities, culture, etc.). Industry-sector delimitations are not clear anymore: for instance, food firms can easily enter in the pharmaceutical market or, by re-using waste materials, can enter the plastic, cosmetic, construction material or textile sectors; engineering and mechatronic companies can easily diversify in several fields of applications and for several types of users; and we can continue.

Asking regions to establish specific priorities and items about where to concentrate research and innovation policies is indeed a complex exercise that implies in-depth analysis, systemic collaboration, choices and responsibilities under political pressures by groups of interest.

For this reason, it is necessary that the strategy must be elaborated through a participative methodology involving the actors of the innovative system, including firms. From a methodological point of view, it is necessary to create matches, schemes and neural maps, for instance:

- matching productive sectors and key enabling technologies (matrix)
- matching emerging with consolidated clusters (matrix)
- individuating specific technology fields, with all possible applications (tree)

Excluding technology fields, in structural terms, according to the different regional conditions and local equilibria, the strategy can be oriented, in various combinations, to (see Table 3.1):

- reinforcing leadership through innovation and strategic diversification
- promoting emerging industries
- "unlocking" hidden resources and
- reinforcing territorial competitiveness and attractiveness

Table 3.1 Objectives, policies and results of supply-side specialization

Objectives	Main policies	Main structural results
Reinforcing leadership	Research/industry collaboration	Leading technology clusters
Promoting emerging industries	Spin-offs and start-ups	Clubs of innovators
Unlocking hidden resources	Training, networking	Potential talents
Territorial competitiveness	Digital agenda, public-oriented research (health, environment)	High-quality contexts

According to this classification, it is possible to see that some regions put greater emphasis on the complex operation of creating several matches between groups of researchers in specific technology areas and their fields of application with consolidated industries. Others concentrated more on the generation of innovative firms and emerging clusters strongly linked to research. Others decided to concentrate research on specific social needs, related to important drivers, considering that it could also create new related industries and closely specialized applied research.

It is possible that, at the individual level, regions can activate new energies by these strategies in their contexts. The main question is in any case how they can have an impact on the state of European cohesion.

It appears that a traditional paradox still works. S3 strategies can be developed more easily and can more easily succeed in excellent regions; they are much more difficult and complicated in weaker regions. Table 3.2 quite clearly shows this problem.

In regions that have strong research and university systems and competitive industries, innovation policies are in some way indicated by the demand side; the promotion of emerging clusters and new start-ups plays a secondary role, but at the same time, this policy can also be easily successful, thanks to the possibility of networking with existing clusters. On the other side, it must be considered that such regions receive little amount of money from Structural Funds, and as a consequence, they can have little additional impact. We can have two different situations:

1   Regions that are able by themselves to activate large amounts of public money for R&D and to obtain relevant funds form European Framework programs, like in several German, southern Scandinavia, Benelux, France and England. In this case, the Smart Specialization Strategy has little relevance and very limited additional impact. It can be casual, but most German *Landers* didn't participate at all in the activities of the S3 Joint Learning Platform.

2   Regions that have almost no other public resources than Structural Funds, like most Northern Italian regions. In this case, the Strategy plays an important role but doesn't have the strength to radically modify behavior of firms and research organizations.

Table 3.2 S3 strategies and productive systems

		Weak	Strong
S&T/R&D system	**Strong**	Investment attraction in technology parks Innovative start-ups	Leading technology clusters Innovative start-ups easily integrated Attractive cities and territories for investment and talents
	Weak	Marginalization	Traditional clusters, price competition
		Weak	**Strong**
		Productive system	

It is true, correctly, that it is recommended not to limit the implementation of the strategy to the Structural Funds but to use it as the milestone of all innovation and industrial policies of regions. Research and innovation measures within ERDF operational programs must indeed be integrated by other measures promoting investment and competitiveness in the same program or in the European Agricultural Fund for Rural Development (EARDF) program, measures for high-level competencies and training in the ESF program, measures for innovation and competitiveness in regionally funded programs, participation in national or European programs, especially Horizon 2020, and private co-financing. In this way, it is possible to achieve a relevant critical mass.

In strong regions, policies for technology transfer and collaborative research and policies for innovative start-ups can work in parallel and reinforce each other. Collaborative research with competitive industries generates innovation for existing firms but also opportunities for new innovative start-ups that, in their turn, will look for further scientific inputs and generate further technology advancement.

In the other contexts, effective policies are highly needed but are not easy. In regions that have good scientific systems but weak industry, it is necessary that universities and other knowledge and research organizations play leading roles in generating new, knowledge-intensive industries through spin-off and start-up promotion and concentrating themselves on the market of research (licensing, knowledge services, etc.), possibly in a worldwide perspective. The risk is that such initiatives can remain isolated poles in the regions and may not find enough cluster synergy around themselves; firms and scientific organizations need to achieve a strong extra-regional, even international, system of relationships.

Regions that are highly industrialized but that lack a highly developed S&T system, at the opposite of the previous situation, need to "import" knowledge in order to promote technology innovation for the local industry. In the absence of this, industry can lose competitiveness, reduce value added and become exposed to price competition.

Finally, regions that are weak both in science and in industry are clearly much more problematic. In this case, the "entrepreneurial discovery" process should be even more careful and able to individuate eventual embryonic excellences and critical resources. They must be connected in strong relationship with external partnerships, avoiding emigration of talents and firms to better contexts, which would confirm the marginal position of the region.

This means that research and innovation policies must consider the local contexts in which they are implemented; they must be internally coherent in order to create synergy and multiplier effects, or at the opposite side, they can spread out their effects on several objectives that are not coherent one to each other, and/or not adequate to the context.

This is particularly evident if we consider education and training. Human resources are the crucial factor for knowledge-based economies, and while in the strongest regions the education and training system is an essential component of the virtuous circle, in other regions, such activities must be highly tailored and supported with other policies in order to effectively contribute to growth and competitiveness. Adequate policies for training and advanced education are essential to contribute to success of smart specialization strategies, if there is not a mismatch with other policies and a lack of coherence with the regional context. If this happens in weaker regions, it can lead to the emigration of talents and further loss of opportunities.

Because of the possibility of largely different performances between the regions, it is indeed very important not to limit regional structural policies for innovation to a sum of strategies close to their territories. There is the concrete risk of accentuating disparities and divergent paths of development, which represents a large threat to European cohesion. The risk is accentuated by the context of monetary integration of large part of the member states of the Union for the last fifteen years (and prepared since several years before); it reduces burdens to mobility but also eliminates any barriers protecting weaker economies, while structural adjustment policies appear not sufficient to recover, or even to compensate for, the restrictive effects of the monetary union.

The same monetary union is itself imperfect, since it was not accompanied by integration at the level of the government of the real economy. The consequence is that those states, or the regions within them, already able to adjust their systems in a context of integration have been further advantaged and could even accelerate their capacity to generate large and powerful innovative ecosystems, able to be competitive at the global level. Weaker regions, at the same time, often don't have the social, political and economic conditions to work in such an integration context, as they could not even make use of the traditional instrument of devaluation and tended to be more marginalized and divergent from stronger regions. Eurostat data on regions show that disparities are increasing between countries but also between regions within countries, and at the level of the Union, it is emerging in a central group of regions, basically around Germany and involving Austria, part of France and Northern Italy and out of this area, some metropolitan areas with all their concentration of high-value-added services but also their contradictions.

In this picture, it is evident that the regional level of industrial development and innovation policies must remain essential and that smart specialization strategy, if implemented according to regional conditions, can help the development of coherent policies. But it is necessary to accompany them by a European level of strategy to recover the objective of cohesion and integration. On one side, it seems that the previous approach of reducing gaps by themselves doesn't work anymore in the new context. The new strategy at the European level should aim, according to Albert Hirschmann's vision, to build complementarities and linkages, in order to connect technology infrastructure, competence centers, large or small innovative clusters, firms and groups of talents.

Especially for weaker regions, it is necessary to create and maintain some points of these networks there to protect regional assets, even if connected with other points in different regions: techno-poles and competence centers, hubs and incubators, clubs of innovators or cluster organizations or training institutes, any kind of factor-generating convenience to remain in the regional system for such critical resources. All of them must be, at the same time, connected in networks with other complementary points in other regions; they are necessary to stay in the network and to make it possible to have something to connect in the network from the local system.

4 Final remarks

In this difficult moment, from the perspective of the European Union, it is crucial to develop an organic policy action to generate a concrete perspective of cohesion in the framework of a knowledge-based and competitive European economy. In this context, the introduction of the Smart Specialization Strategy approach is an important conceptual innovation for developing coherent innovation policies at the regional level to better finalize policies to sustainable specialization pathways based on innovation capacity.

The Smart Specialization Strategy can be an instrument to give stronger identity to regional innovation ecosystems and to make them more convergent on specific issues, where it is clear that a region can have a real competitive advantage. What we wanted to emphasize in this contribution is that we cannot think that this approach is in itself a final solutions to orient all regions to positive and successful trajectories.

There are several questions that need to be considered.

While leading regions are in conditions to further reinforce their position, weaker regions must be involved in complex processes of adjustment. Smart Specialization Strategy is, in some way, a flexible policy approach of vertical character. Nevertheless, structural and institutional adjustment is necessary to make it work efficiently.

First, in most cases, it is necessary to rethink the mechanisms regulating the regional ecosystem, that is the relationships between the various knowledge organizations and the productive systems. It implies a process of institutional reform, involving the education and training institutions and research organizations, to make them play as leading actors of change for the economy and the societies.

Second, at the policy level, there is the need of a greater capacity to combine and converge the various policy instruments and funds (starting from ERDF and ESF) to coherent objectives in a framework of complementarity. It is evident that critical situations can be found both in marginal regions, despite the availability of large European funds, and in regions in intermediate position, which receive less European funds. The policy objective to create an efficient innovation system implies an effort to integrate funds for knowledge institutions but also to work, to a larger extent, at looking for other synergies and involving other actors, for instance, the financial actors, rarely proactive in innovation, administrations and private organizations.

Finally, as shown in the evidence, there is a strong need for building inter-regional linkages in order to avoid an increase in gaps in competitive performance and social change. Connecting regions according to specific technology specializations individuated by the strategies, but also inducing reforms and investment for establishing stable points in such networks, is essential to obtain, in the medium-to-long term, a more equilibrated picture of the Union in its regional segmentation. This must be one basic priority for the future of the Union, to be implemented and monitored with an active role and supervision at the European institutions.

Bibliography

Benhabib, J. and Spiegel, M.M. (1994), The role of human capital in economic development evidence from aggregate cross-country data, *Journal of Monetary Economics*, 34, 143–173.

Benhabib, J. and Spiegel, M.M. (2005), Human capital and technology diffusion, in P. Aghion and S. N. Durlauf (eds.), *Handbook of economic growth*, vol.1 Part A, Amsterdam, Elsevier, pp. 935–966.

Bianchi, P. (1998), *Industrial policies and economic integration: Learning from European experiences*, London, Routledge.

Bianchi, P. (2009), *Le nuove politiche industriali europee*, Bologna, Il Mulino.

De Melo, J. and Panagariya (eds.) (1993), *New dimension in regional integration*, Cambridge, Cambridge University Press.

European Commission (2012), *Guide to Research and Innovation Strategies for Smart Specialisation (RIS3)*, Luxembourg, Publications Office of the European Union

Foray, D. (2014), *Smart specialization. Opportunities and challenges for regional innovation policies*, London, Routledge.

Georgacopolous, T., Paraskevopoloulos, C. and Smithin, J. (eds.) (1994), *Economic integration between unequal partners*, London, Elgar.

Howitt, P. and Mayer-Foulkes, D. (2002), *R&D, implementation and stagnation: A Schumpeterian theory of convergence clubs*, NBER, Working paper No. 9104, August.

Mankin, N.G., Romer, D. and Weil, D.N. (1992), A contribution to the empirics of economic growth, *Quarterly Journal of Economics*, 107 (May), 407–437.

Nelson, R.R. and Phelps, E.S. (1966), Investment in humans, technological diffusion, and economic growth, *American Economic Review*, 56 (1/2) (March), 69–75.

Romer, P.M. (1989), *Human capital and growth theory and evidence*, NBER, Working paper No. w3173, November.

Romer, P.M. (1990), Endogenous technical change, *Journal of Political Economy*, 98 (5), S72–102.

Solow, R.M. (1956), A contribution to the theory of economic growth, *Quarterly Journal of Economics*, 70 (1), 65–94.

I.2 Smart city

4 Issues and challenges for smart cities

Nicola De Liso and Luca Zamparini

1 Introduction

Cities constitute a crucial hub of socio-economic reality: it is worthwhile mentioning that, in the European Union, 70% of the population lives in urban areas (Eurostat, 2013). Cities present aspects that contribute to improving the quality of life. However, they are often characterized by critical points ranging from congestion to the presence of areas of poverty to waste disposal issues, among others.

The definition of "city" should be carefully considered. On the one hand, we have the delimitation in the administrative sense, given the boundaries that are (legally) well defined. On the other hand, it is ever more important to consider "metropolitan cities", in which urban areas previously distinct merge as a result of the expansion of the originating areas. In this respect, it is possible to refer to the definition of *greater cities* proposed by the European Union (Eurostat, 2013).

Although the main focus of this chapter will be the city, it is important to remember that cities can be part of larger "communities", or aggregates that have an organic unity, examples being industrial districts or consortia of municipalities in a mountain area. It is worth remembering that both of these aggregates have a formal definition within the Italian legal system. Such aggregates are characterized by sharing certain characteristics and problems. The mountain area consortia, for example, share issues such as the limited availability of certain services (broadband internet, hospital care, schools); difficulties related to transport (snow on the roads in winter); and migration to larger towns and cities.

The legal, economic and social dimensions of a city intersect, and we have a juxtaposition of different actors – public and private – that contribute to the development of a society in which, as mentioned earlier, 70% of the population lives in cities.

A recent document by the European Commission devoted to smart cities and communities has proposed the following perspective:

> European cities should be places of advanced social progress and environmental regeneration, as well as places of attraction and engines of economic growth based on a holistic integrated approach in which all aspects of sustainability are taken into account.
>
> (European Commission, 2012, p. 3)

Further definitions of smart city were presented in a contribution by Chourabi et al. (2012):

1   A city well performing in a forward-looking way in economy, people, governance, mobility, environment, and living, built on the smart combination of endowments and activities of self-decisive, independent and aware citizens (Giffinger et al., 2007, p. 11)
2   A city that monitors and integrates conditions of all of its critical infrastructures, including roads, bridges, tunnels, rails, subways, airports, seaports, communications, water, power, even major buildings, can better optimize its resources, plan its preventive maintenance activities, and monitor security aspects while maximizing services to its citizens (Hall, 2000)
3   A city "connecting the physical infrastructure, the IT infrastructure, the social infrastructure, and the business infrastructure to leverage the collective intelligence of the city" (Harrison et al., 2010)
4   A city striving to make itself "smarter" (more efficient, sustainable, equitable, and liveable) (Natural Resources Defense Council, 2013)
5   A city "combining ICT and Web 2.0 technology with other organizational, design and planning efforts to dematerialize and speed up bureaucratic processes and help to identify new, innovative solutions to city management complexity, in order to improve sustainability and liveability" (Toppeta, 2010)
6   "The use of Smart Computing technologies to make the critical infrastructure components and services of a city—which include city administration, education, healthcare, public safety, real estate, transportation, and utilities—more intelligent, interconnected, and efficient" (Washburn et al., 2010)

Two main visions of the smartness of a conurbation appear to emerge. On the one hand, the areas with respect to which these innovative solutions can be usefully implemented to improve the sustainability and liveability of urban contexts are indicated in a comprehensive way. On the other hand, the emphasis is on innovation and on ICTs as important engines for the affirmation of the smartness. The next section is devoted to a discussion of several different contexts in which the first vision can usefully be implemented for the development of smart cities.

2   Operational contexts of a smart city

As indicated in some of the definitions provided in the introduction to this chapter, the idea of smart city can have different specifications. One set of specifications that we find particularly useful is the one applied by the *Technische Universität Wien*, which leads a small group of research units working on smart cities since the early 2000s – the first report is dated 2007. The specifications referred to are the smart economy, smart mobility, smart environment, smart living, smart people and, finally, smart governance. The next sub-sections aim at providing a general overview of each of these specifications. To avoid confusion, let us point out that we add our own ideas to the concepts as elaborated by the *Technische Universität*, so that what follows does not necessarily reflect the original contents.

2.1 Smart economy

The first dimension that can be considered in order to verify the degree of smartness in a city is the one that refers to the economy. In this context, a city is considered smart to the extent that it allows the generation of virtuous processes that increase competitiveness, both at the national and international levels. In this context, the smartness in economic terms allows a city to become the reference point in investment and financial development, especially with respect to innovative processes. Among the elements that can be considered to assess the degree of economy smartness of a city, we can mention (1) innovation spirit, (2) entrepreneurship, (3) the economic standing that characterizes the city, (4) productivity, (5) flexibility of the labour market and (6) the extent to which this city is part of international economic clusters.

Innovative spirit can be measured, consistently with the economic literature on innovation, by the number of patents that are generated by businesses referring to the urban territory. Alternatively, it is possible to consider the percentage of companies that provide advanced services. In addition, the degree of entrepreneurship of a city clearly refers to the density of enterprises, which can be measured with respect to the number of inhabitants or with respect to the spatial dimension (businesses per inhabitant or firms per square kilometre). The economic standing of a city is difficult to quantify, and it refers to its perception by external stakeholders and economic agents. A good proxy for the economic standing of the city might be represented by the number of companies held by non-residents in the city itself. The productivity of a city can be measured by the indicators proposed by traditional economic theory, such as the cost of labour per unit of product. Flexibility of the labour market can be measured by means of a plurality of indicators: (1) the proportion of self-employment on overall employment, (2) the cost of turnover, (3) the presence of atypical work, (4) forms of social protection and (5) the weight of social security contributions on the cost of labour. Finally, the extent to which a city is inserted in international economic clusters refers to the share of imports and exports relative to the total amount of income that is able to generate, to the international linkages of universities in the city and so on.

The economic dimension is also important because it allows pondering (and validating) all the proposed changes in the other dimensions that will be considered in the context of effectiveness and efficiency. It also enables ensuring that there is a priority on the most interesting projects and a preference for the most economically feasible ones. It also emphasizes the need to jointly consider specialization and strategic integration among projects. It then promotes a clear awareness of the criticalities and of the important issues required to develop projects that have the ability to determine virtuous development paths. Finally, the economic dimension appears important to direct the governance of the city towards clear and verifiable results.

From a dynamic viewpoint, these efforts must be aimed at a smart growth that can be measured by taking into account the increments in the indicators mentioned earlier (innovative spirit, entrepreneurship, the economic standing that the city has to offer, productivity, flexibility of the labour market and the extent to which this city is inserted in international economic clusters). This is particularly relevant for those cities that start from a disadvantaged position in terms of smartness but that may, through the adoption of appropriate policies, reduce the gap with those cities that are characterized by higher levels of performance.

2.2 Smart mobility

Mobility is a key aspect to be considered within "smart city" analyses. It concerns not only the city residents but all of those who gravitate around the city for whatever reason (work, study, tourism, shopping). Mobility thus represents an important dimension that allows a city to improve its level of competitiveness and to foster virtuous paths of smart development. It is necessary to take into account both the degree of connectivity to national and international transport networks and the efficiency and effectiveness of local transport systems. With respect to the first dimension, the nodes of the international and national networks (ports, airports and trade infrastructure such as intermodal logistic platforms, distriparks) that are geographically located within the city area or in easily accessible places must be considered. Given that most of the cities cannot represent main nodes within large national and international networks, the accessibility between local nodes and the main national/international ones should represent the focus of smart policies leading, i.e. to the possibility for citizens to reach their business or leisure destinations and return on the same day. National and international freight transport movements that originate from, pass by or have a destination in the city should be developed if they lead to important economic impacts to the local territory.

Smart mobility should be also considered at a strictly local level by analyzing, in particular, how urban mobility is managed and carried out. Local policies should be aimed at fostering the passage from private motorized means to other modes that could prove to be less polluting both for passenger and for freight transport. An important prerequisite to reach this goal is represented by the enhancement of the degrees of safety and security of eco-friendly transport modes (i.e. through the creation of dedicated bicycle paths, limited traffic zones and tighter monitoring policies for the arcs and the nodes of the urban transport networks). An alternative to raise the degree of safety of mobility can be the reduction of the speed limit to 30 km/h in the city centres. This is efficient in terms of the reduction of fatalities, and it also allows avoiding the financing of dedicated bike lanes.

The provision of more frequent public transport is another element to be considered in order to improve the smartness of city mobility. In this context, policies should be aimed at improving the accessibility and quality of public transport options, at allowing modal integration and thus at enabling a larger use of public transport. Moreover, they should meet the user demand to the greatest possible extent. Lastly, the connections between eco-friendly transport modes and local public transport should be made more efficient both from an economic and from a time viewpoint. Good connections to the nodes mentioned earlier of the national and international networks involving the city of reference (ports, airports, etc. mentioned earlier) should also be pursued.

Another important element to take into account is the fact that large shares of local transport will still be represented by private motorized vehicles. Policies based on the construction of ever larger infrastructures for nodes and arcs of transport have often resulted in an increase in the rate of motorization with the consequent deterioration of mobility. Increased congestion, longer average transport time, higher rates of accidents, higher fuel consumption and a more marked impact on the environment have consequently been observed. Smart mobility policies must also privilege the use of cars and motorbikes with low environmental impact. This implies penalizing cars with high rates of particulate and other pollutant emissions and rewarding the use of small sized and new generation cars.[1]

2.3 Smart environment

The environment and its quality represent one of the elements that a smart city must necessarily consider, with a view that is not just linked to competitiveness but also to sustainability over time. In order to achieve this goal, in the first place, an efficient use of resources such as water and energy must be put in place. This requires clear policy guidelines, good governance and the participation of all (private and public) stakeholders, which may contribute to obtaining a smart environment using good practices designed to safeguard nature. The assessment of the quality of the urban environment requires the use of multiple indicators. Among these, it is possible to mention the percentage of days in which the permitted share of particulates emitted into the atmosphere is exceeded, the amount of smog and ozone pollution and the percentage of individuals who suffer from diseases of the respiratory system that can be traced back to the aforementioned causes of pollution. Moreover, it is possible to measure the percentage of green spaces that are present within the city area and policies (for example on the subject of mobility) that are put in place in order to minimize the environmental impact of activities in the city.

A document of the European Commission (2012) has divided the measures that can lead to an environmentally sustainable development in four different categories. (1) The first, defined as "reaction", encompasses legislative interventions and administrative actions that take into account the situation and propose solutions to improve efficiency. (2) The second category, so-called "incremental" measures, is based on renewable energy sources, on conservation, on initiatives of the local communities to limit the impact of pollution and on the attempt to give an economic value to the environment. (3) The third category, defined as "radical", includes measures that seek to define a trajectory of growth that takes into account the sustainability and that is able to make a difference in the behaviour of the community. Radical innovations are based on technological change and amend or surpass traditional solutions. (4) The last category, named "transformative approach", attempts to provide a new paradigm for what regards the pattern of production, consumption, the forms of mobility and labour, etc. This last approach requires the presence of cooperative behaviour and of synergy among all the components of a smart city.

A study by Carvalho et al. (2013) has shown that the main questions related to energy and to the environment that a smart city must consider are the following: (1) what are the observable changes in behaviour of urban households and businesses? (2) Which new ways of production, distribution and consumption of energy are emerging in cities? (3) What types of energy policies are planned in cities? The answers to these questions can be provided in some cases in an autonomous way, but in others, it is necessary an international network for the dissemination of best practices and virtuous processes.

The trends that seem to be emerging in order to "respond" in an efficient manner to the earlier questions are linked to a widespread use of new forms of more eco-friendly energy production (by increasing the percentage of renewable resources compared to fossil fuels in the share of the energy production); to the implementation of more efficient solutions for the distribution of energy (favouring the decentralization of energy on a local scale with respect to the established practice of large power plants); and to the integration of ICT, mobility, environment and energy production systems.

2.4 Smart living

A further indicator, or perhaps more properly a meta-indicator, of the level of smartness of a city is represented by smart living, i.e. by all those conditions and requirements that generate a given level of quality of life for citizens. This indicator is of great importance as higher quality of life allows for better performance in terms of competitiveness of the city (Newton, 2012) and acts as an attractor for new highly skilled human resources (see, in this regard, Section 2.5 of this chapter).

Many international contributions concerning smart cities have highlighted a whole series of areas that must be considered in order to classify the degree of smart living. The first one is represented by all the elements that characterize health. For example, it is possible to mention life expectancy, the number of inhabitants per hospital bed, the number of inhabitants per doctor and the degree of satisfaction with respect to the quality of the health care system. Moreover, the emphasis is also on security, which can be quantified by the general crime rate, by the rate of murder and by crimes against property. It is important to consider both the current situation of these dimensions and their trends in order to assess the effectiveness of the investments that the city makes or has made in this regard.

Another element that contributes to identifying smart living is the quality of the dwellings that can be quantified by taking into account the percentage of homes that meet the minimum requirements in terms of quality, heating and, as evidenced in recent years, energy class. Moreover, the mean area that every inhabitant has at his or her disposal and the prices of homes must be computed. With respect to this last indicator, there is a certain ambiguity. On the one hand, high home prices may be an index of the attractiveness of the city, but on the other hand, these prices may also act as a deterrent to individuals wishing to move to a given city. At the international level, for example, it is possible to make the comparison between London or Paris, which are characterized by high average home prices, and Berlin, whose average values in the real estate market are much lower. Thanks to this element, Berlin has emerged in the last few years as a young and dynamic city.

Another indicator of smart living is constituted by the quality of institutions and of the physical infrastructure related to education (Shapiro, 2006). In this context, it is possible to consider the number and variety of upper secondary schools and, in the case of cities that have universities, the schools and degree courses offered by the local university. It is also possible to quantify the percentage of students with respect to the overall population, the degree of satisfaction with the quality of the educational system and its accessibility.

A very important component in determining the quality of life in a city is definitely represented by the cultural events that take place there. Several indicators can be used to measure this attribute. By considering supply, it is possible to mention, although not exhaustively, the number of cultural associations weighed by the number of inhabitants; the number of cinemas, libraries, gyms, bars and restaurants (considered both from a quantitative and a qualitative point of view); facilities for musical performances and/or theatres. On the demand side, it is possible to consider the average spending per individual for theatre and cinema, concerts, exhibitions and for sporting events, as well as the average expenditure for books and food and wine. More generally, the degree of smart living must be quantified by also taking into account the social cohesion policies that the city is able to implement to minimize the rate of poverty among the population. In addition, support policies, implemented in order to provide services and social assistance to the most disadvantaged segments of the population, must be considered and assessed.

One last element that can be analyzed is the ability of a city to impose itself as a renowned tourist destination. This indicator can be measured by the number of overnight stays in accommodation facilities weighed for the residents, the number of tourist attractions that are present and the number of cultural events that take place. The tourism economic literature has highlighted in particular the effects of the tourism phenomenon on the quality of life of a given destination of reference (see, among others, Deery et al., 2012; Kim et al., 2013). Less attention appears to have been devoted to the importance that the indicators of quality of life can have on the development of the tourism sector in a city.

2.5 Smart people

A city is essentially constituted by the individuals who inhabit it or who have it as their main centre of interest and of activity under various perspectives, which for example encompass the professional work life, the human and the administrative-political relationships and leisure. It is therefore essential to consider the human factor as one of the main drivers of a smart city. The international literature (Florida, 2002; Glaeser and Resseger, 2010; Antonietti and Cainelli, 2012 and others) has therefore highlighted the links, the interactions and the complementarity between cities and human capital (smart people). The availability of human capital is one of the key elements in the choice of location for firms. The presence of smart people can be measured with a series of indicators. First, it is possible to take into account the percentage of residents who has a bachelor's degree or other higher qualifications (Master's, Doctorate). Moreover, the educational and vocational possibilities throughout the course of life must be considered. In this regard, it is possible to mention the number of training courses and (re)qualification or the number of books purchased and/or borrowed weighted by the resident population in the city and also courses for the elderly. This last element (jointly with all other indicators that relate to the provision of training, i.e. the number of research institutes, universities and other educational institutions located in the territory, as well as their variety) attains both the smart people and the smart living dimensions.

With respect to the professional/working dimension, it is possible to measure the amount of individuals who work in creative fields or in the advanced tertiary sector. In addition, the possibility of finding a job and the time required to do this should be considered through an analysis of the flows in the labour market. Another important indicator is the presence of entrepreneurial capability in the city (Boschma and Fritsch, 2009). In this respect, it is possible to consider the number of entrepreneurs with respect to either the total population or the geographical dimensions of the city. The economic literature has highlighted the strong synergetic processes between the presence of a creative class, job opportunities and the dissemination of entrepreneurship. From this point of view, the study by Boschma and Fritsch (2009) has shown, within six European countries, a remarkable territorial heterogeneity. The widespread presence of creative industries within a given territory also allows the dissemination of knowledge spillovers that can trigger additional virtuous processes of local development (see, among others, Capello and Faggian, 2005).

A further element that testifies to the degree of smartness in the resident population in a given city concerns the participation of individuals to its political and administrative processes. In this regard, it is appropriate to consider the percentage of individuals who participate in the local elections; the composition by age, sex and place of origin of candidates to administrative roles of the city itself; and the degree of participation in voluntary bodies and in civic committees that try to influence the administrative choices on the basis of the needs of citizens.

Further elements are constituted by the ability of a city to attract human capital and its multicultural composition (Florida et al., 2008). It is possible to consider, on the one hand, the percentage of individuals that have good knowledge of one or more foreign languages as well as the rate of participation in language courses. On the other hand, policies aimed at attracting human capital coming from other countries must be taken into account, taking as a starting point the percentage of foreigners who work in the city and the number of citizens that were born abroad. These quantitative indicators can be accompanied by a series of qualitative indicators that assess how the processes of immigration are managed by considering the policies and administrative measures put in place for this purpose.

2.6 Smart governance

First of all, we have to recall the distinction between *government* on the one hand and *governance* on the other (for a broader analysis, see Chapter 14 by Antonelli and De Liso). The former is made up of the body(ies) in control of an aggregate, be it a municipality, a nation or a firm; it includes the legal framework according to which it is legitimate and can operate. The latter consists of the governing activity, that is the act and manner of governing that results from the actual process of taking decisions, implementing measures and so on.

Even taking the city, and thus the city council or city government, as the aggregate on which to focus, complexity is a structural feature that one must necessarily consider. In fact, local councils, however large their autonomy can be, have to operate in accordance with other governmental bodies and rules, which are often hierarchically superimposed. Furthermore, when we refer to the European area, we observe the existence of a variety of institutional set-ups, each with its own characteristics, even though more and more affected by the European legislation. Thus, for instance, in the UK, one finds the district, London's boroughs, the county and the main subdivision among England, Scotland Wales and Northern Ireland – each with its devolved administration; in Germany, we have the *Stadt*, the *Landkreis*, the very powerful *Land*; in Italy, we have the *Comune* and the increasingly powerful *Regione*, while recently the *Provincia* – as a rule, one had two or more *Province* in a *Regione* – has been abolished, leaving room in selected cases to the *Città metropolitana*. The list ought to be long (just think of Spain's autonomous cities and autonomous communities), but the main point is the richness of the institutional set-ups, each characterized by different capabilities of action.

Besides the role of the public institutions just indicated, we have to consider the fact that the actual working of the city depends also on the presence of other institutions and organizations ranging from the chamber of commerce to the university and other agents and lobbies.

Firms play a fundamental role in the overall performance of a city. Firms respond to policies – they can be attracted or pushed away – but are also active policy players, particularly when they are big or organized in groups (just think of industrial-district firms). Once more we have to consider the variety of firms: private and public-sector, for profit and non-profit; and the relative weight of service, manufacturing and agricultural firms. Firm size, as we hinted earlier, is an important issue: just think of the evolution through time of the importance of Nokia for the greater Helsinki metropolitan area or to the impact of the presence of a car manufacturer (e.g. Volkswagen in Wolfsburg, Germany; Volvo in Gothenburg, Sweden; Fiat in Torino, Italy).

Given these premises, it is clear that to conceive and implement smart policies is not an easy task. The European Commission (2012) has explicitly indicated three dimensions on which to focus, namely energy, transport and information and communication technologies.

Smart governance is often indicated as that kind of governance that fosters the positive aspects of the economy, mobility, environment and the other dimensions that have been referred to up to now, the weapon almost invariably being the ICTs, which become an explicit tool for urban regeneration. ICTs are also often indicated as a tool capable of improving political efficiency and effectiveness, as well as to bring citizens closer to the institutions – the latter phenomenon being favoured by on-line interaction.

The governance process may well lead to improvements in the economy and all of the other dimensions, but it can also lead to indications on how to change the institutions and laws in order to remove barriers to growth.

While much emphasis is laid broadly on economic aspects and use of the potentialities of ICTs, for a city to be considered as smart, other key issues must be addressed. In fact, one has to be aware that active policies may sometimes backfire, leading to an erosion of social capital and to a social, cultural and spatial polarization (see Hollands, 2008, p. 312).

Transparency, inclusiveness, gender equality, participation, accountability and democracy are nice words that are invariably used in the broad literature, ranging from policy documents to research papers, concerned with smart cities. However, we should never forget the importance of those forces within society that tend to promote and perpetuate divides (a reading of Rousseau's *Discourse on Inequality*, published in 1755 is still highly recommended).

3 Smart cities, innovation and development policies

Innovation is the key word. It relates to a plurality of dimensions, and the first one that comes to one's mind relates to technology. However, institutional innovation also plays a fundamental role. At the basis of innovation – in all of its dimensions – is knowledge, and often the study of smart cities is associated with the themes concerned with the knowledge economy.

Starting from the status quo, policies that aim at increasing the degree of smartness of a city must take into account the institutional, technological and economic opportunities. On the latter point, economics has been characterized for a long time as the dismal science of studying the efficient allocation of scarce resources. Economic theory has taught us that there are no free lunches; however, sticking to the metaphor, as Mokyr (1990) has pointed out, through the diffusion of technological change, some free lunches have been made available while definitely many cheap ones have been on the table.

Innovation applied to the city is a very complex phenomenon and obviously depends on the specific context in which we are trying to be innovative. Let us consider an example of possible innovation in *local mobility*. Mobility must be safe, secure, reliable, fast, with a low degree of pollution and integrated with national and – where airports or seaports exist – international transport networks in order to allow the largest possible number of people to reach their desired destination (see, for a broader discussion, Section 2.2 in this chapter). Technology offers various means of transport (i.e. the bicycle with or without engine, the private car, the bus, the underground, the tramway). Road conditions can be modified to some extent through the introduction of reserved bus lanes or of dedicated bicycle paths. On the other hand, the structure of the urban road network should be considered in order to check whether the proposed solutions may be practicable. If the road is too narrow, it is not possible to create a bike lane separated from car lanes.

Several strategies can be implemented to reduce pollution: (1) strengthening the public transport using preferably the trolleybuses, (2) encouraging the use of cars with hybrid engines, (3) synchronizing the traffic lights, (4) promoting intermodality (for example by providing switching parks where one can leave the car and take public transport), (5) promoting the use of bicycles and so on. The range of possibilities is very wide, and as can be seen clearly, the alternatives that will be specifically activated depend on legal, technological and economic aspects. One issue that should not be underestimated is related to the citizens' preferences: if, for example, there is a strong preference for the use of private vehicle – car and motorcycle – the incentives to induce people to change their habits should be particularly stringent (in positive terms, low fares and high frequency of the public transport; in negative terms, making it more difficult to stop and severely punishing anyone who parks illegally).

It clearly emerges that even changing one single feature is a complex problem, while even when the technology is available it must be affordable. The consequences for all the dimensions of smartness should be carefully considered before implementing whatever policy. In many cases, the lack of economic feasibility obviously limits the opportunities actually available. For example, the underground can constitute a solution that is technically highly effective to carry many passengers in a short time and without burdening the traffic of the surface. However, big cities that do not already have active underground lines may hardly conceive the development of an underground network from scratch due to budget constraints.

Sometimes innovation can also consist in reverting to systems that were, at some point, abandoned. Once again an example may be of help: the city of Manchester, UK. In the 1980s, the need for public transport in the Greater Manchester area increased steadily. However, the creation of an underground network was not economically viable. The solution consisted in the creation of a new tramway network, integrated with the local trains system. This network could in part be based on old railway tracks, but in the central area of the city, the tramway had to be built from scratch. The costs of this operation were incomparably lower than those related to the construction of an underground network. Moreover, the construction time was relatively fast. At the end of 1989, the policy was adopted, and in June 1992, the line stretching from north to south (31 km long) was already in use. Since 1994, this line has been systematically used by more than 10 million passengers per year. This first line was designed to be integrated with other lines, which were built over time. In 2014, the network was constituted by more than 90 km of lines – a considerable figure if we consider that we are talking about an urban area. The number of passengers that have used the network of trams in 2014 amounted to 29.2 million.

The creation of this infrastructure has prompted political decisions of the central and local governments, selection procedures for procurement and the solution of technical problems of various kinds. With regard to the latter, we mention first of all laying the tracks and providing proper electric power in the city centre, the creation of a centre for the control of the network, the realization of the system of road signs and special semaphores, the harmonization with the existing road infrastructure and the solution to the problem of the voltage on the power lines from which the trams get energy – as we mentioned, outside the city centre trams made use of old train tracks on top of which was an electric power line that made use of a special voltage.

More in general, it is evident how innovation is based on all of the dimensions of knowledge, which means not only what technology and science can offer but also what the legal, social and economic dimensions offer, both in terms of opportunities, but also in terms of constraints. Urban reality is characterized by a large number of players whose interests can be in conflict, and any policy aimed at changing something can generate tensions.

Technology and science provide a stream of new possibilities and opportunities, but their economic viability is not granted, and resources have to be found (usually through taxation). The stratification of laws – from the European rules to ordinances of the city council – provides the framework according to which we ought to know what is obligatory, what is forbidden and what is permitted. However, the social acceptance of (urban) innovation is also a fundamental aspect.

4 Conclusions

The concept of smart city, which has gained more and more importance within the economic research in the last decade, has been the subject of this chapter. First, it should be highlighted as a clear definition of this concept is still debated among scholars – which have provided alternative meanings. What appears to be embracing all definitions of smart city is its proactive character and the long-term horizon of the various policies and interventions in this area.

Six dimensions of smartness seem to emerge, dealing with economy, mobility, environment, living, people and governance. It should be noted that these dimensions represent six complementary aspects for the improvement of the quality, efficiency and competitiveness of an urban or metropolitan area. It is therefore necessary to privilege a holistic approach to the overall improvement of the smart city. This usually involves behaving with the future in mind, knowing that trade-offs always exist.

A long-term perspective ought to inform policy action. Two difficulties, though, are always present. The first has to do with the political cycle: political incentives may well be short-term, so that long-term projects may be set aside. The second difficulty lies in identifying the drivers of long-term development: fifty years ago, development was synonymous with the construction of large industrial plants. Today many of these plants (e.g. the biggest European steelworks located in Taranto, Italy) have lost any driving force and have often become an environmental, social and economic problem. In hindsight, it is easy to say that that was a mistake, but to identify a different road at the time was far from obvious.

However, these and other similar (bad) experiences have led to the inclusion of "sustainability" in policy planning, while a general environmental awareness has emerged and involves the largest majority of private firms. In fact, for quite a few years, it has not been unusual for producers of goods that may have a disposal problem to take into account this problem from the outset. Sometimes policy action has been also important. A good example is that of the car industry. For decades, car producers did not think about what happened to cars at the end of their lives. Today, when a new car is designed, the dismantling, recycling and reuse of some components are explicitly part of design itself.

Smart policies, which take into account what technology and science offer, together with the incentives and constraints provided by the institutional and juridical sides, can sometimes become a reality.

Note

1 The issues discussed in this subsection will be further developed and analyzed in Chapter 16 on "Urban Mobility in a Smart Development Perspective".

Bibliography

Antonietti, R. and Cainelli, G. (2012), KIBS and the city: GIS evidence from Milan, *Economia Politica*, 29 (3), 305–318.

Boschma, R.A. and Fritsch, M. (2009), Creative class and regional growth: Empirical evidence from seven European countries, *Economic Geography*, 85 (4), 391–423.

Capello, R. and Faggian, A. (2005), Collective learning and relational capital in local innovation processes, *Regional Studies*, 39 (1), 75–87.

Carvalho, L., Germini, M., Lazzerini, I., van den Berg, L., van der Borg, J. and van Tuijl, E. (2013), *Research project energy transition in cities. Lifestyle, experimentation and change. Background, review and a frame of analysis.* First case study: Stockholm, Working Paper 1/2013, Enel Foundation.

78 *Nicola De Liso and Luca Zamparini*

Chourabi, H., Taewoo, N., Walker, S., Gil-Garcia, J.R., Mellouli, S., Nahon, K., Pardo, T.A. and Scholl, H.J. (2012), Understanding smart cities: An integrative framework, in *Proceedings of the 45th Hawaii International Conference on System Sciences*, pp. 2289–2297.

Deakin, M. (ed.) (2014), *Smart cities. Governing, modelling and analysing transition*, London, Routledge.

Deery, M., Jago, L. and Fredline, L. (2012), Rethinking social impacts of tourism research: A new research agenda, *Tourism Management*, 33, 64–73.

De Liso, N. (2008), ICTs and the digital division of labour, in R. Leoncini and S. Montresor (eds.), *Dynamic capabilities, firms' organization and local systems of production*, London, Routledge, pp. 346–374.

EC – European Commission. (1997), *Green paper on the convergence of the telecommunications, media and information technology sectors, and the implications for regulation*, Brussels, European Commission.

European Commission. (2012a), *Connecting smart and sustainable growth through smart specialisation. A practical guide for ERDF managing authorities*, Bruxelles.

European Commission. (2012b), *Smart cities and communities – European Innovation Partnership*, Bruxelles, COM 4701.

Eurostat. (2013), *Eurostat regional yearbook 2013*, Luxembourg, Publications Office of the European Union.

Florida, R. (2002), *The rise of the creative class, and how it's transforming work, leisure, community and everyday life*, New York, Basic Books.

Florida, R., Mellander, C. and Stolarick, K. (2008), Inside the black box of regional development – Human capital, the creative class and tolerance, *Journal of Economic Geography*, 8, 615–649.

Giffinger, R., Fertner, C., Kramar, H., Kalasek, R., Pichler-Milanović, N. and Meijers, E. (2007), *Smart cities: Ranking of European medium-sized cities*. Vienna, Austria, Centre of Regional Science (SRF), Vienna University of Technology.

Glaeser, E.L. and Resseger, M.G. (2010), The complementarity between cities and skills, *Journal of Regional Science*, 50 (1), 221–244.

Hall, R.E. (2000), The vision of a smart city, in *Proceedings of the 2nd International Life Extension Technology Workshop*, Paris, France, September 28.

Harrison, C., Eckman, B., Hamilton, R., Hartswick, P., Kalagnanam, J., Paraszczak, J. and Williams, P. (2010), Foundations for smarter cities, *IBM Journal of Research and Development*, 54 (4), 1–16.

Hollands, R.G. (2008), Will the real smart city please stand up? *City*, 12 (3) December, 303–320.

IBM. (2009), *How smart is your city?* IBM Institute for Business Value, Somers, IBM Global Service.

IBM. (2012), *How to transform a city. White Paper*, Armonk, IBM Corporate.

IBM. (2013a), *How to reinvent a city?*, Armonk, IBM Corporate Citizenship.

IBM. (2013b), *Insatiable innovation. From sporadic to systemic*, Somers, IBM Institute for Business Value, IBM Global Service.

IBM. (2013c), *IBM annual report 2012*, IBM.

Kim, K., Uysal, M. and Sirgy, M.J. (2013), How does tourism in a community impact the quality of life of community residents?, *Tourism Management*, 36, 527–540.

Licklider, J.R.C. and Taylor, R.W. (1968), The computer as a communication device, *science and technology*, April [reprinted by the Digital Equipment Corporation, downloaded from the DEC web page].

Mokyr, J. (1990), *Twenty-five centuries of technological change*, London, Routledge.

Natural Resources Defense Council. (2013), What are smarter cities? Available at: http://smartercities.nrdc.org/about.

Newton, P.W. (2012), Liveable and sustainable? Socio-technical challenges for twenty-first-century cities, *Journal of Urban Technology*, 19 (1), 81–102.

Rousseau, J.J. (1755, Engl. Tr. 1984), *A discourse on inequality*, London, Penguin Books.

Shapiro, J.M. (2006), Smart cities, quality of life, productivity, and the growth effects of human capital, *Review of Economics and Statistics*, 88 (2), 324–335.

Toppeta, D. (2010), *The smart city vision: How innovation and ICT can build smart, "Livable", sustainable cities*, The Innovation Knowledge Foundation, available at http://www.inta-aivn.org/images/cc/Urbanism/background%20documents/Toppeta_Report_005_2010.pdf.

Washburn, D., Sindhu, U., Balaouras, S., Dines, R.A., Hayes, N.M. and Nelson, L.E. (2010), *Helping CIOs understand "smart city" initiatives: Defining the smart city, its drivers, and the role of the CIO*, Cambridge, MA, Forrester Research, Inc.

5 Human capital and the new geography of jobs

Luca Cattani, Giovanni Guidetti and Giulio Pedrini

1 Introduction

The importance of the city as a geographical unit of analysis of the economic development has gained popularity due to, among other factors, the increasing role acknowledged to the economics of agglomeration, as outlined in the contributions of this volume. Quite paradoxically, as globalization speeds up off-shoring processes, the drivers of economic development become more and more spatially concentrated in urban areas. As the global value chains increase their geographic lengths, a set of economic activities with a high content of know-how settles down around urban agglomerations. Cities change their identities in response to radical transformations taking place in the cobweb of social and economic interactions within them. In these evolving cities, technological spillovers and, more generally, the establishment of complementary relationships among human and physical capital are at the basis of processes of economic growth and social change. Actually, this has major consequences on the creation and development of human capital as well as on its spatial allocation. Technological spillovers result into a continuous interaction among different labour markets and the establishment of career paths involving different firms and, hence, distinct internal labour markets. Therefore the process of skill formation can proceed along an inter-firm, or even an inter-sectoral, track. Furthermore, these processes of geographical concentration affect earnings, the income distribution between wages and profits and, last but not least, the efficiency of the institutional architecture regulating the overall economy and the operation of the markets for goods and services.

This contribution pursues three distinct but interconnected aims. First, this article outlines the recent theoretical approaches to the economic analysis of urban development. Particularly, this article explains the rationale for the concentration of specific economic activities in urban areas. In this respect the economies of agglomeration, due to either inter-sectoral or intra-sectoral technological spillovers, play a pivotal role as drivers of these phenomena of spatial concentration of productive activities. The complex dynamics of economic interactions among firms, implied by technological spillovers, cannot be neutral for human capital development. Actually, not only do technological spillovers favour the foundation of new firms, but they also affect, both directly and indirectly, the structuring of the workforce into skills, occupations and earnings. Additionally, this approach investigates the role played by the relations of complementarity among segmented labour markets in the determination of relative wages.

Second, this contribution discusses the statistical indicators needed for the analysis of these labour markets and the understanding of the spatial distribution of jobs (the so-called geography of jobs). Special attention will be devoted to the analysis of job flows indicators. In this way the focus is centred, not only on the stocks in the labour markets, but also on the dynamics of job creation and destruction. Furthermore, this approach allows analyzing the dynamics of job posts and workers separately.

2 Human capital externalities and urban development

Urban areas characterized by high productivity and high output levels tend to grow faster and faster while, on the other hand, less dynamic cities lose both employment and population. This polarization[1] can be observed nowadays in much of the Western world and can no longer be considered as random. Quite the contrary, it calls for a careful study on the root causes of such phenomena, which are probably to be found in structural changes due to major changes in the production processes and in the increasing openness to international trade.

As observed by Reich (1991) at the beginning of the 1990s, describing economies as national vessels engaged in the global competition can no longer be considered as realistic. In this view, the leading companies and regions/cities of a given country were to be favoured by governments due to the fact that they were able to "pull" the country as a whole at the lead of the global competition. It is hard to adapt such scenario to the present world, strongly characterized by outsourcing and relocation practices. Increasing openness to international trade and technical progress have gradually eroded starting from the 1970s the employment potentials of many urban areas that specialized in traditional manufacturing productions, through the increased labour productivity and the strong global competition from new emerging economies with large reserves of relatively cheaper unskilled labour. On the other hand, urban areas characterized by highly innovating capacities face increased global competition starting from a comparative advantage and thus exploiting new localized yet globally interconnected development paradigms. A central role in the success of these innovative hubs is played by human capital where firms' innovative and learning capacities transcend the mere infrastructural endowment in terms of ICT and include the production of knowledge, cultural and innovative services, thus generating a virtuous effect of population and economic growth through the attraction of additional human capital.

Some studies (Glaeser, 2000; Glaeser and Mare, 2001; Shapiro, 2006) emphasize the role of the localization of high-skilled workers in the expansion of employment of many American cities even in not strictly high-tech areas. Others (Moretti, 2004) point out how this concentration will not only bring benefits in terms of employment but also in terms of wages.[2] In such brain hubs, not only do scientists and engineers benefit from the economic growth but from an entire eco-system in which the most dynamic companies will find an atmosphere conducive to the production of new knowledge.

This great divergence between increasingly dynamic and increasingly depressed metropolitan areas can be explained by referring to the so-called brain-gap, a peculiar path-dependent phenomenon first described by Glaeser and Berry (2006). In recent years, cities with an initially small advantage in terms of high-skilled workers have been able to expand this gap with increasing speed, exploit-ing the complementarities between productivity and the urban dimension. The more urban areas react positively to the presence of highly skilled workers by increasing the quality of life, the number and the quality of amenities and local services, the more this human capital accumulation process will depend on the initial conditions. Highly educated individuals, in fact, interact with each other, increasing their own and others' levels of knowledge and skills (Lucas, 1988). Meanwhile this urban concentration produces Porter externalities in a signifi-cantly higher rate than large areas equipped with the same levels of education (Mathur, 1999; Glaeser and Saiz, 2004).

Empirical evidence tends to show that an initial advantage in the localization of human capital produces positive effects more than proportionally over time in terms of productivity, income and economic growth. This evidence can be explained in several ways. First, reference can be made to direct effects through the exploitation of positive externalities arising from agglomeration such as tech-nological spillovers, be they intra-sectoral (MAR externalities) or inter-sectoral. In this light, the concentration of smart people promotes the accumulation and production of knowledge, increases the speed of learning capacities of workers (Lucas, 1988) and enables better interactions between physical and human capital (Acemoglu, 1996). In fact, learning processes evoke a dimension of social inter-action in which either skilled and unskilled workers more rapidly increase their knowledge and skills and, consequently, their productivity.

Second, human capital localizations have a positive effect on the economic growth via two different channels:

1   The reduction of social costs (and related negative externalities) such as pol-lution, bureaucratic inefficiency, crime and alcoholism (Moretti, 2004; Ace-moglou et al., 2005)
2   The increase in the consumption of certain goods and services typically demanded by well-paid and highly educated workers, be they cultural (Glaeser et al., 2001; Florida, 2002), personal (Reich, 1991; Moretti, 2012) or amenities (Shapiro, 2006)

3 The new geography of jobs in an international perspective

The first conceptualization on the new geography of jobs stems from the central role of human capital in fostering urban development in the US. Since the late '70s, the economic and demographic performance of American cities has been increasingly dependent on the educational attainment of their inhabitants thanks to dynamic externalities in the accumulation of human capital in the city (Duranton and Puga, 2004). More recently, this trend has also been observed in Britain and, to a more limited extent, in continental Europe and Italy. According to this evidence, the level of education, qualification and skill becomes the crucial factor of spatial divergence and income inequality. Interestingly, since the very beginning, the concept has been applied to urban areas in a multi-dimensional way by looking at technological and economic aspects together with those related to the quality of life. Special attention has been paid to social interactions and cooperation among firms, with a special focus on relational capital and ecological factors along with the complementarity between physical and human capital. Thriving ecosystems based on innovative businesses are therefore the result of a plurality of forces of attraction (Marlet and Woerkens, 2007) that determine the spatial pattern of economic phenomena. Despite the importance of location decisions for the prosperity of economic activities, however, these ecosystems maintain a high degree of connection with the international dimension, which is crucial from both a purely economic and a cognitive point of view. On the one side, innovative enterprises are fully engaged in global value chains (GBV) and capable of maintaining high levels of competitiveness thanks to inter- and intra-regional technological flows and knowledge spillovers (Hudson, 1999). On the other side, the institutions in charge for education/training are committed to international mobility and exchanges in order to attract and retain highly educated individuals and provide current and future workers with the required knowledge and skills to increase firms' absorptive capacity.

Actually, this international dimension, along with the concentration of human capital determines new opportunities for the economic development of urban areas in Western countries. On the one hand, the international competition of new emerging economies such as Brazil, China or India generates a job destruction process in traditional industries. On the other hand, Western cities grounded on innovative activities can benefit from the supply of relatively cheap intermediate goods from those same developing countries where unskilled workers are abundant and less costly. This is in line with a model based on comparative advantage and implies an international division of labour in which each system is specialized in that stage of the value chain where they enjoy such an advantage. It is worthwhile to refer to the concept of value chain: one can easily think of many instances of consumption goods, such as an iPad, whose manufacturing process is subject to outsourcing and relocation in developed countries, while other activities, such as design, planning and marketing, continue to be performed in the US. The main difference with the past lies in the increasing internal divergence inside national economies.

This effect is particularly remarkable in the US, as described by Moretti's "three Americas" (2012) and Reich's "three jobs of the future" (1991). Moretti draws a picture of a country, the United States, that, at the end of the long period of transition from an industrial to a service economy, can be divided into three areas. The "first America" is that of the manufacturing industry, which has lost half of its employees since 1979 and continues to lose jobs at a rate of 350,000 posts per year. Cities such as Flint, Detroit and Cleveland continue to lose jobs and population and are characterized by traditional industries, low levels of human capital and poor wages. The "second America" is that of innovation hubs, represented by cities like San Francisco or Seattle, which attract entrepreneurs, financial capital and human capital while experiencing a substantial demographic and economic growth. In particular, Moretti highlights the multiplier effect that moves along with human capital: the creation of a job post in the high-tech industries in these cities will create the conditions for employing five people in other sectors that are not necessarily innovative but still sheltered from international competition, such as personal care services. The rest of American cities (the "third America") lay in an intermediate position. They are more and more unstable and on the edge between catching up to the second group and falling into the first one. The distinction between job creation potentials of different industries is thus hinged to the presence or absence of international competition. Personal services that are away from competition can experience employment growth as long as they are driven by localized leader industries capable of turning global competition into an engine of growth instead of a factor of decline. From this point of view, although some attempts to define smart city primarily refer to environmental sustainability as part of the quality of urban life, this concept is not compatible with a "degrowth" scenario. In fact, a body of highly productive activities is needed in order to achieve smart development and address sustainability issues.

Reich envisaged the development of three macro-categories of jobs in the future US economy. The first one, which we might label as routine work,[3] corresponds to the old set of "blue-collar" professions and fits well to the traditional manufacturing currently in crisis as well as to new forms of occupational routines induced by new technologies. The second category, which is labelled as "symbolic-analytical", mainly refers to occupations characterized by a high density of human capital in knowledge-intensive services. These jobs are also exposed to global competition, but they are able to turn it into a strength. With a little forcing, this second set of occupations can be viewed as a precursor of the notion of creative class proposed by Florida (2002) because of their similar ability to spur urban growth. Finally, the third category of jobs includes those personal services (waiters, barbers and many others) that, for their intrinsic nature, cannot acquire an international dimension and whose demand depends on the rise of "symbolic-analytical" occupations.

The effects of the concentration of human capital on economic development, however, do not only stem from high-skilled and experienced workers. The associated demand for new cultural facilities and personal amenities does not explain the entire wage premium enjoyed by unskilled workers living in these areas. One should also refer to agglomeration economies as recalled in the previous section. According to them, skilled cities generate productivity enhancements because they accelerate the learning processes of workers and/or take advantage of complementarity between physical and human capital. In this respect, internal migrations between American urban areas a can be viewed as an empirical confirmation of the effect of wage divergence generated by these economies. Migrant workers not only enjoy a wage increase due to the higher productivity of firms located, but they also benefit from the increase of individual productivity engendered by their own accumulation of knowledge generated by the migration. In the former hypothesis, we would just have a typical wage-level effect potentially offset by the return of the worker in his/her home town. This does not happen, however, in the latter case in which both highly qualified workers and low-skilled and non-experienced workers would manage to maintain their premium once they leave the town and move back to less productive areas. This, coupled with the empirical evidence of an higher acceleration in the accumulation of human capital for both groups of workers, led the economic literature to identify a wage-growth effect specifically associated with urban areas (Glaeser and Mare, 2001; Glaeser and Resseger, 2010).

The presence of educated people also favour cities' quality of life through the growth of consumption amenities (such as green areas) and reduction in crime and pollution. In particular, the newer approach that focuses on consumption and quality of life and the preferences of consumers and workers can be related to the smart city concept through the common feature of the citizens' standpoint (Glaeser et al., 2001). Quality of life in turn stimulates employment growth of both skilled and unskilled workers through "consumer city amenities". In this respect, although the term "creativity" is fuzzy and cannot be conflated with years of schooling (Markusen, 2006), it is a useful bridge to emphasize the human component in which every experience of smart city is necessarily rooted. Moreover, despite the fact that the existence of a direction of causality from creativity to urban growth is questionable, once we control for educational attainment (Glaeser, 2009) and that factors such as tolerance could not act on their own in promoting urban and regional development, the idea of semi-independent locational preferences among selected groups of workers should be taken into account in the elaboration of smart cities policies. For instance, the shares of artists among the employed rose sharply in the metropolitan areas of the United States, especially in Los Angeles and San Francisco, where commercial employment in media, arts, advertising and arts tourism became important magnets for artists (Markusen et al., 2004).

Theoretically, we could therefore assume that concentration of human capital is positively associated with both productivity growth and quality of life. In this respect, the existing estimates suggest that 40% of the migration to US cities are related to amenity and consumption effects, while 60% is related to human capital and wage differentials (Shapiro, 2006), although there are differences between different regions (Glaeser et al., 2014).[4] On the other hand, in Europe, the "amenity effect" seems to operate only on smaller population and geographical scales (Cheshire and Magrini, 2006; Biagi et al., 2011).

4 European perspective

Studies applied to the US have often crossed the Atlantic to capture similar dynamics of agglomeration in order to test the applicability of the model (Glaeser, 2005; Glaeser et al., 2006; Moretti, 2012). The image of a Europe that is segmented into three distinct economic areas in parallel to the division of the US can be very impressive. The first area is the one of northern Europe, which is highly innovative and competitive and positively engaged in the creation of global value. Second, we find Mediterranean Europe, which is lagging behind the rest of the continent. Third, there are a smaller and smaller number of areas in the intermediate group that have either advanced to the top group or have been relegated in the second. Even within the same countries, divergence among different urban areas may increase and accelerate. Highly innovative areas continue to co-exist with depressed ones that are still specialized in the production of traditional goods.

Further attempts to extend the model consisted in including additional socio-cultural and Europe-specific growth-enhancing factors and in putting these factors beside the concentration of human capital. In the Netherlands, for example, the confirmation of the growth potential of human capital pooling in urban areas[5] leaves room for taking also into account the role of amenities and social diversity in fostering urban development, together with the diffusion of other economic and cultural activities within cities.

Another issue lies in the relationship between smartness and social sustainability, which represents a traditional concern at the institutional and policy level, especially for the European Commission. Actually, smart community policies can be an opportunity to reduce inequality, although their results can be counterproductive when not designed appropriately. The blurring lines between the two different outcomes can be spotted in the long-term sustainability of these inequalities between and within metropolitan areas. In case these prove not to be sustainable, smart city and smart community projects should aim at improving trade and exchanges between forerunning and runners-up. Otherwise, incentives may be introduced along with further institutional solution intended to facilitate the acceleration of forerunning cities in their effort to become "smart". These considerations can be applied to the smart city framework as well as to the S3 framework. When reference is made to urban areas, agglomeration theories emphasize the complementarity between physical and human capital as the main advantage of economic development. However, such theories raise questions concerning the existence of inequalities among workers that are not merely due to different levels of education or their locational choices. In particular, by expanding the frontier of technological possibilities, such complementarity incessantly produces new knowledge and organizational routines. This causes a substantial change in the return to a certain type of skills and a shift in the assignment of skills to tasks. As a result, the organizational knowledge and skills held by some groups of workers, in particular those workers that are less likely to upgrade their skills or specialize in other areas/production, will become obsolete. Technical change can thus generate knowledge and skills obsolescence suitable to "crowd out" low-skilled and low-qualified workers. In turn, this "crowding out" effect can exacerbate social inequalities, which is hardly compatible with the concepts of smartness, sustainability and inclusiveness. In this regard, the provision of technical education and vocational training can trigger such skill obsolescence when combined with a relative abundance of human capital and the intervention of R&D-oriented public and private policies supporting such programmes.

This process of skill obsolescence follows the dynamics of a skill-biased technical change (SBTC) model. By assuming the complementarity between new technologies and high skills and the existence of substitution possibilities between different skill groups, SBTC can favour one type of worker and penalize another one, both in terms of real wages and job flows (Acemoglu and Autor, 2011). From this point of view, the concept of SBTC goes beyond the explanation of the performance gap between different areas (such as the "three Americas") or even countries. It also affects individuals that work in the same urban area and generates further within-city inequality, even within those cities that can be considered as smart.

However, it is also important to notice that the positive effects of human capital concentration are not limited to "smart" people. High-skilled workers are highly dependent on an underclass of service occupations performed by low-skilled individuals (Peck, 2005; McCann, 2007). Cities–skills relationship should not be taken for granted, especially in the European context. Many European local systems, in fact – unlike what happens in the United States, where the link between concentration of high-skilled workers and expanding employment origin from high-tech sectors – are still characterized by low demand for high-skilled human capital, with labour demand exclusively driven by trade and accommodation and catering services, along with some branches of professional and business services, education and health. The increased productivity spurred by human capital concentration, however, is mainly attached to skilled jobs. When assessing whether a job can be considered as "high skill" or "low skill", the cognitive content associated with the constituent tasks of that jobs is the main discriminant (Asheim and Hansen, 2009). The dominant field of knowledge (or domain) of each location thus becomes a place-based characteristic that affects locational choices of firms and workers.

5 Smart jobs for smart cities: the case of KIBS industries

In the previous section, we have acknowledged the idea that a highly educated population stimulates local productivity through knowledge spillovers. Cities may benefit from dynamic agglomeration economies if knowledge spillovers and flows of ideas stimulate innovation across sectors, leading to the creation of new goods and services in the long run. Innovation can foster interactions between physical and human capital by creating new jobs for educated workers at the expense of less educated workers (which, on the contrary, would face a destruction of jobs due to the advancement technical skill biases), thus giving rise to a high re-allocation of work. On the other hand, if the increase in productivity is associated with learning processes, we should expect less volatility in jobs, accompanied by a high mobility of highly skilled graduated workers that move to and between large cities. Overall, in the perspective of smart development, the concentration of high-tech activities and research centres is one of the factors that drive urban and regional development by positively interacting with human capital.

In this respect, interesting specificities could arise from the concentration of the so-called knowledge-intensive business services (KIBS) in urban areas

(Table 5.1). Although there is little consensus on their exact boundaries, KIBS are deemed to rely on professional knowledge based on labour qualifications and the quality of human capital (Muller and Doloreux, 2009) where knowledge is not only a key production factor of the firms, it is also the "good" they sell further to an in-depth interaction and cumulative learning process between supplier and user and both parties (Strambach, 2008). Accordingly, as the determinants of KIBS growth lie in the inter-related roles of intermediate demand, knowledge and ICTs, the combination of spatial proximity with human capital density favour the diffusion of KIBS rather than physical production or consumption. In KIBS industries, both agglomeration economies and related variety are in place. In particular, among the reasons for the gains of producing KIBS in urban areas, we find local division of labour and labour pool (Overman and Puga, 2010), knowledge and experiences that they "inherit" from their founders' and core employees' prior places of employment (Campell et al., 2012) suitable matching in the markets of production factors, better learning opportunities (Glaeser and Resseger, 2010) and higher reputation attached to urban locations.

Table 5.1 KIBS industries

NACE rev. 2	Description	NACE rev 1.1	Description
62.01	Computer programming activities	72.21	Publishing of software
62.01	Computer programming activities	72.22	Other software consultancy and supply
62.01	Computer programming activities	72.4	Database activities
62.02	Computer consultancy activities	72.1	Hardware consultancy
62.02	Computer consultancy activities	72.22	Other software consultancy and supply
62.03	Computer facilities management activities	72.3	Data processing
62.09	Other information technology and computer service activities	72.22	Other software consultancy and supply
62.09	Other information technology and computer service activities	72.6	Other computer related activities
63.11	Data processing, hosting	72.3	Data processing
63.11	Data processing, hosting	72.4	Database activities
63.12	Web portals	72.4	Database activities
64.2	Activities of holding companies	74.15	Management activities of holding companies
69.1	Legal activities	74.11	Legal activities
69.2	Accounting, bookkeeping and auditing activities; tax consultancy	74.12	Accounting, bookkeeping and auditing activities; tax consultancy

Table 5.1 (Continued)

NACE rev. 2	Description	NACE rev 1.1	Description
70.1	Activities of head offices	74.15	Management activities of holding companies
70.21	Public relations and communication activities	74.14	Business and management consultancy activities
70.22	Business and other management consultancy activities	74.14	Business and management consultancy activities
71.11	Architectural activities	74.2	Architectural and engineering activities and related technical consultancy
71.12	Engineering activities and related technical consultancy	74.2	Architectural and engineering activities and related technical consultancy
71.2	Technical testing and analysis	74.3	Technical testing and analysis
72.11	Research and experimental development on biotechnology	73.1	Research and experimental development on natural sciences and engineering
72.19	Research and experimental development on natural sciences and engineering	73.1	Research and experimental development on natural sciences and engineering
72.2	Research and experimental development on social sciences and humanities	73.1	Research and experimental development on natural sciences and engineering
72.2	Research and experimental development on social sciences and humanities	73.2	Research and experimental development on social sciences and humanities
73.11	Advertising agencies	74.4	Advertising
73.12	Media representation	74.4	Advertising
73.2	Market research and public opinion polling	74.13	Market research and public opinion polling
74.2	Photographic activities	74.2	Architectural and engineering activities and related technical consultancy
74.9	Other professional, scientific and technical activities	74.14	Business and management consultancy activities
74.9	Other professional, scientific and technical activities	74.2	Architectural and engineering activities and related technical consultancy

Source: European Commission (2009).

6 Measuring employment dynamics in urban areas from a labour-demand standpoint

From a demand-side standpoint, an analysis of the dynamics of skilled jobs in urban areas could be grounded on jobs flows as measured through job creation/job

Table 5.2 A selection of job flows indicators

Indicator	Definition
Job creation (JC)	The sum of positive employment changes in the expanding or opening plants i of the industry s in the period t. $$JC_{c,t} = \sum_{i=1}^{P} \sum_{s=1}^{Z} \frac{e_{i,s,t+1} - e_{i,s,t}}{e_{i,s,t}}$$ $$\Delta E_{i,s,t} > 0$$
Job destruction (JD)	The sum of negative employment changes in contracting or shutting plants i of the industry s in the period t. $$JD_{c,t} = \sum_{i=1}^{P} \sum_{s=1}^{Z} \frac{e_{i,s,t+1} - e_{i,s,t}}{e_{i,s,t}}$$ $$\Delta E_{i,s,t} > 0$$
Net employment change (NEC)	$NEC_{c,t} = JC_{c,t} - JD_{c,t}$
Gross employment reallocation (GER)	The sum of all employment variation of the industry s in the period t. $$GER_{c,t} = \sum_{i=1}^{P} \sum_{s=1}^{Z} \left| \frac{e_{i,s,t+1} - e_{i,s,t}}{e_{i,s,t}} \right|$$
Churning flow (CF)	$NCF_{c,t} = GER_{c,t} - NEC_{c,t}$

destruction at plant-level (Davis et al., 1996). According to this methodology, gross job creation (JC) is the sum of all the new jobs registered in all plants expanding or starting up in the period, while gross job destruction (JD) is defined as the sum of all job losses (see Table 5.2). From this point of view, JC and JD can be defined as the result of a breakdown of employment changes in two components that relate to expanding and contracting plants, respectively. The net change in employment (NEC) is thus given by the difference between JC and JD and is equal, by definition, to the change in total employment in the official statistics in the period of interest. In this way, one can distinguish between two measures: the first one is the gross job reallocation (GJR), which is the absolute sum of all these changes (positive or negative); the second one is the gross reallocation of workers (GWR), which is equal to the sum of all workers that alter their employment status during the year. Finally, the churning flow (CF) is given by the difference between GJR and NEC and measures the extent to which job destruction exceeds the amount necessary to produce the observed net employment change ("excess sector churning"). The level of industry churning and job mobility in urban areas, which is usually high, does not always correspond to major changes in city-wide employment. Employment increases in rising industries can be offset by analogue decreases in declining sectors, and eventually local industry shocks may not necessarily cause substantial turbulence in the urban structure. Actually, net employment gains/losses across industries are usually larger than the overall population change.

On the other hand, however, there is systematic evidence that once urban employment fluctuations occur, they can be often explained by local industry shocks rather than from aggregate shocks. According to the empirical findings, within-city government, manufacturing and service sector employment shocks explain considerably more of industry employment growth variation than do aggregate shocks (Carlino et al., 2001). In this respect, analyses that use this methodology have found some differences between Europe and the US. These differences can be explained by the institutional features in labour market regulations and by the lower labour mobility that characterize European countries. Both aspects influence the spatial distribution of economic activities.

In this regard, it is important to assess the churning flow in order measure, not only the dynamics of labour demand, but also underlying structural changes across industries and the churning of industries across locations in order to disentangle job flows driven by intra-sectoral flows from those that are driven by the variety of productions associated with agglomeration effects (Duranton, 2007).[6] In this way, one can take into account both the industrial composition of employment structure and the overall dynamics labour demand and eventually discriminate cities according to their potentials and weaknesses. For instance, as one of the main specificities of smart development in urban areas to be taken into account is the dominant role of the tertiary sector, it is important to assess the relationship between the greater weight of the service sector with the rate of mobility in terms of jobs and workers compared to the one associated with manufacturing (Davis et al., 2006). The service industry has been found to be among the most important source of employment fluctuations in many US cities. As a consequence, modern urban economies with relatively large shares of jobs in the services are not immune to employment fluctuations. These indicators can be used to assess firm and job mobility in high-tech industries, which is characterized by substantial turbulence compared to traditional sectors (Black and Henderson, 1999). This issue may apply to European cities as well, given the net creation of jobs that they have enjoyed in recent years and the dominant role of the tertiary sector in the employment composition. Indeed, despite the crisis by the average NEC of European capital cities during years 2009–2013 is positive in most of the areas while the proportion of employment in manufacturing industries is lower than 10% in 12 out of 15 cities and is lower than 5% (see Table 5.3). In turn an industry shock can be easily transmitted to related sectors following the smart specialization logic, thus causing significant cross-sector pervasiveness of technological changes on a local basis.

Table 5.3 Net employment change (NEC) in European capital cities (2009–2013)

Cities	Average net employment change (NEC) 2009–2013	Proportion of employment in manufacturing industries (2011)
Brussels	0.10%	4.6%
Sofia	2.04%	10.7%
Copenhagen (greater city)	0.29%[a]	3.1%
Berlin	2.08%[b]	8.5%
Tallinn	4.97%	16.8%
Dublin	7.94%[c]	4.9%
Madrid	24.17%	3.9%
Paris	0.41%[b]	6.5%
Roma	n.a.	n.a.
Amsterdam (greater city)	0.33%	4.6%
Vienna	1.77%	9.1%
Warsaw	0.05%	9.1%
Ljubljana	−0.66%	11.2%
Bratislava	9.73%	9.5%
Stockholm (greater city)	1.78%	6.0%
London (greater city)	3.12%	3.0%

Source: Own elaboration from Eurostat Urban Audit data.

Looking across different sectors, it is important to notice that NEC is higher in KIBS industries on average. This finding is in line with the hypothesis that these industries greatly benefit from urban agglomeration. In these industries, the employment increase in European capital regions during the years 2009–2013 shows a positive trend in the majority of areas and industries, despite the double deep crisis that plagued the continent (Table 5.4). Even capital regions of Mediterranean countries, where the crisis has been more severe, report job increases in some of these industries. This evidence suggests that human capital is positively related to cities' resilience in case of an adverse economic shock. The ability of an urban area to respond to a negative exogenous shock, such as the financial crisis of 2007–2008, will depend on its human capital endowment.

Moreover, an analysis of jobs flow that discriminates on the basis of the level of education required, as well as by business segment, would evaluate in what terms agglomeration economies translate into new jobs. Skills may impact labour demand mainly by increasing average firm productivity and secondarily by increasing the number of entrepreneurs and therefore the number of establishments in an area. The use of plant-based job flows could decompose the aggregate effect on labour demand into the relevant components. On the other hand, urbanization economies may have a greater role for the high-tech sector than for the other industries, although with substantial differences across high-tech subsectors. Additionally, the effect of human capital on employment growth can be more important in some sectors, such as KIBS, or subsectors, than in other sectors. Accordingly, the measure of job creation in these industries could be a good indicator of smart development of urban areas in terms of their capability to reap

Table 5.4 Average employment growth in KIBS industries (Nace code rev. 2) in European capital regions 2009–2013

Cities	J62	J63	M69	M70	M71	M72	M73	M74
Brussels	0.8	16.7	1.5	5.4	3.8	10.7	-6.7	-6.8
Prague	2.6	0.05	2.4	7.6	-3	0	-1	5.5
Berlin	11	17	-0.8	10.2	3.9	1.1	3.9	10.2
Attiki (Athens)	-1.2	9.9	-4.8	-0.9	-4.9	2.7	-6.3	1.9
Madrid	0.1	-0.1	-0.8	7	-3.2	11.5	-4.3	-5.5
Île-de-France (Paris)	1.6	4.6	4.4	5.9	2.1	60.8	-2.2	26.9
Lazio (Rome)	1.5	-3.9	0.6	-1.4	-1.2	-7.9	2.2	-1.4
Central Hungary (Budapest)	3.1	4.1	2.1	2.3	-2.1	8	-3	-4.2
South Holland (Amsterdam)	3.2	-1.2	-1.6	-12.2	0.6	-0.4	-11.4	40.4
Mazovia Province (Warsaw)	9.6	11.2	12.2	5.9	5	11.6	1.6	-8.5
Lisbon	4.5	-1.4	-1.6	3.7	-9.3	-12.6	-6.4	0.2
Bucharest	8.7	-2.9	1.6	-0.2	-4.1	-7	0.2	0.3
Stockholm	1.7	1.8	3.8	7.1	4.5	-6	-1.4	3.4
London	3.4	2.1	4.5	10.3	3.5	1.8	5.1	-0.4

Source: Own elaboration from Eurostat SBS data.

the benefits coming from thick labour markets, knowledge spillovers, matching mechanisms and human capital attractiveness.

These indicators can be also related to worker mobility between urban areas. Heterogeneity in productivity between plants is likely to influence both job flows and worker mobility, thus entailing a correlation between these variables. High wage dispersion is likely to coexist with high levels of churning flows. Workforce characteristics can also influence this indicator if it is assumed that they influence its mobility. On the one hand, educational attainment may have a strong influence on churning flows. The presence of educated workers is likely to increase the number of quits since their skills are adaptable to various tasks. In turn, since quits lead to replacement hiring, the churning rate of plants with educated workers should be higher than plants with a less-educated workforce. On the other hand, there can be opposite effects if skills are firm specific and education increases the adoption of skills on the job or if educated workers receive more training.

An empirical model that aims to specify NEC and CF across industries as a function of human capital would therefore analyze the effect of the share of educated people on job flows variables. Distinctive control variables, according to our theoretical framework, would be given by the employment level in related industries in the same area, with similar natural amenities and congestion. Other controls are represented by tax and expenditure policies, regulatory differences, the endowment of transport infrastructures and public services. Further variables to be account for in the smart city logic could concern the level of ICT infrastructures and the development of e-government services in the urban area.

7 Conclusions

This chapter has discussed the emerging path of development of the most advanced economic systems on the basis of recent economic approaches. The American case, described thoroughly by Moretti and Reich in two distinct strands of research, outlines the geographical polarization of the American economic system. On the one side, there are the urban areas, which have risen on the development of traditional manufacturing firms, whose origins date back to the aftermath of the Second World War. On the other side, there are those urban agglomerates, which have become hub of innovation in the so-called KIBS industries and have sprung up much more recently in the last two decades of the previous century. Interestingly, most of these new poles of economic development have not developed from highly industrialized areas, but they have rapidly become the engine of technological innovation and the attractors of financial and human capital and start-ups. In this way, one can observe a geographic polarization of the productive fabric into two separated tiers: an innovative segment, made up of clusters of innovative firms and kept together by some form of economy of agglomeration such as technological spillovers, and a traditional segment of firms striving for their survival in a globalized world. The firms of the innovative tier operate in the KIBS industries, partly protected by international competition, while the traditional firms operate in traditional sectors, with a high exposure to competition in international markets. In between these two poles, there are those cities that have not taken one of the two paths yet; the first one would lead to economic success whereas the second one seems to be bound to lead to economic decline. Each of these poles is characterized by a specific occupational structure. Particularly, this contribution explores the dynamics of employment in the innovative urban areas. These dynamics result from the complex effects of technological spillovers and, more generally, the economies of agglomeration.

This theoretical analysis has significant consequences on the structuring of both labour markets and income distribution. Each tier defines a specific path of economic development characterized by its own way to recruit and develop human capital. This chapter explains in depth how, in the innovative cities, the increasing demand for highly skilled labour services also affects positively both the productivity of low-skilled workers and their wages. In addition to that, in these areas, the demand for highly skilled workers favours the inflow of employment into the services sectors. Shifting the attention to the main European cities, this chapter also provides evidence on how, even in a severe recession, KIBS industries have contributed positively to employment dynamics. This seems to indicate that these sectors play a key role as employment generators in European countries, similarly to what happens in the US.

The spatial polarization of economic activities does not coincide with the polarization of the labour market since some unskilled workers are attracted in the highly innovative areas; the polarization of the labour market does not match the polarization of the productive sectors. In any case, this theoretical framework combined with the SBTC (skill-biased technological change) approach can provide the rationale for job polarization and its rise, evolution and spatial distribution. As a matter of fact, the growth of the innovative sectors not only gives rise to an increase in the size of highly skilled workers but also in the level of demand for low-skilled workers, as claimed by both the SBTC and the approach of the new geography of jobs. In this case, polarization in jobs changes the distribution of income with an increase in both the upper and the lower tiers. The observed distribution of income is different if the growth of an economic system depends on the traditional manufacturing sectors. In this circumstance, one may well observe an increase in the relative size of the demand for low-skilled workers. This structural change in labour demand causes an increase in the lower tier of the income distribution.

Conclusively, these two different models of economic development lead to two different structures of income distribution. The model based on the growth of KIBS industries tends to exhibit a bimodal income distribution, whereas the model based on traditional sectors shows a unimodal, skewed-to-the-right distribution of income. The choices in the economic policies taken in the past and those selected for the future can drive the economic systems towards one of these two models of economic growth and development.

Notes

1 What Moretti (2012) calls the "Great Divergence".
2 For instance, an increase of 1% in the share of graduates on the total population in a given metropolitan area would increase by 0.6%–1.2% the level of wages of unskilled workers as well, operating through an increase in the demand for particular services and

an increase in labour productivity attributable to a higher innovative propensity of the entire metropolitan area.

3 More recent studies focussed onto the British context use the term "drones" to identify qualified workers that are employed in new routine occupations, such as data collection, string command replication etc. (Brown et al., 2011).

4 Glaeser finds out that in the Midwest and in the South labour demand was significantly higher in skilled areas, but in the West, skilled cities are rather associated with faster amenity growth.

5 It has been calculated that a 1% increase of the number of graduates is associated with an increase by 0.82% of the employment rate in urban areas (Marlet and van Woerkens, 2007).

6 As a matter of fact, Duranton finds out that GER is on average more than twice than NEC for both US and French cities.

Bibliography

Acemoglu, D. (1996), A microfoundation for social increasing returns in human capital accumulation, *The Quarterly Journal of Economics*, 111 (3), 779–804.

Acemoglu, D. and Autor, D. (2011), Tasks and technologies: Implications for employment and earnings, *Handbook of Labor Economics*, 4 (B), 1043–1071.

Acemoglou, D., Johnson, S., Robinson, J. and Yared, P. (2005), From education to democracy?, *American Economic Review*, 2 (95), 44–49.

Asheim, B. and Hansen, H.K. (2009), Knowledge bases, talents, and contexts: On the usefulness of the creative class approach in Sweden, *Economic Geography*, 85 (4), 425–442.

Biagi, B., Faggian, A. and McCann, P. (2011), Long and short distance migration in Italy: The role of economic, social and environmental characteristics, *Spatial Economic Analysis*, 6 (1), 111–131.

Black, D. and Henderson, J.V. (1999), Urban evolution of population and industries in the United States, *American Economic Review (Papers and Proceedings)*, 89 (2), 321–327.

Brown, P., Lauder, H. and Ashton, D. (2011), *The global auction: The broken promises of education, Jobs and Incomes*, New York, Oxford University Press.

Campell, B.A., Ganco, M., Franco, A. and Agarwal. (2012), Who leaves where to and why worry? Employer mobility, entrepreneurship and effects on source firm performance, *Strategic Management Journal*, 33 (1), 65–87.

Carlino, G.A., DeFinab, R.H. and Sill, K. (2001), Sectoral shocks and metropolitan employment growth, *Journal of Urban Economics*, 50 (3), 396–417.

Cheshire, P. and Magrini, S. (2006), Population growth in European cities: Weather matters – but only nationally, *Regional Studies*, 40 (1), 23–37.

Davis, S., Haltiwanger, S. and Schuh, S. (1996), *Job creation and destruction*, Cambridge MA, The MIT Press.

Duranton, G. (2007), Urban evolutions: The fast, the slow, and the still, *American Economic Review*, March, 197–221.

Duranton, G. and Puga, D. (2004), Microfoundation of urban agglomeration economies, in J.V. Henderson and J. Thisse (eds.), *Handbook of regional and Urban economics*, Vol. 4, Amsterdam, Elsevier, pp. 2063–2117.

European Commission. (2009), *Knowledge-intensive business services in Europe*, Luxembourg.

Florida, R. (2002), *The rise of the creative class, and how it's transforming work, leisure, community and everyday life*, New York, Basic Books.

Glaeser, E.L. (1999), Learning in cities, *Journal of Urban Economics*, 46 (2), 254–277.

Glaeser, E.L. (2000), The new economics of urban and regional growth, in G.L. Clark, M.P. Feldman and M.S. Gertler (eds.), *The Oxford handbook of economic geography*, Oxford, Oxford University Press, pp. 83–99.

Glaeser, E. (2005), Four challenges for Scotland's cities, in D. Coyle, W. Alexander and B. Ashcroft (eds.), *New wealth for old nations: Scotland's economic prospects*, Princeton, Princeton University Press.

Glaeser, E.L. (2009), Entrepreneurship and the city, in D.B. Audretsch, R. Litan and R. Strom (eds.), *Entrepreneurship and openness: Theory and evidence*, Cheltenham, Edward Elgar, pp. 131–180.

Glaeser, E.L. and Berry, C.R. (2006), Why are smart places getting smarter? in Rappaport Institute for Greater Boston and Taubman Center for State and Local Government Policy Briefs, mimeo.

Glaeser, E.L., Gyourko, J. and Saks, R.E. (2006), Urban growth and housing supply, *Journal of Economic Geography*, 6 (1), 71–89.

Glaeser, E.L., Kolko, J. and Saiz, A. (2001), Consumer city, *Journal of Economic Geography*, 1, 27–50.

Glaeser, E.L. and Mare, D.C. (2001), Cities and skills, *Journal of Labor Economics*, 19 (2), 316–342.

Glaeser, E.L., Ponzetto, G.A.M. and Tobio, K. (2014), Cities, skills and regional change, *Regional Studies*, 48, 7–43.

Glaeser, E.L. and Resseger, M.G. (2010), The complementarity between cities and skills, *Journal of Regional Science*, 50, 221–244.

Glaeser, E.L. and Saiz, A. (2004), The rise of the skilled city, in *Brookings-Wharton Papers on Urban Affairs*, 5, 47–94.

Hudson, R. (1999), The learning economy, the learning firm and the learning region: A sympathetic critique of the limits of learning, *European Urban and Regional Studies*, 6, 59–72.

Lucas, R.E. (1988), On the mechanics of economic development, *Journal of Monetary Economics*, 22, 3–32.

Markusen, A. (2006), Urban development and the politics of a creative class: Evidence from the study of artists, *Environment and Planning A*, 38 (10), 1921–1940.

Markusen, A., Schrock, G. and Barbour, E. (2004), *Making the city distinctive: A guide for planners and policymakers*, WP 159, Humphrey Institute of Public Affairs, University of Minnesota.

Marlet, G. and van Woerkens, C. (2007), The Dutch creative class and how it fosters urban employment growth, *Urban Studies*, 44, 2605–2626.

Mathur, V. (1999), Human capital-based strategy for regional economic development, *Economic Development Quarterly*, 13 (3), 203–216.

McCann, E.J. (2007), Inequality and politics in the creative city-region: Questions of livability and state strategy, *International Journal of Urban and Regional Research*, 31 (1), 188–196.

Moretti, E. (2004), Human capital externalities in cities, in J.V. Henderson and J.F. Thisse (eds.), *Handbook of urban and regional economics*, Vol. 4, Amsterdam, North-Holland, pp. 2243–2291.

Moretti, E. (2012), *The new geography of jobs*, New York, Houghton Mifflin Harcourt.

Muller, E. and Doloreux, D. (2009), What we should know about knowledge intensive business services, *Technology and Society*, 31, 64–72.

Overman, H.G. and Puga, D. (2010), Labour pooling as a source of agglomeration: An empirical investigation, in E.L. Glaeser (ed.), *Agglomeration economics*, Chicago, University of Chicago Press, pp. 133–150.

Peck, J. (2005), Struggling with the creative class, *International Journal of Urban and Regional Research*, 29 (4), 740–770.

Reich, R. (1991), *The work of nations*, New York, Vintage Books.
Shapiro, J. (2006), Smart cities: Quality of life, productivity and the growth, *The Review of Economics and Statistics*, 88 (2), 324–335.
Strambach, S. (2008), Knowledge-intensive business services (KIBS) as drivers of multi-level knowledge dynamics, *International Journal of Services, Technology and Management*, 10, 152–174.

6 Smart cities, social goods and demand-side outcomes in a regional policy perspective

Gilberto Antonelli

1 Introduction

In our lifetime the greater share of the world GDP is created within the boundaries of large towns and metropolitan areas. This share will very likely increase in the future through particularly dynamic and competitive processes.[1] Although variety in spatial location is a common feature for economic development, this implies that the main challenge for local and global development will be played in this kind of spatial setting, which turned out to be more able in fostering internationalization processes and more capable in breeding and attracting investments in human, real and financial capital.

For this reason, especially countries[2] whose spatial location of economic activities has traditionally taken place following decentralized patterns have to take stock of their historical production paths and adapt them to the new and less new global trends.[3]

What is more, we leave in a world strongly affected by the global crisis from which we are still suffering, and also before the crisis, repeated evidence was showing that profound changes in the economic and social structure should take place in order to satisfy minimal requirements of economic, environmental and social sustainability.

The creeping perception that negative congestion, pollution and other externalities can transform services into disservices and goods into bads has grown more and more together with the evidence on high social costs imposed by the assortment of market and government failures. In parallel to the materialization of new preferences, fed also by the unbinding of supply chains in markets and societies, this has encouraged the search for new ways to increasing prosperity while reducing its dependence on natural and environmental resources and energy. In the meantime also, the fundamentally social and economic origins of many environmental issues are being recognized, and in this perspective, suggestions have emerged to pay attention to the principles of the circular economy and sharing economy.

In order to cope with such quick structural and social change, strategic actions are required by well-equipped (smart) governments, firms and households.

Therefore, the capability of a country or region to take stock of its "deviant" production paths, which in certain instances has been persistent over centuries,[4] depends heavily on their ability to mobilize both the demand and the supply potential of their economies and societies in support of the new strategies.

2 Key concepts and their absorption in economy and society

In my opinion, the capability of regional policies in being fitted to the task depends mainly on the ability of the different levels of governments and of private organizations to single out the appropriate elements of synthesis and connection between four sets of key concepts helpful in planning and shaping suitable policies.[5]

The four key concepts can be listed as follows: smart cities and smart specialization, on the one side, and smart networks and smart learning, on the other side. These can be sorted in two pairs of synthetic nodes addressing different components of the economy and emphasizing different key factors.

The first pair concerns smart cities and smart specialization, which together can bring to "smart development". In this case two steps come out to be crucial to chase in the domain of structural change. The first one concerns the capacity of the country or region involved to run after and exploit the synergies between smart specialization and smart city strategies through the promotion of smart development in the economic sphere – a core element of synthesis and connection between these two strategies.[6] The second step refers to their ability to take fully into account the real economic nature and characteristics of the services that are at the core of this structural transformation, in order to derive from this understanding a substantial drive for change. This second step is very often not enough carefully taken into account when, as it happens in the majority of the studies and prescriptions concerned with smart city, especially the hard side of processes and technologies is addressed to, in order to foster the ease of access to smart services.[7] Instead, understanding both steps can help in better designing economic policies concerned with industrial development and to derive from them the implications concerning the formation of human capital and the creation of jobs and employment.

But structural change, even if important, is only one part of the allegory underlying smartness. Reasonably coherent social change has to take place together with it in order to avoid failures or even disintegration patterns. Social sustainability and inclusiveness are focal constituents of development as we are slowly learning to recognize both at the local and global levels.[8]

The second pair of concepts concerns smart networks and smart learning, which together can bring to "smart communities". Also in this case, which falls in the domain of social change, two crucial steps must be faced. The first one concerns the capacity of the country or region involved to favour and make use of the synergies between smart networks and learning communities through the creation of smart communities in the social sphere – again a coupled core element of synthesis and connection between these two strategies.[9] The second step refers to their ability to take wholly into account the social nature and characteristics of the services that are at the core of the overall transformation in order to derive from them another significant drive for change.[10] By itself, getting the drift of both steps can help in better designing economic policies concerned with local development and to derive from them the implications concerning the formation of social capital and the creation of forward-looking labour and social conditions.

In any case, in order to better exploit these sources of change and innovation both in the economic and the social sphere, we must pay some attention to the new notions of well-being and development and recognize that, apart from normative considerations and value judgements, the majority of the services involved in this momentous change encompass a social nature that leads to significant transformations in standard constraints and objectives of the consumer behaviour.

3 Sustainability, development and demand for new goods and services in an unequal environment

Due both to supply side and new production needs and to the demand side and choices based on new preferences, a deep rethinking of the notion of well-being and development is being carried out. This is leading to a growing agreement on the idea that it arises "from a combination of what a person has, what a person can do with what they have, and how they think about what they have and can do" (IDS, 2009).

Along this line of reasoning, well-being embraces three basic components: (1) the material and economic one, stressing welfare conditions, standards of living and economic values; (2) the relational one, emphasizing personal and social relations; and (3) the subjective one, highlighting, moral values and perceptions, side by side with option and existence values. The three components are merged together, and their boundaries are highly fuzzy (McGregor, 2007; Sumner and Mallett, 2013).

This, in turn, has induced a multi-layered revision of the notion of inequality, thanks to which nowadays also experience and intuition suggest that inequality is a multi-dimensional phenomenon including symbolic features – so many are its features and the circumstances in which it can be felt, conditional on culture, gender, ethnicity, religion, race, geographic location, age and other characteristics – relevant for human well-being, both across individuals and groups.

Looking from this perspective, we can work out that maximizing well-being amounts to trying to minimize one or more dimensions of inequality and that access to material goods and immaterial services can help in this fight, in which appearance and reality intertwine each other and leave room to communication and other symbolic aspects. High-quality goods and services supplied in city environments, on the one side, foster multi-dimensional inequality together with variety and, on the other side, satisfy needs and lessen feelings of inferiority in a never-ending game.

It is important to note that the multidimensional nature of inequality and well-being concerns both each basic component per se and the connections between the three of them. I mean that, even separating the material and economic dimension from the others and limiting ourselves to consider inequalities and welfare in each of the proxies for the standards of living, since this can concern diverse variables such as income, wealth, education, health and nutrition, the multidimensional nature of inequality leaks out. Of course multidimensionality becomes broader if the three basic components are allowed to interact.

Among the non-economic components, an essential role is played by ethnicity, gender and religion. In any case, beneath them, access to many wants is often unevenly distributed and limited by economic constraints that are differently distributed in different contexts. Limiting ourselves only to very immediate examples, we could mention the option to use[11] sophisticated drugs and cures, safe transports, qualified information and knowledge, natural and environmental resources of higher purity and also a safe neighbourhood in which to raise children. Direct and indirect linkages connect material and immaterial components of inequality and welfare. Income constraints can easily bring about fragilities and drive persons to suffer from non-economic dimensions of inequality. Information and knowledge constraints can definitely impact on the earning power of individuals and groups.[12]

The unequal access to goods and resources and the limits to an inclusive growth are often augmented by complementarities among goods and the increasing relevance of "network products"[13] that characterize the actual conditions of consumption.

Moreover, the increasing diffusion of not-purely private goods,[14] contrary to what could be envisaged, can contribute to increase inequality and decrease inclusiveness. If we acknowledge the multiple natures of the economic goods, this depends on the specific composition appropriate in the case under investigation and the prevailing regulation structure for their provision.

In all cases, the quality of consumption is influenced by the ease of use of related conditions and externalities. This multidimensional vision of welfare and inequality lies at the roots of the recently agreed agenda for sustainable development, which will lead for the next fifteen years the whole strategy of the UN.[15] Sustainable consumption and production patterns are crucial goals within it[16] and get involved in different targets. A lot of attention is also devoted to sustainable urbanization and to the strong deployment of creativity and innovation in solving sustainable development challenges.

Services play a dominant role on the supply side as well as on the demand side. This is why sustainability is conceived as heavily dependent on our capability to recognize that "sustainable urban development and management are crucial to the quality of life of our people" (UN, 2015, p. 8) and that, in EU terms, the availability of smart services can be a crucial prerequisite in order to be able to sustainably manage both sides.

But we have to recognize that this has a strong theoretical implication: due to the relevance, if not the predominance, of social goods and services in a field in which multidimensionality submits each individual move to the test of social interaction, we are not allowed to work exclusively with standard economics.

4 How relevant are social goods and services in overall demand?

In our analysis, therefore, high priority should be assigned to social goods and services.[17] In this respect, we should note that, even if for a long time economic theory had simply concentrated on the category of private goods, economists were also able to learn that economic development requires the joint availability of a plurality of goods.

We will select the examples nearer to our study, but several other can be easily made in different areas.

The experience of many less-developed countries and regions, with massive demographic imbalances can show that the access to services like education and social insurance, which are not straightaway conceivable as private services, is, especially when we consider the female population, one of the main determinants of household fertility choices.[18] Furthermore, social services produced and delivered within social and migration networks, positioned in religious hubs, like mosques or social fraternities like the one of Muriti from Senegal, consist in educational and welfare activities that lie at the border between the household, the market and the state. This is again true for the so called welfare mix activities, which have been put on trial in different Italian regions in order to face the fiscal crisis of the state.[19]

Surely enough, this exemplification is not comprehensive. In the production plans of the contemporary firms, techniques are portrayed that give a significant role to "prosumers"[20] in the production, use and distribution of network digital contents or in the implementation of "smart electricity grids" for the production, use and distribution of electric power through bidirectional digital technologies. Also services, like basic research, in which shifting roles and social interaction are substantial, could be interesting study cases.

The suggested instances, referring both to developing and developed countries and regions, lead us to think that the roots of economic development lie in the availability of a plurality of goods: public[21] and social goods, side by side with private goods. Furthermore, this plurality could turn out to be one of the necessary ingredients for sustainable development.

The circumstances that lead each good to belong to a particular category can be non-permanent and pertain to particular historical phases and contexts. Therefore, we deal with categories that evolve over time and in the space.[22] On the other side, the category of social goods has not yet been well codified by economic theory, while in the prevailing opinion this seems the case for public and private services.

This is why, given the fact that this specific category is at stake, it can be useful in the present essay to delve into its theoretical underpinnings.

4.1 Defining the nature of goods and services

We have to recognize, first of all, that the body of economic literature to be surveyed is rather large and includes at least two strands of research that deserve a wider analysis with respect to the analysis we will be able to do in this essay. The first one concerns general microeconomic theory, which amounts to the analytical frame of reference of the present paragraph. The second strand, which will not be addressed to in the present work, deals with the study of the so called social market economy, which envisages going beyond the pure analysis of demand and supply (Röpke, 1958).[23] We could only say, at the present stage, that the latter could be conceived as a container particularly suitable to learn the functions of social goods in a macroeconomic setting.

The first strand of microeconomic literature includes many contributions strictly linked to the present analysis. Chiefly, the historical and anthropological studies proposed by Karl Polanyi (1954) and its statement of the "reciprocity principle", together with the exchange and redistribution ones, perform a founding task. To the extent that they are concerned with activities connected to social networks, and not simply to self-consumption of single households, the concept of "basic commodity", suggested in the frame of its general theory of the allocation of time by Becker (1964) and that of "unpaid work", suggested in the domain of gender studies (Picchio, 2003), outlines significant research lines on individual choices faced with different sorts of social interaction.

The concept of "social capital", put forward in several and variegated studies on economic development by sociologists (Bourdieu, 1980, 1985), political scientists (Putnam, 1995) and economists (Dasgupta and Serageldin, 1999), has provided a relevant investigation basis in a meso-economic perspective.[24]

The interpretations on the expansion of non-profit organizations[25] and the considerations pointed out by Quadrio Curzio (2002, 2007, 2010) on the subsidiarity principle in the framework of the European and Italian structural development, provide a research path open to the interactions between economics and institutions.

In the '80s the concept of "relational goods" has been introduced in the theoretical debate by scholars like Donati (1983), Nussbaum (1986) and Uhlaner (1989) and has also been utilized in the economic literature.[26] They can "provide a theoretical explanation for the puzzling fact that rational individuals engage in collective action" Uhlaner (2014, p. 47) and can help us to relate human capital with social capital in economic development.

More recently, a literature mostly concerned with a functionalist and positive approach is flourishing. It focuses its attention on the implications of information and communications technologies (ICTs) in the rise of the so-called "collaborative consumption" or the "sharing economy".[27] Collaborative consumption, by the way, even though its implications in terms of fiscal and royalty policy are unclear, is expected to contribute to foster social, environmental and economic sustainability, by means of alleviating societal problems such as hyper-consumption, pollution and poverty by lowering the transaction costs within communities.

This very synthetic account of parallel research lines in social sciences shows that, following different paths, we can find room in actual markets for a new category of goods, which I will call, for the sake of generality, "social". This category includes active principles rooted in interpersonal and social relations not shrinkable to pure exchange, not only in the stages of access to and final consumption, but also in those of production and distribution.

This fact goes together with the finding that, both at the local and global level, ups and downs of the economies are often firmly linked to the cumulative successes and failures of markets performance and governments strategies. Therefore, side by side with effectiveness and efficiency problems, related with production, exchange and distribution of private and public goods, typical of the so called *homo faber* and *homo economicus*, we are confronted with the problems related to the needs of resilience, reciprocity, participation, altruism and sustainability, typical of *homo socialis*.

In any case, when taking into account empirical experience, the study of the general principles for determining the economic nature of goods does require greater attention than the one mainstream theory is ready to pay to them. In fact, within its frame of reference, it becomes clear that the first and unique principle employed, which focuses on the conditions prevailing in the final consumption stage (non-rivalry and non-excludability as in Table 6.1), is certainly relevant for the analysis but is hardly exhaustive.[28]

We should be aware of the fact that all the features that characterize a given market structure and performance are contingent upon the nature accredited to the goods exchanged by the agents acting on its demand and supply side. Therefore, the meaning and relevance of the number of firms acting in the market, the kinds of entry and exit barriers, the implications of product differentiation, the role of information and the forms of strategic interaction strictly depend on the type of the goods traded in the market.

We should also note how strong is the contradiction between the fragility of this taxonomy in terms of definition capability and its altogether strong prescriptive

Table 6.1 Goods taxonomy based on the conditions prevailing in the final consumption stage

	Excludable	*Non-excludable*
Rival	Pure private goods	Common resources
Non-rival	Natural monopolies or public utilities	Pure public goods

influence on public policies. The awareness of this influence, given also its possible distortive outcomes, strengthen the call for a greater caution in general and, in particular, for greater attention to the evolutionary character of the economic nature of goods and their social role.

Consequently, it is more than convenient to restart from a careful evaluation of the set of basic principles to be followed in order to remodel a more representative taxonomy of the pluralism of economic goods. In this attempt of remodelling the most influential characteristics affecting definitions as well as interpretation are to be identified from the very beginning. Moreover, more than simply finding a role also for the supply side, the consequences of the interaction between demand and supply have to be explored.

4.2 Defining social goods and services

From a strictly theoretical point of view, the two mostly harmed categories in the mainstream taxonomy seem to be those concerning "public utilities" and "commons". This is because they are confined to include fuzzy objects if compared to the two core categories and maintain a residual character that is left to further exploration only at a lower level of abstraction.

According to the mainstream approach, markets can fail for several reasons. It is well known that subsidies and taxes may favour social cohesion, but they may also distort an efficient incentive structure. Moreover, market power, imperfect information, externalities and public goods can lead to states in which price signals are not effective and efficient anymore. On the other side, also the governments can fail. This happens when the relevant level of government makes "omission mistakes", not doing its best to improve economic performance, or makes "commission mistakes", implementing actions that worsen it. Public intervention in the economy is therefore constrained on a razor's edge by these two types of failures.

Within this framework, one is led to think that, at the origin of every crisis, we should find a single failure as a specific determinant, in a very straightforward and linear chain of bad economic consequences. The exit strategy is always based on a common principle: the implementation of liberalization and privatization measures leading to the fitting incentive structure. And, if properly followed, the exit strategy is supposed to succeed in every case with efficient solutions.

When we come to the case of commons, the so called tragedy of the commons could lead us to think that something similar to a "systemic failure" is likely to happen, while this is ruled out in the other cases. And, anyway, the risk of systemic failure can be thwarted resorting to the appropriate tools. In fact, a safety net is always available, in the mainstream view, if we are able to curb market and government failures altogether.

However, very often in the real world crises, multiplicity in triggering events, discontinuous nature of the crisis, path and cumulative effects play a dominant role. As the global economic crisis has also shown, the risk of systemic failure concerns all the four categories of Table 6.1. Moreover, the very category at the heart of the global crisis has been the one concerning financial assets. These assets, after the extended process of deregulation and privatization taking place in the last twenty years or so, have become even more akin to private goods in terms of global tradability, flexibility and mobility.[29]

The problem is that, in the real world, market and government failures can merge together and cumulate in explosive paths, instead of becoming two distinct sources of normative prescriptions leading to balanced solutions. Unmanageable failures can actually happen at the micro- as well at the meso- and macro-level. This is the reason why we are asked, apart from defining it, to develop a solid and consistent theory of systemic failure, capable of including the theory of market or government failure as a special case. This is even more relevant in contexts in which the actions of the state are split between different agents or levels of government and overlapping can easily occur, for omission or commission motives, at the local and national level as well as at the international level.[30] Systemic failure can, therefore, happen at a local as well as at the national or international levels.[31]

Unfortunately, a complete and satisfactory theory of systemic failure is not available yet, but the need for such a theory was made evident by the global crisis, and by contrast, it is enhanced by the emphasis nowadays placed on the economic prospects of what we could call "systemic sustainability". This theoretical lack can be considered as one important rationale behind the speculative bubbles that are becoming a common fact of economic life and gives an increasingly relevant role to contingency management in basic (private as well as public) economic choices.

Possibly a first step in the new direction can be done by investigating five key principles, based on the theoretical and empirical knowledge accrued in this field, which can enlarge our perspective.[32]

1   The first principle refers, of course, to the conditions prevailing in the final consumption stage for individual customers and pertains to the behaviours on the demand side: precisely, non-rivalry and non-excludability in final consumption. In this case, we are dealing with pure exchange conditions simply drawn from the mainstream theory.

However, in order to make explicit the different kinds of interdependencies that contribute to determine the very economic nature of goods we have to add to the first one at least four other principles. This does not imply that we can always attain consistent categories when using different key principles. But the basic idea is to expose the main categories to a test of economic significance. Afterward, further studies should be carried out in order to test other features of interest.

2   The second key principle we can use refers to the material, natural and legal characters of the economic goods that match both exchange and production

activities. Among the former, inter-industry exchanges have to be considered. These characters are particularly influenced both by technological and organizational change and by regulatory transformations, and in turn, these determinants together are strongly influenced by the evolution of knowledge and its economic organization. In this case, I am mainly referring to the supply side of the market, but also the interactions between demand and supply side are relevant. Table 6.2 shows the main dynamic pushes deriving from this principle, which are able to influence the evolution of the economic classification of goods over time. An important implication of this analysis is that, depending on each country's capability to manage the economic organization of knowledge, the evolution can be determined in a totally exogenous way or in a partially endogenous one.

3   The third key principle draws on the contribution of Ronald Coase and Karl Polanyi and refers to actions based on reciprocity and subsidiarity (but also on mutuality), which can take place between the different agents in exchange relationships. This principle again concerns mainly the demand side. Table 6.3 shows the result of its adoption in the economic classification of goods. The category of "social goods" becomes explicit as a joint result of reciprocity and horizontal subsidiarity. The underlying assumption is that, in the case of social goods, like in that of public goods, transaction costs are not irrelevant. Some similarities can be found between this category and that of club goods,[33] which in the mainstream theory represent the outcome of social aggregations in terms of production and provision of relevant goods, especially at a local level. A collateral advantage of this taxonomy is the possibility to detect money among the public goods.[34]

Table 6.2 Goods taxonomy based on the prospects of evolution in their character

	Weak technological change	*Strong technological change*
Weak transformation in regulation	Low probability of evolution (stationary state)	Average probability of evolution (middle evolution)
Strong transformation in regulation	Average probability of evolution (mid evolution)	High probability of evolution (fast evolution)

Table 6.3 Goods taxonomy based on their degree of mutuality in the exchange phase

	Non-reciprocity	*Reciprocity*
Vertical subsidiarity	Private goods	Public goods[35]
Horizontal subsidiarity	Private goods	Social goods

Table 6.4 Services taxonomy based on the interaction of the agents involved

	Separation between producer and consumer	*Proximity between producer and consumer*
For-profit organizations	Private goods	Common resources
Not-for-profit organizations	Public goods[37]	Social goods

4   The fourth key principle refers to the identification of the agents involved in the supply of services and to the sharing of tasks and functions among them, in a context of social division of labour that also refers to the production activities.[36] In this case, interaction and reciprocity consist mainly in "proximity" between producers and consumers. Reference is made to the supply side and the interaction between demand and supply. Table 6.4 shows the consequences of the adoption of this principle. Further characters of social services are portrayed with reference to the typology of the production organization and the proximity between producer and consumer. Even in this case, it is possible to sort out money among the public services.

5   The fifth and last key principle refers to the greater or lower capacity, related to the utilization of the different goods, of generating and increasing social interaction. From this point of view, consumption and investment decisions, both at the individual and collective level, may induce direct and indirect networks effects. In the case of the so called *network products*, social interaction matters because of its influence on consumers choices of the products and services they buy. Market characteristics like complementarity, compatibility and standards, externalities, switching costs and lock-in and scale economies are the main forces leading consumers to shop for integrated systems (Shy, 2001). Reversing the causal chain, in our case, we could speak of "*services-led networks*" for which social interaction is the outcome of the agents' decision to use specific services. The goods whose use is capable of generating immediate network effects are many, especially if we take into consideration leisure time consumption.[38] Less frequent are the goods that are able to generate networks effects persisting over time, and these are the very goods considered here.

In other words, as an outcome of decisions referring to the use of definite goods, side by side with private benefits, social benefits may arise, which allows for the strengthening of networks of origin.[39] Thus, for instance, in the case of investments in the service we call education, side by side with the private returns, social returns are attainable. The latter may depend on production externalities as well as on other kinds of externalities. With reference to the first class of externalities, an important role is played by the increases in overall productivity linked to innovation and *knowledge spillovers* that are fostered by education. With reference to the second class of externalities, social benefits may be increased by the increase in so called *peer effects* in school, the reduction in incentives to breaking the law, the restraint of behaviours causing health risk and the increase in the degree of political freedom, often associated with a higher level of education (Cingano and Cipollone, 2009).

Table 6.5 clarifies how this analysis and the current example lead to thinking that, while the use of a pure private service or a common resource generates only affects individual well-being, the use of a public service or a social service leads to networks effects.

The five key principles play their roles starting from given configurations in the objective functions of the agents and markets organization and in the actual regulation and institutional frame, as well as in the social behaviour and structure. All this leads to a prevailing incentive structure (North, 1990) whose evolution affects the structural classification of the different goods.

Notably, changes in this classification can be due to three principal events:

1   in the formation or transformation of the initial system under the impulse of technological change and/or according to a specific model of capitalism (e.g. different paths of liberalization, privatization and decentralization in local systems);
2   in the life cycle of a particular good when, for instance, from an initial stage in which the perception of its need is confined in a self-consumption setting to the state in which the good becomes increasingly standardized and offered in the marketplace (relevant examples can be found in services like information packages whose supply shifts from the public sector to a social network and, then to the market; or welfare services in transition from a non-market to a market setting, only after the latter has been established); and
3   when different alternatives for the production of a service co-exist and are linked, for instance, to the political and social value associated to pluralism (relevant examples can be found in the case of education and vocational training).

We could conclude that the category of social goods can acquire its own autonomy and that, if we limit ourselves to the exchange principle and to the demand side, leaving aside production activities (with firms, human capital and natural capital as key constituents) and income distribution (with the

Table 6.5 Goods taxonomy based on effects after their use

	Self-reliance effect	*Network effect*
Individual choice	Private goods	Public goods
Collective choice	Common resources	Social goods

different social groups as contractual players), the risk is high of ignoring the essential characters of the different categories of goods, all crucial for economic development, and of misplacing the role of the different economic agents (Quadrio Curzio, 2010, p. 4). This, on the other hand, makes it even more difficult to identify the most effective policies helpful in achieving system's sustainability.

5 Regulation and infrastructural requirements

After paying attention in the previous chapters of this section to the main issues and challenges of the conceptualization and strategies based on the selection and promotion of smart cities, in this chapter we are trying to derive the implications concerning the demand-side outcomes originating from this strategy.

A first point to be emphasized is that the overall demand envisaged for the future in the markets and value chains implied when speaking of the six dimensions concurring in the basic definition of smart city[40] includes a very wide subset set of goods and services defined as social in the previous paragraphs.

Moreover, public services, made by immaterial and material components, like electricity, gas, water, waste, heating/air conditioning and mobility, which are more and more frequently and pervasively used by the citizens,[41] shares many of the social characters described in the previous taxonomies and play a crucial role in this frame.

Second, from our previous analysis on the nature of social goods and services, we have learned how a balanced attention should be paid to the regulatory framework that is going to be established. In fact, future demand cannot be assessed independently from the rules that will be established in the future markets and their governance. This in turn implies that some interaction has to be allowed in between demand and supply forces. And, as soon as we take into consideration this interaction, infrastructural drivers become crucial.

When citizens are the key decision makers in the demand for goods, several outcomes can occur depending on the different degree of economic and social cohesion and integration that prevails. We could think of a continuum of alternatives that goes from a context in which the community is made by perfectly rational and atomistic agents to a context in which the community is made by agents subject to limited rationality.

Independently from the social context, all the citizens probably will concentrate on some classic requirements of the goods they are looking for: (1) their quality[42] and uniformity in the pertinent geographical area; (2) their cost–benefit profile; and (3) their reliability (and, therefore, their resilience).

But when these classic requirements are delivered in the marketplace, context specificity becomes crucial because it conditions the very performance of the market. In fact, also in this case, we are confronted with a continuum of alternatives that can go from perfect competition performance to failure of the markets.

This suggests that a knowledgeable regulation perspective can help when implemented in order to face the specific nature of the goods and services exchanged in the market. When the exchanged goods and services own a social nature, specific regulation can help even more in pushing for a participation process shaping the characteristics of the demand side. Innovation in this case can derive both from supply push[43] and demand pull from consumers. Furthermore, to the extent that crucial goods can be produced and supplied as joint products, a multi-service perspective can improve the effectiveness and efficiency of the process.

A third relevant point deals with the prevalently closed nature of many of the markets and value chains considered. Goods and services provided in the expected developments of smart cities are, at least in the baseline, largely offered by local and national firms. The search for efficiency and innovation can be, therefore, slower than in open contexts due to poorer competitive pressures. This implies again that, if we need change, a substantial push should be looked for in the mutually sustaining links both on the demand and the supply side. Otherwise, actual supply can exert strong constraints on the demand side.

Fourth, as will be better explained in Chapter 7, these links can be found in the knowledge spillovers taking place between the different sectors of the local system and especially between the technologies employed in these sectors, as the notion of related variety helps to understand.

6 Conclusion

If these four deductions are correct, the main implication is that we cannot expect a spontaneous process of change on the demand side leading to an undifferentiated development of smart cities. We cannot be too optimistic because quite a few dangers are present and a powerful rhetoric is at work (Vanolo, 2014); however, a pivotal role for the success of smart cities is played by human capital (only one part of the smart people dimension) and social capital. Firms' innovative and learning capabilities go well beyond the presence of ICT infrastructures and extend to the production of knowledge, innovative and cultural/creative services.

Therefore, in order to exploit the potential of human capital and social capital a back-up platform is needed to actually extract the linkages relevant for making explicit the demand for new goods and services accruable in this frame. This platform cannot be built without long-term investments in social capabilities, which consist in the availability of general and specific technical and cultural skills (highly correlated with the level and quality of education, training and professional experience) and of political, financial and industrial institutions (highly correlated with the capability in organizing complexity both in the financial and in the production sphere). Social capabilities can be interpreted as a social "infrastructure" (Steinmueller, 1995) generated partly by explicit and partly by implicit investments and are incorporated in the rules governing the economy.

However, since we cannot always pretend to have the ultimate results of an optimal path of investments generating an optimal back-up platform available, we are led to explore in our economies the second best solution. In the case of smart or metropolitan cities, the second best solution can possibly rely on the multi-utilities' know-how. These corporations, to the extent they are sustainable and efficient in the complex markets in which they operate, can perform ancillary roles as the material and immaterial infrastructures for smart city development. At least in some regions,[44] they seem to be one of the few tools available for a planned development of metropolitan areas.

Notes

1 Even if more detailed predictions are needed, a widespread anticipation is that:

> The urban world is shifting. Today only 600 urban centers generate about 60 per-cent of global GDP. While 600 cities will continue to account for the same share of global GDP in 2025, this group of 600 will have a very different membership. Over the next 15 years, the center of gravity of the urban world will move south and, even more decisively, east.
>
> (MGI, 2011, p. 1)

2 And among them Italy for sure. See also Chapter 7 in this volume.
3 Therefore when one speaks, for instance, of "strength of territories", as it has become common in the recent public debate in Europe and Italy, one has to specify exactly what is speaking about, otherwise this risks being only a further example of wishful thinking.
4 And this is again true for Italy: see, for instance, Idse-Cnr (1999, Chapter 2).
5 Since large part of the volume is concerned with the motivation of this scientific tax-onomy, I will take the chance of being vey schematic in this chapter.
6 Part I.3. of the present volume is devoted to the analysis of this first step.
7 The present chapter will deal with this second step.
8 As scholars of economic development, like Irma Adelman (2000), have pointed out already long ago.
9 Part III of the present volume is devoted to the analysis of this first step.
10 The present chapter will deal also with this second step.
11 Or even the benefit of knowing that a chance of utilization exists in the future.
12 For a broader account of the topic see, for instance, Antonelli et al. (2014).
13 For a comprehensive study, see Shy (2001).
14 And this is certainly the case when we are concerned, for instance, with services like public utilities, which are crucial in a growing urban development and at the same time increasingly affected by technological and organizational innovation.
15 See, for instance, Point 3 of the declaration in UN (2015, p. 3).
16 Goal 12, among the 17 goals and 169 targets selected in the 2030 agenda.
17 In the present chapter, the terms "goods" and "services" are used in an equivalent way, and in our view, the increasing role in the economy of services cannot rule out the important tasks performed by material goods. Therefore, we will usually employ the term "goods" for both of them.
18 See, for instance, Ray (1998, Chapter 9).
19 A study of a local experience can be found in Antonelli et al. (1999).
20 This word results from the contraction of either the word "professional" or "producer" with the word "consumer".

21 In this frame, it might be useful to stress that, in a seminal phase for the development of the public goods theory, Musgrave used the world "social good" rather than "public good". See, for instance, Musgrave (1969, pp. 102–107).

22 As Atkinson and Stiglitz (1987, p. 483) suggest, the characteristics that mark the distinction between private and public goods cannot be univocally and absolutely defined but change over time and space, according to the technological and institutional structure of reference.

23 In this respect, reference could be made to Rotondi (2011).

24 Following (Portes, 1998, p. 4), the first systematic contemporary analysis of social capital is due to Pierre Bourdieu, who defined the concept as "the aggregate of the actual or potential resources which are linked to possession of a durable network of more or less institutionalized relationships of mutual acquaintance or recognition" (Bourdieu, 1985, p. 248, 1980).

25 With reference to the literature on not-for-profit organizations, see, for instance, Antonelli and Nosvelli (2003).

26 Relational goods has been defined by Uhlaner (1989, p. 254) as goods that "can only be possessed by mutual agreement that they exist after appropriate joint actions have been taken by a person and non-arbitrary others": "These are goods which cannot be acquired by a person in isolation, but which only exist by mutual agreement as part of a relationship with specific others; moreover, sharing the good provides part of the value" (Uhlaner, 2014, p. 48).

27 Collaborative consumption is defined as "the peer-to-peer-based activity of obtaining, giving, or sharing the access to goods and services, coordinated through community-based online services." (Hamari, Sjöklint and Ukkonen, 2015).

28 See, for instance, the taxonomy employed by Mankiw (2007, p. 224).

29 This is why the suggestion put forward by authors like Schwarcz (2008) to interpret the present crisis as a "tragedy of the commons" seems totally misleading.

30 In the European setting, the overlapping between different levels of government is fostered by the implementation of the subsidiarity principle.

31 Apart from the global crisis, quite a few multi-layer instances can be found, for instance, in the collapse of the US civil defence after Hurricane Katrina in New Orleans in August 2005, in the world's inability to face the tsunami in the Indian Ocean in December 2004, in the local crisis in the field of waste disposal, going on from 1994 in Naples and Campania and in the fraud at the Société Générale triggering the black Monday on 21 January 2008.

32 I am building here on a previous proposal to analyze the notion of social goods made in Antonelli (2011).

33 They are defined as excludable but partially rival (Cornes and Sandler, 1996) and represent another intermediate case between pure public goods and pure private goods.

34 Money is born as a private good and then transforms itself in a public good when it becomes *fiat money*. Such a definition is suggested, for instance, apart from various works by Alberto Quadrio Curzio, in the "*Chartalist*" approach, by Hyman Minsky (1986) and in the studies on "*global public goods*" (Camdessus, 1999). A public good is defined as global when the two standard proprieties of the public goods (non-excludability and non-rivalry) are coupled with availability at a world scale (Popescu, 2009). In other definitions, the fact is stressed that universality in the availability of the good must refer at the same time to the different countries, to the different groups in the population and to the different generations (Kaul et al., 2003).

35 Including money.

36 Like in the so called sharing economy.

37 Including money.

38 For instance, foods, beverages, games, sports.

39 For instance, increasing mutual trust, teamwork, social cohesion, friendship.

40 That is smart economy, smart mobility, smart environment, smart living, smart govern-ance and smart people.
41 And very likely it will happen in the near future.
42 Which includes innovation when relevant.
43 That is through technological and organizational change fostered by firms and governments.
44 And among them, in some Italian regions.

Bibliography

Adelman, I. (2000), Fifty years of economic development: What have we learned?, Paper prepared for the World Bank European Annual Bank Conference on Development Eco-nomics, World Bank, Washington, DC.

Antonelli, G. (2011), Global economic crisis and systemic failure, *Economia Politica, Journal of Analytical and Institutional Economics*, XXVIII (3), 403–434.

Antonelli, G., Bianchi, R., Cainelli, G., Galli, N. and Nosvelli, M. (1999), *Indagine sul sistema del welfare locale nella Provincia di Forlì-Cesena*, Forlì, Consorzio per la Formazione Professionale.

Antonelli, G., Calia, P.P. and Guidetti, G. (2014), Approaching an investigation of multi-dimensional inequality through the lenses of variety in models of capitalism, *Quaderni-Working Paper*, Department of Economic Sciences, University of Bologna, 984, 1–46.

Antonelli, G. and Nosvelli, M. (2003), Opportunità e problemi aperti delle organizzazioni non profit, *Non Profit*, IX (2), 181–226.

Atkinson, A.B. and Stiglitz, J.E. (1987), *Lectures on public economics*, London, McGraw-Hill.

Becker, G. (1964), *Human capital: A theoretical and empirical analysis, with special refer-ence to education*, Chicago, The University of Chicago Press, First edition.

Bourdieu, P. (1980), Le capital social: Notes provisoires, *Actes de la Recherche en Sciences Sociales*, 31, janvier, 2–3.

Bourdieu, P. (1985), The forms of capital, in J. Richardson (ed.), *Handbook of theory and research for the sociology of education*, New York, Greenwood, pp. 241–258.

Camdessus, M. (1999), International financial and monetary stability: A global public good?, IMF/Research Conference on "Key issues in reform of the international mon-etary and financial system", Washington D.C., May 28.

Cingano, F. and Cipollone, P. (2009), I rendimenti dell'istruzione, *Questioni di Economia a Finanza*, 53, September.

Cornes, R. and Sandler, T. (1996), *The theory of externalities, public goods and club goods*, Cambridge, Cambridge University Press.

Dasgupta, P. and Serageldin, I. (eds.) (1999), *Social capital: A multifaceted perspective*, Washington, World Bank.

Donati, P. (1983), *Introduzione alla sociologia relazionale*, Milano, Franco Angeli.

Hamari, J., Sjöklint, M. and Ukkonen, A. (2015), The sharing economy: Why people par-ticipate in collaborative consumption, *Journal of the Association for Information Sci-ence and Technology*, July, 1–13 (in print).

Idse-Cnr. (1999), *Trasformazioni strutturali e competitività dei sistemi locali di produzione. Rapporto sul cambiamento strutturale dell'economia italiana*, Milano, Franco Angeli.

Institute for Development Studies (IDS). (2009), After 2015: Rethinking pro-poor policy, *IDS in Focus Policy Briefing*, 9, available at https://www.ids.ac.uk/files/dmfile/IF9.1.pdf.

Kaul, I., Conceicao, P., Le Goulven, K. and Mendoza, R.U. (eds.) (2003), *Providing global public goods. Managing globalization*, Oxford, Oxford University Press.

Mankiw, N.G. (2007), *Principles of economics*, Mason, Thomson/South-Western, Fourth edition.

McGregor, J A (2007), Researching well-being: From concepts to methodology, in I. Gough and J.A. McGregor (eds.), *Wellbeing in developing countries*, Cambridge, Cambridge University Press, pp. 316–350.

McKinsey Global Institute (MGI). (2011), *Urban world: Mapping the economic power of cities*, Washington, McKinsey & Company.

Minsky, H.P. (1986), *Stabilizing and unstable economy*, New Haven, Yale University Press.

Musgrave, R.A. (1969), Cost-benefit analysis and the theory of public finance, *Journal of Economic Literature*, 7 (3), 797–806. Reprinted in Layard R. (1974), Cost-benefit analysis, Harmondsworth, Penguin, 101–116.

North, D.C. (1990), *Institutions, institutional change and economic performance*, Cambridge, Cambridge University Press.

Nussbaum, M. (1986), *The fragility of goodness: Luck and ethics in Greek tragedy and philosophy*, Cambridge, UK, Cambridge University Press, Ch. 12, The vulnerability of the good life: Relational goods.

Picchio, A. (ed.) (2003), *Unpaid work and the economy*, London and New York, Routledge.

Popescu, A.C. (2009), Money as a global public good, *Annals of the Faculty of Economics*, West University of Timisoara, mimeo.

Portes, A. (1998), Social capital: Its origins and applications in modern sociology, *Annual Review of Sociology*, 24, 1–24.

Putnam, R. (1995), Bowling alone: America's declining social capital, *Journal of Democracy*, 6, 65–78.

Quadrio Curzio, A. (2002), Sussidiarietà e sviluppo. Paradigmi per l'Europa e per l'Italia, Milano, Vita e Pensiero.

Quadrio Curzio, A. (2007), Riflessioni sul liberalismo comunitario per lo sviluppo italiano, in Quadrio Curzio A. and Fortis M. (eds.), *Valorizzare un'economia forte. L'Italia e il ruolo della sussidiarietà*, Bologna, Il Mulino, pp. 361–387.

Quadrio Curzio, A. (2010), *Le Fondazioni e la sussidiarietà: Il ruolo sociale per uno sviluppo creativo e solidale*, Paper presented at the Conference: Fondazioni: Eredi di comunità, figlie del Parlamento, Roma 10 June.

Ray, D. (1998), *Development Economics*, Princeton N.J., Princeton University Press.

Röpke, W. (1958), *Jenseits von angebot und nachfrage. Ein klassiker der sozialen*, Erlenbach-Zürich, Eugen Rentsch Verlag (trad. it. Al di là dell'offerta e della domanda, Catanzaro, Rubbettino Editore, 2015).

Rotondi, C. (2011), Economia sociale e di mercato: la "via italiana" tra liberalismo, liberismo e stato sociale, in Antonelli G., Maggioni M.A., Pegoretti G., Pellizzari F., Scazzieri R. and Zoboli R. (eds.), *Economia come scienza sociale: teoria, istituzioni, storia. Studi in onore di Alberto Quadrio Curzio*, Bologna, Il Mulino, pp. 113–133.

Schwarcz, S.L. (2008), Systemic risk, research paper n. 163, Duke Law School Legal Studies, March.

Shy, O. (2001), *The economics of network industries*, Cambridge, Cambridge University Press.

Steinmueller, W.E. (1995), Technology infrastructure in information technology industries, in M. Teubal, D. Foray, M. Justman and E. Zuscovitch (eds.), *Technological infrastructure policy: An international perspective*, Kluwer, Amsterdam, pp. 117–138.

Sumner, A. and Mallett, R. (2013), Capturing multidimensionality: What does a human wellbeing conceptual framework add to the analysis of vulnerability?, *Social Indicators Research*, 113 (2), 671–690.

Uhlaner, C.J. (1989), Relational goods and participation. Incorporating sociability into a theory of rational action, *Public Choice*, 62 (3), 253–285.

Uhlaner, C.J. (2014), Relational goods and resolving the paradox of political participation, *Recerca. Revista de Pensament i Anàlisi*, 14, 47–72.

UN. (2015), *Transforming our world: The 2030 Agenda for sustainable development*, New York, United Nations, 1 August.

Vanolo, A. (2014), Smartmentality: The smart city as disciplinary strategy, *Urban Studies*, 51 (5), 883–898.

I.3 Smart development

7 Smart development, local production systems and related variety

Gilberto Antonelli and Riccardo Leoncini

1 Introduction

A fundamental element that emerged from the debate on smart specialization strategy (S3) and smart development is related to its regional/local dimension. In particular, the EU's cohesion policies made great references to the so-called place-based policies. This happened in spite of the stronger emphasis that the proponents of S3 policy put originally on sectoral types of policy, which are usually 'by definition' space neutral (see also Chapter 1 for a deeper discussion).

From this new viewpoint, in fact, the concept of S3 is rapidly becoming an important tool to revise and readdress European regional policies. For example, the flagship initiative, the 'Innovation Union', developed within the Europe 2020 Strategy, represents an important example of how the EU deems important the concept of smart growth and smart development. They should be implemented by means of policies stressing the differentiation between regions to maximize the use of scarce resources through the creation of the necessary synergies. In fact,

> Regional Policy can unlock the growth potential of the EU by promoting innovation in all regions, while ensuring complementarity between EU, national and regional support for innovation, R&D, entrepreneurship and ICT. Indeed, Regional Policy is a key means of turning the priorities of the Innovation Union into practical action on the ground.
>
> (European Commission, 2010, p. 2)[1]

The concept of smartness however is not, strictly speaking, about advanced technologies but rather about the smart utilization of even low technologies either by using previously used technologies in a different way through a reorganization of their processes or by using low technologies together with the support of high technologies. In both cases, the idea of co-specialization comes to the fore and becomes very relevant especially within contexts where previous technological specializations already existed.

It is in the light of these elements that the relationships between smart development and regional economic growth take on a very important role in order to fully understand how the concept of smart development is to be developed and how new perspectives on regional policies can be brought about by following this route. Therefore, the present chapter aims at focusing and answering a research question that is very relevant when studying issues of local and industrial development in Italy and Europe. This question can be framed in two steps.

In a first step, we inquire whether, in the perspective of a smart development strategy,[2] a redefinition of the relationships between cities and metropolitan areas, on the one side, and industrial districts, on the other, can help both in interpretation and policy.

In a second step, we ask ourselves if betting too much on industrial specialization in non-urban manufacturing areas[3] can be understood as one of the determinant of the long-term decline in international competitiveness and productivity of the Italian economy.

First of all, these questions have a hermeneutic appeal, in that they comply with the interpretation of the decline in the last twenty-five years or so of an economy based on the predominance of industrial districts and also with the strategic perspective more appropriate for fostering its growth in terms of higher competitiveness and value-added creation in the near future. Moreover, their range of application is not only local or national, but due to the task acquired in the economic literature by this sort of territorially diffused development as an alternative to more typical forms of industrial organization in capitalistic economies, it can be shown to be fruitful in several discourses focusing on the role of SMEs firms in present economic development.

2 Variety, specialization and industrial development

At least from the second half of the 1970s, the scientific debate, first on industrial development and subsequently on territorial development in Italy, has been structured around the core concept of the industrial district.

In the traditional definition suggested by Becattini and his school (Becattini, 2000), the industrial district is defined as an organizational form in which two different dimensions interact: (1) the productive dimension and (2) the social dimension.

The productive dimension refers to a specific productive structure in which a multiplicity of small and very small firms manufacture for a single market and benefit from agglomerative effects. In fact, the action of spatial concentration of productive activities induces – following the by now classic Marshallian triad – three different effects named, respectively, *knowledge spillover*, *labour pooling* and *input-sharing* (Marshall, 1920, chapter 10).[4]

The social dimension instead refers to the specific set of social, political and cultural values of the local community prevailing in the industrial district. It is not by chance that, in the original definition of Becattini, the industrial district is defined as an 'interpenetration' of the set of local firms with the local population.[5] This amounts to saying that the industrial district is not only a form of productive organization, but it can be conceived as an outright form of capitalism where society matters and as a system that, under appropriate conditions, can be transferred both to other local systems in the same country and to other countries.[6]

In this line of thought, the notion of the industrial district has become the bedrock in the history of local development in Italy, both in its interpretative features and, more gradually, in its prescriptive implications.

At first, from the beginning of the 1970s, a series of actions were undertaken at the regional level. The constitution of Ervet in Emilia-Roma and Irpet in Tuscany, for instance, gave support to decentralized policies focusing on the synergic role of the service centres. In other regions, different attempts at implementing policies in support of local production systems were also performed. From the early 1990s, the first general action in support of the expansion of industrial districts took the form of a national law for the innovation and development of small firms (Law October 9th 1991, N. 317).

The institutionalization of the notion of the industrial district in the scientific and policy debate was therefore accomplished in the 1990s. In this frame, the conceptualization of the typical local production system, in spite of being export-led, was basically closed with respect to upstream linkages and more apt to protect the local economy than to promote effective innovative activity. The community of people involved, mainly for demographic reasons, was essentially local and self-contained. The fitness of human resources relied more on work-based learning than formal education acquired, and skill availability in the industrial basin was warranted by the thickness of the connections between workers and employers in the local labour markets.

In this framework, the notion of the industrial district became the key element along which to interpret the evolution of the economy and to conceive industrial and territorial policies in Italy. However, this happened precisely when massive empirical evidence on the decline of the Italian economy was becoming available.

On the one side, ISTAT developed an algorithm capable of extensively identifying the existing industrial districts, starting from the so-called 'local work systems' (*Sistemi locali del lavoro*) (Sforzi, 1987). On the other side, several in-depth analyses have been carried out by the Study Service of the Bank of Italy, in order to identify the major characteristics and the way of functioning of these local production structures. In this way, even the databases useful for applied research and policy analysis have been founded on this conceptualization of local development.[7]

However, as it has been observed in a report on the structural transformation in local production systems and competitiveness in Italy issued by Idse-Cnr (1999), thinking too closely in terms of this industrial district definition led to too much emphasis on the advantages connected to patterns of sectoral specialization. This emphasis, almost inadvertently, but in coherence with an historical habit, helped to underplay the fundamental role of cities in generating economic development, not only through the support given by their material and immaterial infrastructures to the manufacturing sector, but especially in terms of the virtuous capacity of urban environments to generate variety (Cainelli and Leoncini, 1999a).

This is not new for urban economics. Already at the end of the 1960s, the American economist Jacobs (1969) was stressing the role of cities and of urban space as an environment in which the coexistence of knowledge, skills and different life styles can generate significant externalities.

In the more recent literature of urban and regional economics, this approach has been extended also to other production structures of local systems, stressing the importance of productive differentiation as a key element favouring the cross-fertilization of knowledge and skills. The idea beneath this approach is very simple: in an environment characterized by strong productive differentiation, it is more likely that knowledge spillovers arise between the different constituent sectors.

Starting from the contributions by Glaeser et al. (1992) and Henderson et al. (1995), a large body of literature has been developed that tried to empirically test if local development (measured in terms of employment growth or total factor productivity) is more influenced by the degree of local specialization or of local variety. Although it could sound odd, this literature has shown that specialization – a sort of proxy of the 'district effect' – generally exhibits a negative impact on local growth, while variety reveals a positive one. And this has been found to hold also with reference to the Italian case (e.g. Cainelli and Leoncini, 1999b).

The discovery of variety as a driver of local development brought about another advancement in the literature of urban and regional economics. In particular, the notion of *related variety* proved to be quite useful in this regard (Frenken et al., 2007). The underlying idea is that knowledge spillovers do not simply take place between the different sectors of a given production structure but develop between sectors that are linked to each other by relationships of a technological nature. All this assumes a vision of the agglomerative process that takes into consideration, not only the spatial proximity between economic agents, but also the technological proximity, which in turn means cognitive proximity. Firms operating in different sectors can benefit from knowledge flows only if they are able to interact and communicate with each other.

In this frame, the conceptualization of the typical local production system changes radically. It becomes basically open, both upstream and downstream, and more apt to innovate than protect. The community of people involved becomes global, also from a demographic point of view. The notion of human capital becomes crucial, and the fit of human resources to global networks relies more on a mix of work-based learning and formal education, which can create a broad production factor (human capital) both specific and general that is internationally mobile.

3 Variety, specialization and role of cities

At this point, it becomes rather clear that, starting from the dichotomy between variety and specialization, we can identify some interpretative frameworks and policy paths impinging on innovation and smartness, based on the crucial role of cities and aiming at re-launching their role in local and national development.

In fact, it is from within an urban environment that effective mechanisms for the generation of spillovers between technologically contiguous sectors can be established. Moreover, we have to take into account that institutions, such as universities, public/private research centres and firms/corporations with high intensity of knowledge, are generally located within the boundaries of cities and that, as a rule, these are the core components of the external and the internal organization of knowledge, respectively. They are in charge of the formation, transfer and storage of knowledge and skills in the so-called 'knowledge-based economy'.

However, the scientific and policy discourse on the Italian economy has been essentially driven by focusing on the dichotomy between centre and periphery that, shifting their traditional tasks, tends to bestow an ancillary role to urban centres. This is mostly due to the peculiarities of the Italian process of long-term historical and political evolution, which led to the strong development of two (not necessarily complementary) forces: a high degree of geographic polycentrism coupled to the poor presence of towns of large dimensions with full vocations to become metropolitan cities. This is the reason why, when we speak of smart development with particular reference to the Italian contexts (or similar ones), we have to come to terms with a real conundrum before finding new analytical answers and/or policy prescriptions.

We are persuaded that the use of the concept of 'smartness' in this analytic setting, that is in trying to derive the implications of variety and/or related variety on the sustainability and competitiveness of this kind of local production systems, implies a rather radical revision of the standard toolbox for the study of territorial development. We need, for example, to redefine the foundations of the structural model and the scope of industrial policies and local development policies in order to leave behind the focus on industrial sectors, in which the pillars typically hinge on the dichotomy small versus large firms, with the corollary of the alleged relevance and dynamism of medium-sized firms.

Therefore, the limits of such a conceptualization become evident when we use an approach based on variety in which, for instance, the high interpenetration of formal/tangible and informal/intangible elements stands out and brings about an increasing 'loss of weight' of techno-economic processes. This in turn implies that firms are usually able to successfully take control only of some of the segments of the innovative chain (invention, innovation, diffusion) by means of elements such as idiosyncratic ingredients, differential absorption capacities and capabilities to exploit alternative channels for feeding the knowledge acquisition process.

Our conceptualization goes in the opposite direction with respect to the typical model of territorial development used for describing the so-called *Made in Italy*, fostering a wide reassessment that starts, not so much from the analysis of the specializations in production, but rather from a greater emphasis on the modalities with which the firms deeply rooted in the territorial context are able to successfully operate in international environments characterized by strong dynamics in learning processes. These learning processes also require high levels of complementarities and need highly interactive environments able to supply, for instance, services with high technological content (and therefore of knowledge). This is even more needed for firms capable of integrating themselves in high-value-added production segments within global value chains. From this point of view, to achieve the expected goals, the subset of the economic system involved should be able (that is should be smart enough) to integrate rather different sectors and knowledge in order to supply an appropriate platform for complex and high-value-added productions. Its aggregating core is built on intangible factors to the extent that the interpenetration of knowledge and skills is capable of feeding new innovation paths (Brasili and Bertini, 2014).

As a result, in this perspective, we need to get away from industrial policies based almost exclusively on the search for synergies coming from the dominant models of vertical specialization within specific industries. But we need also, and in a symmetrical manner, to get away from intra-sectoral policies aimed at horizontal specialization models between similar segments of different sectors.

To this aim, the peculiar structure of the Italian production system (in which a high degree of techno-economic specialization at a regional/provincial level coexists with high diversification at the national level and with a high degree of international integration) could represent a critical element in order to trigger a transformation of the economic system in a decentralized way. A strategy of this kind would need, on the supply side, a strong integration among sectors and technologies that are now far from each other. This could be made possible through the implementation of complex productions exploiting the advantages of integration between intermediate productions of different sectors, between diversified specific knowledge/skills and between organizational competences, often non-complementary. On the demand side, the capability to start complex techno-economic processes to produce high-quality goods requires a final demand from groovy consumers, willing to reward the production of high-quality goods and services.

In this respect, large urban areas can be legitimate candidates for becoming gravitational hubs able to foster the diversification processes of the productive system. In this way, it then becomes possible to take into account both the inter-linkages deriving from the techno-economic specializations needed to compete at the global level and the formation of more and more sophisticated needs that require, apart from new goods and services, also new skills. The development of new inter-sectoral skills is therefore needed in order to satisfy new and more sophisticated needs, such as those emerging in urban areas. In this way, it is perhaps possible also to bypass lock-in phenomena in traditional specializations from which it would be otherwise difficult to run off. To do this, it would need to identify, on the one side, technological diversification processes and, on the other side, the existence or the emergence of new needs that deserve smart innovation policies.

The concept of proximity can lend itself very well to delivering the various dimensions along which to implement these new and complex learning processes. Yet, the recent literature (Boschma, 2005) has stressed how it cannot be linked simply to the notion of geographic proximity, but also to the other dimensions (cognitive, organizational, social and institutional proximity). These are the dimensions that are gradually acquiring a predominant weight. A simple implication of this burgeoning of the relevant dimensions of proximity is that we need to focus our attention on the study and the political actions relevant in order to innovate in environments characterized by high levels of interconnection and complexity. This raises the related problem of how to act in a strategic way within industries that can include (and typically include) different sectors, based on knowledge and innovation activities that are idiosyncratic. From them, it is then possible to develop the potential positive externalities to the end of effectively implementing cross-fertilized processes.

A new technological trajectory focusing on smart development could therefore start from the redefinition of the role of cities as fly-wheels for industrial and local development. In this respect, the recent literature on related variety can offer interesting cues. As we have seen, this research line stresses the need of a sort of technological specialization among contiguous industrial sectors for the development of a local system. We need to identify sets of industrial sectors having these characteristics and exploiting the role of urban areas, where each node specializes in the supply of specific goods (private, public, commons, social). In this direction, polycentrism can become a resource on which to set up policies, not so much oriented to encourage specialization in production, but rather aimed at fostering growth processes. They would be based on the entire set of input–output connections available in a local system and on the specificities of cities operating as nodes of wider urban networks. All this, including the international linkages that new technological trajectories can stimulate, could configure the transition from a model of industrial and local development based on specialization in production (that in Italy sounds like industrial district), to a model based on the synergy between smart cities and smart specialization.

4 Concluding remarks

The territorial element within which the concept of S3 is deemed crucial is represented by geographical areas within which rather different technological levels coexist. However, as system theory claims, the global performance of a system is conditioned by the slowest of its elements (which generates what is called a reverse salient that can be seen as either a limit to system performance or as an opportunity for faster growth[8]), the concept of co-specialization and of co-development, as portrayed by the proponents of the S3 strategy, becomes crucial.

Within the geographical environment furnished by the Italian industrial districts (IDs), it is possible to delineate some important differences that allows for a further understanding of how the new conceptualization could work. In particular, starting from the differentiation between economies of specialization and of variety, it is possible to stress how IDs are heavily based on a mono-dimensional index of performance (such as profits or export), while the S3 strategy is usually based on multi-dimensional indexes of performance (the rankings are in general built by means of statistical methodologies based on, for instance, cluster analysis or principal component analysis). They are usually based on (mainly arbitrary) choices of a set of variables, of proxies and of related weights. Moreover, while inter-relations are a prerequisite of IDs (as the community of people acts as an essential element that determines the structural characteristics), they constitute one of the targets of S3, if not the main one. Indeed, S3's aim is to get inter-relations as a result, as smartness operates to induce virtuous behaviours that become thus interactive.

Last, but not least, IDs operate in a direction that goes from economic performance to sustainability. Indeed, the main aim in this case is to obtain high levels of performance that later are amenable towards particular coordinates, for instance, ecological and sustainable performance. However, S3 goes in the opposite direction, as economics is subject to the decisional, normative, process that determines priorities and directions, from which the ensuing economy will thus result.

Notes

1 A series of actions are identified, which through regional policy and related financing will fulfil the targets of smart growth of the Europe 2020 strategy (European Commission, 2010, Annex 1).
2 Which in this volume is understood as smart specialization coupled with smart cities.
3 On the side of economic research as well as on that of policy prescriptions and achievements.
4 We should remember, however, that the industrial districts studied by Alfred Marshall where located in rather large towns. The city of Sheffield, site of a cutlery works district, in 1901 was inhabited by almost half million people (451,195), while in the same period the city of Birmingham, site of a metalworks district, was inhabited by around 630,000 people. The population dimension of these towns was rather large in comparative terms.
5 It can be argued that the possibility of inter-penetration was much easier in the period considered in small and medium-sized municipalities. And, in fact, very often small and medium-sized municipalities and suburban areas were considered in debates focusing on the advantages of "small is beautiful".
6 The international interest on this topic is witnessed by the sizeable volume of foreign literature focused on industrial districts in Italy. See, for instance, Amin (1999); Granovetter (1973); Harrison (1992); Piore (1986); Sabel (1982); Storper (1989); Piore and Sabel (1984).
7 For instance, the methodology followed by ISTAT in devising the so-called "local work systems" is based on the conceptualization of a closed industrial district and suffers from its emphasis on self-contained systems.
8 See, for instance, Hughes (1987) on the concept of reverse salients within system theory. See also Dahmen (1991) on the concept of development blocks.

Bibliography

Amin, A. (1999), The Emilian model: Institutional challenges, *European Planning Studies*, 7 (4), 389–405.
Becattini, G. (2000), *Il distretto industriale*, Torino, Rosenberg & Sellier.
Boschma, R. (2005), Proximity and innovation. A critical assessment, *Regional Studies*, 39, 61–74.
Brasili, C. and Bertini, S. (2014), Città e sviluppo locale, in W. Vitali (eds.), *Un'Agenda per le citta'. Nuove visioni per lo sviluppo urbano*, Bologna, Il Mulino, 219–236.

Cainelli, G. and Leoncini, R. (1999a), Dinamica della struttura produttiva: l'industria manifatturiera, in Idse-Cnr, *Trasformazioni strutturali e competitivita` dei sistemi locali di produzione. Rapporto Idse-Cnr sul cambiamento strutturale dell'economia italiana*, Milano, Franco Angeli.

Cainelli, G. and Leoncini, R. (1999b), Externalities and long term local industrial development: Some empirical evidence from Italy, *Revue d'économie Industrielle*, 90, 25–39.

Dahmen, E. (1991), *Development blocks and industrial transformation*, Stockholm, Almqvist & Wiksell International.

European Commission. (2010), Regional Policy contributing to smart growth in Europe 2020, SEC(2010) 1183 COM(2010) 553 final, Bruxelles.

Frenken, K., Van Oort, F. and Verburg, T. (2007), Related variety, unrelated variety and regional economic growth, *Regional Studies*, 41, 685–697.

Glaeser, E., Kallal, H., Scheinkman, J. and Shleifer, A. (1992), Growth in cities, *Journal of Political Economy*, 100, 1126–1152.

Granovetter, M. (1973), The strength of weak ties, *American Journal of Sociology*, 78 (6) May, 1360–1380.

Harrison, B. (1992), Industrial districts: Old wine in new bottles?, *Regional Studies*, 26 (5), 469–483.

Henderson, V., Kunkoro, A. and Turner, M. (1995), Industrial development in cities, *Journal of Political Economy*, 103, 1067–1090.

Hughes, T. (1987), The evolution of large technological systems, in W. Bijker and T. Hughes and T. Pinch (eds.), *The social construction of technological systems*, Harvard, MA, MIT Press, pp. 51–82.

Idse-Cnr. (1999), *Trasformazioni strutturali e competitivita` dei sistemi locali di produzione. Rapporto Idse-Cnr sul cambiamento strutturale dell'economia italiana*, Milano, Franco Angeli.

Jacobs, J. (1969), *The economy of cities*, New York, Vintage.

Marshall, A. (1920), *Principles of economics, eight Edition*, London, MacMillan.

Piore, M.J. (1986), Perspectives on labour market flexibility, *Industrial Relations*, 25 (2), 146–166.

Piore, M. and Sabel, C. (1984), *The second industrial divide*, New York, Basic Books.

Sabel, C.F. (1982), *Work and politics*, Cambridge, Cambridge University Press.

Sforzi, F. (1987), L'identifcazione spaziale, in G. Becattini (ed.), *Mercato e forze locali*, Bologna, il Mulino.

Storper, M. (1989), The transition to flexible specialisation in the film industry: The division of labour, external economies, and the crossing of industrial divides, *Cambridge Journal of Economics*, 13, 273–305.

8 Smart development as a criss-crossed outcome of smart specialization and smart city strategies

Gilberto Antonelli

1 Introduction

As argued in Chapter 6, the capability of a region to take stock of its historical production path in trying to adapt to future trends heavily depends on two crucial steps. The second step[1] refers to the ability of the different levels of government involved to take fully into consideration the real nature and characteristics of the goods and services playing a crucial role in the transformation paths pursued. This can become a substantial driver of change and enhance their competences in managing local development.

The first one, on which we will focus in this chapter, concerns the capacity of the different levels of government involved to run after and exploit the synergies between the two different strategies of governance we are concerned with in this part of the volume: the smart specialization strategy (S3), on the one side, and the smart city strategy (SCS), on the other.

In Part III, we shall see that, since non-pure, private goods are at the core of the transformation paths and given the fact that markets are efficient allocation mechanisms only for private goods, for a relevant part of the economy, coordination mechanisms of a different sort are strongly needed.

We will argue there that these can be implemented through the creation of 'smart communities', which can make available two sorts of tools relevant for overall equilibrium. On the one side, they can elaborate rules capable of attributing economic values to production processes and the supply of goods and services with a social nature. These rules help in regulating the system and ensuring its compliance. This leads to tackling the structure of value chains for social goods. On the other, smart communities can help in adapting the very objectives of individuals, households and organizations to the constraints posed by social values on the subjective behaviour in the consumption of private goods. This leads to modifying the structure of value chains also for private goods. In this way, another source of synergy can be derived bridging the joint lessons coming from the study of smart development and smart communities.

But, in the present chapter, we are still focusing on the first source of synergy, and in order to set up our analysis in a more explicit way, it is better to state the plan of our presentation. First, the reasons for which it can be relevant to explore these strategies will be presented. Afterwards, the key research question that is important to answer will be raised. In third place, the linkages between S3 and SCS leading to smart development as a synergic outcome will be discussed. In the conclusion, the main results achieved are summed up with particular emphasis on the economic impact of development based on smart specialization and the smart city.

2 Why it can be relevant to explore S3 and SCS against the evolution of industrial policies

As far as SCS is concerned, the EU has incrementally assembled a common vision of a sustainable urban development since the 1990s, and in a coherent way, the EC has recognized for a long time the implications of the environmental challenges on dwelling in urban areas for human health, the quality of the citizens' lives and the efficiency of their management. The *smart cities and communities* scheme was started in 2011, and this approach was anchored in the Europe 2020 strategy in 2012.[2]

On the side of S3,[3] it can be observed that the adoption of this approach by the Council of the EU in December 2013 marks a discontinuity with respect to the previous strategies based on the approach of national innovation systems, studied in the 1990s and implemented in the First Action Plan for Innovation in Europe in 1997.[4] From this, one could deduce that the Lisbon Strategy (LS) of 2000 was recognized as not smart enough.

The essential idea under the LS was that, with the aim of maintaining the so called European social model, an extraordinary attempt would have to be made in order to get "the most competitive and dynamic knowledge-based economy in the world capable of sustainable economic growth with more and better jobs and greater social cohesion" (Rodrigues, 2005, p. 4). A reset of the strategy was arranged in 2005 with the aim of decentralizing the responsibility for regional and national innovation systems. But apparently this effort was also not enough persuasive and left room for new options.

Soon after the global economic crisis blew up and the member states belonging to the Eurozone were hampered, in particular from 2009 onward, in regaining price competitiveness through competitive depreciation and pushed to trigger very harsh competition on cost competitiveness through internal devaluation. The most disturbing outcomes of this practice have been the low level of investments both in physical and human capital, as well as the high waste in human resources.[5] Quite the opposite, we know that, among industrialized countries at least from the beginning of 1990s, what prevails is 'knowledge-based competition' (Reich, 1991), anchored in high investments and soaring labour quality.

The problem is that, after the choice made at the EU level around the second half of the 1990s to substitute innovation policy for industrial policy, the decentralization trend could lead S3 and SCS to follow an even more partitioned approach in the framework of EU economic policies. Yet this partitioning could be at least partly curbed if S3 and SCS were implemented together with a consistent design. Therefore, a first reason in favour of the search for linkages and coordination between the two strategies can be traced back to an attempt to avoid further scattering in European economic policies addressed to the real economy, after the fragility shown by them in the last twenty years.

A second reason in favour of the search for coordination and linkages between the two strategies can be found in the aim to draw a broad, but better organized, picture of the distinctive features of smartness when it joins economic development. This reason will be discussed in Section 5 in this chapter because the first reason can be substantiated if we look at the evolution of industrial systems and industrial policies in the long term. This is why it can be useful to summarize here some its main features relevant in our study.

3 Evolution of industry and economic organization of knowledge

The role of knowledge in economic development is not a novelty. Joel Mokyr has been able to offer a convincing explanation of the phenomenon called 'modern economic growth' subsequent to the first industrial revolution and to clarify why the West is so much richer today than it was two and a half centuries ago. In his view, an appropriate answer should pay full attention to the importance of 'useful knowledge' in the Western milieu.

> This does not necessarily mean that each individual on average knows more than his or her great-great parents (although that is almost certainly the case given the increased investment in human capital), but that the social knowledge, defined as the union of all pieces of individual knowledge, has expanded.[6] Greater specialization, professionalization, and expertization have meant that the total amount of knowledge that society controls is vastly larger than ever before. The effective deployment of that knowledge, scientific or otherwise, in the service of production is the primary – if not the only – cause for rapid growth of western economies in the past centuries.
>
> (Mokyr, 2005, p. 287)

On the other side, in his view, "it is very difficult to argue that the scientific revolution of the seventeenth century . . . had a direct impact on the pivotal technological breakthroughs of the Industrial Revolution" (Mokyr, 2005, p. 288). All over Europe, this process of forming a new technical and scientific community autonomous from science academies and universities had technical establishments, administrative bodies and training schools as the core players.

On the other hand, "[i]n the nineteenth century the connection between science and technology became gradually tighter yet is sufficiently gradual and heterogeneous to make any dating very hazardous" (Mokyr, 2005, p. 290).

The sweeping technical change taking place in the course of the second and the third industrial revolutions paved the way to the growth of mass production in industry. Meanwhile, in the second half of the 1970s, technological and organizational innovation was raising huge opportunities for change, especially in the field of industrial automation, through a massive application of electronics, telecommunications and information technologies. Also biotechnologies, with a lag with respect to the discovery of DNA, took off in the second half of the 1990s.

In the midst of the shocks caused during the 1970s by the crisis in the markets for energy and non-energy raw materials and the availability of new technological opportunities put forward by innovation, the US model of capitalism, then based on high volumes of production, turned out to be undermined by Japanese and European firms (Reich, 1991).

The main reaction strategies experienced in the US at that time did not function very well. The protectionist strategy, which, by the way, had been already taken up from the end of the previous century, did not allow persistent effects. Not even the strategy known as 'lean and mean', which was based on sizable wage cuts, production rationalization and first implementations of direct investments abroad, was able to recover profitability for large US corporations. Neither was the third strategy, based on a financial dexterity, fully satisfactory. This is why a change in the model of capitalism was required.

In an altogether new model of capitalism,[7] from the end of the twentieth century, individual firms try to position themselves in the global web looking for networks or clusters that allow them to compete internationally and pull out the highest values from the markets. It is the satisfaction of specific needs enforced by particular clients, often corresponding to other firms rather than final consumers, which represent the guiding principle in the effort to search for new markets and to fix prices to allow for the highest values. Multi-national corporations in the meantime changed into trans-national corporations and were turning more and more into facades under which autonomous groups or subgroups, localized all over the world, were continuously re-contracting among them their tasks in the networks or clusters by means of unbundling.

The transition from the first to the second model of capitalism, partly pushed by exogenous shocks and partly induced by reorganization processes endogenously designed by firms, did not evolve in a harmonic way but through trial and error, by fits and starts, in a frame of increasing risk and progressive financialization of the economy. In fact, the production system and its position in the overall economy have been drastically changed, increasing the role of the meso-economy and giving new functions to network hubs, which are often located in large towns. While authors like Harrison (1994) were scrutinizing whether Italian industrial districts could have been a useful answer for the downsizing of giant US corporations, now it becomes clear that industrial policies can play a complementary role to human development, if they are able to avoid a centralistic approach and become able to browse in an federalist institutional frame capable of stimulating private investment through partnership agreements.

In knowledge-based competition, the availability of specialized professional skills able to face variety linking together very specific technologies employed in different sectors or markets is the new 'entry barrier'. These skills have been classified by Reich (1991, pp. 84–85) in three subsets: (1) *problem-solving skills*, oriented to identifying and solving production problems; (2) *skills required to help customers understand their needs*, oriented to identifying markets opportunities; and (3) *skills needed to link problem-solvers and problem-identifiers*, oriented to fostering a strategic brokering between the first two subsets.

Such a deep change in the model of capitalism went together with the deep transformation of the traditional and homogeneous production factors into 'broad production factors' (Antonelli, 1997). This concept helps in stressing how firms have become able to employ blends of always more varied quantities and qualities of heterogeneous labour and human resources, physical and financial capital with technological change and natural and environmental resources. The increasing interaction, recombination, complementarity and international mobility of production factors helps to make them more flexible and operational in an innovative organization of networks and clusters.

The long-term evolution in the economic role of 'usable knowledge' and in the creation of new knowledge suggests to us to undertake a study with greater attention the evolution in the 'economic organization of knowledge'.[8]

Its three main objectives are (1) to preserve, reclaim and select acquired knowledge; (2) to transmit, transfer, use and diffuse acquired knowledge; and (3) to create new knowledge. This crucial subset of the modern economic and social organization can be split into an internal and an external section with respect to the firm. In fact, three key 'engines' enhancing productivity through knowledge can be envisaged (Antonelli and Pegoretti, 2008). The first one corresponds to work-based learning, and in this case, knowledge is generated as a by-product of the production process within the firms. The second engine corresponds to the general learning process, which is partly internal to the firm and partly external. The external component takes place in the educational and training public/private agencies. The third engine works through process and product innovation, which is originated by investments in new capital (technological innovation) and in new organizational methods.

Moreover, in order to better conceive the sequences of interactions and trade-offs originated by the organization of knowledge internal and external to the firm it can be helpful to classify these sequences in terms of two categories of 'professional competence pipeline': the first concerning the supply side and the second the demand side of labour markets.

As it is by now widely recognized[9] in real-world settings, the diffusion of knowledge and innovation requires new approaches based on advanced industrial policies and human development policies, able to bypass the ambiguities and illusions fostered before and during the years of the global crisis as well as to come out from vicious circles perpetuating low investment and high waste in human resources. And in this scenario EU is losing ground in comparison with the US and also with some of the emerging powers. It becomes clear how only policies based on high investment in R&D and human development can avoid low productivity, underinvestment in human capital and the poverty traps associated with them.

The suggestions derived from this scenario are emphasized when the perspective of the so-called fourth industrial revolution or 'Industry.04' is taken into consideration. As it is well known, this perspective has been wished for by sectors of the business industry with contents very close to the scientific and technological progress in the field of cyber-physical systems, big data or cloud computing. This wish or prediction seems to be one of the follow-ups of the debate on S3. In this framework, an important role is played by the notion of 'smart factory', which is very close to the idea of the representative agent we have in mind when speaking about the supply side of smart development. Focusing on a small subset of the overall proposal, in particular when looking at the actual requirements raised to the different levels of government, one of its main objectives seems to be addressed to improving the economic organization of knowledge in order to adapt it to the new needs of economic networks acting in the international markets. More concretely, this implies a better coordination finalized to allow for more effective and efficient exchanges of 'pieces' of information, education and training among the private partners and between public and private agents participating in the networks.

In the light of this long-term evolution, we can better understand why it can be considered effective to support the development of meso-level networks by means of agencies, but not necessarily coordinated among them, that finance R&D and foster the creation of clusters amongst firms, scientists, entrepreneurs and financial agents[10] also in local and urban environments. This support is explained by the need to arrange organizational structures that can be able to bypass the boundaries of each single firm through the making of networks, clusters and districts in order to generate S3 and SCS. These agencies are decentralized both from the organizational and geographic point of view and act in order to prevent network failures, as suggested by the industrial policies underneath pursued in the US in the last thirty-five years or so.[11]

4 Key research questions

In this frame, three relevant research questions should be investigated.

1   First of all, we could ask ourselves what linkages can be envisaged between S3 and SCS and why it can be helpful to recognize them. From this, derives our interest in deepening our understanding of what we are defining just smartness or, better, smart development and in distinguishing between what can be considered as smart and what cannot. This distinction, in fact, cannot be left just to the technological or organizational interest of single trial product. The literature on this latter aspect is rather large. Conversely, the literature trying to compare S3 and SCS and to find a common framework in order to analyze their joint outcomes seems to be more limited. An upstream and almost unspoken question concerns the interest of the EU to rely on these new key words, forgetting the previous ones.[12]

2   The second question refers to the way smartness can actually impact on the functioning of cities and local production systems. The literature trying to

answer this research question lags behind and seems still in evolution, given also the complexity to be faced when measuring a multi-layered and complex phenomenon.

3   The third research question is conditional on the answers that can be given two the first two and, above all, on the capacity to measure the phenomenon under analysis. This question relates to the role of the different levels of government in managing S3 and SCS, that is smart development. What are the ingredients and rules suitable for more effective governance?

While the present chapter will mainly try to answer the first question, the second will be taken into account in Part II and the third in Part III.

5   Linkages and coordination between smart specialization and smart city strategies

For interpretative and policy purposes, it is helpful to keep in mind that, in EU political jargon, the smart label portrays a figure of speech that goes beyond its literal meanings of intelligent and cunning and recalls the deeper and allusive meanings of sustainable and inclusive. In any case, probably for practical reasons, priorities have been focused more in terms of economic growth than in terms of economic development.

In this frame, planning a smart initiative entails the capability to generate transformations offering simple but, at the same time, meditated answers to a rather complex range of issues. The attribute smart represents therefore a successful example of a semantic box accumulating diffuse consensus while giving origin to a rather wide variety of conjugations more or less linked to the need to develop coherent artefacts, life styles, projects, strategies, institutional processes, analytic methods, evaluation tools and all that goes with it.

However, the definition of smartness changes over time, even drastically and often in relation to the most favoured features of growth and development. Figure 8.1 gives evidence of the evolution in the concept of the smart city.

Together with the very nature of smartness, this reminds us that we are dealing with a multidimensional notion. Again with reference to the smart city, Figure 8.2 outlines the current state of the art concerning our reception of its dimensions.

If this can be understood as one of the problems to be faced when studying this subject, it is at the same time a source of the proliferation of reports concerned with the description of its main characteristics and the introduction of indicators aiming at allowing for a ranking of the different cases under analysis. However, the actual impact of smartness on the functioning of cities and local production systems is less explored. Table 8.1 shows how the volatile results in the case of major Italian cities aspiring to the label of 'smart city'.

In our analysis, we try to focus our attention on this impact. But, in order to do so, and therefore answering the second research question of Section 3 in this chapter, we deem it essential to build up a theoretical scheme that is preliminary to every attempt to answer this question.

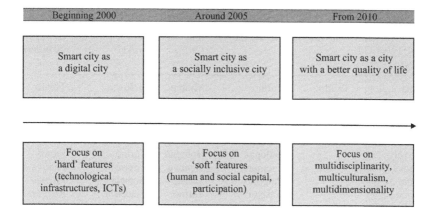

Figure 8.1 Evolution in the definition of the smart city

Source: Our elaboration based on ABB and Ambrosetti (2012, p. 70).

SMART ECONOMY	SMART MOBILITY	SMART ENVIRONMENT
innovation entrepreneurship branding productivity integration manufacturing capacity	accessibility infrastructures, ICTs sustainable, innovative, safe transport systems	pollution control environmental protection sustainable management of resources

SMART LIVING	SMART GOVERNANCE	SMART PEOPLE
culture health security housing education social cohesion	participation to decision making public services transparency policy strategies and perspectives	human capital lifelong learning pluralism flexibility creativity participation

Figure 8.2 The smart city as a multidimensional notion

Source: Giffinger, Fertner, Kramar, Kalasek, Pichler-Milanović and Meijers (2007).

We did find a simplifying principle in the implementation a logic frame focusing on development[13] because it allows for an enhanced, and more disciplined, integration of economic growth with sustainability and inclusiveness. Therefore, as maintained before, a second reason in favour of the search for linkages and coordination between the two strategies can be found in the aim to draw a broad, but better organized, picture of the distinctive features of smartness when it joins economic development.

In order to carry on the comparison between S3 and SCS in a way conducive to a better understanding of their relationships with economic development, we

Table 8.1 Smart cities rankings in the Italian case

Creativity Group Europe (2005) [first 20 cities]	Giffinger et al. (2007)	Caragliu and Del Bo (2011)	ABB and Ambrosetti (2012)	Between s.p.a. (2013) [first 20 cities]	Forum PA (2013) [first 20 cities]
Roma	Trento	Torino	Milano	Bologna	Trento
Milano	Trieste	Trento	Roma	Milano	Bologna
Bologna	Ancona	Milano	Venezia	Roma	Milano
Trieste	Perugia	Reggio Calabria	Bolzano	Reggio Emilia	Ravenna
Firenze		Bologna	Bologna	Torino	Parma
Genova		Cremona	Genova	Firenze	Padova
Torino		Palermo	Trieste	Brescia	Firenze
Parma		Caserta	Torino	Piacenza	Reggio Emilia
Rimini		Cagliari	Palermo	Parma	Torino
Perugia		Ancona	Napoli	Monza	Venezia
Modena		Sassari	Verona	Cremona	Bolzano
Padova		Potenza	Firenze	Vicenza	Genova
Pisa		Catanzaro	Bari	Forlì	Siena
Reggio Emilia		Venezia		Pisa	Modena
Ravenna		Taranto		Modena	Aosta
Terni				Genova	Ferrara
Verona				Bari	Udine
Siena				Verona	Bergamo
Piacenza				Bergamo	Rimini
Pesaro-Urbino				Padova	Pisa

have to look for their main connecting vectors. To this aim, it is useful to single out three different stages that can help us in structuring, even if in a very synthetic way, our analysis.[14]

In a first stage (Figure 8.3), we deem it appropriate to take into account the stylized facts helping us to contextualize the phenomenon under investigation. In a very synthetic way, we propose to isolate four main waves of change pushing for smart specialization and smart city to become core ingredients in the economic development of the different models of capitalism. Figure 8.3 shows how this trend has been fostered by the transition from high volume to high value in the micro-economic setting and industrial development, the diffusion of unbundling and off-shoring in international commerce, the increasing role of intangible assets and broad production factors in the macro-economic setting and the changing shape of meso-economic structures in their interaction with global development.

In the second stage (Figure 8.4.), the main determinants are outlined by the dramatic structural transformations leading to accrue in our century the strategic role of cities in sustaining industrial and economic development.

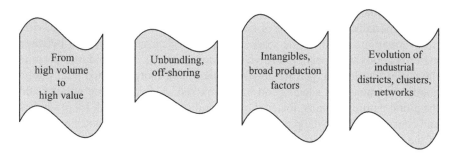

Figure 8.3 Waves of structural change leading to smart development in models of capitalism

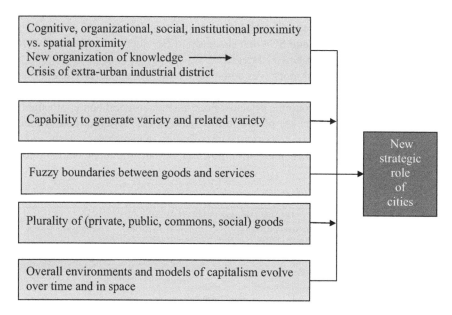

Figure 8.4 Structural transformations leading to a new strategic role for cities in economic development

Five factors – some of them well recognized and some others less known in the literature – are to be taken into account. Especially in territorially diffused industrial systems, the structures accommodating cognitive, organizational, social and institutional proximity are performing better than structures accommodating only spatial proximity. This implies a radical change in the organization of knowledge internal and external to the firms at a global level. In this respect, the crisis of industrial districts has to be better understood[15] in the implementation of new development strategies.[16] Furthermore, the capability to

generate variety and related variety in local production systems becomes a crucial determinant of their international competitiveness.[17] Side by side with these
changes pertaining mainly, if not exclusively, to the production systems, vital
transformations occur in the marketplace. The clear-cut distinction between
material goods and immaterial services disappear and fuzzy boundaries become
the norm. In addition, private goods are more and more matched with public
goods, commons and social good in the markets. The increasing number and
the plural nature of goods, fostered by unbundling, available both for producers
and consumers, entail the planning of new rules on the demand and supply side
of the markets and, what is more important, on the overall environment to be
ruled.[18] At a more general level, ecosystems and models of capitalism evolve
over time and in space. Some of them can disappear; others can evolve maintaining their peculiar characteristics; and still others also can converge towards
different models.[19] Figure 8.4 presents a synthetic account of these processes.

Finally, in the third stage (Figure 8.5), we undertake the task of interpreting
the linkages between S3 and SCS that shape smart development and can support
coordination between these two strategies.

First of all, we can ask ourselves some very basic questions referring to the
static and dynamic characteristics of S3 and SCS that emerge when they are
positioned in concrete economic systems. Four essential aspects come into sight:
(1) the side in which they are placed in the markets, (2) the opportunities they
can generate for the internal and external organization of knowledge, (3) the critical factors in assessing their innovation potential and (4) the tools available for

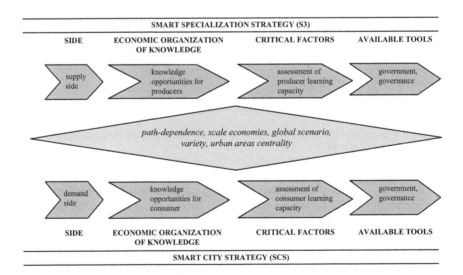

Figure 8.5 Static and dynamic linkages between smart specialization strategy (S3) and
smart city strategy (SCS) in shaping smart development

government and governance. Second, we can consider the parallel vectors taking shape when the implementation of these four aspects takes place along each of the two strategies.

Coming to the results obtained using this method, we can initially note that, while S3 insists on the supply side of the markets, SCS is clearly focused on their demand side. This is a crucial economic principle to be used when we try to address structures and behaviours of the different agents operating in the markets having in mind a coherent plan of action.

Following a similar line of reasoning, while S3 helps to discover new opportunities for developing the internal and external organization of knowledge especially, even if not exclusively, on the side of producers, SCS stresses our attention on new opportunities for developing the internal and external organization of knowledge especially, even if not exclusively, on the side of consumers. This categorization can be very useful even when 'prosumers'[20] can have a room for action.

When coming to explore the section where more dynamic factors prevail, it is easy to note that, in the case of S3, the innovation potential rests mainly on the learning capacity of producers, while in the case of SCS the innovation potential rests largely on the learning capacity of consumers, which is often underestimated.

Lastly, both S3 and SCS have to rely on government and governance for shaping the appropriate regulation structures and overall environments in which they perform. In this respect, an easy prescription is that the division of labour between the different levels of governments has to be forward-looking and the application of the subsidiarity principles well designed. More vital and controversial is a second prescription following from this scheme. Investments fostering material and immaterial infrastructures have to be enhanced at all levels of government and given higher priority over current expenditures. Moreover, new decentralized industrial policies and new local development policies have to be tested, both at the local, national and supra-national level,[21] side by side with policies for the development of human capital and social capital development policies.

In between the two vectors, the main 'chromosomes' of the global environment in which agents act are portrayed. They can work both in the form constraints, as, for instance, path-dependence can do, as well in the form of drivers for change, as, for instance, variety can do. Figure 8.5 tries to present a very schematic account of the dynamics that lead to smart development.

6 Conclusion on the economic impact of development based on smart specialization and smart city

In this section, a distinction is made between conclusions and further thoughts that can help in future research. One of the most important conclusions reached in this chapter is that economic development, and not only growth, is the core issue and that urban areas and metropolitan cities are increasing their relevance in the new geography of development. Therefore, looking for synergies between S3 and

SCS and implementing them is crucial at both the local and global levels. This chapter tried to focus on the reasons for which it can be relevant to explore these strategies. Afterwards, it raised the key research questions we have to answer. Third, it discussed the linkages between S3 and SCS leading to smart development as a synergic outcome.

A second conclusion is that, while S3 insists on the supply side of the markets, SCS is clearly focused on their demand side. This is a crucial, even if static, economic principle to be used when we try to address structures and behaviours of the different agents operating in the markets having in mind a coherent plan of action.

Moreover, while S3 helps to discover new opportunities for developing the internal and external organization of knowledge especially, even if not exclusively, on the side of producers, SCS stresses our attention on the new opportunities for developing the internal and external organization of knowledge especially, even if not exclusively, on the side of consumers.

When coming to explore these dynamic factors, it is easy to note that in the case of S3 the innovation potential rests mainly on the learning capacity of producers, while in the case of SCS the innovation potential rests largely on the learning capacity of consumers, which is often underestimated.

Lastly, both S3 and SCS have to rely on government and governance for shaping the appropriate regulation structures and overall environments in which they perform.

In this respect, an easy prescription is that the division of labour between the different levels of governments has to be forward-looking and the application of the subsidiarity principles well designed.

More vital and controversial is a second prescription following from this scheme. Investments fostering material and immaterial infrastructures have to be enhanced at all levels of government and given higher priority over current expenditures.

In between the two vectors, the chief 'chromosomes' of the global environment are considered: path-dependence, scale economies, global scenarios, variety and the centrality of urban areas. They can operate both in the form constraints, as, for instance, path-dependence can do, as well in the form of drivers for change, as, for instance, variety can do.

The more critical broad production factor in this framework centred on sustainability is human capital, combined with environmental capital and financial capital.

The 'smart factory' can be interpreted as the form of firm capable of developing and employing its internal organization of knowledge in a way that is capable of interacting effectively with the external organization of knowledge and of performing on the supply side being able to forecast and evaluate the evolution of demand. This means that this class of firm is able to manage appropriately the broad production factors defined and to transform sustainability form a constraint to an opportunity.

Coming to the policy implications, we can reinforce the idea that the capability of a region of taking stock of its historical production path in trying to adapt to future trends heavily depends on two crucial steps.

The first one concerns the capacity of the different levels of government involved to run after and exploit the synergies between S3, on the one side, and SCS, on the other.

The second step refers to the ability of the different levels of government involved to take fully into consideration the real nature and characteristics of the goods and services playing a crucial role in the transformation paths pursued. This can become a substantial drive for change and enhance their competences in managing local development.

As said before, further thoughts that can help in future research. A first aspect that can be highlighted is that the economic sectors, the technological trajectories and, in general, the drivers of economic development, including scientific research, are more and more interconnected, even if not in a mechanical way, among them and with the model of capitalism in which they coexist. This is true, not only with reference to the country or local system in which the city is located, but also with reference to the Euroregion in which it will move forwards in the future. In other terms, the model of capitalism co-determines the path-dependence in the evolution of each form of economic system. Moreover, institutional complementarities with further procedures and/or institutions existing in the economic system do influence in a significant way each administrative strategy.

A second and complementary aspect to be taken into consideration is that, even if the distinction between material goods and immaterial services became obsolete and the boundaries between goods and services are fuzzy, the manufacturing sector in new forms is still vital, and in many cases, it is the real hub for development.[22]

In Italy, but this could be the case also of other European countries, soon after the end of the cold war and the enlargement of EU, the understanding of the adjustment to the fundamental new features of the economic transition and its actual occurrence has been very slow and lacking and, in particular, it gave rise to a risky form of myopia, or better, a deviation of the range of vision. The attention paid to the apparently abundant new margins of discretion that this transition was generating, have been often misinterpreted as signals in favour of devolution and fragmentation of the production systems and this generated a diversion with respect to the main attractors applicable to global development.

In this frame, the study of the evolution of the model of capitalism in the US made by Reich (1991) is useful also to look for an answer to two interrelated topical questions relevant today. The first one can be expressed in the following way: when and where can we locate the true origin of smart development? This question has been already answered looking at the European experience in the background of industrial development at the global level.

The second question can be address to as follows: in the end, what is the real difference between innovation and smart development? In order to answer this question, it is useful to stress that the various suggestions offered when trying to define the notion of smart city, or even that of models of capitalism, lead to the conclusion that, on the one side, innovation plays a role of necessary, but not sufficient, condition for the activation of processes giving rise to smartness. Perhaps, looking at the study of small specialization rather than at that of smart city, one can notice how the relevant economic environment and policy practices acquire a heuristic value when looking for the reasons of continuity and discontinuity denoting the innovative path of the different strategies.

On the other side, we could say that smart development and technological innovation do not always exactly overlap. That is, in various cases, technological innovation does not play the role of being the necessary condition for smart development. For instance, we can envisage wide room for the smart employment of databases concerning capital assets through organizational innovation in the banking and insurance sectors.[23] In any case, organizational innovation implies the investment of additional resources in tangible and intangible assets.

Finally, it could be emphasized that, when innovation analysts are engaged in smart development projects, they are led to face a very tough task indeed: they are supposed to learn how to be able forecast and solve (while at the same time satisfying customers) small technical troubles in the implementation of new tools and procedures that are now relegated to the grey area, which confuses the adoption of new devices with the implementation of new rules.

Notes

1 Whose theoretical bases are considered in Chapter 6 and policy implications are presented in Chapter 14.
2 For a more comprehensive review, see Chapter 4 and European Commission (2006, 2010a, 2011a, 2011b, 2012a, 2014), European Environmental Agency (2006), European Parliament and European Council (2003), European Parliament (2014) and Eurostat (2010, 2011, 2013).
3 For a more comprehensive review, see Chapter 1 and European Commission (2009, 2010b, 2011c, 2012b).
4 Cowan and van de Paal (2000, p. 9) state, "We adopt a systemic approach to innovation and innovation policy, as developed in the 1993 Maastricht Memorandum and taken up in the Action Plan for Innovation in Europe." The First Action Plan for Innovation in Europe was issued in 1997. The new rules and legislation governing the EU Cohesion Policy investment for 2014–2020 have been formally endorsed by the Council of the EU in December 2013.
5 In terms of higher unemployment, higher Not in Education, Employment, or Training (NEET) and insecure jobs.
6 This recommendation sounds even more appropriate today when we should remember that 'restless capitalism', even in its phase of knowledge-based economy – or smart economy – continues to behave as a 'distributed system of ignorance' (Metcalfe et al., 2012, p. 3).
7 Allowing, by the way, the US to recover their leadership in industrial development, even if it involved new trade-offs with emerging powers.
8 In this frame, we should ask ourselves questions relating to the formation of the creations of the 'mind' in its different dimensions. What are the activities and agencies in

which the 'pieces of individual knowledge' have been formed after the earlier stages? Who has been in charge for creating and supplying the technical skills needed to implement this very complex social process? Which are the core actors in the future? Can universities have a greater role than in the past and at which conditions? Can tertiary education play a greater role? In continuity with or apart from higher secondary technical education? Is there a division of labour between the fulfilment of radical innovation and incremental innovation, and what are the organizations more effective in the two activities?

9 Only to mention one of the last ones, we can refer to Samans et al. (2015).
10 Managing venture capital.
11 For a more detailed account, see Wade (2015), Schrank and Whitford (2009) and Reich (1991).
12 A partial attempt to answer this often unspoken question is made in Section 2 in this chapter.
13 We refer to the meaning give to the concept of economic development, as distinct from economic growth, by Irma Adelman (2000, p. 1). She includes (1) self-sustaining growth (2) structural change in patterns of production; (3) technological upgrading; (4) social, political and institutional modernization; and (5) widespread improvement in the human condition. The recent evolution in the literature suggests also adding (6) economic, environmental and social sustainability.
14 We regret that, for length constraints, we cannot deal extensively on these steps in this chapter. However, many helpful ideas can be found in the other chapters of this volume, as well as in Antonelli (2011) and in Antonelli et al. (2014).
15 Chapter 7 can be helpful in better understanding the crucial evolution experienced by industrial districts.
16 For European countries like Italy, smartness can represent a way out to the long-term stagnation and decline traps in which they are at present caught.
17 These issues are dealt with in Chapter 7.
18 These issues are dealt with in Chapter 6.
19 For a further analysis, see Antonelli (2014).
20 As it is well known, this word results from the contraction of either the word professional or producer with the word consumer.
21 As in the case of EU for European countries.
22 This is why the notion of an undifferentiated 'innovative sector', as in the case of Moretti (2012), cannot be accepted.
23 This could be true, for instance, also in the case of big data development.

Bibliography

ABB and Ambrosetti. (2012), *Smart cities in Italy: An opportunity in the spirit of the Renaissance for a new quality of life*, Milano, ABB and The European House Ambrosetti.

Adelman, I. (2000), Fifty years of economic development: What have we learned?, Paper prepared for the World Bank European Annual Bank Conference on Development Economics, World Bank, Washington, DC.

Antonelli, G. (1997), Broad production factors and technological systems, in G. Antonelli and N. De Liso (eds.), *Economic analysis of structural change and technical progress*, London, Routledge, pp. 86–106.

Antonelli, G. (2011), Global economic crisis and systemic failure, *Economia Politica. Journal of Analytical and Institutional Economics*, XXVIII (3), 403–434.

Antonelli, G. (2014), Knowledge based competition, convergence in labour markets and models of capitalism in Europe, *Transcience. A Journal of Global Studies*, 5 (1), 79–90.

Antonelli, G., Calia, P.P. and Guidetti, G. (2014), Approaching an investigation of multi-dimensional inequality through the lenses of variety in models of capitalism, *Quaderni-Working Paper*, Department of Economic Sciences, University of Bologna, 984, 1–46.

Antonelli, G. and Pogoretti, G. (2008), Knowledge endowment and composition as dynamic capabilities, in Leoncini R. and Montresor S. (eds.), *Dynamic capabilities between firm organization and local systems of production*, London, Routledge, pp. 289–323.

Between, S.P.A. (2013), *Smart city index. Confrontarsi per diventare smart*, Milano, Between, SPA.

Caragliu, A. and Del Bo, C. (2011), Smart cities in Europe, *Journal of Urban Technology*, 18 (2), 65–80.

Cowan, R. and van de Paal, G. (2000), Innovation policy in a knowledge-based economy, Merit study commissioned by the European Commission, Publication N. EUR 17023 of the Commission of the European Communities, Luxembourg.

Creativity Group Europe. (2005), *L'Italia nell'era creativa*, Milano, Creativity Group Europe.

European Commission. (2006), Communication from the Commission to the Council and the European Parliament on Thematic strategy on the urban environment, COM/2005/0718.

European Commission. (2009), *A technology roadmap*, SEC 1295, Bruxelles, European Commission.

European Commission. (2010a), *World and European sustainable cities*. Insights from EU research, Luxembourg, European Union.

European Commission. (2010b), *A strategy for smart, sustainable and inclusive growth*, COM 2020, Bruxelles, European Commission.

European Commission. (2011a), *Strategic energy technology plan (SET-Plan) – Smart cities and communities initiative*, Bruxelles, European Commission.

European Commission. (2011b), *Cities of tomorrow – Challenges, visions, way forward*, Luxembourg, European Union.

European Commission. (2011c), Proposal for a Regulation of the European Parliament and of the Council laying down common provisions on the European Regional Development Fund, the European Social Fund, the Cohesion Fund, the European Agricultural Fund for Rural Development and the European Maritime and Fisheries Fund covered by the Common Strategic Framework and laying down general provisions on the European Regional Development Fund, the European Social Fund and the Cohesion Fund and repealing Council Regulation (EC) No 1083/2006, Comunicazione della Commissione COM(2011) 615, Bruxelles, 6.10.2011.

European Commission. (2012a), *Smart cities and communities – European innovation partnership*, COM 4701, Bruxelles, European Commission.

European Commission. (2012b), *Connecting smart and sustainable growth through smart specialisation. A practical guide for ERDF managing authorities*, Bruxelles, European Commission.

European Commission. (2014), *Investment for jobs and growth. Promoting development and good governance in EU regions and cities – Sixth report on economic, social and territorial cohesion*, Bruxelles, European Commission.

European Environmental Agency. (2006), *Urban sprawl in Europe: The ignored challenge*, Luxembourg, European Union.

European Parliament. (2014), *Mapping smart cities in Europe*, available at www.europarl.europa.eu/studies, accessed 10 March 2014.

European Parliament and European Council. (2003), Sixth community environment action programme, Decision No 1600/2002/EC of 22 July 2002.

Eurostat. (2010), *European regional and urban statistics reference guide*, Luxembourg, Publications Office of the European Union.

Eurostat. (2011), *Eurostat regional yearbook 2011*, Luxembourg, Publications Office of the European Union.

Eurostat. (2013), *Eurostat regional yearbook 2013*, Luxembourg, Publications Office of the European Union.

Forum, P.A. (2013), *ICity Rate. La classifica delle città intelligenti italiane*, Roma, Forum, PA.

Giffinger, R., Fertner, C., Kramar, H., Kalasek, R., Pichler-Milanović, N. and Meijers, E. (2007), *Smart cities: Ranking of European medium-sized cities*, Centre of Regional Science (SRF), Vienna University of Technology.

Harrison, B. (1994), *Lean and mean. The changing landscape of corporate power in the age of flexibility*, New York, Basic Books.

Metcalfe, J.S., Gagliardi, D., De Liso, N. and Ramlogan, R. (2012), *Innovation systems and innovation ecologies: Innovation policy and restless capitalism*, OPENLOC Project, Working Paper No. 3.

Mokyr, J. (2005), The intellectual origins of modern economic growth, *The Journal of Economic History*, 65 (2), June 2005, 285–351.

Moretti, E. (2012), *The new geography of jobs*, New York, Houghton Mifflin Harcourt.

Reich, R.B. (1991), *The work of nations*, New York, Vintage Books.

Rodrigues, M.J. (2005), For the national strategies of transition to a knowledge economy in the European Union, Background Paper BP5, European Commission's Advisory Group, SSHERA Project.

Samans, R., Blanke, J., Corrigan, G. and Drzeniek, M. (2015), *The Inclusive growth and development report 2015*, Geneva, World Economic Forum.

Schrank, A. and Whitford, J. (2009), Industrial policy in the United States, *Politics & Society*, 37 (4), 521–553.

Wade, R.H. (2015), The role of industrial policy in developing countries, in A. Calcagno, S. Dullien, A. Márquez-Velázquez, N. Maystre and J. Priewe (eds.), *Rethinking development strategies after the financial crisis*, Volume I: *Making the case for policy space*, New York and Geneva, United Nations, pp. 67–79.

Part II

Measuring and applying smart local development

9 Smartness indicators in the European urban framework

Dorel Nicolae Manitiu and Giulio Pedrini

1 Introduction

The concept of urban smartness has become a leitmotiv in the debate on urban development models in the academic, governmental and industrial domains. Although in each of these domains the term "smart city" emphasizes different aspects of urban systems and it is not possible to reach a single definition of the term "smart city", the objectives of technological innovation, sustainability and inclusiveness are widely acknowledged as the main achievements for urban areas that aspire being considered as smart. In particular, the theoretical and institutional debate currently calls for diversifying the debate and going beyond the mere criticism on the dominance of IT vendors in urban smart city strategy, while emphasizing the intrinsic multi-dimensionality of smartness and its tight relationship with the sustainability principle. The sustainability principle interacts with all different dimensions attached to the smart city concept either implicitly or explicitly and can thus be considered as a cross-conceptual criterion that allows a comprehensive assessment of smart city strategies in accordance with the framework of the Europe 2020 agenda.

This wide range of objectives, themes and sectors included in the definitions of smart city leads to a fragmentation of the concept when applying it in the activity of planning, monitoring and evaluating urban development policies. Accordingly, there is a growing need for specific assessments that provide an adequate picture of each city through appropriate sets of indicators in order to distinguish between different types of urban areas. Within this framework, a preliminary step in order to put European cities at the centre of the policy effort to promote a smart, sustainable and inclusive growth is the elaboration of appropriate indicators that take into account the different characteristics of the smart city concept as it has been applied in the European Union.[1] In this way, researchers and local administrators could identify the appropriate measures for each specific situation and, at the same time, take full advantage from the exchange of information throughout the European Union. This would help local authorities to conceive their city as a unique, sustainable urban system already from the outset of the smart city initiatives and to acknowledge the close inter-relation among competitiveness, division of labour, inequality, environment and attractiveness.

According to these premises, this chapter aims at defining a set of indicators applicable to European cities in order to jointly assess their degree of smartness and sustainability. For each of the dimensions taken into account (social, environmental and cultural) and following the DPSIR model (Driving Force, Pressure, State, Impact, Response), we build up a system of indicators that allow a thorough comparison among urban systems, bringing to the debate quantifiable tools through the selection of proper indicators could contribute to design sound "smart city" policies in each urban region. In the light of the smart city concept, the construction of multidimensional indicators is the preliminary step for any activity to compare the ongoing initiatives, while taking into account the latent differentiation of the underlying objectives arising from cities' heterogeneity.

The paper is structured as follows. Section 2 briefly reviews the relationship between the smart city concept and the sustainability principle. Section 3 synthesizes the Europe 2020 strategy for urban areas. Section 4 explains the main characteristics of the DPSIR model. Section 5 selects the relevant indicators. Section 6 shows the results. Section 7 concludes.

2 The concept of smart city in a sustainability perspective

"Smart city" is a very popular label that has been developed in three different contexts: the international scientific community, governmental institutions and large multinational companies. The divergent approaches and purposes that characterize each domain have led to the elaboration of various meanings of the concept. However, it is possible to identify the very first definition of smart city, which had been provided by Hall in 2000. He emphasizes the image of a city

> that monitors and integrates conditions of all of its critical infrastructures, including roads, bridges, tunnels, rails, subways, airports, seaports, communications, water, power, even major buildings, can better optimize its resources, plan its preventive maintenance activities, and monitor security aspects while maximizing services to its citizens.
>
> (Hall, 2000, p. 634)

This definition, centred on physical infrastructures, is influenced by other related concepts centred on ICT technology: wired city, technocity, digital city, creative city and knowledge-based city. All of them emphasize the novelty the technological paradigm, considering the smart city as a place that guarantee better quality of life for residents through the incorporation of ICT technologies and digital information into new products and/or their use in specific areas of intervention (e.g. Marsa-Maestre et al., 2008). Further studies added the notion of sustainable urban development as one of the core conceptual components of smart city (Hollands, 2008; Toppeta, 2010; Nam and Pardo, 2010). In these definitions, sustainability is primarily understood in environmental terms, but it is also related to social aspects through the inclusion of the objectives of inclusiveness, the promotion of social capital and participatory governance. Additionally, the domain of culture is embedded in the idea of sustainability and has been tightly linked to the smart city concept "thanks to its ties with citizens' involvement, service co-creation, technologies, urban policies, tourism and public governance" (Tregua et al., 2015, p. 5). Indeed, the smart city has been considered as an ecosystem formed by a complex infrastructure that combines together different "soft" components among which we find the connections between cultural systems, social networks and communities and various forms of social inclusive principles (Zygiaris, 2013). The smart city thus requires the construction of networks that go beyond the technological element and extend to those intangible assets related to knowledge-intensive business services (KIBS), the organization of knowledge and cultural activities. This approach also underlies the existence of a positive relationship between human capital and cities' attractiveness and the endogenous characteristics of the transformation driven by innovation and creativity that the concept entails. All things considered, smart cities are required to combine together different visions of urban life in an integrated way.

However, several trade-off arises from the intrinsic nature of the challenge faced by European cities, i.e. "combining competitiveness and sustainable urban development simultaneously" (Giffinger et al., 2007, p. 5). Additionally, the wide spectrum of objectives, themes and sectors causes a fragmentation of the concept when projects are actually put into practice. In order to deal with the pursuit of such heterogeneous objectives the smart city has thus been conceived as a "framework for policies supporting technological and ecological urban transition . . . and fertilising national and local political agendas" (Vanolo, 2014, p. 894). Meanwhile, an original and complex set of indicators is needed for providing additional evidence able to capture the multidimensionality of urban environment.

In this perspective, sustainability would act as a transversal principle and not just as a cliché-like combination of economic-social-environmental spheres. Moreover, sustainability can be seen as a cross-conceptual criterion to analyze the outcome of smart-oriented urban policies. It joins together different aspects and issues of urban life, while it is related to other smart city dimensions via the objective of quality of life (Inoguchi et al., 1999; Satterthwaite, 1999; Polese and Stern, 2000) or liveability. In turn, the nexus between liveability and sustainability imposes a constraint on smart cities projects ensuring that the improvement in the quality of life is positively correlated with urban environmental quality. Indeed, one of the main challenges of smart cities is "to enable both urban liveability and environmental sustainability" (Newton, 2012, p. 88).

Following this line of reasoning, the analysis of the mechanisms of production of smart and sustainable urban conduct can be grouped in three broad and heterogeneous dimensions: environmental, social and cultural. The environmental dimension primarily deals with the effects (including externalities) of urban activities on natural resources, pollution and health conditions, all of which are complex and inter-related. Social sustainability promotes inclusiveness in urban initiatives. Different communities living in urban areas can take advantage of new opportunities offered by the integration of different social groups, thus promoting the interaction between creativity and technological innovation (Cohendet and Simon, 2008). Moreover, smartness is grounded on creativity (Florida, 2002); human and social capital (Caragliu and Del Bo, 2012); and amenities (Gottlieb and Glaeser, 2006; Shapiro, 2006). These partially overlapping "soft" factors positively contribute to make urban areas more competitive and attractive. All together, they can be clustered under the cultural domain (Hawkes, 2001[2]), which includes cultural diversity, arts, entertainment, tourism, innovative services, entrepreneurship, an open atmosphere and access to social capital and networks (Nijkamp and Kourtit, 2013). Overall, the cultural dimension supports the creation of new development opportunities for the whole urban community, taking into account the existence of a multiplicity of stakeholders. In this way, one can refer to three policy-useful "pillars" based on both hard and soft indicators, whose relative weight is comparable across the three dimensions. The underlying logic is similar to the one adopted by Giffinger et al. (2007) who identify six characteristics (Economy, People, Governance, Mobility, Environment, Leaving), thirty-one factors and seventy-four indicators for operationalizing the smart city concept under a multidimensional approach.

3 Smart cities and sustainability in the Europe 2020 strategy

Urban areas in Europe represent the main places for implementing smart development policies. They are unanimously deemed as the core engines of economic growth, as well as nodes of innovation networks and social progress. Larger cities also show a higher endowment of human capital, and they usually host high-value-added services that channel a great amount of knowledge and information. Overall, cities account for almost 80% of the EU's gross domestic product, while in 2011 the proportion of Europeans living in urban areas was almost 72% in EU-28 (European Commission, 2014) and is expected to reach 83% of the population by 2050 (European Commission, 2010b). Employment is concentrated in urban areas as well: in 2011, 62% of EU employment could be referred to metropolitan regions. Additionally, employment per head in urban areas grew by 0.7% between 2000 and 2008 compared to an average of 0.5%. However, during the economic crisis (2008–2011), urban areas did not prove to be more resilient than the rest of the continent. The reduction in employment per head was in line with the average, while productivity experienced a lower increase than in non-urban regions. Still, GDP per head is 22% higher in metropolitan regions than the EU average (European Commission, 2014).

On the other hand, cities are seen as unrivalled providers of "the basic ingredients for quality of life in all its senses: environmental, cultural and social" and are thus called to reconcile "economic activities and growth with cultural, social and environmental consideration" (European Commission, 2010b, p. 42–43) in line with a holistic model of sustainable city development. Since 2006, the European Commission has been acknowledging the role of urban areas in delivering the objectives of the EU Sustainable Development Strategy: "the environmental challenges facing cities have significant consequences for human health, quality of life of urban citizens and the economic performance of the cities themselves" (European Commission, 2006). This recognition follows the 6th Environment Action Programme (6th EAP), which called for the development of a Thematic Strategy on the Urban Environment for contributing

> to a better quality of life through an integrated approach concentrating on urban areas [and] to a high level of quality of life and social well-being for citizens by providing an environment where the level of pollution does not give rise to harmful effects on human health and the environment and by encouraging sustainable urban development.
>
> (European Parliament and European Council, 2003)

However, cities have to cope with negative effects of urbanization and international division of labour. Many environmental and social problems are concentrated in the cities. European urban areas consume 70% of energy, which accounts for 75% of the EU's total greenhouse gas emissions (GHG), while congestion costs in Europe accounts for about 1% of GDP every year, most of which arise from urban areas (European Commission, 2012). This concern is at the base of the tendency of the European Union to interpret the themes of smartness mainly in terms of pollution reduction and energy. In 2012, the European Commission launched the Smart Cities & Communities (SCC) Initiative in order "to make Europe's cities more efficient and more sustainable in the area of energy, transport and information and communication technologies" (European Commission, 2012). In turn, the Communication of 10th July 2012 embodies the SCC initiative into the Europe 2020 (European Commission, 2010a) strategy whose first objective is to promote a "smart, inclusive and sustainable growth in Europe and to provide a framework for the EU to emerge strengthened from the current financial and economic crisis" (European Commission, 2012, p. 2). Specifically, it calls for European cities as "places of advanced social progress and environmental regeneration, as well as places of attraction and engines of economic growth based on a holistic integrated approach in which all aspects of sustainability are taken into account" (European Commission, 2012, p. 3). To achieve this purpose, European policy-makers suggest differentiating projects and interventions according to the heterogeneous strengths and weaknesses of each single urban area. Before approving every kind of technology-based project, cities should find a balance among conflicting and sometimes contradictory objectives, while moving towards holistic models of sustainable development. This objective entails a major challenge for the EU: designing and adapting cities into smart, efficient and sustainable places able to offer both a high quality of life to present-day citizens and benefits for future generations. The importance of technology is not in the technology itself but relies on the opportunities that technology makes available to improve the ways cities meet the changing needs and preferences of their residents. ICT-based solutions are thus seen as a tool to address public issues on the basis of a multi-stakeholder, municipality-based partnership (European Parliament, 2014).

The European policy is thus committed to creating a high-quality urban environment and to making Europe an attractive place to invest and work by "avoiding urban sprawl through high density and mixed-use settlement patterns offers environmental advantages regarding land use, transport and heating contributing to less resource use per capita" (European Environmental Agency, 2006). As a consequence, sustainability goals must be taken into account in the evaluation of smart city projects that are flourishing throughout the continent. In particular, the complex mix of challenges faced by European cities requires building up an approach able to guarantee sustainable urban development through investments in infrastructure (transport, housing, centres of learning, cultural facilities), and through policy measures supporting socio-economic development and inclusion. Under a place-based approach, which takes into account both the potential of a city along with its needs, smart city policies should be tailored to these contexts. This need for differentiation is increasingly recognized in policy spheres and underlies the place-based debate around the new EU cohesion policy.

4 The DPSIR model

The existence of a heterogeneous bundle of aspects covered by the same attribute raises the need for suitable inter-related indicators to measure cities' smartness, leading to the development of a great variety of multidimensional rankings. Our proposal is to align smartness characteristics with Europe 2020 targets, most notably sustainability, by building a set of indicators based on the DPSIR model (Driving Force, Pressures, State, Impact, Response), which has been developed by the European Agency for the Environment grounding on the previous Pressures, State, Answers (PSA) model, developed by the OECD (1998, 1999, 2004).

The model relates to the state of the environment in the functioning of the driving forces that determine pressure on the environment. At the same time, the DPSIR model entails a policy intervention as it provides indicators on the actions (responses) undertaken by the policy maker, thus allowing to check whether the policy intervention has produced the desired effects.

The five families of indicators are divided as follows:

1   D (*Driving Force*): underlying factors influencing a variety of different variables;
2   P (*Pressure*): indicators referring to the variables that cause environmental problems;
3   S (*State*): indicators showing the present condition of the environment;
4   I (*Impact*): indicators describing the ultimate effects of changes of state;
5   R (*Response*): indicators demonstrating the efforts of society (i.e. decision-makers) to solve the problems.

The main properties and functions of each family of indicators in the DPSIR framework are the following ones:

1 *Driving Force* indicators usually are not *responsive ("elastic")*. The monitored phenomena are driven by powerful economic and demographic forces, and therefore it can hardly be expected that these trends will change in future. However, these indicators are useful to calculate a variety of pressure indicators, to help decision-makers, and to plan the actions ("responses") needed to avoid future problems and shape the scenario for long-term planning.
2 *Pressure* indicators point directly at the causes of problems. One specific feature of pressure indicators is that they should be *responsive*, that is a decision-maker has indeed a chance to affect the indicator (and thus the problem) by launching appropriate actions. They also serve as an incentive for rational answers, since they may validate the effectiveness of the political action early enough to hold the decision-maker responsible.
3 *State* indicators mainly serve to make an *ex ante* assessment of the situation. In contrast, as their changes are slow, they are suitable for evaluating the policy intervention only in the long run.
4 *Impact* indicators react even more slowly than state indicators. Their main purpose is to make evident the DPSIR patterns, in particular *cause–effect chains*, and to facilitate informed discussions about actions to avoid negative impacts in future.
5 *Response* indicators are very fast, since they monitor the *measures* that are intended to make the slow socio-economic system move. There is no *a priori* guarantee, however, that political responses will be effective; the monitoring of their *success* can be performed only through pressure and state indicators.

The DPSIR model fits well to our perspective because it allows the selection of an inter-related multidimensional set of indicators that are combined together into the three chosen dimensions that in their turn represent a possible application of the "smart and sustainable" binomial. Through the DPSIR model, we can achieve a flexible integration among the economic, social and cultural indicators, while taking account the evidence that previous research on European cities shows consistent evidence of a positive association among smartness indicators such as urban wealth, the presence of creative professionals, the quality of urban transportation network, ICT diffusion and human capital (Caragliu et al., 2011). Moreover, as each dimension is still too broad for being the object of a correlation-based analysis, through the DPSIR model, it is possible to divide the three dimensions into subcategories in accordance with the relevant objectives and domains of interest.

5 Dataset and indicators

Our empirical study is grounded on the European Urban Audit dataset, which is "a set of reliable and comparative information on the quality of life in selected urban areas in Europe" (Eurostat, 2010, p. 203). It includes 323 cities in 27 member states, plus 47 cities from Switzerland, Norway, Croatia and Turkey, relying on more than 300 indicators dealing with different aspects of urban life, e.g. demography, housing, health, crime, labour market, income disparity, local administration, educational qualifications, environment, climate, travel patterns, information society and cultural infrastructure. Although the actual coverage of the survey is still partial and asymmetric, the European Urban Audit represents one of the most important sources for applied studies on the smartness of European urban regions (Caragliu et al., 2011; Caragliu and Del Bo, 2012; Kourtit et al., 2012).[3]

For the environmental dimension, we take into account those indicators that refer to mobility and natural resources: public transport network, air pollution and natural resources consumption. Driving Force indicators deal with demographics and mobility. Pressure indicators are related to the consumption of natural resources, notably water and waste. State indicators are measured by air pollution and landfill waste. Impact indicators concern the negative effects of mobility inefficiencies and pollution. These effects are proxied by health damages caused by respiratory diseases and car accidents. Finally, Response indicators deal with a wide variety of "green" public services": local transport, parking availability, green areas and waste recycling.

The social dimension is one of the most critical issues attached to the smart city concept. Smart cities have to address the risk of exacerbating inequality further to ICT-based projects (Graham, 2002). Although smart cities are expected to favour everyone's access to information technology, this does not avoid the risk of creating "two-speed" cities, namely cities facing economic decline with growing difficulties in facilitating socio-economic insertion due to the lack of jobs and the reduction of public budget. Smart cities are requested to mitigate this risk by strengthening urban social infrastructure, which is viewed as an indispensable endowment of sustainable urban systems. In this perspective, following Hollands (2008), we consider indicators related to wealth, education, employment, activity rate, security, business crisis and migration. All these indicators regard social sustainability as they affect the sense of well-being and provide confidence in the future. Driving Force indicators deal with demographic and social variables and affect both wealth and employment. Pressure indicators deal with the change in Driving Forces indicators, together with indicators related to people's capability to satisfy their basic needs (Atkinson, 2002), such as housing. Some of them are also related to the cultural dimension to the extent to which they measure cultural diversity. In particular, the presence of immigrants is a source of both ethnicity- and language-based diversity, which in turn is positively associated with amenities and higher productivity (Alesina and Ferrara, 2004) but negatively associated with public goods provision (Glaeser and Alesina, 2005). State indicators deal with direct measures of employment, poverty and housing needs. Impact indicators deal with urban crime indicators, the only available figure that represents a widely recognized effect of poverty and social exclusion. Finally, response indicators concern policy answer in terms of childcare, health services and education.

The cultural dimension deals with the vitality, participation and attractiveness of an area. When applying this definition to urban areas, we immediately think to human capital externalities (Glaeser and Maré, 2001; Moretti, 2004; Glaeser et al., 2010) and to the concept of the creative city (Florida, 2005) joined with technological innovation. Human capital externalities are generated by the concentration of skills in the city, which is again proxied by the concentration of graduates. This concentration attracts other skilled workers thanks to higher productivity (and wage premiums) attached to knowledge-intensive industries located in urban areas and other local knowledge spillovers, thus becoming an attractive and retaining factor for educated and skilled households. Notably, the city serves as an ideal pool of human capital accumulation and as a hotspot of complementarities between human capital and knowledge-sensitive capital. Creativity is attached to new ways of thinking and acting and ensures that the urban area is attractive for a highly skilled workforce. It is rooted on technology, tolerance and talent ("the three Ts"). Technology in a smart city perspective is directly related to ICT investment and, more generally, to access to knowledge and information. Tolerance deals with the openness to socio-cultural diversity that characterizes modern urban areas, rooting on the valorization of differences within an inclusive society. In the perspective of smart city initiatives, it also stimulates the degree of participation by government, private sector entities and civil society. Talent is measured by the presence of creative people, but according to Glaeser (2002), it can also be captured by the level of human capital and, in particular, by the availability of a highly educated workforce. Moreover, we introduce tourism and urban amenities as measures of urban attractiveness driven by arts, natural and cultural heritage and recreational activities. This is also consistent with the "consumer city" approach (Glaeser et al., 2001), or the amenity view (Poelhekke, 2006), which emphasizes the great varieties of services and consumer goods provided in the cities, such as the density of restaurants and libraries and the supply of public services per capita, as attractive and retaining factors for educated and skilled households. Merging these theoretical and applied insights in the cultural dimension, we derive an articulated set of indicators. Driving Force indicators deal with the age structure of the population and its level of educational attainment, which is unequally distributed across cities of the same country. Pressure indicators measure changes in young and educated populations, together with the number of tertiary education students, with a separate indicator for female students. State indicators are given by the share of business and financial sector on the urban economy, and by the development of tourism, entertainment and cultural industries. Impact indicators measure the proliferation of new businesses, the diffusion of local units providing business services, and the intensity of tourism supply. Response indicators concern the diffusion of libraries, the use of digital services by local governments (as a proxy of e-government), and the proportion of women elected in local councils (as a proxy of gender policies).

After having omitted redundant indicators and those indicators whose values are missing for too many cities, we end up with twenty-three environmental indicators, twenty-two social indicators, and twenty-one cultural indicators. For those indicators that are not available for the 2007–2009 period, we refer to data coming from the previous waves of the survey. Although missing data are a serious drawback of this exercise (for instance, data on French cities are missing in most of the cases), the number of observations is still considerable, ranging from 78 to 202 cities and covering a population from thirty to eighty million of residents.

6 Results

Once we selected the indicators, we performed a principal component analysis (PCA) for each step of DPSIR model followed by an orthogonal rotation and selected those components explaining at least 75% of variance (except for two cases in which the last additional component is clearly redundant).[4] In this way, we sorted the most crucial characteristics of the European cities with regard to their capabilities of activating and effectively implementing smart and sustainable initiatives. Additionally, through PCA, we reduced the number of indicators and standardized their values in order to make their aggregation possible to build up synthetic rankings based on the DPSIR model.

6.1 Environmental dimension

The PCA on the environmental domain generates twelve factors (Table 9.1). Each step of the model is described by two factors. Mobility and Environment are the main aspects that are measured by these components. Some of them concern the accessibility of the urban area as well as the availability of multimodal transport systems (CITY_ACC, TRANS_NETW, ROAD_ACC). Others are related to pollution (PRIV_TRANS, POLL_AIR), and their effects (MOR<65), and to resource management (RES_CONS, WAT_PRICE, WAS_LAND). The rest of the factors join together both characteristic (PRIV_TRANS, GREEN_SER).

6.2 Social dimension

The PCA on the social dimension generates twelve factors (Table 9.2). Their distribution throughout the different steps of the model is concentrated in the Driving Force and Pressure indicators. Each of them is explained by three factors. The main related features are demographic patterns and dynamics, structural economic weaknesses, social conditions and quality of life. Demographic aspects are measured by DEM, IMM, POP_TREND and MIGR_NONEU. Economic issues refer to business crisis (CRISIS) and unemployment and low educational attainment (UNEMPL). Social conditions include basing housing needs (HOUS_NEED) and urban crime figures (CRIM and THEFTS). Quality of life is related to household size (HOU_HOL) and public services supply (PUBL_GOODS, CHILD).

Table 9.1 Environmental indicators and factors in a DPSIR model

Components	N	Description	Indicators	DPSIR
1D. CITY_ACC	178	City accessibility	1. Rail accessibility (2003–2006) 2. Multimodal accessibility (2003–2006)	Driving Force Driving Force
2D. PRIV_TRANS	178	Diffusion of private transport means	1. N. of cars per 1,000 pop 2. N. of motorcycles per 1,000 pop	
1P. RES_CONS	142	Resources consumption	1. Water consumption (m^3 per annum) per inhabitant 2. Collected solid waste per inhabitant and year	Pressure
2P. WAT_PRICE	142	Water price	1. Price of a m^3 of domestic water	Pressure
1S. POLL_AIR	108	Air pollution	1. N. of days Pm10 exceeds 50 $\mu g/m^3$ per year 2. Annual average concentration of NO_2 3. N. of days ozone exceeds 120 $\mu g/m^3$ per year	State
2S. WAS_LAND	108	Landfill waste	1. Proportion of solid waste processed by landfill	State
1I. MOR<65	176	Mortality rate for < 65 related to heart diseases and respiratory illnesses	1. Mortality rate for < 65 2. Mortality rate for < 65 due to heart diseases and respiratory illnesses	Impact
2IROAD_ACC	176	Deaths and injuries in road accidents	1. Number of deaths in road accidents per 10,000 population 2. Number of persons seriously injured in road accidents per 10,000 population	Impact
1R.TRANS_NETW	85	Transport network	1. Length of public transport network divided per land area 2. N. of stops of public transport per km^2	Response
2R. GREEN_SER	85	Green services	1. Length of public transport network per inhabitant 2. Green space (in m^2) per capita 3. Proportion of solid waste processed by recycling	Response

Table 9.2 Social indicators and factors in a DPSIR model

Components	N	Description	Indicators	DPSIR
1D. DEM	120	Demography	1. Share of pop aged 75+ 2. Demographic dependency 3. Share of pop aged 0–4	Driving Force
2D. IMM	120	Immigrants and females	1. Female to male proportion 2. Non-EU nationals as a proportion of pop	Driving Force
3D. HOU_HOL	120	Household size	1. N. of persons per household	Driving Force
1P. POP_TREND	92	Population trend	1. Pop change over 1 year 2. Pop change over 5 years	Pressure
2P. MIGR_NONEU	92	Migration from non-EU countries	1. Prop of nationals that have moved to the city during the last 2 years 2. Prop of non-EU Nationals that have moved to the city during the last 2 years 3. Prop of non-EU Nationals and citizens of a country with a medium or low human development index (HDI)	Pressure
3P. CRISIS	92	Business crisis	1. Prop of companies gone bankrupt	Pressure
1S. UNEMPL	118	Unemployment and low human capital endowment	1. Unempl. rate (1999–2002) 2. Prop of working age population qualified at level 1 or 2 ISCED (1999–2002)	State
2S. HOUS_NEED	118	Basic housing needs	1. Prop of dwellings lacking basic amenities (1999–2002) 2. Prop of overcrowded households (1999–2002)	State
1I. CRIM	202	Urban crime	1. N. of recorded crimes per 1,000 pop 2. N. of domestic burglary per 1,000 pop	Impact
2I. THEFTS	202	Thefts	1. N. of car thefts per 1,000 pop	Impact
1R. PUBL_GOODS	148	Health services, education	1. Empl. in public administration, health, education 2. Children 3–4 in day care per 1,000	Response
2R. CHILD	148	Children daily care	1. Children 0–2 in day care per 1,000	Response

6.3 Cultural dimension

The PCA on cultural indicators derives thirteen factors (Table 9.3). The wide variety of issues covered by the cultural domain keeps the number of explaining factors relatively high compared to the number of indicators. Indeed, the selected components are related to four out of six of the characteristics proposed by Giffinger et al. (2007): Economy, Living, Governance, People. Economic aspects are measured by entrepreneurship (ENTR) and the diffusion of innovative knowledge-based and support services (KIBS, PERS_SERV). Living is related to the degree of attractiveness of the area (ATTR), the amount of tourism supply (TOUR) and the openness to culture (TOLER). TOLER is also related to Governance through the degree of gender parity in political participation, together with the diffusion of e-government services for citizens (E-GOV).

Table 9.3 Cultural indicators and factors in a DPSIR model

Components	N	Description	Indicators	DPSIR
1D. ACT_POP	144	Active population	1. Share of pop aged 15–64 2. Share of pop aged 25–34	Driving Force
2D. HUM_CAP	144	Human capital	1. Share of pop aged 20–24 2. Share of pop aged 15–64 qualified at tertiary level (ISCED 5–6)	Driving Force
1P. HUMCAP_GROW	168	Human capital growth	1. Students in tertiary education per 1,000 pop 2. Students in higher education (ISCED 5–6) per 1,000 pop aged 20–34 3. Change in the proportion of pop aged 25–34	Pressure
2P. FEM_STUD	168	Proportion of female students	1. Share of female students in higher education (ISCED level 5–6)	Pressure
1S. PER_SERV	152	Personal services	1. Share of employment in trade and restaurant industry	State
2S. ATTR	152	Attractiveness	1. Overnight stays per year per pop 2. Share of employment in culture and entertainment industry	State

(Continued)

Table 9.3 (Continued)

Components	N	Description	Indicators	DPSIR
3S KIBS	152	Knowledge intensive business services	1. Share of employment in financial Intermediation and business activities	State
1I. ENTR	78	Entrepreneurship	1. New business registered 2. Local units providing ICT services per 1,000 companies	Impact
2I. TOURSUPP	78	Tourism supply	1. Available beds per 1,000 residents	Impact
1R. TOLER	163	Openness to culture and gender parity	1. Women elected city representatives per 1,000 residents 2. Libraries per 1,000 residents	Response
2R. E-GOV	163	Digital services offered by local authorities	1. Administrative forms that can be submitted electronically (2003–2006) 2. Daily internet visits on the official site	Response

7 Conclusions

One of the main peculiarities of the smart city concept is that successful, sustainable and inclusive urban development can be only achieved through a balanced mix of accomplishments in different fields in order to enhance citizens' welfare in a holistic and sustainable way. In this respect, a multidimensional assessment could lead to a thorough comparison of the needs and potential of European cities within the Europe 2020 strategy and relate them to the policy responses that have been adopted by the communities. Which aspects should eventually prevail? It depends on the cities' objectives and the residents' needs and wants.

By using the DPSIR model, which has been created for addressing sustainability issues, this study identifies a bundle of indicators that can be used those cities that have achieved satisfactory results along three dimensions of interests: environmental, social and cultural. In particular, our multi-dimensional indicators are able to keep together short-term and long-term issues along three different domains of the smart city concept. Within each domain, our proposal takes into account pillars that are crucial to achieve both smartness and sustainability targets: demography, pollution, mobility, health, education, crime, living conditions and digital services. This approach can be at the root of possible future developments of appropriate methods and indicators for measuring the success of smart cities initiatives at the European level.

This bundle of indicators may help in understanding the relationship among economic crisis, sustainability objectives and inequality issues in urban contexts. In order to become smart and sustainable, cities needs a fertile environment guided by responsive administrators. Such indicators should facilitate a comparative assessment as policy solutions should "circulate, migrate and mutate on an international scale and with growing speed" (Vanolo, 2014, p. 886), while acknowledging that the evaluation of urban areas also depends on local context, on administrators' vision and, more generally, on idiosyncratic cities' challenges. Indeed, through this set of indicators, urban policies can be tailored to local needs and opportunities without abandoning the most challenging goals and priorities attached to the smart city concept. On the other hand, as the rhetoric of smartness runs the risk of losing a critical approach on the enthusiastic and celebratory images illustrated by the techno-centred vision of smart cities, our approach has the advantage of taking into account urban resilience through the inclusion of long-term indicators. Urban development policies could thus gain in farsightedness in the elaboration of meaningful and consistent strategies directed to the pursuit of Europe 2020 objectives.

The main limitations concern the restrictions of available observation that plague every indicator. In particular, in terms of cultural sustainability, the dataset does not include any possible measure of social capital, which plays a crucial role in the development of diversified and knowledge-based local economies. Governance issues are also partially left behind in this approach. Cultural sustainability measures would need to include indicators of democratic urban pluralism in order to address this topic through the DPSIR model. These limitations, however, are typical of this type of study, which, in general, can easily be biased depending on the selected criteria. Our bundle of indicators does not escape these drawbacks, but it provides useful tools for uniting the environmental, social and cultural dimensions when comparing European cities from the perspective of smart and inclusive urban development.

Notes

1 It is worthwhile to notice that two-thirds of the smart cities mapped by the European Parliament (2014) address more than one characteristic and that the overall average of involved characteristics is 2.5.

2 Hawkes (2001) argues that the pillars of sustainability are actually four, instead of the traditional three (environmental, social, economic): cultural vitality, social equity, environmental responsibility and economic viability.

3 Caragliu et al. (2011) provide six indicators of smartness: GDP per capita, number of employed persons in cultural and entertainment industry, multimodal accessibility and length of the network of public transport, e-government and human capital. Caragliu and Del Bo (2012) focus on three aspects: culture (proxied by the number of visitors to museums per resident), mobility (proxied by the length of public transportation) and e-government (proxied by the number of administrative forms available for download from official web site). Kourtit et al. (2012) analyze cities' environmental sustainability using data on the employment structure of the urban workforce, on the degree of business and socio-cultural attractiveness and on the presence of public facilities and of

sophisticated e-services. Using European Urban Audit data for years 2007–2009, we select the indicators according to the different steps of the DPSIR model and to the sustainability dimension they are attached with.
4   Detailed results of the PCA are available upon request.

Bibliography

Alesina, A. and Ferrara, E. (2004), Ethnic diversity and economic performance, NBER Working Papers, No. 10313.

Atkinson, T. (2002), *Social indicators: The EU and social inclusion*, Oxford, Oxford university press.

Caragliu, A. and Del Bo, C. (2012), Smartness and European urban performance: Assessing the local impacts of smart urban attributes, *Innovation: The European Journal of Social Science Research*, 25 (2), 97–113.

Caragliu, A, Del Bo, C. and Nijkamp, P. (2011), Smart cities in Europe, *Journal of Urban Technology*, 18 (2), 65–82.

Cohendet, P. and Simon, L. (2008), Knowledge-intensive firms, communities, and creative cities, in A. Amin and J. Roberts (eds.), *Community, economic creativity, and organization*, Oxford, Oxford University Press, pp. 227–253.

European Commission. (2006), *Communication from the Commission to the Council and the European Parliament on Thematic Strategy on the Urban Environment*, COM/2005/0718.

European Commission. (2010a), *A strategy for smart, sustainable and inclusive growth*, COM 2020.

European Commission. (2010b), *World and European sustainable cities: Insights from EU research*, Luxembourg, European Union.

European Commission. (2012), *Smart cities and communities – European innovation partnership*, COM 4701, Bruxelles, European Union.

European Commission. (2014), *Investment for jobs and growth Promoting development and good governance in EU regions and cities – Sixth report on economic, social and territorial cohesion*, Bruxelles, European Union.

European Environmental Agency. (2006), *Urban Sprawl in Europe: The ignored challenge*, Luxembourg: European Union.

European Parliament. (2014), *Mapping smart cities in Europe*, available at www.europarl.europa.eu/studies, accessed on 10 March 2014.

European Parliament and European Council. (2003), *Sixth community environment action programme*, Decision No 1600/2002/EC of 22 July 2002.

Eurostat. (2010), *European regional and Urban statistics reference guide*, Luxembourg, European Union.

Florida, R. (2002). *The rise of the creative class, and how it's transforming work, leisure, community and everyday life*, New York: Basic Books.

Florida, R. (2005), *Cities and the creative class*, London, Routledge.

Giffinger, R., Fertner, C., Kramar, H., Kalasek, R., Pichler-MilaNović, N. and Meijers, E. (2007), *Smart cities: Ranking of European medium-sized cities*. Centre of Regional Science (SRF), Vienna University of Technology.

Glaeser, E.L. (2002), Review of Richard Florida's The rise of the creative class, *Regional Science and Urban Economics*, 35 (5), 593–596.

Glaeser, E.L. and Alesina, A. (2005), *Fighting poverty in the US and Europe: A world of difference*, Oxford, Oxford University Press.

Glaeser, E.L., Kolko, J. and Saiz, A. (2001), Consumer city, *Journal of Economic Geography*, 1, 27–50.

Glaeser, E.L. and Maré, D.C. (2001), Cities and skills, *Journal of Labor Economics*, 19 (2), 316–342.

Glaeser, E.L. et al. (2010), The complementary between cities and skills, *Journal of Regional Science*, 50 (1), 221–244.

Gottlieb, J.D. and Glaeser, E.L. (2006), *Urban resurgence and the consumer city*, Harvard Institute of Economic Research Discussion Paper No. 2109.

Graham, S. (2002), Bridging urban digital divides: Urban polarization and information and communication technologies, *Urban Studies*, 39 (1), 33–56.

Hall, P. (2000), Creative cities and economic development, *Urban Studies*, 37 (4), 633–649.

Hawkes, J. (2001), The fourth pillar of sustainability: Culture's essential role in public planning, Common Ground Publishing with Cultural Development Network, VIC.

Hollands, R.G. (2008), Will the real smart city please stand up? Intelligent, progressive or entrepreneurial?, *City*, 12 (3), 303–320.

Inoguchi, T., Newman, E. and Paoletto, G. (1999), *Cities and environment. New approaches for the ecosociety*, New York, UN University Press.

Kourtit, K., Nijkamp, P. and Arribas, D. (2012), Smart cities in perspective – A comparative European study by means of self-organizing maps, *Innovation: The European Journal of Social Science Research*, 25 (2), 229–246.

Marsa-Maestre, I., Lopez-Carmona, M.A., Velasco, J.R. and Navarro, A. (2008), Mobile agents for service personalization in smart environments, *Journal of Networks*, 3 (5), 30–41.

Moretti, E. (2004), Human capital externalities in cities, in J.V. Henderson and J.F. Thisse (eds.), *Handbook of urban and regional economics*, Vol. 4, Amsterdam, North-Holland, pp. 2243–2291.

Nam, T. and Pardo, T.A. (2010), Conceptualizing Smart City with Dimensions of Technology, People, and Institutions, *The Proceedings of the 12th Annual International Conference on Digital Government Research*, 282–291.

Newton, P.W. (2012), Liveable and sustainable? Socio-technical challenges for twenty-first-century cities, *Journal of Urban Technology*, 19 (1), 81–102.

Nijkamp, P. and Kourtit, K. (2013), The "New Urban Europe": Global challenges and local responses in the urban century, *European Planning Studies*, 21 (3), 291–315.

OECD. (1998), *Towards sustainable development, Environmental Indicators*, Paris, OECD.

OECD. (1999), Improving evaluation practices. Best Practice Guidelines for Evaluation and Background Paper, PUMA/PAC(9)1, Paris, OECD.

OECD. (2004), *Evaluating local economic and employment development, how to assess what works among programmes and policies*, Paris, OECD.

Poelhekke, S. (2006), Do amenities and diversity encourage city growth? A link through skilled labour, EUI Working Papers No. 2006/10.

Polese, M. and Stern, R. (2000), *The social sustainability of cities: Diversity and the management of change*, Toronto, University of Toronto Press.

Satterthwaite, D. (1999), *Sustainable cities*, London, Earthscan.

Shapiro, J.M. (2006), Smart cities: Quality of life, productivity, and the growth effects of human capital, *The Review of Economics and Statistics*, 88 (2), 324–335.

Toppeta, D. (2010), *The smart city vision: How innovation and ICT Can build smart, "livable", sustainable cities*. The Innovation Knowledge Foundation, Think!Report 005.

Tregua, M., Amitrano, C. and Bifulco, F. (2015), Cultural heritage and multi-actors innovation. Evidence from smart cities. Proceedings of XXVII Sinergie Annual Congress.

Vanolo, A. (2014), Smartmentality: The smart city as disciplinary strategy, *Urban Studies*, 51 (5), 883–898.

Zygiaris, S. (2013), Smart city reference model: Assisting planners to conceptualize the building of smart city innovative eco-systems, *Journal of the Knowledge Economy*, 4 (2), 217–231.

10 Smart development and smart utilities

An international comparison

Andrea Paliani, Giuseppe Cappiello
and Gianluca Di Pasquale

1 Introduction

1.1 The forces driving our future

Megatrends are large, transformative global forces that impact everyone on the planet. Ernst & Young (EY) has identified six megatrends that define our future by having a far-reaching impact on business, society, culture, economies and individuals. While each of the megatrends stands on its own, there is clear interactivity. Digital, big data, sensors and social applications are closely intertwined with expected transformations across other megatrends. Digital technologies will drive the realization of tomorrow's "intelligent cities".

Digital oil fields will also lead to increased savings and output in the energy space, while "smart grids" will revolutionize the production, delivery and use of electricity globally. The ability to create digitally based business models has lowered the barrier to creating new and innovative ventures for entrepreneurs around the world.

In some cases, successful outcomes in one megatrend are related to developments in another. As the world urbanizes to the tune of 750 cities contributing 61% of global GDP by 2030, urban areas will require sustainable and resilient solutions to optimize resources, reduce risks and promote the well-being of all citizens. The economic promise of an increasingly global marketplace will be dependent on major investments in infrastructure and related financing in both new and existing cities.

Economic power continues to shift eastward with the emergence of new markets and new trade linkages. The boundaries between industry sectors are blurring. New entrants that are digitally native are overturning existing business models. Existing players in one sector (technology) are entering other sectors (energy, transport) with exciting new propositions.

This chapter will first set out the main drivers of the change in course, and then it will attempt to define the role of utilities in this scenario by outlining a vision for the time to come.

1.2 The future is digital

The push for innovation as a solution to global competition is giving birth to new business spaces, generated by the intersection between the physical and digital worlds. Fuelled by the convergence of social, mobile, cloud, big data and growing demand for "anytime anywhere" access to information, technology is disrupting all areas of the business enterprise.

One-third of web pages are viewed from mobile phones, and by 2018, one-third of the top-20 firms in most Industries will be disrupted by industry-specific data platforms.

Disruption is taking place across all industries and in all geographies. Enormous opportunities exist for enterprises to take advantage of connected devices to capture vast amounts of information, enter new markets, transform existing products and introduce new business and delivery models. However, the evolution of the digital enterprise also presents significant challenges, including new competition, changing customer engagement and business models, unprecedented transparency, privacy concerns and cybersecurity threats.

Bridging technologies characterizes this new competitive arena and triggers the new technological and business paradigm of the "Internet of Things" (IoT).[1] This market includes all those applications and services made possible by the evolution of ICT and the increasingly wide deployment of sensors, as well as the growing diffusion of mobile devices.

Cisco's Internet Business Solutions Group (IBSG) estimates that 12.5 billion devices were connected in 2010 and predicts that some 50 billion devices will be connected by 2020. McKinsey estimates that the Internet of Things has a total potential economic impact of $3.9 trillion to $11.1 trillion per year in 2025. On the top end, the value of this impact – including consumer surplus – would be equivalent to about 11% of the world economy in 2025 (Manyika et al., 2015).

Big players from the ICT industry, the telecommunications industry[2] and Internet companies[3] are already set to occupy the new market spaces opened up by IoT. Expectations of growth for these applications in the energy and transport industries are also high: according to the Cisco IoT Survey, 86% of transportation companies and 89% of utilities plan to increase their IoT investments in the next three years.[4]

Partly thanks to the rise of IoT, Intel enjoyed record sales of microprocessors, and its stock prices are now 30% higher than in the past few years. Suppliers are developing their solutions in a supply-driven market on the verge of becoming demand-driven. Businesses in all sectors increasingly perceive and understand the potential benefits that IoT solutions can generate in terms of efficiency, business processes transformation and revenue. Consumers are witnessing and experimenting smart homes, smart vehicles, and life-changing innovations that disrupt their approach to daily activities.

As we finish writing this chapter, Drayson Technologies has announced that it as just found the technological solution to providing perpetual energy to sensors.[5] The "Freevolt" system stems from wanting to transform so-called electromagnetic pollution into a source of energy for the Internet of Things. A small hardware system capable of transforming the external radio frequencies (2G, 3G, Wi-Fi, TV) can surround us in "perpetual energy" sources. The basic idea is that we will live in closed areas of the smart object, able to monitor the environment, detect temperature changes, monitor the safety of some areas, etc. Not by chance, one of the first products made is a sensor for measuring environmental pollution, called CleanSpace Tag.

1.3 Urbanization of "old" and "new" cities will require effective infrastructure investment

The number and scale of cities continue to grow across the globe, driven by rapid urbanization in emerging markets and continued urbanization in mature markets. The United Nations (UN) reports that 54% of the world's population currently lives in cities, and by 2050, this percentage will increase to 66%.

In order to harness the economic benefits of urbanization, policy-makers and the private sector must do effective planning and attract sustained investment in railroads, highways, bridges, ports, airports, water, power, energy, telecommunications and other types of infrastructure. Effective policy responses to the challenges that cities face, including climate change and poverty, will be essential in making cities of the future competitive, sustainable and resilient.

1.3.1 Global cities will accrue greater economic power

A 2014 study conducted by Oxford Economics and EY[6] projected that the pace and scale of global urbanization are set to continue, with Asia and Africa urbanizing at the fastest rate among regions. Rapid urbanization will drive the world's future economic growth. The impact will be seen in the shift in spending power to urban areas. Growth in spending on non-essential products for the world's largest cities will outpace growth in consumer spending on essential items, reflecting the rising affluence of urban residents across the globe.

The largest urban explosion of young people will be in Africa, with cities such as Lagos, Abuja, Dar es Salaam and Luanda seeing extremely rapid growth of their young populations. In fact, a full 90% of the 0–14 age group residing in cities from the top 750 cities list will live in Africa in 2030. By contrast, 122 of the top 750 cities have populations that are expected to shrink by 2030, in part due to aging populations. Most of these cities are located in Eastern Europe, Germany, Italy, Japan, South Korea and China.

1.3.2 An urban world requires major investment in infrastructure

Nearly all cities have a growth agenda: high-quality infrastructure contributes to well-functioning, growth-primed cities that can attract new residents and make sure existing ones stay. Many emerging nations face the challenge of building new urban infrastructures from scratch, while many developed nations face the problem of aging infrastructures. The B20 Infrastructure and Investment Taskforce's six recommendations for actions that G20 nations should take include setting specific targets for infrastructure in their national growth plans, establishing a Global Infrastructure Hub and increasing the availability of long-term financing for investment.

With the challenges facing government budgets around the world, many will continue to finance infrastructure projects using public–private partnership (PPP) models, with new "flavors" emerging to meet local needs. Infrastructure funds and pension funds are expected to invest more in infrastructure, as investors focus on alternative assets for diversification or potentially higher returns. Those markets that harness the promise of urbanization by finding creative solutions to financing infrastructure needs will be those that enjoy greater economic growth.

1.3.3 Sustainable and resilient urbanization will be instrumental to the world's future prospects

While urbanization affords economic opportunity, it also presents significant resource risks. Rapid urbanization is contributing to global resource depletion, while some of the effects of climate change (e.g. rising sea levels around coastal cities and extreme weather events) will hit cities the hardest. The World Health Organization (WHO, 2014) reports that 7 million people died – one in eight of total global deaths – as a result of air pollution exposure in 2012, a large proportion of which resided in urban areas.

Roughly 50% of the urban population currently being monitored (representing just 12% of the total global urban population) is exposed to air pollution, which is at least 2.5 times higher than WHO recommended levels (Kneebone, 2014). Local and national policy-makers, along with other important stakeholders, will need to work closely together to plan, build and govern more sustainable cities.

"Green" and "smart" will become important features of the sustainable and competitive city. Green cities will have energy-efficient buildings, reduce waste and rely heavily on renewable energy sources and energy efficient transportation systems. Enabled by the digital, competitive cities will also make use of state-of-the-art information and communication technology (ICT) to build smart mobility solutions, smart grids and other solutions.

2 A new role for utilities

2.1 A game-changing business model to learn from

The IoT is the enabling factor for a great number of applications that take advantage of diffused intelligence by improving industrial processes, improving existing products or creating new ones and opening new prospects for smart city services, such as traffic management, smart lighting, smart buildings, smart parking, waste management, noise/pollution maps etc.

Moreover, sensors and Machine-to-Machine communication can be utilized in several industrial sectors, including the energy industry, from production to add-on and complementary services. Thanks to the IoT, innovative applications have been developed for logistics, fleet management, supply chain management, automation and smart metering, as well as for cross-functional applications in the fields of security, surveillance and maintenance.

2.1.1 Electricity and the sharing economy perspective

The concept of the sharing economy applied to the utility industry has the potential to reform the paradigms of the electricity market and the relationship between consumers and producers. Business models built upon centralized infrastructure such as power plants and long distance transmission lines are set to evolve as distributed energy resources (intermittent renewable power, smart metering, battery storage) become more diffused. The sharing economy is driven by energy efficiency and demand-side behavior in improving asset utilization rates and reducing system and consumer costs.

Peer-to-peer markets will be essential for distributed energy resources to carry forward and apply the principles of the sharing economy. As P2P platforms become more mature and trusted by market stakeholders, they will play a key role in bypassing the incumbents of the electricity market: utility companies. Emerging business models that deliver their products and services through shared networks are directly contributing to increasing the utilization of the electricity system and distributed energy resources. P2P markets allow underutilized assets to be identified and to create opportunities and value from them by providing access and information about ways to diversify goods and services.

Today, metering tools in the utility industry fail to account for distribution and utilization issues such as emission reduction, peak load reduction and network congestion. The sharing economy market has created solutions to infrastructure-related problems that can alleviate utility companies from having to deliver or purchase electricity in periods of high demand or in the event of network congestions. An optimally deployed supply of power unlocked by distributed energy resources can reduce the gap between base and peak load curves, which will improve system load and utilization factors.

Services like these are game-changing elements in sectors that have not yet been affected by the Collaborative Common. Disintermediation in the production and distribution of energy poses non-negligible threats to traditional electric utilities, forcing them to react by defining new models for their businesses. The dream for utility companies to become holistic energy managers of the future has been jeopardized by the sharing economy. In Germany, 46% of renewable energy generation derives from private individuals and farmers, whereas only 5% originates from the "Big 4" power providers (RWE, EnBW, E.ON and Vattenfall) (Bershidsky, 2014).

Today, several start-ups across the globe are taking advantage of these opportunities to gain first-mover advantages and place themselves competitively on the market.

Box 10.1   Vandebron

Vandebron is a Dutch start-up company that pairs electricity buyers and sellers on a proprietary, virtual, online peer-to-peer market. Founded in 2013, it currently hosts 30 producers, which have generated till now enough electricity to power 35,277 households. Vandebron distinguishes itself by catering to individual consumer needs by offering advice and assistance, as well through its network, which brings together suppliers with excess electricity and consumers interested in diversifying their residential energy mix.

An advanced algorithm allows existing clients or interested individuals to estimate their monthly electricity and gas consumption based on what type of house they have and the number of people who live in it. The information provided is then processed to produce a list of suppliers ranked according to various criteria (residual availability, price per month, savings per year, type of renewable energy generated and geographic location) who are available to supply their excess renewable electricity. Upon selecting the desired supplier, technical and contractual information is then summarized and presented in a transparent and easy-to-view format, illustrating a yearly estimate of the expected electricity and gas consumption, the tariff per kWh, and CO_2 emissions abated. The service provided also gives advice on how to obtain electricity at lower prices with long-term contracts.

Overall, the Vandebron model offers a user-friendly intuitive service that allows users to switch energy providers in less than 3 minutes and save on average up to euros75 per year. The business model completely excludes traditional utility companies from the exchange and directly contributes to supporting local renewable energy. Additionally, gas purchased from their platform originates from gold-standard, high-quality emission-reducing projects that contribute to furthering sustainable development worldwide.

Box 10.2   YelOha

YelOha is a solar panel service provider that has created a network based on the principles of electricity sharing. The Israeli start-up has been considered the "Airbnb of electricity" and claims to have created the first solar power sharing network in the world. The collaborative network is composed of hosts and partners, which given their mutual interdependency can save on monthly utility bills as well as power their homes with solar electricity.

The YelOha model is composed of two key actors and supports increasing the share of solar power-generated electricity in urban areas. Solar power hosts, in exchange for giving their consensus, receive free solar panels and a portion of the electricity generated. Partners on the other hand, are those individuals who choose to purchase solar panels to be installed on other people's roofs if their own residential infrastructure is unsuitable (for example metropolitan apartments). This framework allows people to contribute and receive renewable electricity regardless of where they are located.

On average, households are expected to save up to $71 dollars per year, offset 5% of conventional electricity usage and save roughly six clean airproducing trees per solar panel. Additionally, YelOha offers a mobile application that lets users track the amount of electricity produced by their solar panels. Currently the company only operates in the U.S. state of Massachusetts; however, their parent company has recently received funding for $3.5 million and is expected to expand.

Box 10.3   Mosaic

Based in California, Mosaic has created a collaborative online investment model that aims to intensify the distribution of solar power in urban areas. The online platform gives visibility to solar projects that need financing and allows investors to contribute to the development of solar projects that otherwise would be too expensive for the recipient to develop. Unlike traditional crowdfunding initiatives, which offer low-value rewards, Mosaic incentivizes investors to participate in their collaborative model by publicizing the prospect of tangible returns. Upon installing the photovoltaic panels, the revenue generated from the solar electricity produced is divided to offset the customer's utility bill and pay investor yields.

One of Mosaic's largest and most recent projects successfully raised $40,000 to install 196 solar panels on the roof of a local organization. According to estimates,[7] the investment is expected generate up to $55,000 in savings over ten years for the organization and $160,000 throughout the life of the project. Despite the intermittent nature of solar power, which can create uncertainty in the capability to remunerate bills and investors, Mosaic has generated a total of $1.1 million and has never had outstanding payments.

2.1.2 *Open energy information and data*

Open Energy information and data are the driving force of the new energy economy and, as concerns the utilities industry, are able to unlock numerous benefits in the interest of both end-users and power distributers. The circulation of information will be essential to address the challenges posed by fast-paced urbanization and the environment. According to the World Bank (2015), Open Data can be a powerful tool to improve the accuracy of market information, increase transparency and achieve local development goals. Being able to communicate with infrastructure and securing access to this channel will lead to the development of new tools and policies that will help shape better defined long-term strategies. Avoiding energy theft, increasing public safety, improving financial control and delivering more accurate feedback are some of many examples of how open data can address issues (even remotely) related to the utility market.

Box 10.4   OpenEI

OpenEI is a wiki-based community in which consumers, innovators and implementers are brought together to gather, produce, access or gain information on the most recent energy related information. The portal offers tools and models built on user-generated and market content, which can be easily interrogated according to several search criteria, as well as a wide variety of datasets and analyses that can be downloaded. Currently, the service caters to fifteen areas with dedicated applications, datasets and communities for each of them.

Finding information, connecting with people and sharing knowledge are the three main objectives of OpenEI. Since being founded in 2009 through a collaboration between the U.S. Department of Energy and the National Renewable Energy Laboratory, 22,142 people have contributed to the community 935,430 times across 190,512 pages. In October 2015, the portal was visited by 71,902 people from 193 different countries, who downloaded 40 datasets and 682 external energy-related applications.

Box 10.5   Green Button

The Green Button initiative is an industry-developed, consensus-driven response to President Obama's Climate Action Plan of 2013, a call-to-action to provide utility customers with easy and secure access to their own energy usage information in a consumer-friendly, computer-friendly, open and standardized format.

The Green Button is a mechanism that allows users to upload ("connect my data" button) or download ("download my data" button) their own personal data. Online, customers are able to download data related to their energy profiles, yet the "button's" most powerful application, is the possibility for third-party service providers to directly access information about their customers from which tailor made solutions can be built from. Greater access to more in-depth data allows consumers to abate their utility bills and defend themselves against inaccurate market calculations. Additionally, the service provided by the Green Button model has supported the development of new applications related to a variety of fields (heating and cooling, real estate, solar, etc.), which incentivizes, not only savings and energy efficiency, but also country-wide collaboration amongst vendors, regulators, state agencies, utilities and other institutions.

Launched in January of 2012, more than fifty utilities and electricity suppliers serving more than 60 million houses and businesses have committed to enable their customers with "Green Button" access to help them save energy and shrink their bills. Of these, over 42 million household and business customers (reaching well over 100 million Americans) already have access to their Green Button energy data.

2.1.3 The growing demand for e-mobility

The automotive market is distressed. The financial and economic crisis of recent years and the increasing price of fuel have affected consumption in general and the automotive market in particular. In Italy, in fact, a substantial decrease in car registrations has taken place from about 2.490 million (2007) to 0.870 million (2015).

2.1.4 The key role of infrastructures

There is a positive correlation between the demand for electric mobility and the availability of infrastructure. In recent years, the number of charging stations has increased considerably, even if their geographic distribution is still uneven. In particular, there are twelve cities, mostly concentrated in South Italy, where charging infrastructures still do not exist, and seventy-two cities, accounting for 62% of the total, in which there are fewer than ten charging stations.

The diffusion of electric mobility in Italy (and the rest of Europe) is growing but it's still at an early stage. The sales figures of "green" cars in fact are rising but their numbers are still extremely low (about 700 in Italy in 2013). Proportionally, their use has increased a lot, since energy consumption has grown by a factor of eight in three years. An increase in battery life and a mix of incentives and restrictive traffic rules are the levers that may help to facilitate the diffusion of electric cars.

2.1.5 From consumption to resource sharing

The idea of sharing gained strong support during the international financial crisis and has expanded to even newer sectors, of which mobility is a clear example.

The great challenge that cities have to face is to change the value from resource consumption ("cowboy economy", e.g. the private car) to resource sharing (sharing economy, i.e. "the astronaut's economy", smart community business models, such as co-working, smart parking, gamification, crowdfunding, crowdsourcing, etc.). Value creation, in fact, is moving from production and possession to the sharing of goods, from ownership to access and from purchase to re-use.

2.1.6 Emerging paradigms of alternative mobility

In the field of mobility, the need to move towards models focused on resource sharing has brought up new paradigms defined as "alternative mobility". Italian cities are showing an increasing diffusion of services like car sharing and carpooling with progressive improvement and strengthening. An emblematic case is the city of Milan: at the end of 2013, the four car-sharing operators (five, as of May 2014) already relied on a fleet of over 1,500 vehicles and more than 90,000 users. Thus, Milan is now considering an extension of this service also to its hinterland.

2.1.7 The city "bicycle scale"

Italian cities' affinity to bike-sharing services is due to their urban characteristics, which by conformation and extension make cycling the most efficient way to get around. In addition, the "Cyclelogistics" project's survey, conducted by the European Cyclist Federation and promoted by the EU, revealed that 51% of all movements of goods within urban areas could be performed by bicycle-based logistic systems, thus diminishing transportation costs, improving delivery speeds and strongly reducing the environmental impact. Italy is beginning to move in this direction, too. Delivery services by bicycle couriers are already offered in twenty-three Italian cities.

2.2 Riding the wave of collaborative economy

Over the past few decades, the digital economy has turned millions of consumers into prosumers and has reduced drastically the energy cost of producing and sharing information goods, such as music, books and news. The transformation brought by the digital economy in the information goods industries will soon be seen also in the energy industry, if similar networks will be put in place following the same principles at the base of the current global Internet network.

In recent years, scientist, economists, social visionaries and companies have been calling for a paradigm shift in our economic productivity, tied to our ability to efficiently use energy. A simple upgrade of the existing infrastructure[8] will bring only small gains since there is lower potential to exploit their productivity. A new scenario instead is offered by the transition to a fully digital economy and industrial internet resulting in a leap in productivity far beyond the productivity gains achieved in the twentieth century (Rifkin, 2011; Evans and Annunziata, 2012).

This new economic paradigm is already flourishing in several fields thanks to services that go under the name of "Collaborative Economy". The Collaborative Economy is now spreading in various domains (collaborative consumption, collaborative production, collaborative education, collaborative finance). The most relevant domain is collaborative consumption, an economic model based on sharing, trading, lending and renting with the objective of gaining access to a product or service, as opposed to individual ownership. The sharing economy is a subsection of the collaborative consumption domain.

In this future expanded digital economy, enterprises and prosumers will be able to connect to the IoT and use big data, creating opportunities to increase energy efficiency and reduce production costs. For example, new energy governance is no longer hierarchical but distributed and collaborative, where billions of people living in our cities will produce energy, buildings will become micro-scale energy production plants and hydrogen applications will make it possible to store it.

We will develop smart communities made up of prosumers who are able to share locally produced electricity with others. In times of over-production, energy costs will be zero. IoT applications will change the processes of energy consumption by taking the energy at times when the cost is lower. Services like these are game-changing elements in sectors that up until now had not been affected by the collaborative economy. Disintermediation in the production and distribution of energy poses a threat to traditional electric utilities if they will not adopt new models for their businesses.

2.3 From battlefields of competitors to business economic systems

The peripheral view will be a necessary capacity for companies dealing with pervasive waves of innovation in their industry. The expansion of the digital economy to new domains and its merger with the physical world requires an attentive view in different sectors in order to be ready to respond and adopt new business models. This economy calls for a constant monitoring of changes in industrial and organizational structures, not only in a company's industry, but also in other ones.

The hyper-connectivity brought by the IoT and the creation of smart cities will change the competitive scenario and call into question the role of single companies in the value chain. New business models are emerging to cope with cross-sector markets that require competences distributed in companies and organizations once based in parallel vertical sectors.

As the impact of companies' activities evolves from being business-specific to inter-functional and ultimately involving the whole system of suppliers, buyers and competitors, relations along the value chain will have to shift from simple optimization and integration to forms of actual collaboration and synchronization.

In this scenario, competitors will come to collaborate with each other in conjunction with customers and other operators, in order to find the best solutions for the market based on data flowing between all the parties. These solutions, either products or services, will increasingly need to be developed and marketed as hybrid bundles that group together interoperable and complementary elements.

Analysts predict that utilities' business models will evolve from generating and distributing power to aggregating networks, through the realization of multifunctional infrastructures for electricity distribution, public lighting, electric mobility and other complementary services (see Figure 10.1).

To be sure, these scenarios will depend on several factors, especially involving the decisions that political and economic stakeholders will take, and it is difficult

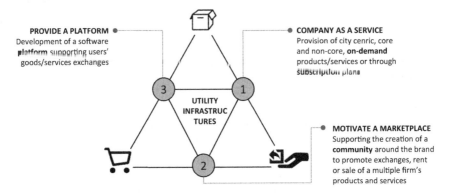

Figure 10.1 Three possible evolutions for multi-functional utilities

Source: Owyang et al. (2013, p. 11).

to determine which players can garner the key role of integrator of the various components. The suppliers of devices, the developers of applications, the ICT platforms and telecommunication companies are all striving to optimize their strategic positioning in order to gain the dominant position. It is very likely that this process will result in different scenarios depending on the geographical market. Smart grids are key components of the IoT ecosystem that an electric utility should leverage to garner the key role of system integrator.

2.4 Big data will be important along the whole value chain

Big data is the phenomenon of our time. The combination of the explosion of data and the rapid development of new technologies capable of storing and processing this information will transform the way enterprises run their businesses.

After an initial period, when big data was an optional extra for most businesses, its value is now widely accepted. Organizations all around the world are racing to exploit the opportunities big data presents, although they have made relatively little progress at a strategic level.

Trends in the power and utilities sector are leading to the emergence of vastly bigger data volumes along the whole value chain. In generation, the decentralization of supply required by decarbonization has created millions of small renewable assets, each generating its own data. Fluctuating and weather-dependent renewable energy production has made it profitable to build weather forecasting data for increasingly sophisticated production schedules. In transmission, the focus on energy efficiency and reliability has grown the amount of data produced by sensors and monitoring equipment. In retail, the trend is moving towards online smart meters and smart home applications, which continuously generate data.

The level of maturity of big data technology adoption varies among the stages of the value chain. The steering of generation plant utilization and energy trading activities already depends on elaborate production and market data models. Here, power and utilities profit from other sectors that are more advanced in big data and analytics, e.g. the financial industry. On the other hand, the full potential of big data in infrastructure operations and retail is still untapped. It is widely unquestioned that big data and analytics are the foundation for improved grid operations and the conversion of customer relationships. Smart meters and smart devices, in particular, are an important new source of data that enables utilities companies to build much closer relationships with customers and to move into new markets.

3 Strategic vision

3.1 The four-layer operating framework to shape the smart city

Needing a new kind of approach, EY has identified a four-layer operating framework to shape the smart city and enterprises vision and strategies (see Figure 10.2).

Today's technological evolution and economic sustainability require a different smart city logical structure, which can be organized based on the following layers:

Basic infrastructure as the enabling factor for the construction of a smart city. This layer includes telecommunications, transport, energy, public lighting, waste and water networks.

A network of interoperable technological sensors related to the "internet of things", aimed at the city's big data collection and at the remote control of its infrastructures. Data originate in the basic infrastructure layer, and user behavior information is collected by connected objects and devices, which are the starting point for the provision of smart services.

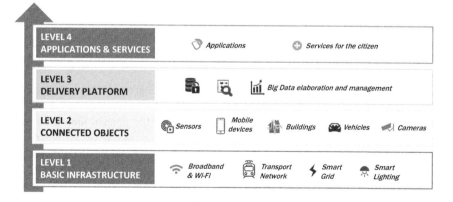

Figure 10.2 The Super IoT platform enabling the convergence of smart city infrastructures

Source: EYs papers.

A delivery platform to evaluate and enhance a territory's big data. A "cloud-based" delivery platform analyzing and elaborating big data generated within the other layers to provide useful information for the improvement of existing services and for the creation of new ones.

A series of applications and services as an additional value for the city, Applications and services represent the contact point with final users and enable the on-demand provision of services based on geo-localization.

A model of vertical silos has to be avoided. The traditional process of innovation and digitalization by vertical silos has to be replaced by a process that exalts interoperability. While in the short term, this may create vertical services, later on it will not be able to exploit the synergy and interoperability with the other subjects and would disfavour economic sustainability.

A peer-to-peer approach may be useful in an early phase, in which the various stakeholders of the city may enhance their previous experiences, their already implemented services and their former planning. Thereafter, however, they should quickly converge to a model of "shared layers".

Smart city governance must be coherent with these settings both on the level of the institutional delegations and responsibilities and by respecting the financing patterns that apply to the different projects.

The process of building the smart city must aim at the creation of a unique basic infrastructure and a unique delivery platform, into which different applications should plug their "sensors" and deliver their services through the integration of data and services collected from other cities. This is the model of approach that will guarantee at the same time-speed, sustainability as well as a wide range of public and private services.

3.2 Tools for utilities to better understand urban trends and pattern of growth

One of the most discussed issues at the global level is the availability of methodologies to measure and compare a city's level of "smartness". The main purpose of these tools is aimed at providing a unique point of view on urban trends, patterns of growth and investment, as well as the effects of political, regulatory or strategic change.

Many indices have been suggested to measure the degree of transformation or innovation of a city, and despite analyzing the same thematic areas, they differ in terms of the indicators used and methodology adopted to present their findings, some of which have been listed in Figure 10.3.

Often their traits are global and thus measure the attractiveness of a city through a variety of fields ranging from finance and investments, to economic growth, brand-identity, transport, culture, sustainability, innovation, and so on. Other limitations may include the fact that many indices are built to only cover cities above a certain population size or GDP or are confined to the performance of their nation due to data restrictions or risk-averse models of data collection. This can result in

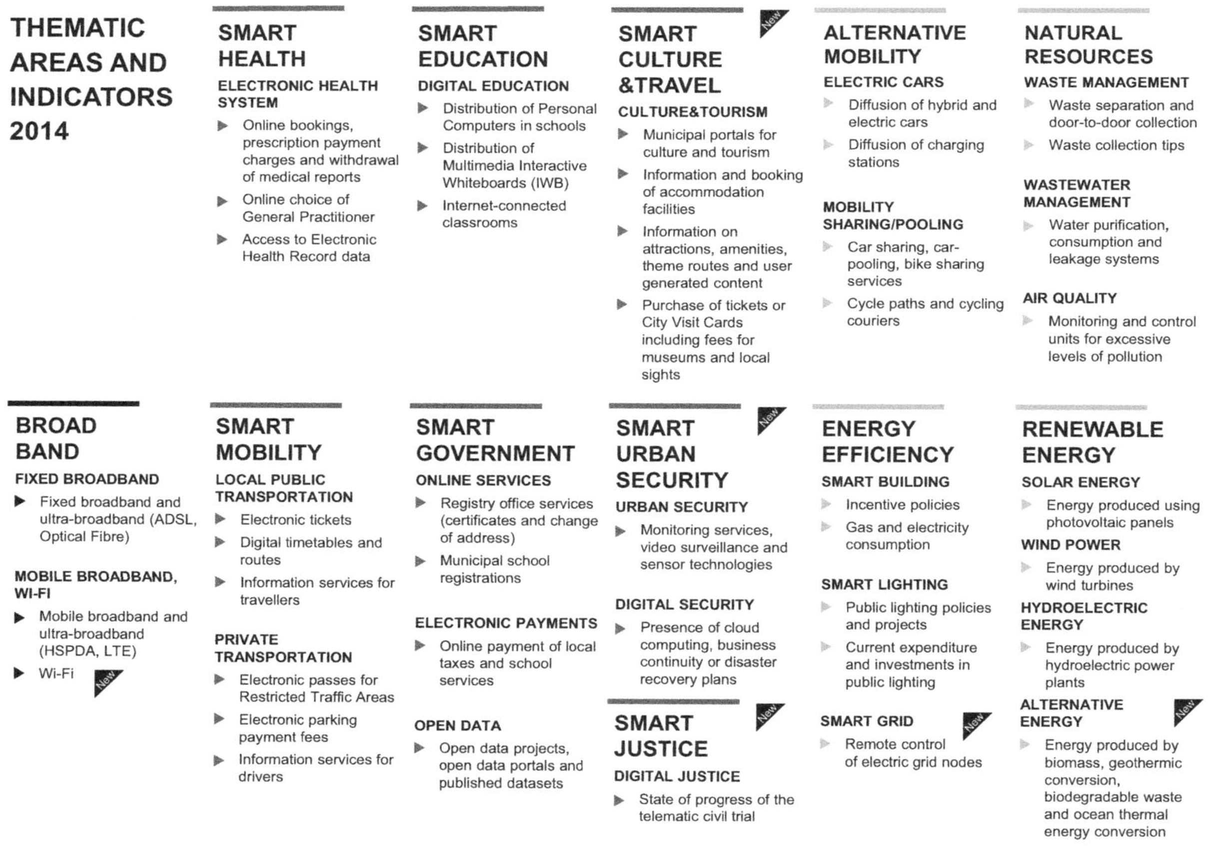

THEMATIC AREAS AND INDICATORS 2014

SMART HEALTH

ELECTRONIC HEALTH SYSTEM
- Online bookings, prescription payment charges and withdrawal of medical reports
- Online choice of General Practitioner
- Access to Electronic Health Record data

SMART EDUCATION

DIGITAL EDUCATION
- Distribution of Personal Computers in schools
- Distribution of Multimedia Interactive Whiteboards (IWB)
- Internet-connected classrooms

SMART CULTURE &TRAVEL

CULTURE&TOURISM
- Municipal portals for culture and tourism
- Information and booking of accommodation facilities
- Information on attractions, amenities, theme routes and user generated content
- Purchase of tickets or City Visit Cards including fees for museums and local sights

ALTERNATIVE MOBILITY

ELECTRIC CARS
- Diffusion of hybrid and electric cars
- Diffusion of charging stations

MOBILITY SHARING/POOLING
- Car sharing, car-pooling, bike sharing services
- Cycle paths and cycling couriers

NATURAL RESOURCES

WASTE MANAGEMENT
- Waste separation and door-to-door collection
- Waste collection tips

WASTEWATER MANAGEMENT
- Water purification, consumption and leakage systems

AIR QUALITY
- Monitoring and control units for excessive levels of pollution

BROAD BAND

FIXED BROADBAND
- Fixed broadband and ultra-broadband (ADSL, Optical Fibre)

MOBILE BROADBAND, WI-FI
- Mobile broadband and ultra-broadband (HSPDA, LTE)
- Wi-Fi

SMART MOBILITY

LOCAL PUBLIC TRANSPORTATION
- Electronic tickets
- Digital timetables and routes
- Information services for travellers

PRIVATE TRANSPORTATION
- Electronic passes for Restricted Traffic Areas
- Electronic parking payment fees
- Information services for drivers

SMART GOVERNMENT

ONLINE SERVICES
- Registry office services (certificates and change of address)
- Municipal school registrations

ELECTRONIC PAYMENTS
- Online payment of local taxes and school services

OPEN DATA
- Open data projects, open data portals and published datasets

SMART URBAN SECURITY

URBAN SECURITY
- Monitoring services, video surveillance and sensor technologies

DIGITAL SECURITY
- Presence of cloud computing, business continuity or disaster recovery plans

SMART JUSTICE

DIGITAL JUSTICE
- State of progress of the telematic civil trial

ENERGY EFFICIENCY

SMART BUILDING
- Incentive policies
- Gas and electricity consumption

SMART LIGHTING
- Public lighting policies and projects
- Current expenditure and investments in public lighting

SMART GRID
- Remote control of electric grid nodes

RENEWABLE ENERGY

SOLAR ENERGY
- Energy produced using photovoltaic panels

WIND POWER
- Energy produced by wind turbines

HYDROELECTRIC ENERGY
- Energy produced by hydroelectric power plants

ALTERNATIVE ENERGY
- Energy produced by biomass, geothermic conversion, biodegradable waste and ocean thermal energy conversion

Figure 10.3 EY country- and regional-level Smart City Index

Source: EY's papers.

misrepresentations of regions and cities with low population density or countries where talent, infrastructure or brand value is mostly absorbed by one or two leading cities (Jones Lang Lasalle, 2015).

To overcome these boundaries, EY has developed a national and regional-wide *Smart City Index* (SCI) highlighting not only cities with long-term and sometimes underestimated assets but also smaller cities, which in recent years have been improving rapidly.

3.3 The need for country-specific instruments to support decision making and strategic investment

The EYs SCI was ideated with the intention of contributing to the development of smart cities in Italy, where this process is slow and inconsistent. All local entities (such as municipalities and other local stakeholders involved in smart city projects) are evolving independently, without benefiting from the experience and lessons learnt from other cities.

It is indeed necessary to respect different realities, but it is also important to build a common curve of experience without unnecessary waste of time and resources, hence the importance of identifying best practices to serve as possible models and the most suitable ones for every type of city or local context.

Nevertheless, the detection of best practices without a shared measuring system is arbitrary and difficult. This is the reason behind the creation of the SCI, an index in which all 116 county towns are ranked based on three distinct elements. In particular, the SCI:

1   Measures what is already "smart and available" inside cities, services and infrastructures, not only data regarding existing projects, structural data or information regarding the quality of life;
2   Collects data from ad hoc surveys directly performed by EY; utilizes original data and is not limited to data from other sources (that may not be uniform);
3   Covers a broad range of application areas, from broadband infrastructures to digital services and sustainable development.

This tool is being used by the following (see Figure 10.4):

1   Operators managing assets and infrastructures, as a tool for stakeholder engagement, to raise the profile of their urban investment and to encourage positive competition between city governments;
2   National entities, to define and support the policies for city innovation providing a common methodology to define best practices and reference models, in order to set up guidelines;
3   Cities, to carry out an assessment of their roadmaps, to be ranked with other cities and to support their candidacy for smart city financing with concrete data;
4   Regions, to define the city benchmarks on their territory, in order to monitor "smart region" programs.

Target: Service and Network Providers (Telcos)

Benefits for the client
- Better understanding of the market context
- Facts based business intelligence and go-2-market strategy
- Affordable and soundly financed BP for new services and new technology deployments

Target: technology vendors

Benefits for the client
- Better understanding of the local market needs, drivers and approach
- Implement better value propositions for new services and client demands
- Assess the impacts of disruptive technologies in the various industry markets

Target: Government (national and local)

Benefits for the client
- Availability of city data for assessing, planning and evaluating smart city programs
- Effective selection criteria for initiatives financed under the European Regional Development Fund and European Social Fund

Target: Utilities

Benefits for the client
- Access to an established framework for the measurement of smart city performances
- Demonstrate with relevant stakeholders within a smart city the contribution a utility can make
- Assume a role in the IoT similar to what a Telco where unable to achieve in the web economy

Key objectives

Support clients, public and private, to monitor, analyze and understand from a business perspective, the smart city market take-off

Main Issues

1. What is the level of "smartness" of cities in the country (+100 capital cities) ?

2. What are the main innovation trends and drivers for market take-off ?

3. How can national and regional public policies and funds accelerate the adoption of solutions at local level ?

4. What are sound sustainable architectural models for Smart City projects ?

5. What are successful stakeholder engagement and go-to-market strategies ?

Figure 10.4 EY country- and regional-level Smart City Index – objectives and benefits

Source: EYs papers.

3.4 Sustainable cities: main trends for 100+ green capitals of Italy

The completion of a smart city has to pursue a pattern that begins with a shared vision and requests a powerful executive ability of the city's political leadership. It does not depend on a single contributor, but rather it takes a community of individuals to design and install improvements to the city, starting from the history and culture that has shaped it.

To build a smart city, rules need to be respected, conditions adapted to and a correct sequence of steps adhered to, so that the highest level of interoperability with the solutions adopted by others is maintained. By nature, a smart city is dynamic, fluid and adaptive. The smart city is multi-faceted and enriched with many applications.

In other words, when does a city become smart? Before now, there has never been a way to show how far from being a smart city the cities in a country are. EY developed a country-wide SCI with the aim of measuring the "smartness" of Italian cities using the most objective and dynamic method possible.

We discovered that many Italian cities are making their way towards being smart cities in an economical context characterized by the shortage of resources and the lack of tangible models as a reference. Hereinafter is outlined a detailed analysis of some of the main trends of the Italian market, assessed on the basis of the green component of the SCI.

A large part of the on-going transformations is created from the collaboration between public and private operators, in particular between local governments and utilities. Utilities, in fact, play an important role in delivering "green" services, such as electric mobility, public lighting, building, energy efficiency, environment and so on.

3.4.1 Italy at the forefront of the European Covenant of Mayors movement

The Europe 2020 growth strategy aims at building a smart, sustainable and inclusive Europe. In particular, the European Regional Development Fund (ERDF) determines that 5% of the resources have to be allocated for integrated actions related to sustainable urban development.

The new challenge for the city was inspired by the need to reconcile economic development with social impact and environmental sustainability. It becomes fundamental to rethink existing growth models that pay more attention to issues such as social equity and accessibility, energy efficiency in the patterns of production, consumption and awareness of individual and collective responsibility. In this perspective, cities play a central role, as they are closest to the centres of production and the consumption of goods and services.

The Covenant of Mayors is the leading European movement encouraging local authorities to increase efficiency through the use of more sustainable natural resources. Out of 5,500 EU mayors who signed the covenant, nearly 50% are Italian (see Figure 10.5). This clearly gives proof of the great interest that our nation

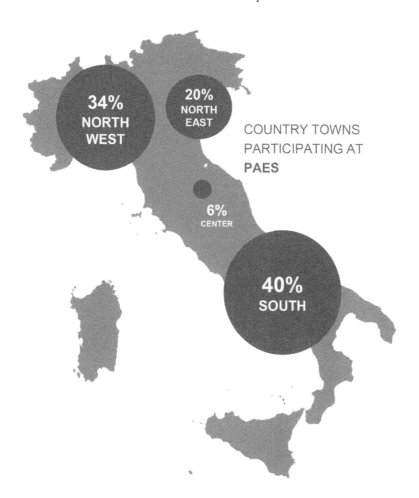

Figure 10.5 Distribution of Italian municipalities that signed the European Covenant of Mayors

Source: European Covenant of Mayors web site.

expresses towards energy matters and environmental sustainability. Attention is paid to these issues nationwide by smaller townships as well as by county towns.

From a "green" podium, Bolzano and Trento have defined a strategy for sustainability that affects simultaneously all "green" determinants. Rome instead, has chosen mobility and energy efficiency as the city's key challenges to be faced.

Notes

1 The IoT can be defined as a network of networks of connected endpoints (or "things") that communicate with each other, as well as with humans.
2 Especially in Europe.

3 Especially in the USA.
4 CISCO, Internet of Everything (IoE) Value Index How Much Value Are Private-Sector Firms Capturing from IoE in 2013?, available at http://internetofeverything.cisco.com/sites/default/files/docs/en/ioe-value-index_Whitepaper.pdf
5 On the order of around 100 microwatts.
6 See EY (2015, p. 34).
7 http://www.mercurynews.com/business/ci_22171412/solar-financing-startup-mosaic-crowd-sources-installations
8 For instance, combustion engines, centralized electricity grids, production plants and transport infrastructures.

Bibliography

Bershidsky, L. (2014), Germany's green energy is an expensive success, *Bloomberg View*, September, available at http://www.bloombergview.com/articles/2014-09-22/germany-s-green-energy-is-an-expensive-success, accessed 12 January 2015.

Evans, P.C. and Annunziata, M. (2012), *Industrial internet: Pushing the boundaries of minds and machines*, General Electric, November, available at http://www.ge.com/docs/chapters/Industrial_Internet.pdf.

EY (2015), *Megatrends 2015. Making sense of a world in motion*, Bahamas, EYGM Limited.

Jones Lang Lasalle. (2015), *The business of cities 2015*, Jones Lang Lasalle, available at http://www.jll.com/Research/jll-business-of-cities-report.pdfhttp://www.jll.com/Research/jll-business-of-cities-report.pdf.

Kneebone, E. (2014), *The growth and spread of concentrated poverty, 2000 to 2008–2012*, Washington DC, The Brookings Institution, available at www.brookings.edu/research/interactives/2014/concentrated-poverty#/M10420, accessed 12 January 2015.

Manyika, J., Chui, M., Bisson, P., Woetzel, J., Dobbs, R., Bughin, J. and Aharon, D. (2015), *The internet of things: Mapping the value beyond the hype*, McKinsey Global Institute, June, available at http://www.mckinsey.com/~/media/McKinsey/Business%20Functions/Business%20Technology/Our%20Insights/The%20Internet%20of%20Things%20The%20value%20of%20digitizing%20the%20physical%20world/Unlocking_the_potential_of_the_Internet_of_Things_Executive_summary.ashx.

Owyang, J., Tran, C. and Silva, C. (2013), The collaborative economy, A Market Definition Report, Altimeter Group. www.altimetergroup.com.

Rifkin, J. (2011), *The third industrial revolution*, London, Palgrave MacMillan.

WHO. (2014), Air quality deteriorating in many of the world's cities, May, available at www.who.int/mediacentre/news/releases/2014/air-quality/en, accessed 12 January 2015.

World Bank. (2015), Exploring-open-energy-data-in-urban-areas, June, available at http://www.worldbank.org/en/news/feature/2015/06/03/exploring-open-energy-data-in-urban-areas, accessed 12 January 2015.

11 Smart development in regional economies

The specificities of Southern Italy in the European frame

Cosimo Casilli, Valentino Moretto and Giulio Pedrini

1 Introduction

The achievement of smart development needs multidimensional interventions that go beyond technological innovation and are not grounded only on the new opportunities offered by ICT networks. Innovative paths should be rooted in the specificities of each region, while enhancing the vocation of each local context in terms of both knowledge and entrepreneurship and social and cultural resources. Accordingly, the existence of distinctive knowledge on a local level ("local knowledge"), defined as "regional knowledge domain" (Cooke, 2012), leverages specific skills and resources to create the conditions for a long-term growth based on regional specialization that is compatible with the economic incentives underlying the globalization process. The capacity of local systems to root economic activity in a place-based cultural, social and institutional environment is at the heart of economic development and success (e.g. Storper, 1997) and can endogenously create and strengthen sustainable comparative advantages.

This capacity requires institutional and infrastructural preconditions. The institutional structure should be able to stimulate and support the reconversion and the reorganization of economic activities by leveraging the complementarities between institutional sub-systems at the regional level. This institutional requirement enables smart communities to create an atmosphere of mutual trust, to address conflicts and to attract resources commitment (Rodrıguez-Pose and Storper, 2006). In fact, the concept of smart community incorporates the adherence to institutional models based on a non-formal bottom-up approach that favour a locally embedded interaction between communities and institutional agents (Farole et al., 2011). On the other hand, the preconditions for smart development concern both material and immaterial infrastructures. The former include ICT networks, while the latter include knowledge infrastructures aimed at generating and disseminating knowledge across the regional economic system. The existence of these preconditions implies that, in their absence, smart development policies should be preceded by the recovery and modernization of the existing endowment of infrastructures.

This issue certainly applies to the communities of Southern Italy. Southern Italy is persistently lagging behind the European regions under many aspects, while the economic gap with the Northern part of the country is still in place and has worryingly increased during the last crisis. This poor baseline entails the risk that the great potential of smart development policies in the realm of theory struggles with serious difficulties in terms of their actual implementation. Accordingly, the issue of giving actual meaning to smart development policies in Southern Italy should be preliminary addressed before analyzing the opportunities that could be grasped by these communities through the reorientation of specificities and vocations of their local systems starting from the existing experiences and grounding on the cooperation between different actors, participation and internal cohesion. On the other hand, like other Mediterranean communities, Southern Italian cities and regions are characterized by a complex interweaving of traditional modern and postmodern conditions (Leontidou, 1993). Additionally, they show heterogeneous conditions and attitudes with regard to their capability to implement smart development policies, showing, for instance, different attitudes in implementing EU policies. Some of them also experienced interesting tracks of endogenous development along the last two decades (Tedesco, 2012), although these advancements have been partially jeopardized by the last crisis. Accordingly, Southern Italy should not be considered as a homogeneous area but as a fragmented setting of regional and urban systems. It is therefore useful to distinguish their cities and communities according either to the specific issues they have to address or to the local resources, competences and capabilities they can count on.

Within this framework, this chapter aims at representing the degree of competitiveness and smartness Southern Italian cities and communities under a bundle of economic, social, environmental and institutional aspects. To achieve this purpose, we summarize the results of the major rankings of competitiveness and smartness that include Southern Italian cities in order to identify the main existing requirements for implementing smart development policies in these areas and to find out the threats and opportunities that characterize these areas. Then we give an overview of the existing projects, by dividing them according to their locations and characteristics. This overview is accompanied by two case studies: the first focuses on the projects that have been developed within the Matera European Capital of Culture initiative; the second analyzes the recourse to innovative financing in the waste management processes in the metropolitan area of Naples. The results of these two case studies will be used to discuss a series of recommendations on the future efforts that Italian "Meridione" should make in order to achieve smart development objectives through the creation of smart communities, while acknowledging that Southern Italian cities cannot be considered as homogenous entities and that each community could pursue specific development policies if it satisfy the relevant infrastructural and institutional requirements.

The rest of the chapter is as follows. The second section discusses the existence of the infrastructural preconditions of smart development. The third section analyzes the economic and social profiles of the main cities of Southern Italy according to the smartness indicators that have been developed by national and international agencies and identify the main opportunities and weaknesses for this area by using a SWOT analysis. The fourth section shows some evidence on best practices of smart communities and describes the implementation of two projects of cultural and financial innovation. The fifth section discusses the main issues raised by the strategic planning for Smart Communities 2020 in Southern Italy. The sixth section concludes.

2 Infrastructural preconditions for smart development

The meaning of smart development is wide and linked to the cogency of developing projects, strategies, institutional processes, metrics and everything else needed to enhance the smartness of regional and urban systems. In our vision, this concept represents the perfect synthesis between smart specialization and smart community paradigms.

On the one hand, smart specialization is essential for truly effective research and innovation investments: the European Commission asks national and regional authorities across Europe to draw up research and innovation strategies for smart specialization, so that the EU's Structural Funds can be used more efficiently and synergies between different EU, national and regional policies, as well as public and private investments, can be increased. In the European Commission's proposal for cohesion policy in 2014–2020, it will be a precondition for using the European Regional Development Fund (ERDF) in 2014–2020 to support these investments (European Commission, 2014).

On the other hand, the concept of smart city, in vogue with different forms since the beginning of the millennium and raised from Caragliu et al. (2011, p. 50), defines it as:

> A city can be defined when Smart investment in human and social capital and traditional (transport) and modern (ICT) communication infrastructures fuel sustainable economic growth and a high quality of life, with a wise management of natural resources through participatory governance.

This definition combines the concepts of sustainability and economic growth to those of improvement of quality of life related to tangible and intangible infrastructure.

Furthermore, the European Commission promotes an integrated Strategy for Smart, Sustainable, and Inclusive Urban Development of European cities and communities to enrich the Europe 2020 strategy.

Urban Europe 2020 smoothly integrates the principal priorities and flagship initiatives as follows:

1   Smart Communities and Cities: developing a communal and urban economy based on knowledge and innovation (innovation, education, digital society)
2   Sustainable Communities and Cities: promoting a more resource efficient, greener and more competitive communities and cities (climate, energy and mobility, competitiveness)

3   Inclusive Communities and Cities: fostering a high-employment communal and urban economy delivering social and territorial cohesion (employment and skills, fighting poverty) (European Commission, 2015a).

Smart development thus requires the twofold capability of local actors to formulate models and tools to face the challenges raised by regional and urban systems' complexity engendered by the knowledge economy. For this capability to emerge, however, it needs to be rooted in a set of preliminary infrastructural requirements, provided that immaterial infrastructures are as important as material ones in supporting smart development pocesses. Accordingly, it is necessary to identify a set of preconditions for implementing multi-objective policies that address issues of economic competitiveness, social equity and environmental performance. Such preconditions can be briefly highlighted as follows (Komninos et al., 2013):

1   A modern technological infrastructure enhancing the richness of networks, data (open), cloud computing and especially IoT (Internet of Things).
2   A vibrant and innovation-driven economy fostered by synergies with advanced research centres and ecosystems able to attract capitals of different nature
3   Human and social wealth to enhance a relational and social skill system in a given industry sector
4   A model of governance designed to enhance citizens' participation in value creation processes and to make them literate about innovation and change

In particular, regarding the last precondition, the governance system plays a strategic and decisive triggering role in building a community able to introduce innovations based on citizens' empowerment, stakeholders' engagement and the innovative use of social capital. This is especially true in the field of common use services, where the efficiency gains of "smart" innovations need to be accompanied by social and economic direct and immediate advantage. Without this correspondence, these tools are likely to increase social scars and jeopardize community cohesion. Indeed, if few resources are invested on this aspect, the gap between those who hold the knowledge means, and get advantages from using these innovations, and those who do not is likely to become wider and wider. This increase of the number of people who are left on the edge will eventually generate unsustainable training and assistance costs.

In the presence of such requirements, cities and communities can develop appropriate strategies towards becoming "smart" characterized by a high level of citizen involvement in all sectors of the economy and society and by the emergence of new forms of collaboration among local governments, research institutes, universities and networks of firms.

3   Southern Italy's communities: the state of the art

The latest report of the European Commission (2015b) on the socioeconomic situation of Italy describes, in a special section, the gap between Northern and

Southern Italy, investigating the causes of these regional disparities. In particular, the European Commission highlights the enormous delays in productivity and labour market of Southern Italy. Furthermore, SVIMEZ (Association for the Industrial Development in Southern Italy) underlines the structural weaknesses of Southern Italy in terms of the governance of the business system and the competitiveness of the education and training system.

Even more worrying is the analytical description that emerges from the last report presented by SVIMEZ on the economic situations of Southern Italy (SVIMEZ, 2015). SVIMEZ draws a picture of a country with deep imbalances and an increasing socio-economic divide, where the South of Italy is losing competitiveness: in 2014, for the 7th consecutive year, the GDP of the South is still negative (−1.3%); the gap in GDP per capita than the rest of the country has returned to 2000 levels; during the crisis years 2008–2014, family consumption in Southern Italy plummeted by nearly 13% and industrial investment by 59%; in 2014, almost 62% of Southern Italians earn less than 12,000 euros per year, compared with 28.5% in the Centre-North.

The same report shows that the South, in the period 2001–2014, had a cumulative growth rate of −9.4% compared with 1.5% in the Centre-North and −1.7% in Greece and +21.4% in Germany. In addition, the collapse of the capital expenditure in Italy has decreased by about 17 billion through 63.7 to 46.7 billion euros. In other words, from 2001 to 2013, spending in the South fell by 9.9 billion euros, rising from 25.7 to 15.8 that is 34.1% of the country's total. (The amount was much lower compared to the programmatic target of 45% set in various planning economic documents.) In conclusion, "the South is now at high risk of industrial desertification, with the consequence that the lack of human, business and finance resources that may prevent a possibile economic recovery of the southern area, transforming the cyclical crisis in a permanent underdevelopment" (SVIMEZ, 2015, p. 12).

The goal of this section is therefore to make a trustworthy analysis of the state of Southern Italian community and in particular of the impact that the smart development can have on communities in the south.

3.1 Strengths and weaknesses of Southern Italy communities: a SWOT analysis

Italian communities are increasingly at the centre of economic and social leadership filled of opportunities and complex challenges.

However, Italian communities, especially those in Southern Italy, show some features that slow down the process of smartness for the following reasons:

1   Marked fragmentation of projects that often present themselves as smart waterproof silos cannot interoperate with each other's solutions
2   Poor planning and high generality of smart solutions at the municipal and extra-municipal level
3   Poor coordination of initiatives with contemporary low rate of reuse and replication of smart solutions

The combination of these factors produces a weakening of the initiatives and solutions not enhancing the specific communities' vocations.

In Table 11.1, thanks to SWOT analysis tools, one can identify the strengths and weaknesses, threats and opportunities of Southern Italian communities, in particular in the environmental, social and cultural domains

As Table 11.1, shows the main strengths are the combination between entrepreneurial dynamism and the widespread existence SME enterprises system and the presence of highly educated young people with enormous untapped potential. Also the natural beauty and the historic cultural identity of the South of Italy is increasingly appreciated. On the other hand, infrastructural gaps and the low level of public–private investments are the main weaknesses that negatively affect the development potential of this region. Additionally, we find a lack of public administration dynamism with bureaucracy and very slow judicial times, which is unanimously considered as one of the main missing preconditions in the Italian "Mezzogiorno".

Among the opportunities, new legislation in terms of procurement and reorganization of local authority systems represents a great occasion for the south of Italy. Equally important will be the opportunity to exploit the Europa2020 program and the growing demand for value-added services. These opportunities are threatened

Table 11.1 SWOT analysis of Southern Italian communities

	Helpful to achieve the objective	**Harmful** to achieve the objective
Internal origin (attributes of the system)	*Strengths* (a) Cultural identities (b) Social cohesion (c) Vivid entrepreneurial activism (d) Resources and natural riches (e) Highly skilled human capital	*Weaknesses* (a) Low level of public–private investment (b) Infrastructural and social gaps (c) High degree of bureaucracy and political instability of local authorities (d) High recourse to judicial disputes (e) Poorly prepared officers in managing complex projects
External origin (attributes of the environment)	*Opportunities* (a) New procurement legislation and reorganization of local authorities system (b) Europe 2020 and Structural Funds (c) Catching up thanks to mature federalism (d) Growing demand of value-added services	*Threats* (a) Crisis of Eastern Europe and the Mediterranean area (b) Widespread diffusion of a shadow economy (c) "Competitive mistrust" (d) Backwardness of training and education system

by a high share of underground economy, the backwardness of the educational system and the persistent crisis of many neighbouring countries surrounding the Mediterranean sea.

3.2 Southern Italy communities as portrayed in the existing rankings

The degree of smartness of Italian communities is measured by dozens of national and international rankings that use different methodologies and degree of detail. However, the multidimensional performance measurement systems adopted by the main international rankings are rather similar with each other and origin from the six dimensions proposed by Giffinger et al. (2007) for defining smart cities.

In particular, we refer to the following three rankings:

1   I-City Rate promoted by Forum PA in collaboration with the National Association of Italian Municipalities (ANCI) and Observatory Smart City
2   The Smart City Index, which is sponsored by a public–private partnership where there are among others Telecom and Agid
3   The European House Ambrosetti, which has been elaborated together with institutional and private partners including Bocconi University

I-City Rate 2014 ranking distinguishes transversely within each of the six dimensions between "standard" and "smart" factors (see Figure 11.1). More than 100 statistical variables and 72 elementary indicators are distributed across six dimensions. Milan, Bologna and Florence lead the rankings, while small cities report a remarkable environmental record. Southern urban areas are far behind in the standings; Cagliari ranks in first place among the capitals in the South in the 60th position of 106 capitals mapped (see Table 11.2).

The Smart City Index 2014 produced by Between (2014) shows a very different structure (see Table 11.3). It identifies 12 main categories with 26 macro areas for a total of over 400 indicators derived from more than 50,000 surveys per year, and maps 116 province capital cities. The Index is divided into three bands according to ranking positions. The first band includes those cities that are placed from the 1st to the 39th place; the second band goes from the 40th to the 78th place, while the third band includes the remaining cities till the 116th place. Among Southern cities, only two (Bari at the 20th place and Napoli at the 33rd) fall within the first band.

Finally, The European House Ambrosetti (2012), in collaboration with Bocconi University, has mapped thirteen Italian metropolitan areas using nine performance indicators that fall within three major areas: Mobility Management, Resource Management, Quality of city life (see Table 11.4). In this ranking Palermo, Napoli and Bari are placed among the worst cities with critical outcomes in all types of analysis performed.

Other organizations such as Pricewaterhouse Cooper, AT Kearney and the Economist Intelligence doesn't map performance cities in Southern Italy, or in any case, these cities are not present in the top 100 European smart cities.

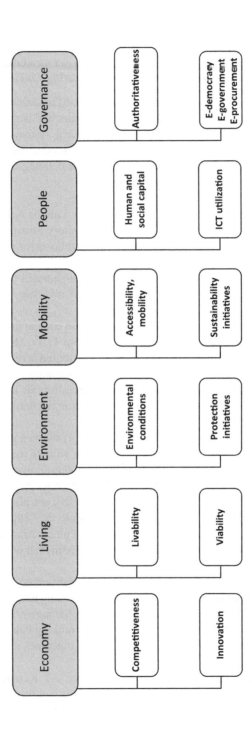

Figure 11.1 I-City Rate dimensions

Source: Forum PA, 2014.

Table 11.2 Smartest cities and top ten Southern cities in 2014 I-City Rate

City	Ranking 2013	Ranking 2014	Standard 2014	Smart 2014
Milano	3	1	7	1
Bologna	2	2	1	2
Firenze	7	3	11	3
Cagliari	47	60	71	45
Pescara	65	62	66	55
L'Aquila	67	64	70	59
Teramo	73	70	68	77
Bari	59	71	78	56
Chieti	66	72	60	88
Sassari	75	74	74	79
Salerno	70	76	80	73
Matera	64	77	76	86
Oristano	93	79	84	82
Napoli	81	80	96	64

Source: Forum PA, 2013 and 2014.

Table 11.3 Smartest cities and top ten Southern Italian cities in the 2014 Smart City Index

Cities	Ranking 2014	Ranking 2013
Bologna	1	1
Torino	2	5
Milano	3	2
Bari	20	17
Napoli	33	50
Lecce	41	36
Catania	43	72
Cagliari	44	40
Palermo	45	64
Foggia	56	49
Sassari	58	66
Potenza	61	34
Matera	63	51

Source: Between 2013 and 2014.

Table 11.4 The European House ranking of Italian metropolitan areas

City	Ranking
Milano	1
Roma	2
Venezia	3
Bolzano	4
Bologna	5
Genova	6
Trieste	7
Torino	8
Palermo	**9**
Napoli	**10**
Verona	11
Firenze	12
Bari	**13**

Source: TEH-Ambrosetti, 2012.

Table 11.5 Suggested interventions along the six dimensions of the smart city

Dimensions		Interventions
Economy	1	Greater competitiveness through increased productivity, encouraging entrepreneurship among young people and women, innovative ways of accessing credit, internationalization
	2	More investment in research and development, no-tax areas (the American model) to boost production of trademarks and patents on an international scale
Living	3	Improvements in living and personal safety conditions, health and social services for the elderly and for children
	4	Essential infrastructural improvement combined with quality of services to ensure efficiency
Environment	5	Mapping of the environmental conditions and sustainable actions for protection of air and water, energy, waste etc.
	6	Huge investments required in smart grid, namely in electrical networks (and others) that integrate, in a smart way, user behaviour and actions
Mobility	7	Necessary improvements and investments in accessibility (area and land) and internal mobility with a focus on the territorial assets policy
	8	Implementation, thanks to ICT, of info-mobility solutions by adjusting fleets and incentive to use public transport for economic and environmental sustainability
People	9	Raising the quality of human capital and student and researcher mobility. Insist also on aspects such as multiculturalism and gender balance with flexibility and fluidity of jobs
	10	Given the socio-demographic characteristics of Southern Italy are required extensive digital literacy policies to allow access to innovative services
Governance	11	Necessary tools, methods and models of e-democracy and e-government in order to ensure participation, recovery of confidence in the institutions with co-design and co-management of works and services
	12	Use of e-procurement practical in order to promote transparency and significant cost savings without neglecting use of Open Data

3.3 Can smart development be implemented in Southern Italy?

The position of Southern cities in national and international rankings allows us to identify what types of projects are helpful in increasing the smartness of the southern communities and what types of tools and investments are necessary to implement (sustainably) smart development in Southern Italy communities along the six dimensions of the smart city (Table 11.5).

4 Best practices and case studies of smart communities in Southern Italy

The goal of this section is to provide a general overview of the initiatives and smart solutions planned and implemented in Southern Italy. Moreover, it includes two case studies that show the liveliness of the initiatives and the importance of smart development for getting the heel of Italy moving again.

4.1 Smart community projects: an overview

The overview on design principles and smart solutions is being carried out thanks to the Italian Smart Cities platform sponsored and realized by ANCI, which collects data on all of the smart projects launched throughout Italy.

Italian Smart Cities then is an operational tool for mapping, collecting and cataloguing projects on smart cities all over the country.

The platform includes just over 1,200 smart projects that involve around 15 million Italian citizens in 117 Italian communes for a total investment of around 4 billion euros.

If we look just at Southern cities it can be seen that the top five cities financed by smart projects are, in order of finance obtained, Bari, Ragusa, L'Aquila, Cagliari and Naples. If emphasis is, on the other hand, placed on the number of implemented projects, the top five changes slightly, and the order becomes Bari, Lecce, Cagliari, Naples and Reggio Calabria.

A more detailed analysis also confirms a trend that is true for all Southern cities and which sees environment and mobility domains far outweighing all other domains for investment. An example is the city of Bari, both as regards the number of projects and investments made.

Figure 11.2 summarizes the domains that have most benefited in terms of financing, from project development in Bari in the last five years.

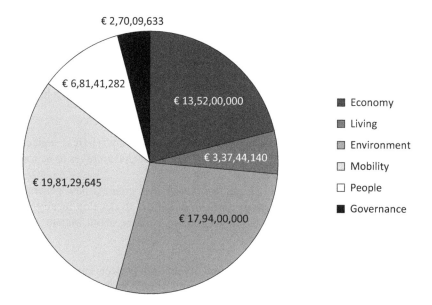

Figure 11.2 Financial amount of development projects in the city of Bari in the last five years

Source: ANCI, 2015 – own elaboration.

A better understanding of their characteristics, rationale and effectiveness can be achieved, however, only through a closer examination. Accordingly, after this brief overview of smart projects in Southern Italian communities, the next two paragraphs will examine two significant case studies:

1   Matera European Capital of Culture: Our analysis will depict how culture and tourism can turn Matera into a smart city.
2   Saving Cost Bonds: We will investigate how innovative financial instruments can help communities to make investments that would be difficult to realize using traditional financial instruments.

4.2 Matera European Capital of Culture

When speaking of Matera, it is impossible not to refer to the fact that the Lucanian capital has been awarded the title of European Capital of Culture (ECOC) for the year 2019. The reasons behind this success can be found on a bundle of key factors that characterize the community of Matera: the presence of highly specialized human capital, the widespread diffusion of ICT solutions strongly based on Open Data and Cloud Computing and the international network that Matera has been able to build up. On the other hand, the active participation of citizens and the high quality of the proposed projects represent the main winning elements of the bid for the title of ECOC.

The ongoing evolution of Matera is intrinsically connected with projects and investments that the city of Matera will implement in the perspective of becoming European Capital of Culture. In particular, all the planning for Matera 2019 is aimed at enhancing its historic-artistic cultural potential and promoting the innovations encompassed in the pursuit of environmental and economic sustainability (Comitato Matera, 2019, 2014). Figure 11.3 shows the main directions that Matera ECOC is taking.

"Open Future", the slogan chosen for the whole Matera 2019 programme, contains fifteen flagship macro-projects (subdivided in their turn into about a hundred subprojects) with two cornerstones:

1   The founding of the demo-ethnic-anthropological Institute (I-Dea), a place in which art and science will meet starting from the shared archives to be found in the region, in Italy and in Europe, and
2   The Open Design school, which, from 2015, will create a new generation of designers with the necessary skills and abilities to develop locally most of the structure and indispensable technology to bring about Matera 2019's programme.

Around these two major initiatives, we find hundreds of projects envisaged by the cultural programme, fifty of which were already present in the candidature dossier. Going on to analyze the system of investments and Matera ECOC's overall budget, one can see that it amounts to around 702 million euros divided into two

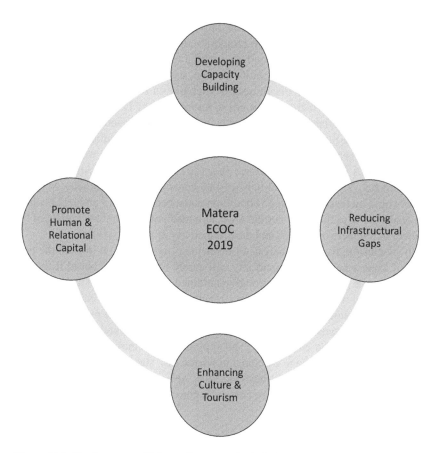

Figure 11.3 The four axes of Matera European Capital of Culture 2019

main categories: operational costs, which come to nearly 52 million euros, dedicated to the cultural programme, and capital investment costs (of almost 50 million euros), for work related to candidature, that is to say infrastructure, transport, urban regeneration, energy, the digital agenda etc.

As for the operational costs, most of the money comes from the public sector (44.7 million euros to be exact, equal to 86%), while it is interesting to note that only 1.5 million come from the European Union (3%) in the form of a prize: 70% of the total resource is dedicated to the cultural programme, 18% is for publicity and marketing and 12% to cover general administration expenses and personal expenses. The total expenditure is spread over a period of nine years, from 2014 to 2022.

Of the almost 650 million euros destined to capital expenditure, 82.4 million euros are to be spent on financing new infrastructure of a cultural character or to the improvement of existing infrastructure, 31 million euros on urban regeneration and 536.5 million euros on public works (constructing a university campus, improving the efficiency of the railway etc.).

The "Studi e Ricerche per il Mezzogiorno" Institute (SRM) has recently estimated what might be the social and economic impact of Matera ECOC through a dedicated survey (SRM, 2015). In its forecast, which is grounded on an analysis of other European capitals of cultures, SRM predicts a 20% growth of the number of visitors in 2019, which corresponds to an increase of 12 million euros of the added value of tourism and 10 million euros of indirect financial benefits. From 2019 onwards, a further increase is predicted in tourism spending (i.e. the additional income generated by each additional presence) in Matera would rise from 79 to 99 euros in the fifth successive year (2023) against Basilicata's 68 euros, Southern Italy's 70.8 euros and Italy's 103.6 euros in 2019. Eventually, Matera's GDP would increase by around 100 million euros between 2019 and 2023, which is equal to 10% of the city's current GDP, as a result of the combined effect of the growth in numbers of tourists and the productivity of tourist services.

In conclusion, from the analysis of investments and potential impact, the process of Matera becoming a smart city will surely move swiftly ahead if the initiatives can be replicated and strongly engrained in the socio-economic context of the city and if these initiatives are strengthened and built on instead of being allowed to fizzle out. The case study also demonstrates that the role of the stakeholders' role is crucial to innovating culture-based services and to achieving the expected goals of the community. The application of innovative approaches to culture and cultural heritage is framed in what cities' stakeholders can do, in line with the conceptualization of "social enhancer" driven by the three dimensions of identity, social cohesion and democracy (Tregua et al., 2015).

4.3 Smart waste and the Saving Cost Bond

During the decade 2004–2013, local authorities' spending fell by a total of 27% (ISTAT, 2014). This has caused a backlog in the provision of infrastructure and a lowering of the quality of local public services that cannot be resolved in the traditional way of resorting to investment, since the overall local finance situation appears to be widely compromised and therefore widely incompatible with a community smartness process. It is therefore necessary to experiment with a range of innovative financial tools and public–private interaction to get investment going again in the smart communities sector. In this regard, the experiment being carried out in Campania, and in particular in Naples, on the management of rubbish appears absolutely novel and pioneering. The issue of waste and plant design in Naples, and more generally in Campania, has been reported in the international press and has become a topical example of the concept of systemic failure (Antonelli, 2011).

The case study seems even more interesting because of the choice of the city government to invest in a difficult sector where change is problematic. In the last two years, the City Council of Naples has repeatedly tried to invite tenders to solve the problem of "closing of the waste cycle", searching for someone or something able to provide waste disposal on site. Eventually, Banca Prossima, which belongs to Intesa San Paolo group, issued the first Italian saving cost bond (SCB) named in Italian as TRIS ("Titolo di riduzione di spesa"). By acquiring this financial derivative, citizens can fund the project through zero-risk bonds that are sold on a secondary market (Figure 11.4).

TRIS will provide the means, thanks to the satellite company of waste management, ASIA, to build an innovative plant that does not combust but rather extracts cold biogas without emitting substances or odours. The structure will be capable of treating around 20,000 tonnes of wet rubbish a year, equal to 30% of the total. The bio-methane produced will be used for local authority consumption or to fuel the fleet of vehicles that collect the rubbish.

The most important aspect, and the origin of the name of the bond, is the significant savings made from the reduction in costs. Currently, ASIA spends 140 euros per tonne for managing the waste collected in other plants, whereas with this type of project and this plant it will spend around 90 euros per tonne, which, considering the volume of collections, will guarantee a savings of around 900,000 euros per year, which will go to finance the underwriters' dividend. The 50 euros per tonne cut in the cost of waste disposal depends on several factors: the innovative pioneering technical project carried out in collaboration with specialized companies, the calculation of costs and time, which represent a considerable improvement over the previous public operation, and finally the speed with which decisions are made and carried out throughout the project.

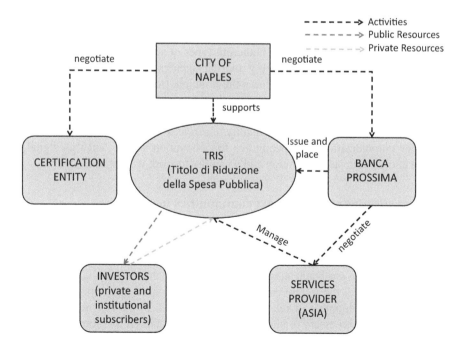

Figure 11.4 The functioning scheme of TRIS

The impact of this operation will be ultimately to do something that is of both practical and social use in the public domain that will have the effect of a reduction in public spending (a yardstick to which the dividend will be linked). That will be performed with the involvement, not only of the companies working in waste disposal, but also of social enterprises that facilitate the employment of disadvantaged individuals (Pasi, 2015).

TRIS thus is the very first Italian prototype of financial engineering to impact on spending, which can be used to address problems of an economic, environmental and institutional nature.

Summing up, the first Italian SCB is noteworthy for the following characteristics:

1   The private investor (private and/or institutional underwriter) contributes at zero risk.
2   The public administration benefits from a sure savings (around 50 euros per tonne in the case of TRIS).
3   The shares/bond will not be floated by the public administration but through a banking institution, Banca Prossima in this instance.
4   It works on reducing public spending by facilitating the process of measuring the socio-economic impact and making a local public service more efficient.

Finally, it seems that tools like the saving cost bond together with ICT-Smart City could have an explosive impact in areas such as health, energy, transport and social housing. The research institute Nomisma estimates that the potential market of SCB in the social sector alone is worth around 30 billion euros from now until 2020.

Thus, SCBs are a tool suited to numerous types of operation in the urban environment capable of creating solidity and management efficiency together with a reduction in costs. It also introduces the principle (too often neglected in Italy and in its towns) of "pay for success", or the payment of investor returns against tangible and particularly measurable results.

Ultimately, smart cities, and the quality of services within them, must combine a clever rationalization of expenditures for innovation actions, such as digital, aimed at the public administration and its ability to work with private sector.

5 Strategic planning for smart communities in 2020 Southern Italy

It appears evident that, in order to face the urgent situation in the South, answers should be formulated in terms of comprehensive economic and strategic policies that favour, on the one hand, an enhanced efficiency in meeting public needs, and, on the other hand, the improvement and consolidation of smart specializations through the development of related-variety industries. In the next few years, it will therefore be necessary to intervene in the labour markets by promoting strategies, investments and active policies that trigger additional demand of skilled labour in emerging industries and by reorganizing education and training to fully exploit human capital and reduce mismatch phenomena.

The logistics and energy sectors are also fundamental for the smart development of Southern regions. The high cost of energy, which is about 20% above the European average, actually penalizes manufacturing production of Southern Italy, in particular small-scale industries. Things are not better in terms of logistics: Southern regions suffer logistics costs 11% above the European average to an equivalent of around 12 billion euros. As a result, the retail distribution of many goods is almost exclusively entrusted to large foreign firms. This bundle of interventions would contribute to the strengthening of pre-conditions of smart specialization in Southern Italy. Alongside them, there is obviously the issue of urban regeneration within the smartening process of Southern communities. Substantially, there are two directions in which private and public entities efforts should be concentrating their efforts and investments:

1   Strengthening institutional capacity building for better use and spending of European structural funds, and that is not all. A recent study realized by the Puglia Institute for Economic and Social Research states that the efficient use of EU Structural Funds would only contribute to a 1% yearly GDP growth in the Southern regions. This means that alongside EU Structural Funds local governments will have to develop new capabilities in the field of innovative financial tools (SCBs are an example), public–private partnerships and innovative public procurement.

2   Setting in motion strategies for sustainable development that promote and enhance the artistic and cultural heritage with projects capable of reviving history and tradition without viewing the concept of smartness as a mere label. On the contrary, technology and ICT should be used as enabling tools for the regeneration and cultural relaunching of Southern communities. It is important to develop new mechanisms for capitalizing on cultural assets and environmental resources and exploiting the induced opportunities for tourism. It would also be profitable to invest in the "social network" paradigm to build ecosystems able to involve companies, public bodies and citizens in "social innovation" paths.

6 Conclusions

In this chapter, we have discussed the actual opportunities for Southern Italian communities to achieve smart development objectives through innovative projects that leverage their internal strengths. Despite the severe and persistent demographic and economic crisis that hit these regions in recent years, and the historical weakness of Italian "Mezzogiorno", interesting improvements are offered by innovative approaches grounded on stakeholder participation and public–private cooperation in the environmental and cultural domain. However, in order to take advantage of locally embedded social and cultural proximities, and grasp the opportunities for smart development, these regions must enjoy the required preconditions for activating concrete manifestations of locally embedded intellectual capital and knowledge not otherwise available. On the other hand, the difficulty of encompassing advanced production factors in a poor infrastructural framework also requires these communities to look for new institutional and organizational tools able to redefine the economic basis of Southern Italy (for instance by broadening the labour supply and breaking the market barriers for individuals that are currently inactive), and increase the overall attractiveness and quality of life of urban areas.

In this respect, two initiatives of Southern Italy's communities are deemed as significant case studies. The former concerns the recourse to a multi-stakeholder approach for increasing the value of a city through cultural programmes in the city of Matera, which has been awarded the title European Capital of Culture in 2019. The latter deals with the public–private interaction aimed at the creation of innovative financial services that has promoted major investments in the field of waste management in the metropolitan area of Naples. Although Southern communities cannot be considered as homogeneous entities, these promising experiences can represent a benchmark for addressing the issue of widespread systemic failures in this region by leveraging on innovative, sustainability-based and multidimensional interventions.

Bibliography

ANCI. (2015), Italian smart cities, accessible at http://italiansmartcity.it/.

Antonelli, G. (2011), Global economic crisis and systemic failure, *Economia Politica*, 28 (3), 403–434.

Between. (2013), Smart city index. Confrontarsi per diventare smart. Report 2013, Milan, Between.

Between. (2014), Smart city index. Confrontarsi per diventare smart. Report 2014, Milan, Between.

Caragliu, A., Del Bo, C. and Nijkamp, P. (2011), Smart cities in Europe, *Journal of Urban Technology*, 18 (2), 65–82.

Comitato Matera. 2019 (2014), *Matera città candidata capitale europea della cultura 2019*, Matera, Antezza Tipografi.

Cooke, P. (2012), The knowledge economy, spillovers, proxmity and specialization, in B.T. Asheim and M.D. Parrilli (eds.), *Interactive learning for innovation. A key driver within clusters and innovation systems*, Basingstoke, Palgrave McMillan, pp. 99–109.

European Commission. (2014), *National/regional innovation strategies for smart specialisation, coehesion policy 2014–2020*, Bruxelles, European Union.

European Commission. (2015a), *Results of the public consultation on the key features of an EU urban agenda*, Bruxelles, European Union.

European Commission. (2015b), *Country report Italy 2015 including an in depth review on the prevention and correction of macroeconomic imbalances*, Bruxelles, European Union.

The European House Ambrosetti. (2012), *Smart Cities in Italia: un'opportunità nello spirit del Rinascimento per una nuova qualità della vita*, Milan, ABB – The European House Ambrosetti.

Farole, T., Rodrìguez-Pose, A. and Storper, M. (2011), Cohesion policy in the European union, growth, geography, institutions, *JCMS: Journal of Common Market Studies*, 49 (5), 1089–1111.

Forum, PA. (2013), *ICity Rate. La classifica delle città intelligenti*, Rome, Forum PA.

Forum, P.A. (2014), *ICity Rate. La classifica delle città intelligenti*, Rome, Forum PA.

Giffinger, R., Fertner, C., Kramar, H., Kalasek, R., Pichler-MilaNović, N., Meijers, E. (2007) *Smart Cities: Ranking of European Medium-Sized Cities*, Centre of Regional Science (SRF), Vienna University of Technology.

ISTAT. (2014), *Conti ed aggregati economici delle Amministrazioni pubbliche*, Rome, ISTAT.

Komninos, N., Schaffers, H. and Pallot, M. (2013), Special issue on smart cities and the future internet in Europe, *Journal of the Knowledge Economy*, 4 (2), 119–134.

Leontidou, L. (1993), Postmodernism and the city: Mediterranean versions, *Urban Studies*, 30 (6), 949–965.

Pasi, G. (2015), Saving cost bond: se la revisione della spesa diventa investimento sociale, *Percorsi di Secondo Welfare*, available at www.secondowelfare.it.

Rodrìguez-Pose, A. and Storper, M. (2006), Better rules or stronger communities? On the social Foundations of institutional change and its economic effects, *Economic Geography*, 82 (1), 1–25.

Storper, M. (1997). *The regional world: Territorial development in a global economy*, New York, Guilford Press.

Studi e Ricerche per il Mezzogiorno. (2015), Matera 2019. L'impatto economico potenziale, Workshop on Matera Capitale della Cultura 2019, 30th June 2015.

Svimez. (2015), *Rapporto sull'economia del Mezzogiorno*, Bologna, Il Mulino.

Tedesco, C. (2012), Urban governance and the "profiles" of Southern Italy cities, in J. Seixas and A. Aòbet (eds.), *Urban governance in Southern Europe*, Farnham, Ashgate, pp. 71–89.

Tregua, M., Amitrano, C. and Bifulco, F. (2015), *Cultural heritage and multi-actors innovation. Evidence from smart cities*. Proceedings of XXVII Sinergie Annual Congress.

12 Smart development in regional economies

The Emilia-Romagna Region in the European frame

Silvano Bertini

1 Introduction

The dramatic shock that affected industrialized economies in the last few years provoked relevant structural changes also in local and regional ecosystems. Even those regions traditionally characterized by strong endogenous dynamism, high competitiveness and high levels of employment suffered huge consequences and needed to undertake intense adjustment processes and efforts for change.

This happened, and it is still happening, also in the Emilia-Romagna region, considered worldwide to be an example of a community able to activate a remarkable experience of local endogenous industrial development, to combine high levels of competitiveness and social cohesion and to activate a wide number of protagonists in the entrepreneurial system.

Having been considered an international case study of success since the end of the '70s, especially in the phase of emergency of the post-fordist industrial economy, it is relevant today to understand how this region reacted during such an external shock and which structural adjustment processes were activated.

It is important to underline that adjustment happened, not only under the context of the long-lasting financial crisis, but also of further important constraints linked to macroeconomic stabilization, competition, system inefficiencies, absence of industrial policy at the national level.

All these elements show that the regional economy is adjusting itself in a very narrow street, a very complicated and unfavourable context. It is possible to say that the main, maybe the only, favourable factor can be individuated, despite all, in the typical "neural" mechanisms consolidated in the past decades in the region: entrepreneurship, social involvement and dialogue, dynamism, attitude to teamworking and networking and clustering. The challenge was to adapt these mechanisms to relevant technological and social changes.

2 From crisis to change

Emilia-Romagna suffered the impact of the international crisis at a larger extent than Italy as a whole (and than most of the other industrialized regions in Italy) for two main reasons.

First, the economy of the region depends very much from its export capacity; Emilia-Romagna is the region with the highest export propensity according to the demographic size. The value of exports is around 37% of GDP, and it is the basic multiplier of the regional economy.

Second, regional exports are strongly concentrated on (or linked to) investment goods and their components or intermediate products, especially industrial and agricultural equipment (near to 50%) or construction components. These goods can be less sensitive to price and currency exchange rates, but they are much more sensitive to demand trends than consumer goods.

As a consequence, a shock on the demand side had a relevant impact on the economy: employment reduction, providers and subcontractors in difficulty, working time and wage reduction. In 2009, real GDP fell of about 4.5%, while the value of exports fell of 23.5%. In both cases the performance was worse than the Italian average.

We can say that those factors normally considered strengths increased the vulnerability of the region. In 2008, before the crisis, unemployment rate in the region was around 3% of the labour force, normally considered a rate near to full employment. Actually, long-term unemployment was only around 0.6%. In a short time, unemployment rate rose to almost 9% of the labour force. This means about 100,000 additional unemployed people of 4.4 million inhabitants and 2.1 million active people (70% of the working-age population). And this impact was even limited by social safety nets for workers.

The recovery of the previous levels of GDP was obtained only in 2013, while for export, already in 2011. The first positive signals in employment appeared only in 2014. It is clear that, both at the single firm and at the ecosystem levels, quantitative recovery was accompanied by changes in the business models and in local relationships. It appears that the secret is in high dynamism, not limited to simple process and product adjustment, but involving immaterial levels at the base of imagination, innovation and reorganization. For a manufacturing system, like the one in Emilia-Romagna, such evolution implies cultural efforts and strong selection processes.

In this new context, the generation of higher value added in the ecosystem seems to be based on the following factors:

1   *Knowledge and technology.* Firms are looking to increase their knowledge networks and technology sources in order to improve their innovative capacity, to provide new original and effective solutions and to diversify products. It is evident that in the last few years firms have made relevant efforts for R&D. The increase of regional share of GDP dedicated to R&D expenditure from 1.1% to 1.63% in a very few years was due only to the firms' component. It is a fact that during the period of crisis firms didn't reduce R&D expenditure and even increased their efforts for innovation. But data on R&D expenditure are not enough to understand the efforts of firms, especially for the smaller ones. Most of this effort is based on the construction of networks, on informal R&D and on quick re-adaptation of

previous results to new solutions. The recovery and increase of previous levels of exports, accordingly to entrepreneurs' declarations, was due for almost 80% to the introduction of new products and models. It is also evident that innovation is increasingly based, not on specific dedicated technologies, but on cross-cutting technologies and interdisciplinary solutions. It can appear a paradox, but this new approach to technology innovation is very suitable for SMEs, since it emphasizes networking and combining different sources of knowledge and doesn't require anymore the big R&D laboratories typical of large firms.

2   *Creativity*. Innovation is not only based on technology but also on the capacity to develop original solutions at a given technology or even to adapt technologies in simple aesthetic dimensions, but also for functional solutions. The region is not considered leading in design, but it has a high concentration of designers; there are more than 5,000, excluding those ones working within manufacturing companies, and they can reinforce a natural attitude of firms to develop dedicated solutions. A second aspect of creativity that is going to be further developed is linked to communication and to human interfaces: computer graphics, creative software, audio-video, wi-fi apps and 3D. Despite relevant progress, in this case, the limited development of the software industry represents a weakness for the regional system.

3   *Social value*. In the last few years, the value of product is determined, not only by its functional use for clients, but also for the advantage of all stakeholders and the community in general. Markets, government rules and people consider very much aspects like environmental sustainability, impact on health and quality of life, accessibility for disable people, information society and simplification of daily life and solidarity. The regional community has a tradition of strong attention to social values; in the past, it was considered a source of additional cost; now firms are increasingly aware that it represents an element of the competitive advantage.

4   Service innovation. Post-production and even after-market phases of value chains are more and more crucial for competitiveness to reinforce fidelity of customers, distributors, communities and institutions. Service innovation regards logistics, distribution, assistance, information, communication, networking, implementation, technical updating and so on. It is a new challenge for many firms, and it represents a barrier especially for SMEs in the region. This weakness depends again especially on the limited use of advanced ICT solutions, but some success cases are gradually coming out.

These are the factors that seem necessary to redesign the regional competitive advantage, for building a smart region and generating new employment. Emilia-Romagna made some progress in the last few years in this direction, but the process is still on going. At the moment, moving from a − to +++, we can estimate the regional position as follows (see Table 12.1).

The creation of a new ecosystem for a smart region is a long-term process that involves all actors, from policy makers, to firms, from social organizations, to individuals. The transformation of the region is an interactive process between

Table 12.1 The position of Emilia-Romagna as a smart region

Knowledge and technology	++	Emilia-Romagna is in the group of "follower" regions in the European Innovation Scoreboard classification.
Creativity	+	The creative sector is weak and little organized, but creative attitude is very strong in any sector.
Social value	+	The feeling for social cohesion, environment, healthcare and assistance is strong, but only in the last few years has been assumed as a source of value by firms.
Service innovation	−	This is the main weakness at the moment, especially due to the firm size and limited application of advanced ICT.

different actors, considering also different levels of awareness, according to the vision of Emilia-Romagna region as a biological ecosystem, with capacity of adaptation. In this sense, it is not a rigid determinism between policies and economic evolution but an interactive evolutionary process and converging strategies and actions.

We can point out some aspects of this ongoing and deep process at the policy, territorial and business levels.

3 Smart specialization strategy (S3) for innovation

The new approach for regional policy strategies is defined, under the new European guidelines, by the smart specialization strategy, which invites regions to focus innovation and development policies on their own knowledge assets and competitive advantages.

Smart specialization implies choosing adequate objectives for reinforcing and renewing the regional industrial system with the support of R&D, starting from industries or from technology resources. Regions should unlock their hidden or actual potentialities, following these main principles:

*   embeddedness (consolidating competitiveness of core sectors);
*   relatedness (promoting diversification through related variety);
*   cross contamination (matching different industries, competencies, technologies); and
*   promoting emerging, knowledge based industries (European Commission, 2012).

The Emilia-Romagna region has approved an S3 strategy focused on four priorities (Regione Emilia-Romagna, 2014b).

1   The first priority is that of reinforcing larger consolidated clusters, typical milestones of the regional economy (mechatronics and automotive, agrifood, construction), exploiting their accumulated knowledge and capacity

to involve several technologies for their modernization and diversification. These vocational systems for Emilia-Romagna are articulated in a mix of subindustries (manufacturing and non-manufacturing) along the value chains or linked to each other by market or technology synergies; they are distributed in the whole regional territory and involve a large number of employees (all together, about 1 million workers of 2.1 million in the whole regional economy). It is difficult to imagine to further increase employment in these activities, but it is crucial to keep present levels and, most of all, to increase added value and competitive advantages.

a   The agri-food system involves around 313,000 employees (more than 16% of regional workforce) distributed in agriculture (80,000), food industries (60,000), chemical and complementary industries (5,400), mechanical engineering (33,500), retail (65,000) restaurants and cafeterias (64,500) and services (2,200). It presents a high degree of specialization and several leaders (often co-operative firms) and popular products at the national and international levels in almost all of its industries (diary, meat, preserves, pasta and cereals, wines and beverages). Agri-food value chains can represent fields of application of a large variety of consolidated and advanced technologies. Very briefly, the strategic objectives are:

   i   Reinforcing innovation capacity and absorbing advanced technologies to better answer new demand exigencies: health, gastronomy, local originality and biological production.
   ii   Better valorizing regional products in the world and increase exports.
   iii Extending value chains to green chemicals and to other convenient destinations for waste or secondary products (pharmaceutics, cosmetics, energy, construction, textiles).

b   The building and construction system suffered the crisis much more than other systems. Nevertheless, it represents a crucial system for the region, not only for the building sector in itself, but for all industries linked to it, especially ceramics, which represents an important regional exporting sector, and finally a unique mix of specialized knowledge and competencies. The construction system counts about 350,000 workers, in which are included construction components (metal, wood, plastic, ceramics, etc., 58,000); mechanical engineering (32,500); the construction sector itself (134,500); public utilities (11,300); retail and real estate agencies (55,000); and architecture, engineering and other services (58,000). The whole system needs shock therapy based on knowledge and a new competitive strategy based on:

   i   intensifying efforts on innovation for upgrading existing buildings through energy efficiency, safety and home automation;
   ii   introducing new concepts for construction and restoration;

iii innovating and diversifying materials toward sustainable solutions; and

iv increasing exports, especially through large integrated projects.

c The mechanical engineering and automotive industries represent the core of the regional industrial system: about 50% of manufacturing employment and 60% of exports. They include several subsectors with several niche leaders and medium sized firms. Main excellences are sport cars, motorcycles, engines and other automotive components; shipbuilding; off shore; industrial automation and robotics; specific industrial equipment (food processing, woodworking, ceramics, industrial logistics, etc.); agriculture machines; oleo-dynamics; earthmoving machines; filtration; elevators; controls and precision instruments; electro-medicals; power technologies; heating; and so on. In total, almost 340,000 workers are employed in such systems, of which 240,000 are in manufacturing, almost 50,000 are in software and engineering, and another 50,000 are in commercial activities. The main strategic need is to remain at the top in terms of quality and specialization and to become more competitive in post-production services. Strategic objectives are:

i diversifying in new product and market niches;

ii quickly developing new solutions based on KETs, especially nanotechnologies, advanced materials, sensors and digital technologies; and

iii adopting new methodologies for approaching the market and providing complementary services.

2 The second priority is that of promoting the development of new industrial vocations in systems with high growth potential and high absorption of young talents in science and technology, in socio-humanistic and even artistic disciplines, in order to promote change and qualified diversification of the regional economy towards new manufacturing, immaterial industries and new business and social models. They have been identified in the health and wellness industries and in the cultural and creative industries. Both of them can also contribute to regenerate traditional industries and typical public activities like welfare and culture, less and less sustainable with public money.

a Health and wellness industries have already a solid base, and they are expanding; they are not yet very strong in pharmaceutics and biotech, but very competitive in biomedical products, medical equipment, prosthetics, wellness and fitness equipment and health and assistance services. The business component of this system counts about 77,000 workers, of which about 14,000 in manufacturing;' 15,000 in trade; and 47,000 in health, assistance and wellness services. In addition, it must be considered that more than 35,000 people work in non-profit organizations and 66,000 in the public health, sanitary and assistance institutions. The strategic objectives in this area are:

i   generating new businesses and new approaches to provide health and sanitary goods and services, also in order to reduce public expenditure, increase efficiency and effectiveness;

ii   exploring new potentialities and new solutions for diagnostics and care of diseases and disabilities; and

iii   improving wellness culture.

a   Cultural and creative industries are still very fragmented and weak, but a lot of young people are strongly interested in such activities, especially in the city of Bologna; without a real business development of such activities and their integration with the rest of the economy, they risk to become a social group of highly educated and underemployed people, or to move to major cities or creative regions in Italy, Europe and the USA. The wide range of activities that can be included count globally 147,000 workers, including also fashion and furniture. The core of the cultural and creative industries are publishing, audio-video, digital communication, arts and culture, entertainment, educational products, design and architecture (about 70,000). People employed in public or non-profit organizations are 7,600. The main objectives of the strategy are:

i   favouring the match between creative, technology and management competencies;

ii   integrating media and diversifying forms of fruition of cultural products and services;

iii   integrating cultural industries with consolidated industries and institutions; and

iv   generating successful start-ups and attracting external firms.

3   Facing big drivers of change: sustainability, quality of people life and social wellness, information and communication society. This priority, in a few words is not industrial, but, let's say, cultural and transversal to all industries. It looks to improve understanding and anticipating crucial social needs and requirements.

a   Sustainable development, green and blue economy: energy efficiency and renewable energy, life cycle assessment, low environment impact, biological and natural products, biodiversity, sustainable tourism

b   Quality of life: healthcare, social assistance, accessibility, wellness, people and social services, quality of urban and rural areas

c   Information society: hybrid products, hybrid technologies, social networking, communication, new business and public services, new organizational models

4   Promoting service innovation. Although two-thirds of economy is based on tertiary activities, it is evident that most of them are widely subordinated

to manufacturing or to the public sector. Most indicators show that the service sector is not very competitive and that most of advanced services are exported by manufacturing industries themselves. The most negative fact is that the service sector, because of its low competitiveness, plays just a small transformative role in modern, smart economies. Even in mostly manufacturing value chains, the service components represent around 50% of added value. The aim of this priority is that of contributing to increase the competitiveness, to favour modernization and to introduce new business models in service industries crucial for regional competitiveness, especially logistics, software and knowledge-intensive services.

In synthesis, the S3 of Emilia-Romagna focuses R&D for competitiveness and growth of five complex industrial systems: three of them traditional and consolidated, to be led to the knowledge economy; two of them essential for new growth pathways for the future. They must be, not only great attractors of technologies, but also promoters of social change and must improve their competitiveness also through service innovation and advanced ICT applications.

3.1 Key technology innovation issues

Once it is established what the key clusters for regional competitiveness are, the second step was to better focus on R&D efforts towards specific industrial needs.

It was elaborated a matrix in which the main matches between all these regional actual and potential clusters and Key Enabling Technologies (KETs, plus digital technologies) were individuated (see Table 12.2). It is clear that there are multidisciplinary linkages between technology and industries. Connecting KETs with industries is the mission of the laboratories of the Regional High Technology Network, developed in the last few years and described later. Such laboratories are not individuated according to specific scientific or technology disciplines but according to their fields of application.

Table 12.2 Key Enabling Technologies (KETs) in Emilia-Romagna

Regional platforms KETs + digital	Mechanics and materials	Agri-food	Building	Life sciences	Energy and environment	ICT
Nanotechnologies	XX	X	X	XX	X	
Advanced materials	XX	X	XX	XX	XX	
Micro-nanoelectronics	XX	X	X	XX	X	XX
Photonics	X	X		X	X	X
Industrial biotechnologies	X	XX	X	X	X	
Advanced production systems	XX	XX	X	X	XX	XX
Digital technologies	XX	XX	X	XX	X	XX

In order to develop a detailed technology agenda (let's say a regional technology forecast), thematic discussion groups were organized in order to share the vision of the main technology issues where to finalize the efforts of research and innovation. In total, about 130 people were involved: researchers, firms, technologists and experts. The result of this work, including an open discussion on the web, after a public workshop, is resumed by Table 12.3, and it represents a relevant effort to design a regional technology forecast, tailored on the regional industrial potential.

Table 12.3 Key technologic issues in the selected thematic areas

Thematic areas	Key technology issues
Agri-food system	
Innovation and sustainability of food products and processes	Sustainable production processes for food industries. Industrial plants and equipment for food industries. Ecodesign, innovative and composite materials, simulation, life cycle assessment. Innovative and sustainable packaging. Compatible and intelligent materials, functional coating, packaging simulation. Food quality and safety. Sensorial and microbiological analysis, thermic impact and energy saving, microbic applications.
Nutrition and health	Functional food, health and nutrition. Optimization of preserving techniques for quality, functional components, biomarkers, personalized diets. Innovative industrial biotechnologies for food. Probiotics, functional ingredients, bio-active additives, bio-based processes.
Smart, integrated and sustainable food value chain	Supply chain management in food industries. Automatic identification, interoperability, logistics and environment impact optimization. Precision and sustainable farming. Innovative genotypes, sensor applications, biomass management. Water management for food industries. Efficiency and re-use, filtration and ultrafiltration through biodegradable nanomaterials and anaerobic membranes. Waste valorization from food processes. Bioconversion of by-products, green chemicals, industrial symbiosis. Smart agro-industry. Data analysis and simulation, ICT applications.
Building and construction system	
Sustainable buildings	Technologies and systems for sustainable buildings. Sustainable and energy efficient building materials with augmented performances and easy demolition, diagnostic techniques, sustainable construction techniques. Functional and sustainable materials. Materials from renewable raw materials, advanced ceramic materials, re-used materials, functional surfaces, geopolymers.

Table 12.3 (Continued)

Thematic areas	Key technology issues
Safety	Evaluation of seismic vulnerability. Methods, monitoring, reinforcement and anti-seismic adjustment, multifunctional construction systems.
	Safety in infrastructure management. Data monitoring and management, intelligent reinforcement systems, flows management.
Restoration, recovery and regeneration	Innovative technologies for building restoring and recovery. Pre-vision non-invasive morphometric technologies.
	Urban mining. Dismantling and reprocessing materials, selection and extraction of materials.
Smart building and cities	Accessibility, comfort, smart automation of living spaces. Integration and inter-operability of home plants and optimization.
	Urban regeneration. Smart buildings and clean energy. Integrated shell-plant solutions, remote control, monitoring of energy consumption, network infrastructure.
Construction and life cycle assessment	Project management. Building information modeling, Augmented reality applications in control.
	Transparency. Open data, business intelligence, digital communication in building.
Mechatronics and automotive	
Human-centred integrated solutions	Advanced design methods. Integrated design, ecodesign, open design and open invention
	Human–machine interaction. Touch and gesture interaction, man–robot co-operation, intrinsic security systems, immersive reality, optic components.
	Advanced maintenance. Smart diagnostics and prognostics, self-maintenance and I-maintenance.
Smart, adaptive, secure solutions	Smart manufacturing. Modularization, simulation, rapid prototyping (design-in-the-loop and hardware-in-the-loop), zero-defeats techniques.
	Manufacturing 2.0: smart products and services, hardware COTS for control systems, post-PLC platforms, open source components, digital manufacturing and social additive manufacturing.
	Autonomous robot systems. Sensors in destructured environments, new actioning concepts, intrinsic secure systems, high-performing materials, energy accumulation systems for heart, air and sea environments.
	Miniaturization. Solutions based on silicon, polymers, biocompatible materials, nanomaterials, microcomponents, micromanufacturing.
	Intelligent transport systems. Innovative and integrated sensors, data fusion, situation awareness, ADAS (Advanced Driver Assistance Systems) and self-driving.

(*Continued*)

Table 12.3 (Continued)

Thematic areas	Key technology issues
Sustainable solutions	Sustainable manufacturing. Efficient and effective solutions, sustainable and energy-saving solutions.
	Systems for generating, storing and distributing energy. Electro-chemical accumulation systems, supercapacitors, KERS, hydrogen systems, simulation and smart grid, cogeneration.
	High-performing materials and surfaces. Micro- and nano- functionalization, intelligent materials.
	Ecological vehicles. Efficient endothermic engines, rational use of energy, innovative systems of propulsion.
Health and wellness industries	
Customized healthcare	Early diagnosis. Biomarkers for diagnosis, prognosis and monitoring, identification and validation of new genomic and protein biomarkers (flow, tissue and genetic), drug testing, biosensors.
	New therapeutic approaches and advanced medicine. Optimization of clinical studies and market readiness, drug screening, nanomedicine, new drugs for rare diseases.
	Regenerative medicine: cell therapies, biomaterials, mixed disposables
	Biomaterials for medical and diagnostic applications.
Independent and active life	Prosthetic and rehabilitation systems. Simulation, prosthetic biosensors, less invasive, patient-oriented prostheses, new materials, medical decision support (MDs) for amputees, prostheses and orthotics for children.
	Telemedicine. Health technology assessment, personal health systems, interoperability, business intelligence for the healthcare system.
Innovation in health processes	Big data. Standards, electronic health files, privacy guarantee systems, decision making systems, mobile applications.
	New therapy applications of biomedical disposables. Blood purification, oxygenation, bioengineering.
	Innovative systems for production of health products. Last-mile health logistics.
Wellness	Healthiness of wellness and sanitary structures. Monitoring and analysis, sanitation and decontamination of air and water in structures.
Cultural and creative industries	
Smart cultural heritage	Technologies for tangible heritage. Acquisition, preservation, monitoring, restoring and maintenance of tangible cultural goods, archiving and digitalization, valorization and fruition systems.
	Technologies for intangible heritage. Acquisition, valorization and restoring through digitalization.
	Interoperability and dematerialization. Semi-automatic extraction, mapping and ontology of data, workflow management.

Table 12.3 (Continued)

Thematic areas	Key technology issues
Creative processes and new business models	Digital production and 3D virtualization. Innovative software interfaces, additive manufacturing, mass customization, home prototyping.
	New business models. Web-based solutions for co-design, virtual living labs, crowdfunding platforms, interactive platforms for creative products.
	Ecosystem services. Knowledge recycling and re-use, use of communication technologies to reduce anthropic impact, remote learning and pervasive communication.
	Materials for creative industries. Light sources, textile materials.
Digital communication and new targets	Digital communication of cultural goods. Management of data and of heterogeneous multimedia, creation of multimedia contents, multilanguage products.
	Technologies for digital natives. Learning, entertainment, media, cultural institutions.

3.2 Policy mix

All these sets of themes of innovation and technology are at the base of research and development measures promoted by the region. Projects are mainly carried out by firms, or those less ready for the market, by research laboratories. In both cases collaboration between firms and laboratories, and, as a consequence, between technicians and researchers, is requested. Firms' projects aim to introduce new products or service to the market, with the support of a research laboratory; projects of laboratories aim to define new technologies, mainly transversal to several industries and to identify possible industrial applications with firms.

But the implementation of the S3 requires other type of measures to increase its effectiveness, especially:

* starting up new innovative firms in the fields of high technology, creativity, service innovation;
* investment and business innovation;
* investment attraction;
* export and internationalization;
* training; and
* integrated tourism promotion, like agri-tourism and gastronomy tourism, cultural tourism, wellness tourism, etc.

By integrating different regional policies and financial sources and further expected national and European resources, and private co-financing, the value of S3 until 2020 is about 2.5 billion euros, and it can be a relevant sum for promoting relevant effects in the regional system.

4 New smart and immaterial infrastructure and networks

The establishment of a new economy based on knowledge and innovation is a long-term process. It can be said that it started in 2002 with the approval of a new law aimed especially at promoting a regional network of structures dedicated to industrial research and to technology transfer, with the scope of establishing systemic linkages between firms and research organizations. This network is today part of the basic infrastructure of the innovation ecosystem of Emilia-Romagna: the Regional High Tech Network (Regione Emilia-Romagna, 2012b).

But technology research is not the only dimension of smart development. We will consider two other emblematic network infrastructures: EmiliaRomagnaStartUp and IncrediBol. As we will see, they are not separate but linked to each other.

4.1 The Regional High Technology Network

As said later, the origin of the Regional High Technology Network was in 2002. Its development didn't follow a linear process. It was quite a new experience for the region, and part of its development was based on a "learning by doing" process. We can even say that its present configuration requires further evolution and new strategic choices by the region and all the other actors involved, basically universities and research organizations.

Before the establishment of the network, relationships between firms and research were based on casual individual relationships and very limited. In the universities there is no formal entity for the so-called "third mission", excluding some external intermediary organization. The law could not reform University organization, but tried to reinforce and design new structures for industrial research and technology transfer. Two types of structures were developed:

- Industrial research laboratories: research units specialized in specific applied research fields aimed at developing new technology solutions, to transfer them to firms, to cooperate with them and answer to their technology needs; laboratories, at present, have the following configurations:
    - research centres within universities or research organizations
    - public–private consortia (or similar)
    - private R&D or research units of firms, after accreditation by the region

- Innovation centres: structures aimed at supporting firms in individuating adequate research partners, understanding their needs, providing various support services for innovation, including funding research. They are normally public–private organizations.

They are complementary organizations. Laboratories must transfer their knowledge and their results; innovation centres must support firms in research and innovation activities. Even if the core of the network is represented by thirty-six laboratories of the main universities and research organizations, there are around a hundred structures included.

In the thirty-six laboratories strongly linked to universities and research organizations there are more than 600 dedicated researchers and about 1,200 other professors and researchers involved. Another 700 researchers and technicians are involved in the other laboratories and innovation centres. It is a community of about 2,500 people.

The laboratories are basically asked to:

• valorize research results for industry;
• developing collaborative research projects, also accessing to further public funds;
• provide technology consultancy;
• give access to laboratory instruments;
• develop, valorize and exploit IPR; and
• generate spin-offs.

The network has no juridical configuration, at the moment. It is simply virtual and coordinated by ASTER, a consortium participated by the region and the main knowledge organizations.

The network is articulated in six thematic platforms dedicated to specific applied research fields:

• advanced mechanical engineering and materials;
• construction;
• food;
• life sciences;
• energy and environment; and
• information and communication technologies.

ASTER's coordination has the scope of promoting and valorizing laboratories with firms, even participating in fair exhibitions or organizing meetings, to promote joint projects and participation to national and European opportunities and to provide facilities for technology transfer. Main instruments developed by the consortium are:

• database laboratory instruments accessible to firms,
• contract models between firms and laboratories,
• a database of experienced researchers available to work for firms,
• a catalogue of research competencies in the network, and
• a technology report on the main results achieved by laboratories.

The network produced several results and changes in the regional ecosystem. Especially, it developed a knowledge community and, in many cases, permanent connections between firms and research units. It still has, in any case, some weaknesses. The most relevant is the lack of institutional solutions in the university system for what concerns the organization of the "third mission" and the recognition of a semi-academic figure (the "industrial researcher"), with possible career mechanisms. Anyway, it represented a basic turning point in the evolution of the regional system.

4.2 EmiliaRomagnaStartup

According to several analyses, Emilia-Romagna is a region with a high rate of generation of spin-offs and innovative start-ups. The support to start-ups was not a policy priority until before the crisis; the region was in a condition of full employment, and the natural process of entrepreneurial natality and mortality could ensure employment maintenance and gradual evolution of the system. Of course, regional policies were not absent, but they let enough space for various local initiatives, normally of little dimension and not great levels of efficiency.

After the crisis, the generation of innovative start-ups assumed greater importance, and beyond the availability of larger funding opportunities, there was the need to create a governance of a fragmented system of incubators and of the variegate panorama of "startuppers".

The creation, again through ASTER, of a web portal (www.emiliaromagna startup.it) was the base to create the start-up community. The portal has the following functions:

- Showing a dynamic map of all incubators, hubs, accelerators and programs aimed at the support of start-up development, indicating locations, available spaces and facilities
- Providing standard business services for all start-ups, especially legal, fiscal, accounting, IPR management, environmental regulation etc.
- Supporting start-ups to contact specialized financial operators in the formal (venture capital) and informal (business angels) markets
- Promoting the creation of networks, partnerships and little clusters between start-ups
- Providing a unique point of visibility for possible investors, partners, finance organizations and consultants
- Providing information about events and opportunities

But the web portal is just part of the community activity. It is the channel to organize animation activities consisting in workshops, seminars, match-making events, meetings with specialized consultants in fields like export and internationalization, investment planning and so on.

There are 336 start-ups registered in the community. Starting from the platforms of the Regional High Technology Network, they are distributed as shown in Table 12.4, matching fields of activity and fields of application. It clearly appears

Table 12.4 Start-ups in Emilia-Romagna by fields of activity and application

Fields of application / Fields of activity	Agri-food	Building	Energy & environment	Mechanics and materials	Life sciences	ICT and creative and cultural industries (CCI)	Others	Total
Agri-food	10	0	0	0	0	1	0	11
Building	0	6	1	0	0	0	0	7
Energy and environment	7	6	18	0	0	0	2	33
Mechanics and materials	1	3	11	16	1	2	3	37
Life sciences	2	0	1	1	24	2	2	32
ICT and CCI	12	5	10	7	3	130	22	189
Others	3	1	3	0	0	2	18	27
Total	35	21	44	24	28	137	47	336

that the distribution is completely different from the typical industrial structure of the region. Digital and creative industries and sustainable activities are dominant in front of consolidated industries.

4.3 Incredibol

Incredibol was originally a simple project promoted by the City of Bologna, capital of the region (and seat of the main organizations in the various fields of creativity), with the scope of supporting and promoting firms and professionals in the creative sectors. It started in 2011. The support is partly from grants and partly from material help, for instance, location in city spaces, training and consultancy and promotion services.

After a very few years, it is a network of private businesses and professionals but also institutions and other organizations involved in the creative movement, step by step extending to the rest of the region. The Region and the City actually agreed to extend the same support scheme to the whole region. At the moment, there are sixty firms, associated freelancers and associations. They belong to various activities (see Table 12.5).

The reinforcement of this network and of connected industries is a priority of the region, and in the next chapter, it will be evident that there are new material opportunities.

5 New physical territorial infrastructure and smart cities

A further element that can contribute to create a smart region is that of physical spaces, as catalyzers for knowledge resources and relationships and the generation of innovation. The realization of such infrastructure is not simply for location. They must change the relationships at the local level and create a new attractive environment, first of all for main cities, which can play a new leading role in this phase. There are three basic physical infrastructures that are going to be realized for reinforcing the innovative function of urban areas: technopoles, smart incubators/accelerators and innovation labs.

Table 12.5 The Incredibol network

Design. Visual and graphic, smell and taste, sound, handicraft, architectural, industrial design	19
Publishing. Services for authors, web publishing	5
Fashion	3
Audio-video. Music, fiction, documentaries, cartoons, radio, TV, web	12
Art	3
Social. Crowdfunding, creative hubs, creative spaces, innovative services, urban regeneration	12
Creative software. Games, makers, innovative services	6

Technopoles are infrastructure dedicated to host industrial research laboratories and to provide facilities for technology transfer and research/industry relationships. They are close, or strongly linked, to universities or research organizations and must link them to firms and to the local community. In technopoles, there are spaces for laboratories of the Regional High Tech Network, other laboratories, facilities for workshops and meetings, spin-offs and private research units. They are not specialized by sector or disciplines; they can be multidisciplinary. Their role is simply to connect and contaminate knowledge and competencies. There are nine technopoles almost completed (some of them with more than one seat). They can be new structures, or sometimes they are located in previous old historical buildings, giving them a new function. There is a project for a great technopole in Bologna, which will be the hub of the network (Regione Emilia-Romagna, 2007).

Smart incubators/accelerators are new networks for making available spaces for developing new projects and business ideas and to make it easier to transform them into firms. They are mostly specialized in the creative economy. They are crucial to creating a new generation of firms especially by young people that need to find collaborative environment and to build their networks. There are thirteen initiatives going to be developed in the major and some minor cities.

Finally, innovation labs are a new initiative still in phase of starting up. Taking experience from the living labs model, widespread over Europe, they are places in which the local community, firms and institutions can be supported in elaborating solutions for various critical aspects of social and economic life, by the means of information society and smart innovation (see Table 12.6). They can be places in

Table 12.6 New smart urban infrastructure

	Technopoles (technologies)	Smart incubators	Innovation labs (not yet approved)
Bologna	Micro-nanotechnologies Energy and environment Automation, sensoristics Life sciences Building engineering ICT – Computing	DAISY – Creative industries LOGISANA – Last-mile health logistics Bologna Design Center	Web economy
Ferrara	Life sciences Water and hearth management Vibroacoustics Architectural restoring	CASERMA VIGILI DEL FUOCO – Creative industries EX MERCATO COPERTO – Creative industries and local excellence products	Sustainable tourism, culture and mobility

(Continued)

Table 12.6 (Continued)

	Technopoles (technologies)	Smart incubators	Innovation labs (not yet approved)
Forlì-Cesena	Aerospace Food ICT	ATR CONTEMPORANEO – Creative industries CESENA LAB – Digital, web and media	Local identity and memory Digital applications
Modena	Automotive, engineering Life sciences ICT Biomaterials	HUB AREA NORD – Creative and digital industries	Arts, music and culture
Parma	Food Life sciences RFID	MILLEPIOPPI – Sustainable and tourism industries	Food, health and culture
Piacenza	Robotics Energy	URBAN HUB – Sustainable and creativity	Mobility and logistics
Ravenna	Shipping technologies Bioenergy Architectural recovery Advanced materials (Faenza)	COLABORA – Cultural and creative industries NIC-NET – Multimedia	To be decided
Reggio Emilia	Mechatronics Home energy Food	TRAIN-ER – Cultural and creative industries	Social innovation
Rimini	Environment Materials for fashion	RIMINI TOURISM VENTURE INCUBATOR – Innovation and tourism	Active wellness

which solutions can be developed quickly, outside bureaucracy, generating effective examples and networking them (Regione Emilia-Romagna, 2014a).

In addition to this, the system of advanced training, beyond universities, must be considered. It is crucial to generate critical competencies for innovation. Some historical training institutes must be valorized in the perspective of smart development, like, for instance, design schools. But the Region reinforced this network with the establishment of a network of Superior Technical Institutes and of support services for new graduates in undertaking projects for start-ups or for innovation projects for selected firms.

6 Clusters, relationships and new business models

The entrepreneurial system is facing evolutionary changes on the base of a consolidated presence of traditional and specialized industries, networks and local clusters and strong territorial linkages.

Traditional local clusters are evolving from simple manufacturing to the knowledge dimension. Local industrial vocations survived, but supply chains are much more complex, partly local, partly much more extended, even at the global level, sometimes for lower production costs, sometimes for quality, specialization and technology levels of components. It seems that the regional distinctive competitive advantage is in the deep and adaptable technical know-how and "know-whom", quick problem-solving capacity, quick learning, attitude to networking and teamwork.

This feature seems to be crucial for firms that need to compete in a dynamic context, in which products and models are constantly renewed and personalized. Firms are more and more concentrated in innovation activities, strongly integrated with the phases of industrialization. Emilia-Romagna seems to be positioned in the global context, and to be attractive, in the areas of producing prototypes, dedicated products, short series and highly qualified products. Firms are increasingly investing in R&D for innovation. ASTER estimates about 4,000 companies constantly or frequently investing in R&D (see Table 12.7).

This evolution also requires establishing new relationships with other specialized firms, with research and competence centres and with knowledge intensive services providers, not always located in the region. Despite the fact that these relationships can be global, it remains in any case necessary to consolidate a regional knowledge and innovation ecosystem. In addition to this, global competition implies also new relationships at the marketing and financial levels, with implications on property and management of firms.

The main phenomena characterizing regional clusters, in terms of relationships and business models, are the following:

1   Increasing penetration of large multinational groups or financial entities like investment funds. In most cases, they are acquisitions of existing successful companies, partly, but increasingly, greenfield or brownfield investments. Some important regional industries, like high-performing cars and other transport means, shipbuilding, agricultural machines, bio-medical products and recently even ceramics, have most of their leaders,

Table 12.7 Firms investing in R&D by S3 priority and system

S3 priorities	S3 systems	Number of firms (*)
Priority 1	Agri-food	1,685 (462)
	Building and construction	1,198 (365)
	Mechatronics and automotive	1,906 (368)
Priority 2	Health and wellness industries	725 (208)
	Cultural and creative industries	1,259 (326)
	Others	398
	TOTAL	3,979

(*) Some companies are present in more than one system; in parenthesis are the numbers of firms that specialize in just one system.

and sometimes specialized SMEs, under extra-regional property. Maintaining and reinforcing attractiveness for such investors is, in this moment, crucial for the region. Investors see strong advantages in highly specialized products; they bring global market networks, finance and organization. We can just mention· Lamborghini and Ducati (Volkswagen-Audi), Ferrari, Maserati, Marelli, VM (FCA), Landini (Argo Tractors), Ferretti Yachts (Shandong Heavy Industries Group), Breda Menarinibus (King Long), Marazzi (Mohawk), Tetrapak, Bellco, Fresenyus Kabi, Sorin and B.Braun.

2   Emergence of local small and medium multinational groups. It is happening in clusters in which there is strong regional leadership, like automation and packaging, machine tools, food industries or wellness. Some of these companies are even cooperative firms. They are strongly concentrated in R&D, engineering and marketing, and they often develop related diversification. They keep their headquarters, core production and research activities in the region. We can mention IMA, GD, SACMI, System, OCME, SCM, Electric80, Jobs, Barilla, Granarolo, Orogel, Valfrutta, Technogym, Rosetti Marino and Micoperi.

3   Growth of dynamic SMEs. Often under strong visionary entrepreneurial management, they are highly specialized, continuously in search of new ways for increasing turnover and profits. Their business models are variegated: some of them emphasize technology and develop multiproduct/multimarket strategies; others are more attentive on increasing value on existing products and developing new solutions. Often they don't have good parameters of efficiency and profitability, since their efforts are concentrated on innovation. Some of them reinforced their specialization through immaterial factors, increasing knowledge, design and service components of their business. Some of them are generating relevant diversification processes, like in aerospace and drone production, in new energy or environment technologies, in green chemicals and in advanced materials; in this way, they increase the level of diversification of clusters, even osmosis and interpenetration between clusters.

4   Emergence of knowledge and creative workers and small firms, still weak in economic terms but strongly motivated in their field of competence. They work in creative software, audio-video, publishing, design, 3D printing, new social services and sustainable tourism.

In this context, it is possible that an agricultural and breeding firm becomes a producer of bioenergy and a strong exporter of hay from Ravenna port to Mediterranean countries, thanks to collaborative research with university for better hay-drying systems or that a company, traditionally producing simple candles, becomes a smell designer for hotels, cars and other public or private places. It can also happen that an engineering company producing machines for ceramic tiles starts producing machines and construction components inspired to bioarchitecture (wood, hemp, corn) or that another mechanical firm gives a start to diversified businesses from environment and energy technology, for packaging equipment or for new light helicopters or that an off-shore company creates a research laboratory on marine technologies and gives a start to a new company for algae-based nutraceutic products.

Knowledge networks seem hard to be formalized; entrepreneurial dynamism moves in multiple directions.

Another phenomenon is a new form of cooperation between medium and large firms, local or not, and local communities. Firms understand the advantage of good relationships and reputation at the local level and invest in training, research and technology transfer (even for apparently different industries) and the generation of start-ups. They develop new locations for these activities, maybe in attractive places in the countryside or in urban centres. We can list the cases of Barilla in food and biotech, Dallara in advanced materials, Technogym in fitness and wellness and Topcon in infomobility. They are developing this experience of so-called "business academies". There is a new perception of the competitive advantage based on knowledge management. It can be developed also promoting different sectors through cross-cutting technologies, through the generation of new business and other forms of contamination.

Local productive systems are changing identification and boundaries. In several cases they are not anymore identified by products, but by concepts. For instance, "wellness valley", "food valley" or "motor valley" don't have a rigid territorial anymore and not even a single sector definition. They involve firms in various manufacturing and service activities, including tourism, cultural heritage organizations and competence centres.

Cluster organizations sometimes emerge not on a territorial base, like aerospace. It doesn't even appear in official statistics, but about forty firms are diversifying from automotive and mechanical components to the aerospace industry. The same is going to happen with electric engines. Not the same seems happening in several cultural, creative and digital industries, in which both firms and clusters organizations are strongly fragmented. Finally, it becomes evident in the presence of knowledge intensive clusters with public and private actors around research infrastructure, like for supercomputing systems in Bologna.

7 Some final considerations

It seems that crisis, domestic constraints, technology opportunities and social changes are stimulating, in Emilia-Romagna, strong attitudes to dynamic competition and innovation within a consolidated and active ecosystem. Despite huge adjustment costs of these years, reasonably it appears that Emilia-Romagna has the possibility to recover employment levels under a changing competitive paradigm.

One positive signal is the elevation of Emilia-Romagna from the "moderate" to the "follower" level in the European Innovation Scoreboard. It is an exceptional case considering the national context. This was due basically to firms that increased their attention and sensitivity to R&D. They represent two-thirds of R&D expenditure.

Some crucial weaknesses still remain. At the business level, there are still delays in management culture and approaches. Firms are facing new challenges, often without adequate awareness and methodologies. Knowledge and design management, additive manufacturing and service innovation are crucial to maximize profits and added value. But there is strong need for innovative management methodologies.

The main areas of resistance in the ecosystem towards the creation of a smart and competitive region are to be found in banks and universities. Banks are strongly reluctant to play the "Schumpeterian" role for innovation and don't even consider it as their institutional task. Universities are still very slow in developing in strategic terms the "third mission", despite increasing demand of R&D services by firms and policy efforts of the region. R&D services have been exported in 2014 for 20 million Euros and imported for 294 million Euros. It is evident that this is the less competitive component of the ecosystem.

Consequently, it is also evident that an adequate reform of universities and public research at the national level is more and more urgent to make regional ecosystems, and the national one, more competitive and efficient.

Bibliography

European Commission. (2010), Unlocking the potential of cultural and creative industries.
European Commission. (2012a), Connecting smart and sustainable growth through smart specialisation.
European Commission. (2012b), Guide to research and innovation strategy for smart specialisation (RIS 3).
European Commission. (2012c), How can cultural and creative industries contribute to economic transformation through smart specialisation?
European Commission. (2013), Smart guide to service innovation.
European Commission and Creative Europe. (2011), A new framework programme for the cultural and creative sectors.
European Commission, Europe. 2020 (2010), A strategy for smart, sustainable and inclusive growth.
European Commission, Horizon. 2020 (2013), The EU framework programme for research and innovation.
Foray, D. (2015), *Smart specialisation – Opportunities and challenges for regional innovation policy*, London, Routledge.
Regione Emilia-Romagna. (2007), ERDF ROP 2007–2013 Emilia-Romagna.
Regione Emilia-Romagna. (2012a), Programma Regionale Triennale per le Attività Produttive 2012–2015.

Regione Emilia-Romagna. (2012b), Programma Regionale per la Ricerca Industriale, l'Innovazione e il Trasferimento Tecnologico, PRRIITT 2012–2015.

Regione Emilia-Romagna. (2014a), ERDF ROP 2014–2020 Emilia-Romagna.

Regione Emilia-Romagna. (2014b), Strategia Regionale di Ricerca e Innovazione per la Specializzazione Intelligente.

13 Smart development in regional economies

The Lombardy Region in the European frame

Armando De Crinito, Marco Baccan, Alina Candu, Enza Cristofaro and Giuseppe Cappiello

1 Introduction

Regione Lombardia understands the smart specialization strategy (S3), not only as a tool to define the new strategy for the future, but also as a gauge of the past choices. In this chapter, first, the regional economic and production context is described as a highly dynamic one, and the results of a SWOT analysis are shown, highlighting the key growth drivers and the path to turn one's own weaknesses into opportunities.

Second, the new vision introduced by S3, the model for selecting the priorities, is described, which consist in new ways of decoding the territorial structure: moving away from a vertical approach, with a perspective on traditional sectors, towards a new horizontal logic based on "systems of competence" (so-called Specialization Areas, or SAs).

Third, in line with the European drivers (social challenges, cross-fertilization, KETs, etc.), we focus on the challenge of Regione Lombardia for the European Programming period 2014–2020, consisting in accelerating the evolutionary process and establishing itself in the market of emerging industries and transformation of the mature industry. It also lunge on specific tools that Lombardia is implementing due to support the establishment of the emerging industries: tools supporting the creation of enabling environments (such as "Cluster Initiative" and Open Innovation Platform) and tools addressed directly to the enterprises, focusing especially on financial instruments, digital growth and pre-commercial public procurement topics.

Fourth, we show how this complex process takes place in parallel with a continuous Entrepreneurial Discovery Process (EDP). Lombardia is beginning to set-up an EDP plant based both on top-down as well as bottom-up approach. The prioritization envisaged by S3 should be the result of an open process through which entrepreneurial actors, from the public and private sector (i.e. companies, research organizations, universities and civil society), would constantly guide the allocation of public resources. Regione Lombardia has applied the process mentioned earlier during the years in different way collaborating with the territorial stakeholders: starts it indeed before the designing phase of the S3. The mechanism for discussion and approval with stakeholders is also described.

Finally, we describe the evaluation and monitoring mechanism that is just one of the relevant elements of a complex research and innovation governance system divided by different processes running or to be still set-up.

2 Regional context – economic and production system

With over 9.9 million residents recorded in 2014, Lombardy is the fourth most-populated region in Europe. Lombardy's gross domestic product, amounting to 33,835.7 Euros per inhabitant (2014), is the fifth largest among European regions. Lombardy's production system is currently one of the most developed in Italy and Europe: at the beginning of 2015, there were approximately 813,000 active firms (compared to some 5,150,000 at the national level), out of which over 99% are micro and small companies,[1] constituting the bases of the regional economy. Manufacturing industry is the leading sector by amount of enterprises and fourth by workforce at a European level. Lombardy's economic eco-system is strongly export-oriented and thus largely exposed to the changes triggered by globalization.

Lombardy's knowledge-based system is extremely articulate; it's specialized in a range of technical-scientific disciplines and includes skills and research groups of international ranking. The knowledge-intensive service industry[2] still has large margins for growth, especially compared to other regions or areas of Europe; the percentage of people employed in Lombardy's knowledge-intensive service industry stands at 32.4% versus London's 67.2% (Eurostat). In Lombardy, there are fourteen academic institutions, which are complemented by a multitude of top-ranking public and private research centres. Thirty-six entities provide business accelerator/incubator services, which have to date helped create over 200 start-ups in Lombardy.

As for foreign investments, Lombardy offers an "Invest in Lombardy" service, providing assistance for international companies planning to set up or expand business in Lombardy, offering a dedicated and professional service at any stage of the project. In 2014, *The Financial Times* published a report "European Cities and Regions of the Future 2014/2015", which places Lombardy first amongst the southern European regions in the number of foreign direct investments, that being a significant improvement compared to the previous edition of the report.

3 Strategy for research and innovation and key growth drivers

A report by the OECD (2012) shows that the Lombard system presents the strengths and weaknesses, as shown in Table. 13.1.

Given the complexity and the wide diversification of the Lombard innovation system, Regione Lombardia intends to **support growth paths** of its own system, not only by aiming to the strengths, but also by turning weaknesses into opportunities, for instance by capitalizing all the different forms of creativity, knowledge and skills within the regional territory and by supporting new globally competitive value chains, capable of accomplishing new market opportunities.

Table 13.1 Strengths and weaknesses of the Lombardia region

Strengths	Weaknesses
High economic production	*High fragmentation* in undercapitalized micro businesses
Strong *diversification* of businesses in the manufacturing and service industries	Tendency towards *"informal" innovation* activities
Strong *relational dynamics* among players in the subcontracting supply chains	*Low turnover rate* of businesses
Widespread presence of *representative organizations*, of deeply rooted production sectors and industrial districts	*Lack of systemic assessment* of business support and development programmes
High *quality of advanced education* and of the private and public research system	*Poor communication* between education, research and production systems
Great *diversification* and wide distribution of industries, particularly in the traditional and modern manufacturing and service fields	

Source: OECD (2012).

Box 13.1   Main growth leverages

- Enhancing synergistic interaction and the **inter-sectoral cooperation** between entrepreneurial and research worlds (districts, clusters, networks, research centres) and across industries, enabling these relations to evolve according to market expectations
- Enhancing the *"demand pull"* approach to intercept the new needs of society and to steer market research (for instance aging population, specialized healthcare. . . .)
- Facilitating the **enabling conditions** to support innovation (in particular **eco and social innovation**)
- Reinforcing the presence on international markets and developing at the same time the capacity to **attract knowledge and investments**
- Planning integrated action in the framework of smart cities, aimed also at increasing the **attractiveness of the Region** by promoting its territorial, environmental and cultural assets.

---

4 Regione Lombardia's priorities

In line with the goals of the "Europe 2020"[3] strategy, and spurred by the fast pace of change in knowledge- and technology-intensive industries and production in the region, Regione Lombardia launched some years ago a strategy built on actions and measures to set up projects and available resources on a handful of priority fields and industries identified as such for their strategic interest or for their potential vis-à-vis the public and private system, specifically on supporting innovation projects in manufacturing.

However, as described in the first chapter, the analysis of the Lombard context shows a dynamic and diversified entrepreneurial and scientific and technological system with excellence in many sectors and fields. Regione Lombardia is aware of the growing difficulty of decoding and governing the changes taking place in the region in order to devise regional policies that address real needs.

There is therefore a strong need to change the way of decoding the Region compared to the past, moving away from a vertical approach, with a perspective on traditional sectors, towards a new horizontal logic based on "systems of competence".

Box 13.2   A new way of decoding the Region

Regione Lombardia, in keeping with the policies implemented over the years, characterized by balanced top-down and bottom-up decisions, has identified, after a period of rationalization, **seven Specialization Areas,** that represent a new radically vision. The Specialization Areas include and well represent a consistent part of the economic and scientific actors situated in the territory and contribute to increasing their leadership in their respective themes.

The Specialization Areas identified so far are as follows:

1   Aerospace
2   Agri-food
3   Green industry
4   Creative and cultural industries
5   Health industries
6   Advanced manufacturing
7   Sustainable mobility

The process of identifying the Specialization Areas in any case requires a continuous and inclusive mechanism always alert to systematically capturing and enhancing new strategic skills.

Changing the way of decoding the Region means, first of all, revising and redefining the competence mapping process. Such a process inevitably implies a transition period towards the new approach that may lead, at an initial phase, to underestimating the potential of the Specialization Areas, particularly in terms of the positioning of the value chain compared to other European regions.

During this phase, in which the Specialization Areas still maintain a significant sectoral connotation, Regione Lombardia can seize the opportunity to facilitate and launch tools and initiatives to support and accelerate this process.

5 Challenges to address: emerging industries

It is widely recognized that the boundaries between traditional industrial sectors are increasingly blurring. As a result, cross-fertilization in the manufacturing and service industries is becoming an important factor to accelerate the process of innovation geared to the emerging needs of the market. Innovation is increasingly driven by the introduction of enabling technologies and of new business and creativity models and by social challenges that the industry needs to address to ensure its competitiveness.

Emerging industries are those industries characterized by high growth rates and great market potentials. They can emerge both in new industrial sectors and in existing industrial sectors that are evolving or merging to engender new industries.

Emerging industries are hard to identify, for the very reason of being emerging, and are clearly recognizable only after a few years, once they have become mature industries. However, it is possible to identify their distinctive and generating factors and to act concretely on these in order to recognize them promptly and support them in an effective way.

A typical example of emerging industry in Europe is given by part of the traditional textile industry that has evolved into a technical textiles industry through the application of textile processes based on new materials in order to meet the needs of advanced manufacturing industries such as aerospace, automotive, biomedical devices, etc.

Box 13.3   The challenge of Regione Lombardia

A system of dynamic, diversified and broad production and scientific skills, crossing the various SAs, such as Regione Lombardia's system, has strong potential for convergence and cross-fertilization, which must be decoded and exploited to accelerate the **evolutionary process and establishment on the market of emerging industries and transformation of the mature industry**.

The challenge that Regione Lombardia faces is therefore to help the production system **seize and intercept new market opportunities** within the SAs through the evolution of their traditional industries into emerging industries, by addressing the needs of the new markets (strengthening the market-driven approach) and helping improve the quality of life of its community (society-driven approach).

In order for the mature industries to evolve into emerging industries, the "smart communities" topic could be a crucial means to intercept new needs by gathering round and aggregating the skills of the Specialization Areas. Among the areas associated with smart communities, emphasis will also be placed on promoting cultural heritage with a view to local attraction (e.g. living labs for the testing of technologies on the ground, such as technologies for security, preservation, traceability and access to cultural heritage) and as a means of energizing the tourism industry and impacting positively on the rest of the production system.

Considering the strong vocation for manufacturing of the Lombard territory, Regione Lombardia has identified the manufacturing industry as the priority for its policies, in keeping with prior policies and could be appreciated also as a driver of the transformation process from mature into emerging industries.

Supporting the manufacturing industry means supporting even the knowledge-intensive service industry, since 11% of manufacturing output goes into the production of goods needed in the creation of services, while occupation in the manufacturing industry generates occupations in services with a ratio of 1:2 (one person employed in manufacturing means two persons employed in the service sector). In particular, Regione Lombardia will support actions having direct or indirect effects on micro, small and medium-sized enterprises, as they make up most of the businesses in Lombardy.

To face the challenges pointed out, Regione Lombardia envisages implementing specific tools and setting up specific lines of action.

6 Tools to be implemented

To support and accelerate the process of establishment of emerging industries, a series of "tools" has been identified supported by specific initiatives. The tools, based on their purpose, can be classified into two categories:

1 Tools supporting the creation of enabling environments for enterprises so they can grow and evolve into emerging industries

    a Clusters and other enterprise aggregations as tools to create enabling environments for the start-up phase and growth of emerging industries
    b Open Innovation, networks and platforms of knowledge sharing in order to stimulate the aggregation of economic and scientific entities and to share best practices, experience, and knowledge (creation of living labs, crowdsourcing environments, etc.)

2 Tools addressed directly to enterprises to facilitate the evolution of the value chain and to develop technologies, products and processes able to meet the new needs of emerging markets

    a Enabling technologies to developed in products and processes that can help innovations make the quantum leap
    b Tools for the dissemination of ICT technologies
    c Tools to stimulate the demand for innovation on specific, functional and performance requirements unmet by the market, such as pre-commercial procurement and public procurement for innovation to stimulate new emerging needs

  d   Tools to promote intersectoral cross-fertilization aimed at stimulating
      the birth of innovations geared to the new market needs (for instance,
      through clusters or open innovation environments)
  e   New forms of collaboration between enterprises, including large ones,
      and research institutions to promote the most effective ways to conduct
      research and innovation activities

Particular attention will be given to clusters and other enterprise aggregations. Through the previously described path, a total of nine Regional Technology Clusters (RTCs) have been created so far in the following areas: agri-food; aerospace; green chemistry; energy, clean tech and sustainable building; intelligent factory; mobility; life sciences; smart communities technology; and living environment technology. According to the principle of full inclusion, Regione Lombardia gives to the local systems the opportunity of aggregating enterprises, research centres and other economic entities in new clusters in strategic fields such as, for example, creative and cultural industries. Regione Lombardia seeks also to turn clusters into effective tools of "soft" governance between the regional territory and the regional administration in order to have trustworthy interlocutors to involve systematically in the planning of regional strategies. In a medium-long term time period, clusters will eventually develop, becoming vigilant sentinels of their specific system of skills. In this process, large enterprises will play an important role as catalysts of skills and attraction of resources, of knowledge and technology with a positive effect on SMEs.

In order to accelerate the growth process of Regional Technology Clusters (RTC), in the 2014–2015 period,[4] Regione Lombardia has planned direct support for the development and enhancement of RCTs, involving also the enlarged regional system, in order to guide the clusters along a structured development path in accordance with best European practices (for example by measuring the growth and development performance of clusters using indicators for "Gold Label" certification by European Cluster Excellence Initiatives[5] [2012]).

An example of RCT governance can be well represented by the Lombardy Aerospace Cluster,[6] which has set up an operational structure that also includes technical and scientific core businesses and universities organized in working groups on fields of interest (for example working groups on research and development to update strategic plans, training, marketing and internationalization).

The Open Innovation tool (networks and platforms of knowledge sharing) will stimulate the aggregation of economic and scientific entities in order to share best practices, experience and knowledge (creation of living labs, crowd-sourcing environments, etc.). Regione Lombardia is launching also in this regard, a pilot project, with ERDF funding (2007–2013 European Community programming period), concerning the creation of a collaborative platform (Open Innovation environment[7]) to integrate an increasing number of "innovation ecosystems" formed of a variety of actors, including large enterprises. This tool will have a start-up and development phase ending by 2015 and will get into full swing in time for the new 2014–2020 programming period.

The model designed by Regione Lombardia, and represented here, links the tools to the S3 challenge – to proceed the evolutionary process into emerging industries (see Figure 13.1).

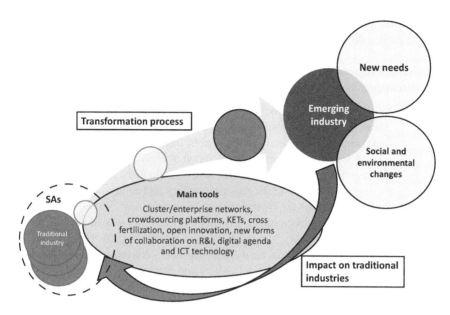

Figure 13.1 The Lombardia model
Source: Regional Resolution 3486/2015.

Regione Lombardia intends to support this process also with the aim of generating indirect effects on the enterprises operating in mature sectors that are not yet ready to embark on this path of change.

7 Lines of action to be set up

A relevant element of Smart Specialization Strategy is the **entrepreneurial discovery process**. The prioritization envisaged by S3 should be the result of an open process through which entrepreneurial actors, from the public and private sector (i.e. companies, research organizations, universities and public society), would constantly guide the allocation of public resources.

Regione Lombardia has applied the process mentioned earlier during the years in different way collaborating jointly with the territorial stakeholders, starting it indeed before the designing phase of the S3.[8]

The roadmap-building process was realized in close collaboration with the regional territory. The entrepreneurial discovery process brings to light confirmations mainly of the strategy that Regione Lombardia intends to pursue in the coming years, intended above all to support an evolution towards emerging industries as golden opportunities for transformation of the entire system. To this day, the EDP is oriented for prioritization applied on emerging industries, considered one of the competitive leverages.

The lines of intervention will propose a number of actions successfully tested in the past and that will be redirected towards the achievement of the new S3 goals. The implementation of the specific actions, the time and methods of their realization will be studied in depth in the Action Plans that makes up the actual Operational Programme.

The path is divided into two parts:

1   Supporting and reinforcing "enabling environments" for enterprises to strengthen innovation governance.

   a   Support to the realization of "major projects" within the Specialization Areas. Support and promotion will be provided for the realization of a limited number of large innovative projects, inspired by the model of Knowledge & Innovation Communities, aimed at connecting the three sides of the knowledge triangle (education, research and innovation) and at having an important impact on the regional territory and on its attractiveness.

   b   Reinforcement of the Open Innovation environment, started in 2013, as an instrument of regional governance for the systematic identification of innovative and technological challenges, which the industrial system can address by applying an ecosystem approach, convey cross-fertilization actions between different technology and production areas and foster an environment conducive to the development of emerging industries.

   c   Development and future reinforcement of RTCs both through internal support activities and support during the exploration of new business opportunities (e.g. analysis of emerging markets, activities aimed at increasing visibility of these clusters at national and international levels, also through the inclusion in extended knowledge networks).

   d   Activities aimed at involving clusters in initiatives at the European level such as technological platforms and the Knowledge Innovation Communities (as "raw materials" and "healthy living and active ageing" and the future "Food4future" and "Added Value Manufacturing") and the participation of the regional territory in projects within Horizon 2020.

2   Interventions addressed directly to enterprises and research system to support the development and transformation of the value chain.

   a   Creation of "pilot plants" or "pilot projects" within the framework of projects identified by Regione Lombardia such as sustainability and social challenges. These pilot plants will act as laboratories promoting know-how, development and application of new priority technologies, especially if enabling the creation of new products and innovative processes by assessing production viability and new business models capable of promoting the innovative potential of Lombard enterprises.

   b   Support and promote innovation by applying the pre-commercial public procurement (PPP) procedure, used to promote the presentation of innovative solutions (including green types) by enterprises. Particular attention will be paid on the projects that provide for development or use of enabling technologies with a high innovation potential.

   c   Actions for the creation of new enterprises focused on social innovation and environmental sustainability, founded by spin-offs, existing businesses and self-entrepreneurship. Attention will also be paid to new companies (newco) established through a corporate restructuring process.

d Complementary actions related to the management aspects of organizational and planning "complexities", to sustain enterprises in the acquisition of advanced services such as, for instance company check-ups, technology audits and strategies, business planning.

e Regione Lombardia has been supporting enterprise networks as an instrument since 2012, and it intends to focus its efforts on encouraging Lombard consortia that create value by exploiting synergies and complementarities among individual businesses that enter domestic and international markets.

f Actions to increase enterprise culture developing synergy also with ongoing training activities to support the growth of enterprises in markets that must satisfy new needs.

8 Mechanisms for discussion and approval with stakeholders

Different mechanisms have been considered.

1 Sharing with regional, national and European stakeholders

   a In defining its strategies, Regione Lombardia has always maintained a constant and fruitful dialogue both internally, among the various Directorates-General, with national institutions (Ministries, Departments, Agencies, other regions) as well as with European institutions (other European regions, European Commission, Joint Research Centre S3 platform, etc.), creating recurring opportunities to gather, discuss and align to the strategies.

2 Sharing with the regional territory – Working Groups (WG)

   a The process of defining the regional strategy is in keeping with a process of self-discovery of the regional territory's potential and the technological potential that the Region can develop in the international context. Next to consolidated methods used by the Region to share its decisions with the regional territory (Development Pact), new tools have been added, such as the Working Group on RTC and the Working Group of Industry and Innovation Experts, created to share the challenges that Regione Lombardia intends to address, and to bring out needs, through a qualified and continuous process of entrepreneurial discovery, and meet them through the effective regional actions.

3 Sharing with the regional territory – Public consultation

   a In order to involve citizens and other subjects that could contribute to the definition or sharing of decisions, Regione Lombardia organized, on the 25th July 2013, the event named "Stati Generali: Ricerca e Innovazione" with the aim of starting a dialogue and a discussion with qualified and institutional actors at the European Community, national and regional level on the activities promoted by Regione Lombardia on research and innovation themes of the past. The event marked the start of a public consultation process (through an online questionnaire) on themes related to the smart specialization strategy to involve the community in regional decisions, in the context of the quadruple helix model. The purpose was to gather feedback and new ideas on research and innovation to improve regional policies (the new ROP ERDF/ESF/EAFRD) vis-à-vis Europe 2020.

4   Outward-looking process

a   In order to plan a proper outward-looking process, in addition to the attendance of various meetings with foreign regions organized by the Joint Research Centre (JRC) platform of Seville, and with Italian regions organized by the Italian Ministry for Economic Development and the Ministry for Education, University and Research, Regione Lombardia has opened a direct dialogue with other public administrations. For instance, Regione Lombardia organized a meeting open to Italian regions with the aim of gathering ideas and/or proposals, comparing the experiences to explore in the context of the ongoing work on smart strategies. Moreover, Regione Lombardia organized a dialogue with foreign regions within the network of the 4 Motors for Europe, focused on the discussion on S3 themes among the 4 regions in the network, also a dialogue within "Vanguard Initiative New Growth by Smart Specialization", etc (Vanguard Initiative, 2013).

9 Financial instruments

With the new 2012 Financial Regulations, financial instruments are defined as EU measures of financial support to achieve one or more specific strategic objectives of the European Union. These tools may take the form of equity or quasi-equity investments, loans or guarantees or other forms of risk sharing and may even be associated with grants if necessary.

This definition outlines the context within which Regione Lombardia is called to compete in order to exploit all the potentialities of the use of financial instruments.

Indeed, Regione Lombardia is aware that, in addition to ensuring greater revolving and additionality of the resources available, effectively planned financial instruments underpin the most significant results pertinent to EC programming, such as achieving sustainability of actions, objectively verifiable in the medium to long term, leveraging the effect of competences deriving from the coming together of different public and private professional skills, required for operating under the same conditions of sub-optimal or "quasi-market" investment.

Over the years, Regione Lombardia has developed high levels of expertise in the preparation and implementation of use of financial instruments for research and innovation, as part of a clear process of integration and complementarity of regional and community planning, encouraging shared methodologies, content and strategy over time, nurturing and reinforcing a continuous path of "capacity building".

In the light of the current economic situation and of the increasing contraction of public resources, the European Commission itself stresses the importance of extending and reinforcing the use of financial instruments as a more efficient and sustainable alternative to traditional funding based on subsidies, thanks to:

1 a greater flexibility in responding to specific market needs effectively and efficiently and in promoting a significant participation of financial institutions and private investors based on adequate risk-sharing;
2 a diversified structuring to better approach the financing needs of the receivers (enterprises, individuals, local authorities, etc.) based on the identification of market failures and therefore supporting the most disadvantaged areas and sectors;
3 a greater simplification;
4 a systematic transversality and complementarity both within 2014–2020 European Structural and Investment Funds and at a general level in connection with all relevant public policies (policies acting in synergy with other financial instruments such as the EIB and/or that can be activated in the 2014–2020 cycle as part of community programmes under direct EU management such as Horizon 2020, COSME, etc.

On the strength of the experience acquired, Regione Lombardia intends to continue along the path it has taken in recent years, also with reference to European Structural and Investment Funds 2014–2020 planning, so as to increase further financial resources in aid of the Region, involving, on one hand, a larger number of private co-financiers and, on the other, those willing to make the most of the contributions received as loans or other forms of financial instruments.

Box 13.4   Guidelines for proposing new financial instruments

1 Gradual replacement of sunk fund logic and dissemination of **transversal board financial instruments**
2 Rationalization of the instruments portfolio activated in the past by creating a **critical mass of resources**
3 **Innovative methods for developing a course of planning** and implementation for financial instruments, through criteria for gradualness,

simplification, standardization and flexibility, that can also be extended at the national and/or interregional levels, able to change the financial market's mindset to the "quasi-market"

4   Expansion of **additionality** through the activation of new funding resources and new channels

5   **Multiplier effect** given by joint leverage and revolving actions that financial instruments are able to bring about.

In the coming years, special attention will be paid to instruments in support of research and innovation policies, and in particular to:

1   the support and promotion of the aggregation of enterprises and research centres in the context of Specialization Areas identified through the involvement of RTCs;

2   the enhancement of infrastructure assets and of the ability to develop excellence;

3   the promotion of investments by enterprises (also in collaboration with large enterprises and research organizations);

4   the support demand of innovation; and

5   the support for the creation of innovative enterprises, by exploring and strengthening risky capital markets through involvement of institutional investors such as venture capitalists and also by involving informal investors (for instance Business Angels and crowdfunding platforms).

The opportunity, given by Financial Regulation, to combine financial instruments with traditional grants, will allow for actions to accompany key players, first and foremost enterprises, providing support with vouchers for training and consulting services, patenting assistance, etc., allowing the creation of a subsidiary framework within which the effect and impact of the actions triggered by regional financial instruments may be maximized.

10 Digital growth in smart specialization

Digital growth represents economic and therefore employment development that originates from a greater and better diffusion of the Internet and from an increasingly pervasive use of next-generation technologies, which play an increasingly important role in social and economic life, as well as being an integral part of the economy to the benefit of all sectors, both public and private.

The smart use of ICT technologies to stimulate demand and the consequent supply of private and public services, and innovative processes, is a prerequisite for achieving any smart specialization for Lombardy. It is therefore necessary to consider ICT technologies and their dissemination as enabling conditions for the efficiency of public administrations, business innovation and quality of life for the community but also as key elements for the transformation of production processes.

The tools available for the enhancement of digital growth in Lombardy, starting from areas of intense specialization, are the Agenda Digitale Lombarda and the regional strategy to support smart communities.

At the end of 2011, Regione Lombardia was the first Italian region to start a process for the simplification and modernization of the Region's system, also based on an analysis of future developments in the field of new technologies, innovation and digitization, which led to the new *Agenda Digitale Lombarda 2014–2018* (Agenda Digitale Regione Lombardia, 2011)[9] that intends to contribute to restoring competitiveness of economic and social growth. Regione Lombardia will drive innovation for its production system, contributing to the development of initiatives integrated in the context of smart communities, recognized as a crucial strategic driver to stimulate the creation of emerging industries, and the use of ICT technologies in businesses related to previously identified specialization areas.

Specific initiatives are envisaged for the dissemination of ICT technologies in different specialization areas identified, for example, by creating synergies with the Specialization Area for "cultural and creative industries" that may represent both a fruitful system of industrial and technological skills and a strategic driver for steering the production system towards emerging markets.

In this context, there will also be support for schemes that aim to realize digital ecosystems in different theme areas, including info-mobility, food excellence, healthcare, attractiveness, culture and entertainment, which may provide information, services and applications to the end user in an integrated way (open services), while setting the conditions for the creation and development of smart cities and communities.

For example, it is possible to envisage the realization of online services to foster sponsoring (for example with possible crowd-funding schemes) for the cultural and creative sector, of on-line services for the promotion of product/service ideas at international level, encouraging interaction with traditional sectors with a view to open innovation.

11 Public procurement of innovation

Public procurement of innovation in R&D services is a means by which public demand can become a stimulus for market innovation, thus contributing to the development of a strategy for enterprise growth and competitiveness.

1   Public procurement for innovative solutions

Regione Lombardia has started a policy of promoting public demand for innovation capable of optimizing public spending, with the aim of raising the quality and sustainability of public services and at the same time of promoting additional private sector investments in innovation. First Region in Italy, Lombardy decided to forsake the role of mere "funder" of innovation to become the "smart customer" and "co-innovator", able to impact R&D plans by enterprises and thereby guide them towards satisfying real public interest.

The public procurement for innovative solutions[10] was recently applied to increase the circulation of the *Carta Regionale dei Servizi (CRS)*, a smart card with multiple functions that can access both traditional and on-line public administration services, containing a private key that ensures recognition of identity while safeguarding privacy.

2   Pre-commercial public procurement

Pre-commercial public procurement is considered by Regione Lombardia a tool to create the so-called "market competition" to foster the advance of enterprises or other innovative economic entities, placing them in a competitive situation before, during and after R&D activities, limiting cases of natural or legal monopoly.

With pre-commercial public procurement, Regione Lombardia aims, in particular, to stimulate innovation by requesting a number of economic entities to develop innovative solutions, starting from the concept behind the original development of a limited volume of first products or services in the form of a test series. At the same time, the enterprises are allowed to develop better products by virtue of a better understanding of demand and, therefore, reducing time-to-market. The first pilot project was developed in the field of healthcare, and it concerns automated devices for moving beds and stretchers.

Sectors in which the public procurement of innovation can be applied include health, water, sustainable building, energy and environment, transport, ICTs and culture.

12 Evaluation and monitoring mechanisms

The importance of analyzing the results and impacts of public investment in research and innovation is linked both to spreading a culture of the public entity's accountability towards the community and of value for money, namely the social and economic value of public investment.

Review of monitoring and evaluation of regional initiatives, even before defining performance indicators, shall start with careful examination of project evaluation mechanisms, at all stages in which this takes place: before, during and after.

Moreover, Regione Lombardia previously put in place discussion and approval mechanisms within the Region itself, with relevant ministerial bodies and the European Commission. In the smart specialization strategy, the intention is to integrate the existing, reinforced system, with new instruments of dialogue and interaction, to enable Regione Lombardia to approach and "listen" more closely to the community.

The main goals are, on the one hand, to provide a larger number of subjects, in a clear and transparent manner and in a "quadruple helix" perspective, with the results obtained by regional initiatives and exploiting the best and, on the other, to gather from the community comments, observations, suggestions for improvement and modification, all to be considered in the review process.

The consulting and approval system can be formed, for instance, by the specific working groups of the clusters who have already contributed to the process of defining the smart specialization strategy.

Another important tool for dialogue and governance of innovation will be represented by the Open Innovation environment,[11] a wide and complex relational environment involving public and private economic actors operating in the innovation system in which ample space will be dedicated to the sharing of results, using suitable IT applications (forums, online questionnaires, communities, etc.) at the end of a systematic and ongoing public consultation of regional initiatives.

The process of analysis and comprehensive review, performed at least once a year, involving the various actions undertaken and a summary of the critical issues identified in a broad vision vis-à-vis the accomplishment of the goals of the specialization strategy, will be governed by Regione Lombardia through the extended regional support system.

This process will become integrated with the process that Regione Lombardia already implements, in accordance with regulatory, monitoring and evaluation constraints of the Operational Programmes in the context of 2014–2020 cohesion policies.

The governance of the S3 monitoring, evaluation and review process will be aligned and will comply with that defined in 2014–2020 Operational Programmes and will be built through "Impact Evaluation and Action plan monitoring", "Knowledge generation" and "Policy learning" processes.

13 Conclusions

In a dynamic, continuous evolution of social challenges and innovative solutions context, it becomes increasingly complex to read and govern the changes taking place in order to design policies to the real needs of the regional territory.

"Smart Specialization" is a major innovation in regional industrial policy, through which it emphasizes and affirms the principle of priorities no longer tied to a traditional vision for industrial sectors but based on a logic of selectivity and concentration of interventions on specific technologies to support specific sectoral areas or new higher-value-added markets.

The "ex-ante conditionality" for ERDF becames an opportunity for Regione Lombardia to "test" concretely new paths of development of the regional territory. It made an important cultural leap in creating a governance system that could be able to seize new opportunities as they emerge from the regional territory, turning them into priorities and then translating them into actions that could evolve the regional economy while also triggering structural changes.

Indeed, the governance system consists mostly in two key activities (direct actions meaning the S3 apart): vertical and horizontal coordination. Vertical coordination is focused on comparison at the national and European levels, and horizontal coordination is addressed inward: Regione Lombardia between different Directorates-General, ERDF and ESF Managing Authority, etc. Thus, the Lombardia Region can support smart development in an economic environment.

Each change requires multiple new tools but also the revival of some existing ones. It is essential to have access to tools that can focus and integrate knowledge distributed on the regional territory, which make up the regional innovation ecosystem as universities, laboratories, end-users, innovative start-ups and small and medium-sized enterprises. For Regione Lombardia, some of them are Lombard Technological Clusters, an expert panel with experts from industry and from academic world, which is going to complete and integrate the first instrument, and the Open Innovation Platform, which is complementing and strengthening the "Entrepreneurial Discovery" Process. It is an instrument of dialogue that consists of the large and complex environment of relationships between public and private economic actors in the innovation system and that represents a real "laboratory" to discover new value chains starting from the real needs of a constantly evolving market.

Notes

1 Definition by EU recommendation 2003/361, with the following main factors: staff headcount, turnover or balance sheet total (medium-sized: staff headcount < 250, turnover ≤ euros50 m, balance sheet total ≤ euros43 m; small: < 50, ≤ euros10 m, ≤ euros10 m; micro: < 10, ≤ euros2 m, ≤ euros2 m).

2 Eurostat Glossary, Knowledge-intensive-services: NACE – High-tech, knowledge-intensive services; Knowledge-intensive market services (excluding financial intermediation and high-tech services); Knowledge-intensive financial services; Other knowledge-intensive services.

3 Europe 2020 is the European Union's ten-year growth strategy. It consists of seven flagship initiatives providing a framework through which the EU and national authorities mutually reinforce their efforts in areas supporting the Europe 2020 priorities such as innovation, the digital economy, employment, youth, industrial policy, poverty and resource efficiency. Regarding innovation in particular, Europe 2020 sees an increase in R&D investment to reach 3% of GDP and, regarding education, an increase to 40% of the population aged 30–34 having completed tertiary education.

4 DGR n. X/707 of the 20th September 2013: Regione Lombardia resolves to allocate an overall amount of euros1,000,000.00 to support the complementary and/or functional activities for the development and enhancement of RTCs.

5 European Cluster Excellence Initiatives are fostered by the European Commission (DG Enterprise and Industry) in order to develop methods and tools to support cluster organizations in improving their ability to manage networks and clusters.

6 www.aerospacelombardia.it.

7 See DCR n. X/733 of 27/09/2013, *Amendments and additions to the guidelines implementing axis 1 of the ROP ERDF 2007–2013. Outline of the 1.2.1.1. line of action "Development of information networks and systems for the dissemination and sharing of information and services among SMEs, among SMEs and research system, and among SMEs and the PA."*

8 For example a dual approach (top-down and bottom-up) was applied during the regional call for proposal "High Technology Districts (DAT)" realized for R&I collaborative projects with the participation of the companies, large and SMEs, research organizations, universities, etc. This measure was also the starting point for the foundation of the RTCs.

9 Contemplated by Regional Law 7/2012 "Measures for development, growth and occupation".

10 See DGR n. IX/2379 del 20/10/2011, *Activation of the procedural path for the awarding of pre-commercial procurement or procurement for innovation of research and development service by Regione Lombardia, on certain strategic themes, aimed at the development of innovative products for use in strategic and priority areas.*

11 See DCR n. X/733 of 27/09/2013, *Amendments and additions to the guidelines implementing axis 1 of the ROP ERDF 2007–2013. Outline of the 1.2.1.1. line of action "Development of information networks and systems for the dissemination and sharing of information and services among SMEs, among SMEs and research system, and among SMEs and the PA."*

Bibliography

Agenda Digitale Regione Lombardia, Trend Analysis, Regione Lombardia and Lombardia Informatica, Milano.

OECD. (2012), *Boosting local entrepreneurship and enterprise creation in Lombardy region (Italy)*, Paris, OECD.

Vanguard Initiative. (2013), New growth by smart specialization. Engagement for the future of industry in Europe, Paperback, Dirk Van Melkebeke, Secretary-General Department EWI Editor, Brussels.

Part III

Governing smart local development

14 Government and governance for smart development in smart communities

Gilberto Antonelli and Nicola De Liso

1 Introduction

Policy, together with polity and politics,[1] is at centre stage of the debate on smart development[2] and smart communities.[3] Being conceived as an intentional action put forward by one or more of the governing bodies operating at a certain level, policy is crucial for implementing new strategies. Governing bodies of any aggregate – like a country, a city, a firm – are constantly concerned with forward-looking perspectives, forecasting and assessing, that is with policy.[4] Even the choice of leaving things as they are is, usually, the result of intentionality.

Globalization has heightened the awareness of the need to keep up with competitors, and we speak of competition between nations, regions, cities, firms and individuals.

Limiting ourselves for a moment to the first three items, more and more emphasis has been on being "attractive": to attract investments, to attract firms, to attract educated people and so on. Thus, a lot of attention has been devoted to explicitly analyze one's institutional architecture in order to undertake those changes that are deemed necessary to reach the desired goal.

The underlying idea is – one is tempted to say, obviously – that we identify some objectives that we want to achieve and act accordingly. Reality shows that objectives can be not as clear, may be difficult or impossible to achieve, that trade-offs are always present and that actions are imperfect both in the private and the public sector and can backfire. A macro-economic example can make immediately clear the difficulties that are incurred when one has to conceive and implement some policy: a look at the long world economic recession that started in 2007, and which we do not know exactly in early 2016 whether is over, ought to make us reflect on our capabilities to understand phenomena, setting targets and acting accordingly.

Reasoning at the meso-economic scale of cities or metropolitan areas does not necessarily imply that things are easier. The quantity and quality of variables to be taken into account is extremely variegated, while local environments are never really "local": that is local environments are always interconnected with larger and international ones. About the latter point, the presence of an airport illustrates the point in that all the levels of government and regulation are involved – from worldwide air traffic control regulations, to safety, to the many services that are necessary to the airport itself, many of which are regulated and supplied at the local level.

When official papers and reports on smart specialization, smart cities and smart communities deal with government's goals, the latter look in general well defined and the task to actually manage them straightforward. For instance, we read, "[C]ities should be places of advanced social progress and environmental regeneration, as well as places of attraction and engines of economic growth based on a holistic integrated approach in which all aspects of sustainability are taken into account" (European Commission, 2012a).

However, when we get closer to the actual implementation of the new policies and strategies, quite a few problems arise. First of all, in the last five years or so, it became increasingly clear that the smart label can cover many areas; most of them are correlated and sometimes overlapping. Each actor, and among the others, European Union, municipalities, corporations, contributes to shape industry, cities and communities. The role of public policy and public administration is recognized as crucial in providing a framework of opportunities and constraints for determining socio-economic development.

Second, although national and local governments play an important role in local economic development, several groups and organizations[5] are involved, and they have to play a role in each strategy.

These features, by themselves, contribute to increasing the complexity of finding positive solutions. But, in third place, we are well aware that this complexity is augmented also by the fact that often the goods and services produced and exchanged in the sectors mostly concerned are not purely private goods. As we argued in Chapter 6, social goods are at the core of the transformation paths and, given the fact that markets are efficient allocation mechanisms only for pure private goods, in a relevant part of the economy – central in our frame – a coordination mechanism of a different sort is strongly needed.

Fourth, recent and less recent economic history suggests that not only at the micro level[6] but also at the macro and meso levels risks and failures are ordinary events. Unfortunately, even representative democracy contributes in making bulky and costly the application of a guiding principle that appears straightforward: "we must know in order to decide".[7]

As we have learned through experience, this is true for all levels of government – local, national, supra-national and sectorial.[8] But also markets can fail both at the sectorial, local, national and global level. Moreover, as in the case of the global economic crisis just mentioned, they can fail simultaneously.[9] On top, networks and clusters can fail as well, and this implies that partnerships can fail too.[10]

Of course, failures foster conflict that is embedded in social interactions, and inequality can be amplified by strong diversity in the economic and social impact of different capabilities to implement smartness. As a consequence, under these circumstances, we cannot assume perfect rationality and optimal behaviours both in the public sector and in the private one. This suggests taking care of resilience in political strategy.[11]

In this book, some of the key platforms that the core actors can and should rally in fulfilling their strategies for smart development have been identified. A first crucial platform relates to the capability to adopt new procedures for data collecting and processing in production and consumption activities. Many decisions crucially depend on data availability and information must be reliable. Nowadays the available tools allow governing bodies to monitor and manage loads of variables, on the side of production as well as consumption, concerning several kinds of flows of goods and services, from electricity to mobility,[12] from finance to education, from housing to food, from potable water piped into networks to waste disposal and many others. An example of application of this capability is what has been called the "sharing economy". In this case, network technologies can mitigate markets imperfections or failures through a solution that implies "commons-based peer production".[13] Yet disruptive effects take place in the industries concerned, but these should be smoothed through new forms of regulation as well as prior planning of structural change.[14]

Another key platform has been identified in a true capability to innovate simultaneously at different levels, both through incremental and radical innovation. This capability can be reached when a full recognition of disruptive effects, failures and opportunity costs of innovation processes is on hand. Different types of knowledge are relevant drivers in this respect: knowledge of technological opportunities, scientific knowledge of the regulatory framework, creation of new knowledge. In this regard, there is room for the typical debate on the role of the public sector in providing incentives and disincentives for an appropriate economic organization of knowledge within and outside the firms. The creation and use of different types of knowledge is a multi-dimensional phenomenon that covers all the domains we have referred to. In addition, knowledge is characterized by a series of interactions that embrace scientific, technological and economic fields. Meanwhile it is related to the demand for satisfying widespread social needs. We need to combine the smartness defined in the document issued by the European Commission (2012b) – in which cities must be places of progress where all aspects of sustainability are taken into account – with the opportunities that emerge from new modes of knowledge production.

A third platform relates to the capability to forecast and implement a provision of human capital satisfying investments as well as consumption needs, for individual agents and for the community as a whole, both on the side of the demand for and the supply of labour.

But, since human capital can be considered as a necessary, but not sufficient, condition for human development and since the latter is crucial in smart development for reaching cohesion and sustainability, the capability to forecast and implement a satisfactory provision of human capital has to be coupled with that of forecasting and implementing the formation of an adequate amount of social capital in smart communities, through a dedicated fourth platform.

Finally, the sector of public utilities can turn into engines able to serve, albeit in a selective way, all the four platforms. This sector is already playing an increasingly important role in the economy, due to the quantitative and qualitative performances of its leading groups. Nevertheless, multi-utilities may become strategic brokers for local systems in which they operate. In particular, they can set in motion new innovative processes able to drive the potential of the new technological infrastructures towards the delivery of new and more effective services thanks to their experience in providing incentives for citizens' involvement and in assessing their needs.

However, having said this, we need to recognize that strategies for smart development face a huge and complex problem: how can it be possible to attain the relevant capabilities and mastering all these platforms together when starting from such a disarming state of affairs concerning policy limits?

We suggest a positive answer to this question in Section 3, while being aware of the complexity of the task and trying to do our best for not simplifying it too much.

The nodal points that we are going to discuss, however briefly, in this chapter are the ones that ought to open the way to smart development in smart communities. The selection of these points might at first sight seem rather idiosyncratic, but they simply reflect the complexity of our societies. The first point to be investigated concerns the role of knowledge and technology – about the latter, we will focus on ICTs.

The second point has to do with the meaning of government and governance as it has evolved in recent decades and may serve for answering our question. These items open the way to a better understanding of what are in terms of policy action the implications for smart development and smart community. Therefore, in third place, we look at the way smart development can be governed through smart communities. Fourth, we focus on the critical role of the public administration and put forward some idea on the facilitation role that selected multi-utilities can play at the local level. The chapter will be concluded with a short list of preconditions and suggestions on how smart development could be managed in smart communities.

The case studies presented in this book, as well as the benchmarks envisioned in the studies of circular economy and in the experiences of the sharing economy, give evident signals of the need for coordination between government and governance in making available highly sophisticated services.

Therefore, the central role of the public administration is stressed in regulating existing infrastructures and in providing new material and immaterial infrastructures. The assessment of future needs in a planning period ranging approximately from ten to fifteen years is becoming more and more important. This cannot be done with a week government and implies a strong cooperation between the private and public organizations.

Crucial nodes for smart development and for an effective connection between the organization of knowledge internal and external to the firms rest on schools and, above all, on universities as providers of fundamental research and radical innovation as well as higher education.

We cannot forget, however, all the limitations that affect the performance of public administration: from debt to failure. This is why a carefully planned division of labour between metropolitan authorities and multi-utility companies can be promising. The latter might enable multiplicative effects in the metropolitan areas through the provision of material and immaterial infrastructures complementary to their ordinary services.

2 Governing the knowledge society and the digital division of labour

Knowledge-based society and knowledge-based economy are recurring expressions in policy documents – and not only. However, it would be interesting to know what policy makers and all of the observers making use of these expressions mean. In fact, any form of production, from artisanal work processes to computer-governed flexible manufacturing systems, implies some form of knowledge, nor is the use of ICTs, per se, an indicator of knowledge possession.

2.1 On some dimensions of knowledge

We hear discussions about "knowledge" as if it is something clearly defined, and very often it is conflated with information – the presumption being that being informed means to know. To begin, as a minimum, knowledge takes place by processing information, that is knowledge is *processed* information. However, information can be wrong, false or misunderstood, and even from the right information, we might derive wrong knowledge. Our age is characterized by the constantly increasing availability of data and the means to process those data – i.e. computers – have also improved at exponential rates. And yet we experience long economic crises, nor is development taking place through a smooth avenue.

Technological knowledge has been at centre stage since the First Industrial Revolution, and it has merged with scientific knowledge afterwards. These changes, together with the *necessary* evolution of the institutional set-up, have revolutionized our societies.[15] A few dimensions must be recalled when we refer to "knowledge": know-why, know-that, know-how and, one should not undervalue the next, know-who.

The first dimension, *know-why*, refers to the deeper understanding of phenomena. An example can clarify the meaning of knowing why: we know that a body falls *because* there exists gravity. This form of knowledge concerns many fields that have an economic and social impact. Just think of biotechnologies, pharmaceuticals or nanotechnologies, each of which has a strong scientific background based on knowing why.

The second dimension concerns *knowing-that*. This characterizes both scientific and technological knowledge. In chemistry for long periods, both scientists and technologists knew that some reactions took place and that the mechanism was reliable without knowing exactly why.

The third dimension, *knowing-how*, typically concerns firms and individuals and is related to specific capabilities and skills. As an example, we can refer to microchip production: in theory, any physicist accompanied by technologists could find codified knowledge on how to produce microchips. However, when one wants to establish such a firm, the difficulties can be insurmountable.

The fourth dimension, *knowing-who*, is increasingly important, particularly in complex societies. Consultancy is the most obvious example: we refer to consultants who can advise us on what is feasible, which are the norms to be complied with and so on. In a globalized world knowing who can be decisive.

Worthy of a comment is the fact that the third and fourth dimensions may have an important tacit component within themselves.[16]

The next step considers the (re)production of knowledge. Knowledge reproduction and production of new knowledge occurs in many places: universities, public and private research laboratories and through any kind of human activity, the latter organized in manufacturing or service firms or small artisanal workshops. We cannot review here all of these spheres. Let us just remind that the role of the state and public authorities has always been important in promoting knowledge, be it for defence or "simple" economic reasons.[17] The institutional framework may well be national (or regional, or sectoral), but the local nodes – i.e. cities – are always important. Given that key players are universities and research laboratories, the ability of cities to establish, attract, keep and develop these entities is fundamental.

A side comment is necessary to point out that in many OECD countries demand for education has been constantly increasing during the last decades. This is reflected in the university tuition fees policy, which has been implemented in many places such as the United States and the UK, but also in Asia. Concentrating on two of the most attractive countries, that is the USA and the UK, we see that their universities have systematically increased tuition fees since quite a few years. In the UK, which for a long time had a system of subsidies that basically have meant free education for the students, fees were introduced in 1998 amounting to £1,000 per year and since 2012 have been raised up to £9,000. In the USA, tuition fees have been constantly increasing every single year since 2000, with the "Ivy League" universities charging today around US$45,000 per year (to which one must add room, board and often health insurance, which add at least US$16,000 per year).[18] Put in another way, as demand for education has increased, so have university fees.[19]

Universities create knowledge communities that have an obvious international dimension, but the local one ought to be carefully considered: one can think of the biotech cluster around Cambridge (UK) or of Amsterdam's science park, which connects education, research and business.

About knowledge, a further aspect can be recalled. If during the First Industrial Revolution the role of science was not as fundamental, from the second half of the nineteenth century, the role of the latter increases all the time: the understanding of chemistry, of some materials, of electricity and so on required the scientific explicit contribution. Science and technology merge and become more and more intertwined, so that the scientist that once was addressed as the "ivory tower" scholar is no longer on top of his or her tower.[20]

The willingness of governments (and thus not only firms) to stay at the forefront of the economy, together with other considerations – typically concerned with defence or environment-related aspects – as well as the active role played by society has led to a new way of developing knowledge that has been called "mode 2".[21] This notion results from a broad range of considerations and

> is intended to be useful to someone whether in industry or government, or society more generally and this imperative is present from the beginning. Knowledge is always produced under an aspect of continuous negotiation and it will not be produced unless and until the interests of the various actors are included.
>
> (Gibbons et al., 1994, p. 4)

This sentence makes evident that continuous efforts should be made to adopt the economic organization of knowledge appropriate to the everlastingly evolution in economic and social needs.

However, this effort should not ignore that the evolution of the different dimensions of knowledge and its conversion in innovation is often punctuated, not smooth and even disruptive, at least in the short run. The discontinuities in technological change recall to us that scientific research is essential and that radical change can be better financed and managed in the public sphere, while incremental research and development are more suitable for the private sector. The disruptive character of technological change should be taken into consideration side by side with compensation effects taking place in the medium and long run,[22] when trying to improve the forecasting and assessment capabilities of the government.[23]

2.2 The digital division of labour: from the macro trends to smart cities

The way in which we work, produce, consume, communicate, learn and run our businesses and whole systems – from railways networks to waste management – depends structurally on ICTs, and this dependence is bound to increase through time. ICT is one of the most pervasive technology humans have ever created and has been classified as a *general purpose technology*[24] as the steam-engine or electricity-based technology.

The key passages are the creation of the first computers in the 1940s,[25] the clear separation between hardware and software and, in the 1960s, the fact that the computer could be used as a "communication device"[26] for active interaction. The latter statement is fundamental: communication does not mean carrying unilaterally whatever message or information[27] or storing and processing more and more data: it means that all the participants of a (computerized) network can, at least in theory, modify and add to the content of whatever is being circulated.

Involved in what we have sketched in these few lines is a revolution that has affected every aspect of human life: the whole socio-economic, political and juridical systems have all been shaken. We can thus speak of a *digital division of labour*.

The juridical and legal side might not to be underestimated; in fact, a whole new set of legal problems emerge. Let us mention just a few examples. Protection of copyright has become a serious issue in the digital world in which one can copy instantaneously at basically zero cost anything, from books to songs, to computer programmes and games. Privacy seems not to exist anymore and the problem is extended to working places where employers can easily find ways of illegally spying on their employees. Tele-work has been a real possibility for many years by now, however it often requires new regulations. Illegal activities[28] can flourish because it becomes difficult to persecute criminals holding their servers in "strategic" countries. Internet companies can withhold and filter information, sometimes in accordance with authoritarian governments. Network neutrality – the principle according to which internet service providers refrain from blocking, slowing down or speeding up (legal) digital content on the basis of source, ownership or destination – is not to be taken for granted.

Digital technologies have changed the way in which we produce goods and services as a minimum since the 1970s, and the process of change has speeded up with networked digital technologies. Computers govern manufacturing processes, while in the service sector many services could be conceived and developed only because there exist computerized technologies. In fact, services, including utilities, are a field in which ICTs have been massively applied and, often as a consequence of this massive use, improved.

ICTs have also changed the quantity and quality of our consumption patterns. Digital technology associates supply and demand that is, in many cases producer and consumer using the same basic technology. The best example one can think of is that of what can be collectively defined as the entertainment industry, which ranges from music to videogames, from cinema to television. More and more of these activities take the form of file downloads to the home computer. Some internet service providers, through ever increasing broadband, are trying to shift TV watching from TV sets to computer screens. Wireless technologies have also experienced big waves of development, particularly in order to expand the range of activities that can be carried out by means of smart phones.

Obviously the processes mentioned earlier have also concerned the public administration so that, in the most advanced countries, much of the interaction between citizens and the public administration itself no longer requires direct contact, but digital interaction.

When we want to match the macro trends just reviewed with local development perspectives based on the smart city strategy, we find useful ideas in the papers proposed by IBM (2009, 2012).[29] The city is the environment in which the actual interaction between citizens, businesses and public administrations takes place. Whatever affects transportation, communications and the utility systems can have a dramatic impact on all the agents. IBM suggests making use of three pillars – which are partly immaterial – in order to monitor and assess the condition of the core systems.

The first pillar is that of *instrumentation*. Instrumentation consists of all those sensors and meters already in use (e.g. gas, electricity and water meters), which will be supplemented by increasingly inexpensive radio frequency identification tags, which will provide a constant flow of data. Infrastructure for data gathering is the first step to address, and solve, many of the challenges cities face.

The second move consists in creating *interconnection*, that is links among data, systems and people. Interconnection is not a new phenomenon; what is new is the scale and the depth of interconnection, which is leading to the so-called internet of things, opening thus up new ways to gather and share information.[30]

The third pillar is called *intelligence*, in the form of new kinds of computing models and new algorithms, states explicitly IBM. Let us quote verbatim:

> Intelligence . . . enables cities to generate predictive insights for informed decisions making and action. Combined with advanced analytics and ever-increasing storage and computing power, these new models can turn the mountains of data generated into intelligence to create insight as a basis for action.
>
> (IBM, 2009, p. 2)

Through these pillars a positive impact can be obtained on the core systems identified as *city services* (in terms of local government administration and public service management); *citizens* (health and education, public safety, government services); *business* (business environment, administrative burdens); *transport* (cars, roads, public transport, airports, seaports); *communication* (broadband, wireless, phones, computers); *water* (sanitation, freshwater supplies, seawater); and *energy* (oil, gas, renewable, nuclear).

If the technical side is within reach for many cities, due to the fact that the cost of sensors and microchips in general is affordable, as is also the elaboration of intelligent models for data analysis,[31] there are other aspects that are part of the game but that have to do with aspects of cities' government and governance. Examples suggested by IBM (2012) are to "break down bureaucratic barriers", "embrace transparency" or "encourage citizen involvement". These are aspects that affect, not only sclerotic management, but also enduring interests and vested rights. Furthermore, things may be not as clear-cut as they might seem at first sight: authoritarian and opaque regimes can, in some cases and conditions, be more effective than democratic ones at solving problems or promoting growth – thus sometimes getting paradoxically, ex post, some real consensus. We enter in this way into the complex ground of government and governance.

3 Government and governance

The words "government" and "governance" are sometimes treated as synonyms, sometimes as distinct concepts, while sometimes the latter is indicated as the evolution of the former. At first, the more one reads about the meaning and the distinctions between the two, the more one risks being confused.[32]

As Plattner has clarified, for a long time, it was not easy to find a consistent differentiation in the meaning of "government" and "governance". Then, from early the 1990s, the use of the word "governance" has experienced a wide success, a landmark in the term's success being a 1992 World Bank report entitled "Governance and Development" (Plattner, 2013, p. 18). Many initiatives have then made use of the noun "governance" or of the expression "from government to governance".[33] Governance has thus irresistibly entered the vocabulary of conferences, institutions and all sorts of publications and eventually is associated with any kind of institution and organization, from international bodies, to national and local authorities, to firms.

Despite the difficulties in disentangling the two concepts, after twenty-five years or so, a fairly clear distinction can be made today. A starting point is that the notion of governance is characterized by the idea of complexity and by the way in which power is exercised. Cariño (2004, p. 2) notes that "[t]o govern is to exercise power and authority over a territory, system or organization. This applies to both government and governance". However, when we think in terms of government the exercise of power takes the form of mere control and enforcement of the rules, when we think in terms of governance, societal development is central. Put in another way, "[i]n governance, all of society are involved in managing public affairs. Yet the state does not shrink into nothingness" (Cariño, 2004, p. 5).

Many observers note that, in advanced democracies, the role of society and of firms is increasingly important when we want to have effective and participatory governance. The weight of various movements, associations and societies (e.g. environmentalists, consumers associations, non-profit organizations) is important in shaping the way in which laws and norms are written and enforced – thus governments at any level, from supranational to city level, do not simply exercise power, but they share it. For-profit firms are also aware of their social role, and "corporate social responsibility" has also become a central issue in governance analyses. The quantity and quality of players has changed and increased. Furthermore,

> Central government is no longer supreme. The political system is increasingly differentiated. We live in "the centreless society" . . . in the polycentric state characterized by multiple centres. The task of government is to enable socio-political interactions; to encourage many and varied arrangements for coping with problems and to distribute services among the several actors.
>
> (Rhodes, 1997, p. 51)

The importance of city governments and local governance is fundamental when we remember, for instance, that 70% of Europeans live in urban areas: this means that local governments, through their governance, directly affect a good deal of citizens daily life, from local transport to traffic limitations in the city centre, to where one can enrol the children to school, to local taxation, to land-use regulations – just to mention a few.

At the city level, the provision and distribution of services among the several actors is immediately visible. As Rhodes clarifies, services, in particular, are provided by any permutation of public local government agencies and the private and non-profit sector. And we may add that in this framework multi-utilities can play a distinctive role. Governance – and especially service delivery – can thus be understood only as a complex network in which one can set the several interdependent actors involved. Networks are a further dimension that sometimes partners with and sometimes substitutes for hierarchies and markets. In the end, governance means self-organizing, inter-organizational networks (Rhodes, 1997, pp. 51–53).

About service delivery, a notion that complements what has just been said and that was strongly emphasized in what we consider a first phase in the diffusion of the model of governance, is that of the *quasi-market* (Le Grand, 1991). Since the 1980s, (local) governments have slowed down dramatically or have stopped completely being both the funder *and* the provider of services. Conflating what Rhodes (1997) and Le Grand (1991) write, the state – by this meaning any government, from national to local – becomes primarily a funder, while the services are provided by private for-profit, non-profit and public companies, all competing with one another. We have thus witnessed an evolution from monopolistic public provision of services to a new situation:

> All these developments thus involve the introduction of quasi-markets. . . . They are "markets" because they replace monopolistic state providers with competitive independent ones. They are "quasi" because they differ from conventional markets in a number of key ways. The differences are on both the demand and supply side.
>
> (Le Grand, 1991, pp. 1259–1260)

Taking into account all this, when we search for hopeful answers to the question raised in Section 1, a crucial principle can be derived from a very simple idea: just as public and private sector can fail together they can also cooperate and govern together by means of government coupled with governance.

The increasing awareness of the limits built in policy and deriving from bounded rationality, conflicts, inequality and failures led to the crisis of the model based on top-down government and to the consolidation of the principle of vertical and horizontal subsidiarity. This has encouraged the diffusion of a new doctrine of the exercise of authority based on the model of governance, which is understood as a multi-centric system including several actors, most of them social organizations, which is emerging sometimes as a rival source of authority, at times as a cooperative resource, at others as competitor and after all as an interlocutor[34] towards the model based on government.[35]

The foundations of governance lie therefore on the effectiveness of regulation much more than on jurisdiction, stimulating the rise of sets of behavioural rules leaving abundant freedom to the private sector.

However, after a first phase in which governance was largely thought as a substitute for government, the new background induced by the global economic crisis and fostered by the European emergencies led to revise this approach. A new challenge is arising between government and governance that contributes to blur and revise the boundaries and the ground covered by these two forms of authority: they are supposed to play together in a persistent way. The diffusion of the public–private partnership (PPP), can be considered one of the most relevant evidences of the transition to a second phase.

In our case, the cooperation between the private and the public sectors can be implemented through the creation of "smart communities", which can make available two sorts of tools relevant for an overall equilibrium.

To conclude this section, let us emphasize that at the local level we probably observe one of the most difficult conditions in which governance occurs. City governments have varying margins of autonomy, but they are affected by many restrictions. Considering the European situation, agents have to know, and often comply with limitations imposed by, EU, national and regional laws. The local political system is affected by the broader aggregates: public policy and mayors in capital cities – and in metropolitan areas or big cities in general – usually are not just local issues. The local economic system is affected by global forces but requires local attention. The broad social system is affected by many forces, and whatever happens, attention is required at the local level – just think of housing or recycling plans.

4 Governing smart development through smart communities

In Part I, we argued that the conceptualization of "smart development" can be derived from the combination of the key ideas lying beneath the strategies of smart specialization (S3) and smart city (SCS). In this chapter, which is taking stock of Part II and the other essays of Part III, we argue that the conceptualization of "smart community" can be derived from the combined ideas of smart networks and collective learning. Furthermore, we suggest that the capability to identify strong synergies between "smart development" and "smart communities" can be essential in the implementation of S3 and SCS through a mix of government and governance capabilities.

In trying to do this, we cannot forget that social organizations, like households and other social groups, share with firms an important limit in the processes of knowledge preservation, creation, retrieval and diffusion. The storability of the pieces of knowledge gained in the past is not easy nor granted. This has to do both with the very nature of knowledge – the question is hanging: is it numerable, additive, superadditive? – and with the characteristics and organization of society.[36]

In any case, substantial problems arise from this limit in the organization of knowledge and its transfer. And each society tries to find new solutions. The formation of stable structures of relations inside a social group, at a local level or in wider contexts tries to provide a basis for patterns of relationships amongst the members that allow improving the processes of knowledge preservation, creation, retrieval and diffusion.[37]

4.1 Smart development as a synthesis of smart specialization and smart city

In Chapter 8, we reached the conclusion that economic development, and not only growth, is the core issue and that urban areas and metropolitan cities are increasing their relevance in the new geography of development.

Another relevant conclusion is that the economic sectors, the technological trajectories and, in general, the drivers of economic development are more and more interconnected, even if not in a mechanical way, among them and with the model of capitalism in which they coexist.

In this chapter, after recapitulating why it is relevant to identify the interactions between S3 and SCS and understand how they shape what we call "smart development" and its main drivers, we will try to focus on the main implications for policy action.

A first aspect to be noted has to do with the state of the art. In fact, the literature trying to compare S3 and SCS and to analyze their impact as well as their joint outcomes is still limited.

Next, we deem it fitting to undertake the task of interpreting the linkages between S3 and SCS in order to support coordination between these two strategies. Coordination is strongly needed due also to the EU tendency to spreading economic policies addressed to the real economy in order to cope with such a strong structural differentiation among Member Countries. This is openly recognized also by the efforts to foster a "political union" rather than a "union of policies".

Third, a joint analysis can improve our capacity to measure the phenomena under investigation and have an impact on the allocation of functions of the different levels of government in managing S3 and SCS looking at the ingredients and rules more suitable for effective governance.

When we start asking questions referring to the static and dynamic characteristics of S3 and SCS emerging when they are positioned in concrete economic systems, four essential features come into sight: (1) the side in which they are placed in the markets, (2) the opportunities they can generate for the internal and external organization of knowledge, (3) the critical factors in assessing their innovation potential and (4) the tools available for government and governance. Moreover, we can consider the parallel vectors taking shape when the implementation of these four aspects takes place along each of the two strategies.

Coming to the results obtained using this method, we start noting that, while S3 insists on the supply side of the markets, SCS is clearly focused on their demand side. This reveals a crucial economic principle, even if with a static character, to be used when we try to address structures and behaviours of the different agents operating in the markets having in mind a coherent plan.

Following a similar line of reasoning, therefore, we note that, while S3 helps to discover new opportunities for developing the internal and external organization of knowledge especially, even if not exclusively, on the side of producers, SCS stresses our attention on the new opportunities for developing the internal and external organization of knowledge especially, even if not exclusively, on the side of consumers. This categorization can be very useful even when "prosumers" can have room for action.

When coming to explore the domain where more dynamic factors prevail, it is easy to note that, in the case of S3, the innovation potential rests mainly on the learning capacity of producers, while in the case of SCS the innovation potential rests largely on the learning capacity of consumers, which is often underestimated. Lastly, both S3 and SCS have to rely on government and governance for shaping the appropriate regulation structures and overall environments in which they perform. In this respect, an easy prescription is that the division of labour between the different levels of governments has to be forward-looking and the application of the subsidiarity principles well designed.

More vital and controversial is a second prescription following from this scheme. Investments fostering material and immaterial infrastructures have to be enhanced at all levels of government and given higher priority over current expenditures. Moreover, new decentralized industrial policies and new local development policies have to be tested, both at the local, national and supra-national level, side by side with policies for the development of human capital and social capital development policies.

In between the two vectors are portrayed the chief "chromosomes" of the global environment in which agents act – that is path-dependence, scale economies, global scenario, variety and urban areas centrality. They can operate both in the form constraints, as, for instance, path-dependence can do, as well in the form of drivers for change, as, for instance, variety can do.

The more critical broad production factor in this framework centred on sustainability is human capital, combined with environmental capital and financial capital.

The "smart factory" – very close to the idea of the representative agent when smart development prevail – can be interpreted as the form of firm capable of developing and employing its internal organization of knowledge in a way that is capable of interacting effectively with the external organization of knowledge and of performing on the supply side and able to forecast and evaluate the evolution of demand. This means that this class of firm is able to manage appropriately the broad production factors defined and to transform sustainability from a constraint to an opportunity.

Coming to policy implications, we can reinforce the idea that the capability of a region of taking stock of its historical production path in trying to adapt to future trends heavily depends on two crucial steps. The first one concerns the capacity of the different levels of government involved to run after and exploit the synergies between S3, on the one side, and SCS, on the other. The second step refers to the ability of the different levels of government involved to take fully into consideration the real nature and characteristics of the goods and services playing a crucial role in the transformation paths pursued. This can become a substantial drive for change and enhance their competences in managing local development.

4.2 Smart community as a synthesis of smart networks and collective learning

Also in this section, we will carry on in the same way. After focusing on why it is relevant to identify the interactions between smart networks and collective learning and understand how they shape what we call a "smart community" and its main drivers, we will try to focus on the main implications for policy action.

In this case, the literature trying to analyze the joint outcomes of smart networks and collective learning it is not necessarily new, but it is still gifted to provide developments in the new scenarios of smart development.

In second place, the interpretation of the linkages between the operation of smart networking and collective learning can offer new insights on how the economic organization of knowledge internal and external to the firms can perform and favour coordinated policies in the two domains.

Third, a joint analysis can improve our capacity to measure the phenomena under investigation and have an impact on the allocation of functions of the different levels of government in supporting the operation of smart networks and collective learning through effective governance.

In our days, it is relevant to focus on the interaction between smart networks and collective learning for understanding how knowledge is managed in economic and non-economic organizations.

Smart network are vehicles of long-lasting interaction between social and economic agents based on knowledge preservation, creation, retrieval and diffusion.

Collective learning can be conceived as one of the main activities involving social and economic agents and aiming at preserving, creating, retrieving, maintaining and diffusing knowledge. At each stage of the historical evolution, it brings about a given level and shape of organization of knowledge for social and economic use, which depends on the connections of private agents conduct with the functioning of public agencies.[38]

Of course, a smart network is a wider notion than that of economic networks, and our scientific field of specialization does not allow us to take into account all the dimensions of such a multidisciplinary concept. However, the notion of smartness, as we have put forward in this volume, implies at least an indirect aptitude to perform cunningly in real economic environments. Therefore, smart networks should interface with economic networks.

An economic network has been defined as: "a group of agents who pursue repeated, enduring exchange relations with one another and, at the same time, lack a legitimate organizational authority to arbitrate and resolve the disputes that may arise during the exchange" (Rauch and Hamilton, 2001, p. 1).

The economic literature went on proposing to split economic networks into three main subgroups: "networks as concentrated exchange", "networks as primordial relations" and "networks as structures of mutual orientation" (Zuckerman, 2003).

Moreover, since the 1980s, a vast non-mainstream literature

> has emerged on "suprafirm" networks, clusters, and value chains, treated as a third elementary institution of firm coordination. In contrast to Marshall and his neoclassical successors, it treats clustering and network building as intentional acts, part of firm strategy; and interprets them with a non-neoclassical economics based on assumptions of limited-foresight, learning, and path-dependency, rather than of equilibrium and rational expectations.
>
> (Wade, 2012, p. 8)

Therefore, following this line of thought, networks are interpreted as a distinct and alternative coordination mechanism with respect to markets and hierarchies, and inter-firm coordination through networks is supposed to have big private and social gains. This is due to the fact that, favouring the access to pooled resources, participation in them can raise learning, productivity and innovation. What have been called the "emergent properties" of networks, such as their competence in absorbing technologies then affect the competitiveness of each firm. The networks themselves, along this causal line, become a source of "increasing returns".

Something similar could be also said about some networks formed by other social organizations, like households and ethnic groups, which can be thought as nth elementary institutions[39] of coordination complementary to households and other social groups.

The more critical driver of change in this sustainability-centred framework is social capital, combined with human capital.

Again in this framework, the "smart factory" can be interpreted as the class of firms capable of interacting with and improving the external organization of knowledge and to perform, not only on the supply side, but also on the demand side of the markets. This means that this kind of firm is able to appropriately manage all the broad production factors defined and in transforming sustainability form a constraint to an opportunity.

As said in advance, in our case, the cooperation between the private and the public sectors can be implemented through the creation of "smart communities", which can make available two sorts of tools relevant for an overall equilibrium. On the one side, they can elaborate rules capable of attributing economic values to production processes and supply of goods and services with a social nature. These rules help in regulating the system and ensuring its compliance. This leads to tackling the structure of value chains for social goods. On the other side, smart communities can assist in adapting the very objectives of individuals, households and organizations to the constraints posed by social values on the subjective behaviour in the consumption of private goods. This leads to modifying the structure of value chains also for private goods. In this way, another strand of synergy can be derived bridging the criss-crossed lessons coming from the study of smart development and smart communities.

5 Conclusion

Policy is a central feature of governance and government, and we have seen that complexity is a structural feature of them. Before summarizing the main suggestions we have been able to put forward, it is useful to list some preconditions, even if they often taken for granted in the political debate. Many preconditions are relevant and, without claim of exhaustiveness, let us consider some of these.

The first precondition concerns the political side: democracy, transparency, participation and accountability are the words that come to our mind. All of the involved political agents would subscribe to these words. However, once the elected rulers are installed in office their behaviour may deviate from those words. We have here a first tension in that rules must be written in such a way as not to allow a drift towards autocracy and corruption, but when rules are too strict, whatever their intention, they can obtain a perverse effect of blocking any possibility of effective governance.

The second precondition concerns knowledge. Knowledge relates to all aspects of our action, that is we need institutional, organizational, scientific and technological knowledge. This means that an updated organization of knowledge within and outside the firm should be made available. One has to be very careful because often one presumes to have the right knowledge, informing his or her action on this presumption to find out that the premises were wrong. Everybody was shocked, for instance, when an FAO report clarified that the biggest source of greenhouse gases came from livestock activities – an activity that before then would have likely been classified within the green economy line. Moreover, as we have stressed in this chapter, knowledge and forecasting, which is strongly associated with it, are based on investments in R&D and innovation.

The third precondition can be addressed as the technological dimension, with particular emphasis on ICTs. Our presumption to possess the "right" knowledge is more and more based on our ability to gather, store and process data. Undoubtedly enormous progress has taken place, and today, we can monitor and assess in real time more and more magnitudes, from traffic to the sewerage system. The "internet of things" is gaining more and more ground and will help a better management of many aspects, providing optimal services where and when they are needed. However, predictive models, particularly when human behaviour is part of the prediction, must be taken with a grain of salt, and fallback arrangements must be planned together with satisfying solutions.

A fourth precondition consists in the acknowledgement of the coexistence of hierarchic, market and network mechanisms in which public, private for-profit and non-profit companies coexist and compete to provide goods and services the nature of which fall the composite taxonomy discussed in Chapter 6, in which the social goods play a relevant role.

Coming to the suggestions we have first of all to stress how the case studies presented in this book, as well as the benchmarks envisioned in the studies of circular economy and in the experiences of the sharing economy give evident signals of what the future requirements and tasks of public policies will be in the next few years.[40] They go so far as to imagine communities in which through government and governance highly sophisticated services will be offered. And the more so when economic, environmental and social sustainability is at stake.

The central role of the public administration in regulating existing infrastructures (for instance, in the field of mobility and energy) and in providing new material and immaterial infrastructures (like, for instance, in the field of R&D and education) is therefore emphasized. Due to the array of requirements put forward by the business community, social organizations and citizens, the public administration has to become more robust and efficient, not only in the management of current affairs, but also in the assessment of future needs. The assessment of future needs in a planning period ranging approximately from ten to fifteen years is becoming more and more important. This cannot be done with a weak government and implies a strong cooperation between the private and public sectors.

Crucial nodes for smart development and for an effective connection between the organization of knowledge internal and external to the firms rest on schools and, above all, on universities as providers of fundamental research and radical innovation, as well as higher education. In the perspective of smart communities, we have to refer also to the positive experiences of corporate university, which can be considered as one of the applications of the PPP principle.

We cannot forget, however, all the limitations that affect the performance of public administration: from debt to failure. This is why a carefully planned division of labour between metropolitan authorities and multi-utility companies can be promising. The latter might enable multiplicative effects in the metropolitan areas through the provision of material and immaterial infrastructures complementary to their ordinary services.

Notes

1 As it is well known, "policy" in general applies to plans of actions adopted by an individual or social group or to a project rationalizing the course of action of a government. "Polity" relates to the form of government of a social organization or to an organized society, such as a nation, having a specific form of government. "Politics" refers to social relations involving schemes to gain authority or power or to the activities and affairs involved in managing a state or a government.

2 As we define the synergy of smart specialization and smart city, see, in particular, Chapter 8.

3 As we define in the present chapter, the synergy of smart networks and collective learning.

4 For repeated clarifications about the relevance of long-term (10–15 years) forecasting for business leaders, policy makers and citizens in relentless environments, see Manyika et al. (2013).

5 For instance, local chambers of commerce, private businesses, business organizations or associations, local universities or community colleges citizen, advisory boards, consumer associations, public–private partnerships, utilities, private foundations, non-profit organizations.

6 We should note that, while at the micro-economic level (for instance the firm) failure reflects, mainly and at least in the long run, efficiency problems of the agent involved;

at the meso and macro level, it especially reveals problems concerning effectiveness of the body involved.

7 As suggested in the famous quote by Luigi Einaudi (1964). The translation is ours. One of the reasons is that, paradoxically, the application of this very simple principle may imply forecast and evaluation activities that can be difficult and expensive in an ever-changing world.

8 In this case, we refer to independent authorities operating in particular sectors.

9 For additional remarks, see Antonelli (2011).

10 For an in-depth analysis, see Wade (2012).

11 That is to take care of the positive roles that redundancy can play in the functioning of actual systems and that a "single best solution" for each problem can be very risky.

12 Take, for instance, passenger and commodity flows in public transport.

13 This idea was first proposed by Yochai (2002).

14 For an in-deep scrutiny aiming at strategy and policy issues, see Manyika et al. (2013).

15 For further remarks, see De Liso (2013).

16 On these dimensions of knowledge, and on tacitness, one can refer to Ryle (1949), Polanyi (1983) and Loasby (1999).

17 The notion of a national system of innovation, which has become very popular in the 1990s, sums up the overall idea, even in a phase in which it has been superseded by the smart specialization approach. Chapters 1, 7 and 8 also deal with this aspect.

18 For data and comparisons, see the various issues of *Education at a Glance* of the OECD, the latest available is OECD (2015); for detailed information about "Ivy League" universities, one can refer to their web pages in which tuition fees are explicitly indicated.

19 We have to point out that recently, in some countries – including the USA and other ones such as Italy – university enrolment has decreased.

20 See also Chapter 8.

21 For an in-depth analysis, see Gibbons et al. (1994).

22 The economic literature has focused in the past on compensations brought about by price reduction effects, technology multiplicative effects and income effects.

23 Even if we have to consider that forecasts and policy evaluation are usually very expensive and imply appropriate skills.

24 The definition is self-explanatory.

25 In the United States, but efforts in the UK and Germany's Konrad Zuse ought also to be mentioned.

26 The latter statement is taken from the title of Licklider and Taylor's (1968) work; for a thorough analysis, see De Liso (2008), on which the present sub-section is partly based.

27 This is, for instance, what happens when we read a newspaper.

28 Such as drugs and weapons trafficking, not to mention the availability of paedophile sites.

29 See also IBM (2013a, 2013b, 2013c).

30 Worthy of a comment here is the fact that the city of Manchester (UK) was awarded an important UK government grant in December 2015 for its *CityVerve* project, which included explicitly the internet of things as an object. As one can read on the web page announcing the award, "The Internet of things adds sensors and data analysis to equipment like streetlamps, vehicles or home heating equipment. These 'smart' improvements will help deliver more personal, efficient and flexible products and services" (https://www.gov.uk/government/news/manchester-wins-10m-prize-to-become-world-leader-in-smart-city-technology, accessed 30th January 2016).

31 Consultants can provide the skills when not available locally.

32 And maybe Plattner (2013, p. 19) is right when he states that "once a term becomes a buzzword, it is all but futile to try to give it a precise meaning". The point can appreciated even more by reading the long review chapter on *governance* in the book by Roe (2013).

33 Two examples being the UN 1999 "World Conference on Governance" and the 2003 Hague conference "From Government to Governance".
34 For a presentation of this doctrine, see Rosenau (1990), March and Olsen (1995), Rosenau (2004) and Iannone (2005, p. 78).
35 According to the Grammarist (2009–2014), "Governance and government are interchangeable in the sense the process of governing, but they differ in other senses. Government often refers to the governing body itself, while governance often refers to the act of governing. So members of a government are engaged in governance." In addition, "Meanwhile, governance is often the better word for the administration of nongovernmental organizations (corporations, for example), while government works better in reference to the public administration of nations, states, municipalities, etc."
36 One can even doubt, following Alfred Marshall, that outside slavery we could even speak of human capital.
37 See also Chapter 15.
38 In this volume, we often refer to this process speaking of organization of knowledge internal and external to the firm.
39 Due to the much larger number of institutions involved in the social domain.
40 In this respect, reference can be made to Ellen Macarthur Foundation et al. (2015) and Montini and Nicolli (2015).

Bibliography

Antonelli, G. (2011), Global economic crisis and systemic failure, *Economia Politica: Journal of Analytical and Institutional Economics*, XXVIII (3), 403–434.

Cariño, L.V. (2004), The concept of governance, chapter 1 in *From government to governance*, UN Public Administration Network, available at http://unpan1.un.org/intradoc/groups/public/documents/eropa/monograph-worldcog-chap1.pdf, accessed 23 January 2016.

Deakin, M. (ed.) (2014), *Smart cities. Governing, modelling and analysing transition*, London, Routledge.

De Liso, N. (2008), ICTs and the digital division of labour, in R. Leoncini and S. Montresor (eds.), *Dynamic capabilities between firm organization and local systems of production*, London, Routledge, pp. 346–374.

De Liso, N. (2013), From mechanical arts to the philosophy of technology, *Economics of innovation and new technology*, 22 (7), 726–750.

Einaudi, L. (1964), *Prediche inutili*, Torino Einaudi, 3–14.

Ellen MacArthur Foundation, SUN and McKinsey Center for Business and Environment. (2015), Growth within: A circular economy vision for a competitive Europe, Ellen Macarthur Foundation, SUN and McKinsey Center for Business and Environment, June.

European Commission. (2012a), *Smart cities and communities – European innovation partnership*, COM 4701, Bruxelles, European Commission.

European Commission. (2012b), *Connecting smart and sustainable growth through smart specialisation. A practical guide for ERDF managing authorities*, Bruxelles, European Commission.

Gibbons, M., Limoges, C., Novotny, H., Schwartzman, S., Scott, P. and Trow, M. (1994), *The new production of knowledge*, London, Sage.

Grammarist (2009–2014), http://grammarist.com/usage/governance/.

Hayek, F.A. (1973) *Law, Legislation and liberty. Volume I: rules and order*, London, Routledge and Kegan Paul.

Heere, W.P. (ed.) (2004), *From government to governance. The growing impact of non-state actors on the international and European legal system*, The Hague, T.M.C. Asser Press.

Hollands, R.G. (2008), Will the real smart city please stand up? *City*, 12 (3), 303–320.

Iannone, R. (2005), Governance: una questione di significati, *Rivista Trimestrale di Scienza dell'Amministrazione*, 2, 57–85.

IBM. (2009), *How smart is your city?*, New York, IBM Institute for Business Value, Somers, IBM Global Service.

IBM. (2012), *How to transform a city. White paper*, New York, IBM Corporate.

IBM. (2013a), *How to reinvent a city?*, New York, IBM Corporate Citizenship.

IBM. (2013b), *Insatiable innovation: From sporadic to systemic*, New York, IBM Institute for Business Value, Somers, IBM Global Service.

IBM. (2013c), *IBM annual report 2012*, New York, IBM.

Keynes, J.M. (1922), A revision of the treaty, being a sequel to the economic consequences of the peace, reprinted in 1971 as Volume III in The Collected Writings of John Maynard Keynes, London, Macmillan.

Komninos, N. (2014), What makes cities intelligent? in M. Deakin (ed.), Chapter 5, pp. 77–95.

Le Grand, J. (1991), Quasi-markets and social policy, *Economic Journal*, 101, September, 1256–1267.

Licklider, J.R.C. and Taylor, R.W. (1968), The computer as a communication device, *Science and Technology*, April [reprinted by the Digital Equipment Corporation, downloaded from the DEC web page].

Loasby, B. (1999), *Knowledge, institutions and evolution in economics*, London, Routledge.

Manyika, J., Chui, M., Bughin, J., Dobbs, R., Bisson, P. and Marrs, A. (2013), Disruptive technologies: Advances that will transform life, business, and the global economy, McKinsey Global Institute, May.

March, J.G. and Olsen, J.P. (1995), *Democratic governance*, New York, Free Press.

Montini, A. and Nicolli, F. (2015), *Filiera ambientale, ciclo dei rifiuti, regolazione: stato dell'arte*, HerAcademy, Background Paper No. 1, December.

Nowotny, H., Scott, P. and Gibbons, M. (2003), 'Mode 2' revisited: The new production of knowledge, *Minerva*, 41 (3), 179–194.

OECD. (2015), *Education at a glance*, Paris, OECD.

Plattner, M.F. (2013), Reflections on governance, *Journal of Democracy*, 24 (4), 17–28.

Polanyi, M. (1983), *The tacit dimension*, Gloucester, MA, Peter Smith.

Rauch, J.E. and Hamilton, G.G. (2001), Networks and markets: Concepts for bridging disciplines, in J.E. Rauch and A. Casella (eds.), *Networks and markets*, New York, Russel Stage Foundation, pp. 1–29.

Rhodes, R.A.W. (1997), Understanding governance, Chapter 3: The new governance: Governing without Government, pp. 46–61, previously published as The new governance: Governing without Government in *Political Studies*, 1996, Vol. XLIV, September, pp. 652–657.

Roe, M. (2013), *Maritime governance and policy-making*, London, Springer.

Rosenau, J. (1990), *Turbulence in world politics: A theory of change and continuity*, Princeton, Princeton University Press.

Rosenau, J. (2004), Strong demand, huge supply: Governance in an emerging epoch, in I. Bache and M. Flinders (eds.), *Multi-level governance*, Oxford, Oxford University Press, pp. 31–48.

Ryle, G. (1949 repr. 1990), *The concept of mind*, Chicago, University of Chicago Press.

Wade, R.H. (2012), Return of industrial policy?, *International Review of Applied Economics*, 26 (2), 223–239.

Wade, R.H. (2015), The role of industrial policy in developing countries, in A. Calcagno, S. Dullien, A. Márquez-Velázquez, N. Maystre Jan Priewe (eds.), UNCTAD-HTW, *Rethinking development strategies after the financial crisis*. Volume I: Making the case for policy space, New York and Geneva, United Nations, pp. 67–79.

Yochai, B. (2002), Coase's penguin, or, Linux and the nature of the firm, *The Yale Law Journal*, 112 (3), 369–446.

Zuckerman, E.W. (2003), On networks and markets by Rauch and Casella eds., *Journal of Economic Literature*, 41 (2), 545–565.

15 Smartness and collective learning processes

The enabling role of public utilities

Alessandro Camilleri[1] and Marco Ruffino[2]

1 Introduction

The authors assume smart cities as collective learning processes, deeply rooted in the ICT resources, but not simply determined by them. The focus is the interplay between technology availability – the "Internet of Things" paradigm – and emerging collective behaviours, an autopoietic, societal process grounded on intentional and unintentional "network thinking" mix. Following this approach, collective learning, rooted in positive values, becomes a key factor in developing a real smart city, seen as a context positively characterized in terms of quality of life, in the wide meaning of the concept. If smartness is necessarily a learning outcome, building a distinctive level of community capacity, enhancing the knowledge opportunities and guiding the spontaneous sensemaking activities are three central issues of the smart city learning management. This implies both a clear commitment and a widespread participation and contribution, by means of a balanced mix between government and governance. Public utilities – highly structured networks with a visible and tangible role in the urban space – can be a smart city and "living labs" key players, supporting and orienting the collective learning with a multi-focal, integrated approach: directly, by service-driven activities proposing and enabling new forms and opportunities of behaviour, and at the sides, reinforcing the place-based knowledge systems. Beyond that, the recurring nature of the public utilities (a balanced mix of public and private shareholders) can favour a positive and innovative agreement between demand (smart city) and supply (smart specialisation) interests, pursuing the improvement of all direct and indirect services. In this view, public utilities are to be seen as learning network organisations, up to favour the cognitive interactions between the diverse players, both at the local and the global scale. From the HR management side, two relevant consequences are more specific skills development and better integrated participation in the educational local system.

2 Smart cities, smart specialisation and collective learning processes

2.1 About the smartness: cities, regions, specialisation and policies

During the last five years, the adjective "smart" has gained importance as a "discourse principle" (Foucault, 1972) with respect to different, interconnected domains. In order to better understand the meaning and the pragmatic role played nowadays by the "smartness" concept and, furthermore, by the wide correlated linguistic area, it is useful to have a brief overlook on this specific landscape. Moving from the smart city reference, we can observe that this label "was born in 1994, but papers regarding this topic are few or zero until 2010, when the European Union started to use 'smart' to qualify sustainability projects and actions in the urban space" (Cocchia, 2014, p. 18). It's not unnatural to think at the role played, since 2007, by the symbolic reference of Apple's iPhone, the first *smart* phone. In fact, the ubiquitous presence of ICTs, surely as a digital media, is one of the most structural characterisations of the smart city reference. Gathering the wide ensemble of adjectives connoting the city's post-fordist transition to a glocal and network space, it's a very useful way to set the semantic area underlying the smart city concept. An incomplete list of terms shows the emergence of two main families.

The first and most populated is the "ICT group", including qualifiers as digital, virtual, cyber, wired, hybrid, information, and obviously e-city (Cocchia, 2014). A growing role is assumed by the Internet of Things (IoT) computing paradigm, going "beyond traditional mobile computing scenarios that use smart phones and portables, and evolv[ing] into connecting every day existing objects and embedding intelligence in to our environment" (Gubbi et al., 2013, p. 1646). In the IoT perspective, a possible, future reference is the

> City Information Model (CIM) . . . based on the concept that the status and performance of each buildings and urban fabrics – such as pedestrian walkways, cycle paths and heavier infrastructure like sewers, rail lines, and bus corridors – are continuously monitored by the city government operates and made available to third parties via a series of APIs, even though some information is confidential.
>
> (Atzori et al., 2010, p. 2797)

In this context, "planning and design is an ongoing social process, in which the performance of each item is being reported in real-time and compared with others" (p. 2797). The second family may be viewed as "cognitive group", gathering terms as knowledge city (Ergazakis et al., 2004; Musterd and Gritsai, 2012), learning city (OECD, 2002; Juceviciene, 2010) and, in a lesser pronounced way, creative city (Hall, 2000). The two ensembles are often joined by the more neutral expression "innovative city". In their turn, knowledge and learning references come from a relatively far approach, applied originally on the organisational functioning (learning organisation, Argyris and Schön, 1978); the post-fordist paradigm (learning economy, Lundvall, 1994); the territorial economy (learning region, Florida, 1995; Maillat and Kebir, 1999; Capello and Faggian, 2005; Asheim, 2012; Rutten and Boekema, 2012; Healy and Morgan, 2012); the competitive production systems (knowledge organisation, Nonaka and Takeuchi, 1995); and the entire human consortium (knowledge society, David and Foray, 2002; learning society, OECD, 2000). Also the urban applying field of the adjective "smart" is widening: "a smart city is one with at least one initiative addressing one or more of the following six characteristics: Smart Governance, Smart People, Smart Living, Smart Mobility, Smart Economy and Smart Environment" (European Parliament, 2014, p. 9). As Nam and Pardo show in a relevant conceptualisation work (2011, p. 283), "Smart is more user-friendly than intelligent. . . . Smart city is required to adapt itself to the user needs and to provide customized interfaces": clearly a part of the more general blurred boundaries between production and consumption.

Another basic topic of the linguistic field is the "smart specialisation" concept, developed in the academic world only in 2008 and very shortly adopted by the EU policy makers as a core reference for the Europe 2020 innovation plan strategy, known as RIS3 (European Commission, 2015). The smart specialisation is assumed as

> a learning process to discover the research and innovation domains in which a region can hope to excel. In this learning process, entrepreneurial actors are likely to play leading roles in discovering promising areas of future specialisation, not least because the needed adaptations to local skills, materials, environmental conditions, and market access conditions are unlikely to be able to draw on codified, publicly shared knowledge, and instead will entail gathering localized information and the formation of social capital assets.
>
> (Foray et al., 2009, p. 2)

On these basis, some authors stress the importance of the context introducing the "knowledge ecology" term (McCann and Ortega-Argilés, 2011, p. 2), linking the potential evolutionary pathways with the inherited structures and the existing dynamics, including adaptation or even radical transformation of the system. The players are regarded as being the agents who use their knowledge-acquisition facilities and resources (human capital, ideas, academic and research collaborations) to scan the available local economic and market opportunities, to identify technological and market niches for exploitation, and thereby act as the catalysts for driving the emerging transformation of the economy. The smartness is clearly expressed by the interplay between local and glocal dimensions of the learning processes, "inherently localized and cumulative, embedded in human capital, interpersonal networks, specialized and skilled labour markets, and local governance systems" (Camagni and Capello, 2013, p. 357). Moving from this assumption, the same scholars propose the correlate concept of "smart innovation policies", defined as "policies able to increase the innovation capability of an area and to enhance local expertise in knowledge production and use, acting on local specificities and on the characteristics, strengths and weaknesses of already-established innovation patterns in each region" (p. 357).

This brief overlook on the linguistic landscape related to the smart concept takes in evidence the core role of the collective learning dynamics in the spatial and relational contexts: above all, innovation – incremental and even more disruptive – is a social process, implying not only the development of new skills, but a more or less "cognitive reframing", producing a different, better quality of life. As the previous quoted European Parliament Report (2014, p. 23) remarks, "while ICT is a definitive component, Smart Cities cannot simply be created by deploying sensors, networks and analytics in an attempt to improve efficiency. Indeed, at worst, this can lead to a one-size fits all, top-down approach". The focus is the interplay between technology availability and emerging collective behaviours – via the intensive use of distributed networks sustaining and managing relationships – reinforcing the communal ability to deal with the local needs. In this view, the "living lab" methodology, despite a lack of theoretical framework (Schuurman et al., 2015) seems to be a possible bridge between smart city and smart specialisation. The "smart" adjective is not neutral in its effects, but demands a relevant functioning progression. Quoting again the European Parliament (2014, p. 18),

> at its core, the idea of Smart Cities is rooted in the creation and connection of human capital, social capital and information and Communication technology (ICT) infrastructure in order to generate greater and more sustainable economic development and a better quality of life.

Scholars also stress the topic, defining a city to be smart "when investments in human and social capital and traditional (transport) and modern (ICT) communication infrastructure fuel sustainable economic growth and a high quality of life, with a wise management of natural resources, through participatory governance" (Caragliu et al., 2009, p. 50). A smart city must have lesser problems than another traditional city; if certain kind of problem persists, we are not in presence of any substantial evolution. In the same time, the gains acquired must be irreversible: the essence of the smart city is sustainability in an innovative community. That's imply that "an uneducated, unhealthy, unemployed, and uninspired citizenry can never become a learning city, irrespective of how many philosophies, policies, or proclamations are handed down" (Scott, 2014, p. 93).

Coming along this way, the smartness reference meet another relevant scientific, politic and practical topic, namely the social innovation, defined – drawing upon once again to a European linguistic source – as "the development and implementation of new ideas (products, services and models) to meet social needs and create new social relationships or collaborations. . . . Social innovations are innovations that are social in both their ends and their means" (EC, 2013, p. 6). As we can easily see, all the matter (from smart city to the social innovation, passing through the smart specialisation) is deeply inscribed in the (endless) transition to a new paradigm, more structured and positive than the current ill-defined "post-fordism", which is another way to reaffirm the learning centrality.

In summary, the focus of the smartness is, in our view, the collective evolution of behaviours and social relations, not necessarily devoted to an explicit, rational end but significant in terms of outcomes (communal well-being), activated and sustained by the ICT spatial-distributed resources. The explicit reference to the sustainability implying also an increased "socio-political capability and access to resources needed to enhance rights to satisfaction of human needs and participation" (Moulaert et al., 2005, p. 1976). Smartness is also a question of inclusion and effective civil rights, strongly linked to a collective empowerment dimension: an innovation not only good for society but also enhancing society's capacity to act. Without appropriate community capacity building (OECD, 2009), smartness is quite impossible.

2.2 The cognitive side: knowledge, competencies and learning processes

As we have seen, taking smart cities as collective learning systems is a wide-spread approach, both in research papers and in political debate. Following Jarvis (2007, p. 100), a learning society is also "one in which the majority of social institutions make provisions for individuals to acquire knowledge, skills, attitudes, values, emotions, beliefs and senses within a global society". And a learning city (UNESCO, 2014, p. 6) is a city

> that effectively mobilizes its resources in every sector to: promote inclusive learning from basic to higher education; re-vitalize learning in families and communities; facilitate learning for and in the workplace; extend the use of modern learning technologies; enhance quality and excellence in learning; and nurture a culture of learning throughout life.

These cities identify and are capable of implementing innovations that inspire and guide public and private organisations, communities and social actors, modifying their behaviour and enhancing the whole life conditions. All that imply a significant cognitive work, distributed and coordinated among a wide ensemble of social, institutional and economic actors. In order to understand the possible enabling roles of the public utilities, it's now useful to focus on a few relevant topics of the cognitive side.

The first one regards the nature of the knowledge involved in (and generated by) the learning processes. Starting from the policy debate, the smart city is easily associated with "smart people", assumed as

> e-skills, working in ICT-enabled working, having access to education and training, human resources and capacity management, within an inclusive society that improves creativity and fosters innovation. As a characteristic, it can also enable people and communities to themselves input, use, manipulate and personalise data, for example through appropriate data analytic tools and dashboards, to make decisions and create products and services.
>
> (European Parliament, 2014, p. 28)

In fact, although ICT skills are a relevant resource in a technology-driven context, they seem quite insufficient facing the smart cities' complex and multidimensional nature. However, the same source, immediately after this assumption, introduce another key characteristic, the "smart living", implying a more wide set of competencies, related to health, safe living, culture, and "high levels of social cohesion and social capital" (ivi). Social and personal skills are not dissociable to the digital ones.

Several scholars, referring to the knowledge-based productive systems (in which we can easily inscribe smart cities), point to other knowledge resources, more extended and locally rooted. For Camagni and Capello (2013, p. 361) starting from formal knowledge in order to identify the degree and capability of each region to innovate is a relevant limit, due to the critical importance of the "informal knowledge creation and development, such as creativity, craft capability, and practical skills". In this way, Asheim et al. (2011) propose a distinction between "synthetic", "analytical" and "symbolic" types of knowledge, clearly oriented to stress the importance of the lesser codified one. For the authors, the former is a combination of existing knowledge, applied by an inductive process (through testing, experimentation, computer-based simulation or practical work) in order to solve specific problems coming up in the interaction with customers and suppliers. The latter "is related to the creation of meaning and desire as well as aesthetic attributes of products, producing designs, images and symbols, and to the economic use of such forms of cultural artefacts" (p. 897) and characterised by a distinctive tacit, context-specific component, based on an informal interplay between actors in a community space. However referred to the productive systems, all of those characteristics are compliant with the creative processes required to the smart cities. The collective sensemaking demands rather specialised abilities in symbol interpretation and creativity than mere information processing. Sensemaking "starts with chaos [and] is about labelling and categorizing to stabilize the streaming of experience, . . . is social and systemic [and] is about action" (Weick et al., 2005, p. 411, et passim). The interpretation of the context leads to identifying and choosing alternative actions. These choices are guided by recollections of past solutions and by a search for other potential models for action. The exploration of new behaviours, instead of using well-established routines, implies relevant cognitive work, favoured by the free interplay between social actors. Obviously, people have a different level of skill, awareness, capabilities, belief and other resources to explore the new opportunities and possibilities. On the one hand, innovation is slowed down by cognitive blocs due to natural risk aversion (Kahneman and Tversky, 1984) and prevailing exploitation behaviour (March, 1991); on the other hand, people tend to adapt to others, implementing other people's ideas rather than generate their own. In any case, the successful performance of individuals and organisations depends on their common understanding of the innovation process as collective learning.

Cultural maturity is often a very relevant constraint, needing focused unlearning actions, moving first of all from decision makers. Speaking about smart specialisation, Foray and colleagues observe, not without a certain irony, the relevant difficulty of learning inside the institutions carrying out the innovation policies. Before becoming a policy hit, the original concept has been assumed by the OECD, EC and so on as a taboo, the idea had been "stifled and repressed as a result of the enormous conformity that has characterised innovation policy research and practices over the last decades in many international policy forums" (Foray et al., 2011, p. 3). Evidently, the speed of the institutional learning process is not always coherent with the policy goals.

The smart city – viewed as a cultural product "translating" data resources in aesthetic symbols, images, (de)signs, artefacts and narratives, part of collective behaviour – demands widespread sensegiving, seen as the means of influencing sensemaking in others. Symbolic leadership is a relevant component of the learning mix. Through this way, digital resources and the Internet of Things gain a structural role in the everyday life, as a "natural" part of common, usual thinking, just to disappearing from the consciousness of the users. The material city is partially declined as a virtual city, "intangible urban dimension where people, relationships and services are virtually joined and shared to build a smarter community" (Cocchia, 2014, p. 32). Besides, "the ubiquitous sensing and processing works in the background, hidden from the user" (Gubbi et al., 2013, p. 1649).

Tacitness, embeddedness and virtuality imply – keeping close to intentional, structured and deterministic learning processes – a relevant role of the incidental learning, defined as

> a by-product of some other activity, such as task accomplishment, interpersonal interaction, sensing the organizational culture, trial-and-error experimentation, or even formal learning. Informal learning can be deliberately encouraged by an organization or it can take place despite an environment not highly conducive to learning. Incidental learning, on the other hand, almost always takes place although people are not always conscious of it.
>
> (Marsick and Watkins, 1990, p. 12)

Intentional and incidental learning are to be seen as the two sides of the same coin. The former dimension is related to explicitly trying to resolve certain problems and/or enhancing certain functions, in the face of technological opportunities; the latter is the creative, emerging adaptation, an outcome of an inductive process of reflection and action, not highly conscious and influenced by chance. If planning the unintentional may be appear oxymoronic, it's possible and suitable to create a positive environment where "people have the need, motivation, and opportunity for learning" (Marsick and Watkins, 2001, p. 28). Unintentional innovations are highly fostered by an intentional use of the ICTs "given the distributed, asynchronous nature of technology-facilitated interactions, more may be learned incidentally by learners reading between the lines" (ivi, 32).

Another reference, more dated but very useful in approaching the cognitive side of the smart city in a knowledge management view, is the "ba" concept, defined by Nonaka and Konno (1998, p. 40) "as a shared space for emerging relationship. This space can be physical, . . . virtual . . . mental (e.g. shared experiences, ideas, ideals), or any combination of them. . . . Ba is a context which harbors meaning". In translating this concept from organisational context to be more wide and fluid, what is important is the idea of unifying in the same space the physical, virtual and mental dimensions. In this perspective, "ba" is "the world where the individual realizes himself as a part of the environment on which his life depends" (ivi, 41). Following our perspective, it seems a valid alternative definition of smart city, stressing adequately the interdependence between individual and collective behaviours, orienting by a common meaning framework, emerging from self-structuring network thinking.

However focused on organisations, the knowledge management literature offers more relevant contributions to understand the urban smartness development. In this way, another useful concept is the interplay between knowledge and knowing; the former is assumed as what is possessed, and the latter is what is part of action. This epistemological distinction, due to Cook and Brown (1999), points one more time to interactions between physical, social and mental dimensions in the

> generative dance between knowing and knowledge, [the] knowledge is a tool of knowing, that knowing is an aspect of our interaction with the social and physical world, and that the interplay of knowledge and knowing can generate new knowledge and new ways of knowing.
>
> (ivi, 381)

Learning and smart city are to be seen as a space housing and stimulating situated interactions in which knowledge, data and information technologies become a tool of knowing, starting off new knowledge creation.

Speaking about situated interaction (as the adjective "situated" must be taken in a wide, virtual dimension), relational knowledge and interplay between individual and collective dimensions leads necessary to assume a network perspective. Networks are multi-level structured spaces, often characterised by a small word properties (Watts and Strogatz, 1998), relevant in developing collaborative creativity (Uzzi and Spiro, 2005). Critical parts of the social network architecture are the so-called weak ties (in an ego perspective, acquaintances, compared with the close friends strong ties): "if social systems lacking in weak ties will be fragmented and incoherent. New ideas will spread slowly . . . and subgroups separated by race, ethnicity, geography, or other characteristics will have difficulty reaching a modus vivendi" (Granovetter, 1983, p. 202). All factors are really incoherent with the smart city requirements. In the learning cities and regions, networking and partnerships are key ingredients, since collective learning and robustness depend on a continuous exchange and flow of information about products, processes and work organisation. As a complex social constructs, smart cites need enabling learning at all city levels (inhabitants and their families, organisations and city administration through networks). "The collective learning of individuals and their participation in partnership networks are especially important" (Juceviciene, 2010, p. 419). Going beyond Florida's traditional approach to the learning region, Musterd and Gritsai (2012) emphasise the importance of the personal networks impacts. These networks include "personal links, professional and social relations and other types of local social connections related to people's life courses" (p. 343).

In this perspective, ICTs play a structural role, linking networks of people, businesses, infrastructures, resources, energy and spaces, as well as providing intelligent organisational and governance tools. ICTs, Internet-based and reinforced by Internet of Things, open up new possibilities for the growth of effective networks of organisations based upon spatially dispersed interaction (OECD, 2002, p. 21) and "stretched" connectivity (Amin and Cohendet, 2004, p. 93), enlarging spatial proximity to organisational proximity.

All the topics briefly examined point to another, final key aspect: the knowledge and learning governance of the smart city or, in other words, of the process enabling and fostering their building. In this way, governance is a collective exercise addressed to activate cognitive opportunities, enable individual and collective actors to freely play with, to share behaviour schemes and to learn from each other. More differentiated is the city context, and more important is taking into account the cognitive distance (and dissonances) within social actors. As remarked by Juceviciene (2010, p. 429) regarding the Kaunas city case study,

> general policies are important for creating learning approaches in the city, but specific spheres of social life benefit from acquiring learning at different times and at different speeds. Learning partnership networks emerge when there is a perceived need for them by the people and organisations concerned.

As the brief outline has shown, some cognitive-related characters coherent with a smart city self-structuring process are:

- the equilibrium among the intentional and the incidental learning;
- the practical and "free at the sides" exploration of opportunities;
- the interplay between knowledge and knowing (with special regards to the ICT skills);
- the network interactions among actors, crossing the societal structure;
- a clear and visible link between smart city's project and local educational policy; and
- the possibility of recognising and celebrating, with adequate collective rites, the new aesthetic and functional values emerging for the practices activated and sustained by the technological drivers.

Quoting one more time Juceviciene (2007, p. 69) "in this way, quality of spiritual and physical life is achieved, and contemporary work competences are created that enable competitiveness and sustainable development within the city and its organizations". In any case, learning is not a goal *per se*, but a key process to achieve the goals of the city and the development of its inhabitants. Using a biological metaphor, a smart city is an autopoietic construct (Maturana and Varela, 1980), self-structuring and evolving via its own collective cognitive and learning work.

2.3 For a learning policy: seeing both the forest and the trees

In order to activate, to orientate and to sustain a positive learning environment, several "enablers" are identifiable.

Moving from digital side, two key aspects are the open data and the networking public resources. The first are to be seen in an extended and not deterministic perspective, addressed to enlarge the inner potential of the information, beyond the obvious original domain. Free, structured and continuous big data can become a strategic resource for creative, unattended applications, adding intelligence to the context and stimulating new collective behaviours. The mere availability is, under certain conditions, a potential learning slack. In a fruitful policy view (EP, 2014, p. 11), "this allows individuals and companies to process and recombine these and other available data in order to create useful resources for the public, for example real-time traffic information". If planning creativity is not possible, creating intentionally a rich, free, stable and structured data environment is a relevant booster. In itself, data are not a real resource without the cheap and extended possibility of access, communication and exchange. The digital network is not only the necessary for carrying infrastructure; it is more a social "infostructure", aiming for people to interact each other, to develop mutual interdependent behaviours and to enlarge weak ties and social capital resources. Ubiquity and pervasiveness in networks can enhance this use. Describing the e-Kaunas smart city case study, Juceviciene (2010, 428) stresses the importance of having

> a network for data exchange that encompasses all sectors (municipality, education, healthcare, transport, culture and others) and a system of information services on the social, economic and cultural life of the city. [Kaunas] creates an electronic card for the city, as well as a website for local and worldwide needs and carries out a public relations campaign of e-city ideas in all types of media.

Another class of enablers is related to collective knowledge resources and their development opportunities. Obviously,

> a learning region requires a human infrastructure of knowledge workers who can apply their intelligence in production. The education and training system must be a learning system that can facilitate life-long learning and provide the high levels of group orientation and teaming required for knowledge-intensive economic organisations.
>
> Florida (p. 532, et passim)

The core point is not (only) the presence level of high-skilled people but the social extent of key competences directly involved in the cognitive processes, looking specifically at "Digital competence; Learning to learn; Social and civic competences; Sense of initiative and entrepreneurship; and Cultural awareness and expression" (EP, 2006). Given the importance of informal and incidental learning, some authors also emphasise

> three conditions to enhance this kind of learning: critical reflection to surface tacit knowledge and beliefs, stimulation of proactivity on the part of the learner to actively identify options and to learn new skills to implement those options or solutions, and creativity to encourage a wider range of options.
>
> (Marsick and Watkins, 2001, p. 30)

Building a smart, learning city implies a relevant and widespread level of capabilities (Sen, 2009):

> the sole power and ability of citizens to construct their own cities appropriate to their needs. This power is based on thinking of education as developing lifelong leaders and discovering learning as practicing experiential solutions to the needs, problems, and opportunities of the community.
>
> (Scott, 2014, p. 92)

Consequently, one strategic question becomes what kind of educational resources may have a smart city. Several authors have focused their attention on this topic, directly or referring to the more wide field of the learning region. Yorks and Barto (2015, p. 35) point to integration between adult education and human resources development "as citizens being learners are confronted with both the challenges of workplace change and the interconnectedness of communities". The citizen-workers are seen as people able to "contribute to organizations and society in ways that have meaning for them"; for this purpose, they propose the creation of inter-institutional connections. Building partnerships and networks is a widespread action scheme. Since 2001, the European political discourse on lifelong learning pinpoints local-level partnership as an essential resource. Moving from previous studies (Nyhan et al., 1999), according to the European Commission, prone to a wide, inclusive and societal approach, partnership

> should include local authorities, schools, universities, other learning providers and related services such as information, guidance and counselling, research centres, enterprises (as part of their corporate social responsibility), public employment services, NGOs working at the local level (e.g. voluntary and community organisations), representatives of particular groups of (potential) learners and actors dealing with gender equality issues.
>
> (European Commission, 2001, p. 11)

In the higher education field, the learning cities are assumed as a natural context to apply the Community Engagement Scholarship (CES) approach devoted "to facilitate development of university–community partnerships and to address societal problems through community-based research and evaluation, service learning and civic engagement, recognition of the value of tacit knowledge, and efforts aimed at the democratization of knowledge" (Fitzgerald and Zientek, 2015, p. 26). One specific CES methodology coherent in the urban context, following the authors, is the "service learning" formula. In this approach,

> students, faculty, staff, partner organizations, and community members are all contributors to knowledge and all have the potential to both teach and to learn. . . . Service learning is about relationships between the learner and the teacher and about the relationship between what's learned and how it is applied to real problems through service and engagement. . . . All [the actors] involved in service learning play the role of both teacher and learner.

The reciprocity involved in service learning creates a diverse community of experts. Those experts, when combined, hold a vast knowledge of the community and have diverse perspectives on how to tackle even the most complex community problems.

(ivi, 29)

Also the ICT may play a crucial role as learning multiplier and accelerator of change, notably in tertiary education, launching free and systematic events by MOOCs, Massive Open On-Line Courses (EADTU, 2015).

A last (but obviously not least) point is the global reinforcement of the social capabilities, looking in specific to the more deprived/lesser-integrated urban actors. Community capacity building has a critical role to play in local development, more pronounced regarding the possible degree of "smartness" of the cities. Without an inclusive and participative action, focused on "enabling all members of the community, including the poorest and the most disadvantaged, to develop skills and competencies so as to take greater control of their own lives" (OECD, 2009, p. 11), it's quite impossible to reach the adequate level of cohesiveness and resilience necessary to deal with economic and social challenges as well as ICT opportunities. The "happy few" or "the have and have not" risks are sensible. As we have seen, the smart city has to be seen as an empowered community, not only to the technological side, but chiefly in autonomy, knowledge, resilience and leadership. Capacity building needs to be seen as an endogenous process where external agencies, such as governments, civil society and businesses, act merely as a catalyst, facilitator (including providing resources) or knowledge broker for communities. On this ground, the smart city meets another key-reference of the new policy agenda: the already cited social innovation concept. One more time, it is a question of networking: social innovation "involves alliances between the top and the bottom, or between what we call the 'bees' (the creative individuals with ideas and energy) and the 'trees' (the big institutions with the power and money to make things happen to scale)" (Murray et al., 2010, p. 8).

Nobody in itself (neither institutions nor charismatic leaders) can ignite and lead the complex, hidden and systemic processes needed to found a sustainable smart city (and the correlated smart community of inhabitants). The active engagement and the interplay between a multiplicity of actors, provided by adequate capabilities, in a multi-network space, are basic conditions. Establishing a sustainable learning policy demands seeing "both the forest and the trees", both the general frame and the single necessities, roles and contributions. It's a matter of equilibrium between "the ethics of possibility" and the "ethics of probability" (Appadurai, 2013, p. 299). Between hope, aspiration, desire, creativity and systematised rationalities, risk management and cost/benefits approaches is a matter of smartness.

3 Position and potential roles of public utilities

The word "multi-utility" brings together two main concepts: the management of a wide range of services in different industries (multi-) and the public interest of the services provided (utility). In Italy, multi-utilities are very heterogeneous in terms of size (economics, customers, employees); territorial presence; range of businesses managed; and shareholder composition. At the same time multi-utilities have at least one characteristic in common: the strong roots in the geographical areas in which they operate, coming both from their typically long tradition and from the type of services provided to their customers. In the last few years, the Italian multi-utilities context has been characterised by an increasing level of competition (both within the market and for the market), fast growing technological opportunities and uncertainty originating from national and local regulation.

Given this context, it is quite simple to predict that playing a key role in a smart development process will be a "must choice" for any multi-utility that aims to maintain and possibly further develop its leadership in the future. There are at least four main reasons why this assumption could be true:

1   Multi-utilities manage several unique points of regular access to their customers in order to run their businesses (e.g. meters for electricity, gas, water and district heating services), naturally producing a huge stream of big data (with relevant potential value for all the actors in the urban space) and, at the same time, linking them in a highly structured, cheap and potentially bidirectional network.
2   Consequently, the technological shift driven by the IoT will have a serious impact on the information that multi-utilities will manage and the way they will interact with their customers.
3   More and more the services provided by multi-utilities will benefit by and/or will need strong interaction with other services, infrastructures and information managed by other public or private players, in order to gain quality and sustainability, through more robust positive externalities.
4   Long local history (despite the actual merging and restructuring processes) has characterised multi-utilities, in the common beliefs and perceptions, as "near-institutional actors", more easily seen as an innovation/learning vector.

3.1 Fostering smartness with HR management: competencies, learning opportunities and educational involvement in the Hera approach

The Hera Group is strictly coherent with this general framework. Hera is one of Italy's largest multi-utilities and operates mainly in environmental services (waste collection and treatment); energy services (distribution and sale of electricity and gas); and water services (waterworks, sewerage and purification). As of the beginning of 2016, Hera operates in the centre-north of Italy, particularly in an extensive area throughout Emilia-Romagna, in part of the province of Pesaro-Urbino and in the provinces of Padua, Udine and Trieste. Hera's goal is to be the best multi-utility in Italy for its customers, workforce and shareholders. It aims to achieve this through further development of an original corporate model capable of innovation and of forging strong links with the areas in which it operates by respecting the local environment. Even if Hera was established on November 2002 and then was listed on Milan stock exchange on June 2003, to better understand its business, it is important to recall that some of the core processes such as gas and water distribution have a long heritage that had begun in the second half of the nineteenth century.

One of the major challenges that Hera is facing to maintain its leadership in the actual smart development context is to match the need of maintaining solid links with the regions in which it operates and the need of generating innovation in all provided services. In this competition, human resources management plays a key role to assure that the company is and will be provided with the best and most useful competences, sustained and empowered by strong learning capabilities. This is the starting point for the development of the "Hera HR smart approach", aimed to reach the best dynamic balance between heritage and innovation through three main HR streamlines such as (1) culture and behaviours, (2) diversity and inclusion and (3) learning and organisation. All the HR activities have been reread and eventually redesigned in order to best fit the goal of creating added value from the composition of traditional cultural values and innovative needs in a fast changing context, driven by the ability of sharing resources and information and pursuing cooperation, both internally and externally.

Focusing on the learning streamline, Hera has further developed, and in some cases redesigned, in an inward/outward integrated perspective. Its approach to education and training follows four main paths:

1   Confirming consolidated initiatives directed to preserve the core competences in the company operating areas, reinforcing the general workforce abilities to teach and learn, seen as an ordinary part of the collective professional behaviour ("School of Crafts")
2   Evolving running initiatives of structured cooperation with secondary technical schools, designed to close the gap between formal learning and business applications ("Hera teaches you a job . . . at school")
3   Developing new initiatives of cooperation with secondary school in order to co-design teaching programmes, provide technical lessons and host students to let them put into place their knowledge in a workplace (an agreement between Hera and the Governmental Department of Education – Emilia Romagna Region for work-related learning in the technical education)
4   Further developing the role of HerAcademy (Antonelli et al., 2013), as of today, the first and only Italian corporate university in the multi-utility industry, assumed as a two-way link between the company and the educational system

Internally Hera has invested on the preservation and adaptation of the technical skills needed to operate in its core traditional business. The company has progressively developed a knowledge management model (see Figure 15.1) designed to cover three main dimensions of knowledge transfer: from trainers to individuals, in interactions among expert workers and junior workers and in collective interactions among workers during daily operational activities.

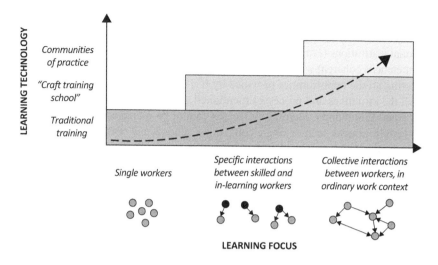

Figure 15.1 Collective learning and communities of practice

The aim is to build an inner company capability to strengthen the connection and coherence between formal training sessions and daily operational applications of theoretical knowledge. Furthermore, in terms of approach Hera uses a combination of:

1   traditional educational methods (such as training sessions, distance learning);
2   specific internal "schools" focused on the interaction between expert senior workers and junior workers and designed to facilitate the integration between formal and non-formal learning, the development of individual capabilities of learning and the interdisciplinary approach to work; and
3   network of practices.

As a matter of fact, over the years, Hera has worked on some specific key factors such as:

1   developing widespread (auto)-capabilities of knowledge representation and management among all human resources through initiatives aimed to "teach to teach" and "teach to learn" that support the transmission of practical knowledge and its own enhancement;
2   recognising and capitalising on "emergent" networks of practice, throughout active approaches of social network analysis and organisational micro-design, all this using cooperating ICT settings such as forums and wikis; and
3   hybridising their own knowledge with a structured openness to the local and global environment, from the structured networks with academic and educational actors to professional communities and emergent phenomena.

These human resources key factors can be seen as enablers that have prepared the company to manage profitable interactions with the educational system, in a typical smart community perspective. On this basis, Hera is cooperating with educational institutions (public or private) to preserve and develop the supply of core competences coherent with the actual and future demand of a smart city, using and fostering all the opportunities provided by ICT development.

All the initiatives and processes mentioned earlier are based on the belief that, in a smart community, learning processes cannot be managed any more in confined environments such as single companies, schools and research centres, needing to be designed, managed and monitored in a cooperative, networked way in which each actor plays a critical role for its own and the collective development. In this context, for a multi-utility (as well as a local company), smartness is necessarily related to the ability to make sure that its growing capabilities really match with the local (smart) community. Looking to the future, Hera's active role in creating smartness is to be a conscious, but not deterministic, network catalyst agent in matching data, information, knowledge and relational and social capital; in distributing learning opportunities; in reducing transactional costs; and in nurturing cohesive behaviour across the local and the global arenas.

4 Concluding remarks

As we have seen, the smartness level in a system is not more than the overall cognitive resources and use-related abilities and opportunities (social capital and collective vision included) that the system owns. Developing this kind of intangible asset is a core part of whatever smart cities design and practice. For a public utility, to be a strategic player in this context implies managing, in an integrated and circular way, at least three orders of resources and processes:

1   The "diffusive interface" between technological innovation and citizens, by service-driven activities proposing and enabling new forms and opportunities of behaviour
2   The distinctive embeddedness in the local governance networks, acting as a market key-actor as well as a co-leading "institution"
3   The real learning capabilities, in itself and in the cognitive and productive situated networks, with a specific focus on the educational and research side, seen as favourite path to understand, explore and free creative opportunities

In this view, human resources management and organisational development are to be seen as an inner component of the more wide enabling role of public utilities toward the smartness, insofar as they contribute to empower the collective learning processes, across the whole context.

Notes

1 Organisation, Learning & People Development Director, Gruppo Hera.
2 Alma Mater Studiorum University of Bologna, DISI.

Bibliography

Amin, A. and Cohendet, P. (2004), *Architectures of knowledge: Firms, capabilities, and communities*, Oxford, Oxford University Press.

Antonelli, G., Cappiello, G. and Pedrini, G. (2013), The corporate university in the European utility industries, *Utilities Policy*, 25, 33–41.

Appadurai, A. (2013), The *future as cultural fact. Essays on the global condition*, New York, Verso Book.

Argyris, Ch. and Schön, D. (1978), *Organisational learning*, Reading, MA, Addison-Wesley.

Asheim, B. (2012), The changing role of learning regions in the globalizing knowledge economy: A theoretical re-examination, *Regional Studies*, 46 (8), 993–1004.

Asheim, B., Boschma, R. and Cooke, P. (2011), Constructing regional advantage: Platform policies based on related variety and differentiated knowledge bases, *Regional Studies*, 45 (7), 893–904.

Atzori, L., Iera, A. and Morabito, G. (2010), The internet of things: A survey, *Computer Networks*, 54, 2787–2805.

Camagni, R. and Capello, R. (2013), Regional innovation patterns and the EU regional policy reform: Toward smart innovation policies, *Growth and Change*, 44 (2), 355–389.

Capello, R. and Faggian, A. (2005), Collective learning and relational capital in local innovation processes, *Regional Studies*, 39 (1), 75–87.

Caragliu, A., Del Bo, C. and Nijkamp, P. (2009), Smart Cities in Europe, 3rd Central European Conference in Regional Science, CERS, pp. 45–59.

Cocchia, A. (2014), Smart and digital city: A systematic literature review, in R. Dameri and C. Rosenthal-Sabroux (eds.), *Smart city: How to create public and economic value with high technology in urban space*, Heidelberg, Springer International Publishing, pp. 13–43.

Cook, S.D. and Brown, J.S. (1999), Bridging epistemologies: The generative dance between organizational knowledge and organizational knowing, *Organization Science*, 10 (4), July–August 1999, 381–400.

David, P. and Foray, D. (2002), An introduction to the economy of the knowledge societies, *International Social Science Journal*, 54 (171), 9–23.

EADTU. (2015), Position papers for European cooperation on MOOCs. Available at: http://home.eadtu.eu/news/95-position-papers-for-european-cooperation-on-moocs, accessed 20 August 2015.

Ergazakis, M., Metaxiotis, M. and Psarras, J. (2004), Towards knowledge cities: Conceptual analysis and success stories, *Journal of Knowledge Management*, 8 (5), 5–15.

European Commission. (2001), *Communication from the Commission 'Making a European Area of Lifelong Learning a Reality'*, Brussels, 21 November2001 COM(2001) 678 final.

European Commission. (2013), *Guide to social innovation*. Available at http://ec.europa.eu/regional_policy/sources/docgener/presenta/social_innovation/social_innovation_2013.pdf, accessed 20 August 2015.

European Commission. (2015), *RIS3 guide*. Available at http://s3platform.jrc.ec.europa.eu/wikis3pguide, accessed 20 August 2015.

European Parliament. (2006), *Recommendation of the European Parliament and of the Council of 18 December 2006 on key competences for lifelong learning* (2006/962/EC).

European Parliament. (2014), *Mapping Smart Cities in the EU*, IP/A/ITRE/ST/2013–02 January 2014.

Fitzgerald, H. and Zientek, R. (2015), Learning cities, systems change, and community engagement scholarship, *New Directions for Adult and Continuing Education*, 145, Spring 2015, 21–33.

Florida, R. (1995), Towards the learning region, *Futures*, 27, 527–536.

Foray, D., David, P. and Hall, B. (2009), Smart specialisation – the concept, *Knowledge Economists Policy Brief*, 9, 1–5, Brussels. Available at http://ec.europa.eu/invest-in-research/pdf/download_en/kfg_policy_brief_no9.pdf, accessed 20 August 2015.

Foray, D., David, P. and Hall, B. (2011), *Smart specialization. From academic idea to political instrument, the surprising career of a concept and the difficulties involved in its implementation*, MTEI working paper. Available at http://infoscience.epfl.ch/record/1/0232/files/MTEI-WP-2011–001-Foray_David_Hall.pdf, accessed 20 August 2015.

Foucault, M. (1972), *Archaeology of knowledge*, New York, Pantheon.

Granovetter, M. (1983), The strength of weak ties: A network theory revisited, *Sociological Theory*, 1, 201–233.

Gubbi, J., Rajkumar, B., Marusic, S. and Palaniswami, M. (2013), Internet of things (IoT): A vision, architectural elements, and future directions, *Future Generation Computer Systems*, 29, 1645–1660.

Hall, P. (2000), Creative cities and economic development, *Urban Studies*, 37 (4), 633–649.

Healy, A. and Morgan, K. (2012), Spaces of innovation: Learning, proximity and the ecological turn, *Regional Studies*, 46 (8), 1041–1053.

Jarvis, P. (2007), *Globalization, lifelong learning and the learning society: Lifelong learning and the learning society* (Vol. 2), New York, NY, Routledge.

Juceviciene, P. (2007), *The learning city. Kaunas Technologija*, quoted in Juceviciene, P. (2010).

Juceviciene, P. (2010), Sustainable development of the learning city, *European Journal of Education*, 45 (3), 419–436.

Kahneman, D. and Tversky, A. (1984), Choices, values, and frames, *American Psychologist*, 39 (4), 341–350.

Lundvall, B-A. (1994), The learning economy, *Journal of Industry Studies*, 1 (2), 23–42.

Maillat, D. and Kebir, L. (1999), "Learning region" et systèmes de production territoriaux, *Revue d'économie Régionale et Urbaine*, 3, 429–447.

March, J. (1991), Exploration and exploitation in organizational learning, *Organization Science*, 2 (1), 71–87.

Marsick, V.J. and Watkins, K.E. (1990), *Informal and incidental learning in the workplace*, London, Routledge.

Marsick, V.J. and Watkins, K.E. (2001), Informal and incidental learning, *New Directions for Adult and Continuing Education*, 89, 25–34.

Maturana, H. and Varela, F. (1980), *Autopoiesis and cognition. The realization of the Living*, Dordrecht, D. Reidel Publishing Company.

McCann, P. and Ortega-Argilés, R. (2011), Smart specialisation, regional growth and applications to EU cohesion policy, *Document de treball de l'IEB 2011/14*, Available at http://www.ieb.ub.edu/aplicacio/fitxers/2011/7/Doc2011–14.pdf, accessed 20 August 2015.

Moulaert, F., Martinelli, F., Swyngedouw, E. and González, S. (2005), Towards alternative model(s) of local innovation, *Urban Studies*, 42 (11), 1969–1990.

Murray, R., Caulier-Grice, J. and Mulgan, G. (2010), *The open book of social innovation*, London, The Young Foundation.

Musterd, S. and Gritsai, O. (2012), The creative knowledge city in Europe: Structural conditions and urban policy strategies for competitive cities, *European Urban and Regional Studies*, 20 (3), 343–359.

Nam, T. and Pardo, T. (2011), Conceptualizing smart city with dimensions of technology, people, and institutions, *The Proceedings of the 12th Annual International Conference on Digital Government Research*. Available at https://www.ctg.albany.edu/publications/journals/dgo_2011_smartcity/dgo_2011_smartcity.pdf, accessed 20 August 2015.

Nonaka, I. and Konno, N. (1998), The concept of "Ba": Building a foundation for knowledge creation, *California Management Review*, 40 (3), 40–54.

Nonaka, I. and Takeuchi, H. (1995), *The knowledge-creating company*, New York, Oxford University Press.

Nyhan, B., Attwell, G. and Deitmer, L. (eds.) (1999), *Towards the learning region. Education and regional innovation in the European union and United States*, Thessaloniki, CEDEFOP.

OECD. (2000), *Knowledge Management in the Learning Society*, Paris, OECD.

OECD. (2002), *Cities and regions in the new learning economy*, Paris, OECD.

OECD. (2009), *Community capacity building. Creating a better future together*, Paris, OECD.

Rutten, R. and Boekema, F. (2012), From learning region to learning in a socio-spatial context, *Regional Studies*, 46 (8), 981–992.

Schuurman, D., De Marez, L. and Ballon, P. (2015), Living labs: A systematic literature review, European Network of Living Labs (2015), *Research Day Conference Proceedings 2015. Open Living Labs Day*, 16–28. Available at https://www.scribd.com/doc/276089123/ENoLL-Research-Day-Conference-Proceedings-2015#download, accessed 08 September 2015.

Scott, L. (2014), Learning cities for all: Directions to a new adult education and learning movement, *New Directions for Adult and Continuing Education*, 145, Spring 2015, 83–94.

Sen, A. (2009), *The idea of justice*, London, Allen Lane.

UNESCO-Institute for Lifelong Learning. (2014), *Conference report: International conference on learning cities: Lifelong learning for all*, Hamburg, UNESCO.

Uzzi, B. and Spiro, J. (2005), Collaboration and creativity: The small world problem, *American Journal of Sociology*, 111 (2), 447–504.

Watts, D. and Strogatz, S. (1998), Collective dynamics of 'small-world' networks, *Nature*, 393, 440–442.

Weick, K. Sutcliffe, K. and Obstfeld, D. (2005), Organizing and the process of sensemaking, *Organization Science*, 16 (4), 409–421.

Yorks, L. and Barto, J. (2015), Workplace, organizational, and societal: Three domains of learning for 21st-century cities, *New Directions for Adult and Continuing Education*, 145, 35–44.

16 Urban mobility in a smart development perspective

Luca Zamparini

1 Introduction

Mobility represents one of the important dimensions that allow a city to improve its level of competitiveness and to foster smart development paths. Policies related to smart mobility need to take into account connectivity with national and international transport network on the one hand and the efficiency of local transport systems on the other. With respect to the first issue, the nodes of the international and national networks that are geographically located within the city area or in easily accessible places must be prioritized. The presence of ports, airports and trade infrastructure such as intermodal logistic platforms, distriparks and the like has to be considered. It should be noted that not all cities can represent main nodes within large national and international networks. On the other hand, investments should in most cases be directed to the connection between the local nodes and the main national/international ones. A report by Caltrans (2010) has listed six possible principles that should be followed when pursuing smart mobility initiatives: (1) location efficiency, (2) reliable mobility, (3) health and safety, (4) environmental stewardship, (5) social equity and (6) robust economy. Location efficiency should foster the integration of mobility and land use policies in order to minimize the need for trip making and the length of trip. Reliable mobility should be based on transportation network management and on multimodal mobility options, with predictable costs and times, to reduce congestion. Health and safety should guide policies to promote management and design practices that lessen exposure to pollution, minimize injuries and fatalities and encourage active living. This should be gained by prioritizing integrated transportation systems and services to reduce environmental risks and the exposure of travellers to hazardous threats and to pose the conditions for efficient emergency responses. This principle is tightly connected to an environmental stewardship that considers the natural environment by supporting policies that aim at reducing emissions of greenhouse gases and of pollutants. Social equity involves both infrastructure provision and system management. It is aimed at prioritizing the mobility of economically, socially or physically disadvantaged people to increase their participation in smart city activities. Finally, the robust economy principle considers the effects of mobility on the competitiveness of the city and on its smart development. This can be measured by the congestion effects on productivity, by the efficient use of system resources, by the network performance optimization and by the return on investment.

Mobility was considered as one of the important domains of smart cities in a taxonomy that was proposed by the *Technische Universität Wien* (see Chapter 4 for a thorough description). More recently, a paper by Neirotti et al. (2014) has included transport and mobility among the important domains of smart development initiatives, jointly with natural resources and energy, buildings, living, government and economy and people. The paper also considered the important sub-domains of mobility: (1) city logistics that should aim at improving the flows of goods within a city through effective and efficient interaction and integration with traffic conditions, geographical, societal and environmental issues; (2) people mobility related to the provision of innovative and sustainable ways to facilitate the movement of persons within the city fostering public and environmentally friendly transport options by taking advantage of technological innovation and by promoting proactive citizens' behaviours; and (3) info-mobility as the distribution of dynamic and multimodal information, both before and during the trip, aimed at improving transport efficiency and at minimizing private and public transport costs. The last sub-domain can be considered as a transversal tool that can be useful to maximize the quality and efficiency of the previous ones. The following sections of this chapter will be devoted to discussing and commenting on the possible smart policies for the movement of freight and persons in a city and to the Information and Communication Technologies (ICTs) that can be usefully adopted to support mobility.

2 Smart policies for urban freight transport mobility

With respect to freight transport, smart policies and infrastructural investments should move from the traditional quantitative measure of transport flows to a more qualitative one. It is not useful to have large flows of goods (perhaps for the presence of a transportation hub) that do not impact economically on the territory and that do not allow the development of value-added activities useful to start or consolidate processes of industrialization or of local development of business activities. A measure of the transport of goods that takes into account the impact on local activity and the ability to activate virtuous processes of smart development should be implemented. Moreover, city planners should carefully consider the implementation of integrated transport and land use policies to optimize the quantity of (public and private) warehouse, logistic platforms and similar nodal infrastructures and to allocate them to areas that cause the minimal amount of pollution and congestion to the neighbourhoods where the majority of citizens live. Urban freight transport (UFT) policies have a manifold relevance. They can be useful to optimize (1) the environmental effect of urban freight movements; (2) the total cost of freight transport and physical distribution that has a significant and direct bearing on the efficiency of the economy; (3) the effect of freight transport costs on the cost of commodities; and (4) the role of UFT in servicing, retaining and improving the competitiveness of the industrial and trading activities of the urban area.

In the recent decades, there has been a growing interest from both academics and policy makers on the efficient deployment of logistics for collection and distribution activities in city centres. UFT evolution is dependent on several socio-economic variables such as trends in land use planning, changes in the population structure and commercial trends in various sectors of urban economic systems. Policies involved in UFT should also take into account their environmental sustainability and social issues (Browne et al., 2012) related, among others, to safety, congestion and use of the roads by residents of the area. Several strategies have been proposed in order to optimize the economic, social and environmental efficiency of UFT. Among them, it is worthwhile mentioning the use of urban consolidation and distribution centres, the provision of freight facilities (parking areas, loading/unloading bays), the use of alternative modes (i.e. cycle-logistics), the design of peculiar vehicles and the adoption of ICT tools. Moreover, the transport economic literature has analyzed UFT by using many different data collection strategies and statistical/econometric techniques. An important issue to take into consideration is related to the different economic actors that are involved in the urban freight distribution activities. Table 16.1 provides a summary of the various categories of peculiar interests related to the various urban freight transport economic actors.

Table 16.1 Different interests of urban freight transport actors

Category	*Actors*	*Main interest in urban freight transport*
Supply chain actors	Shippers	Delivery and pick-up of goods at the lowest cost while meeting customers' needs
	Transport companies and logistics providers	Low-cost but high-quality transport operations, satisfaction of shippers' and receivers' interests
	Receivers (megastores, small shops)	On-time delivery of products, with short lead times
	Consumers	Availability of a variety of goods near the centre
Other urban freight transport affected actors	Other economic actors in the urban area (manufacturers, service providers, craftsmen)	Site accessibility and on-time delivery
	Residents	Minimum hindrance caused by goods transport
	Visitors/shoppers	Minimum hindrance caused by goods transport and a high variety of the latest products in the shops

(Continued)

Table 16.1 (Continued)

Category	Actors	Main interest in urban freight transport
Resource supply actors	Infrastructure providers	Cost recovery and infrastructure performance
	Infrastructure operators	Accessibility and infrastructure use
	Land-owners	Profitability of local areas
Public authorities	Local government	Attractive city for inhabitants and visitors, minimum hindrance but effective and efficient transport operations
	National government	Minimum external effects by transport, maximum overall economic situation

Source: Marcucci et al., 2013.

By considering the various stakeholders and their main interests in urban freight transport, several considerations emerge. First, it is evident that the various private economic actors (supply chain actors, other urban freight transport affected actors and resource supply actors) are characterized by heterogeneous needs that determine important trade-offs among the satisfaction of the various interests. Second, the main categories that emerge are the need to deploy effective and efficient transport operations, the minimization of hindrance to residents and visitors and the reduction of transport operation costs. Lastly, public authorities (and especially local ones) have the main task of reconciling the various and conflicting interests.

3 Smart policies for urban passenger transport mobility

With respect to passenger transport, a city is characterized by a good accessibility to the national and international transport networks to the extent that, for example, it is possible to have a return trip on the same day when travelling on business or for leisure. Smart mobility should be also considered at a strictly local level by analyzing, in particular, how urban mobility is managed and carried out and to which extent it determines smart development possibilities. Goodwin (2008) has proposed a taxonomy of possible incentives that can alter mobility decisions towards smarter options. Table 16.2 proposes the list of the considered incentives on the basis of the traditional partition of travel demand models following the four stages of route choice; mode choice (or modal split, i.e. the percentages of movements that are carried out with the various modes of transport); destination choice; and number of trips.

By analysing the various incentives that are listed in Table 16.2, it is possible to notice that some are related to specific characteristics of urban neighbourhoods

298   *Luca Zamparini*

Table 16.2 Incentives to the various stages of travel demand decision to modify mobility

	Key incentives
Route choice (assignment)	Relative journey times, sometimes money costs
	Information and expectation about routes, e.g. as implied by colour and thickness of roads on maps, broadcast news reports
	Real time route guidance, in-vehicle (e.g. satellite navigation systems) and on road (e.g. variable message signs, recommended detours, speed limits)
	Traffic management, e.g. limited access to residential areas or shopping centres restricting through routes
	Pleasantness of scenery, landmarks, iconic sculptures
	Fear of certain types of road or area
	Availability of facilities on some routes (toilets, shops, etc.)
	Differential priorities for different vehicles, e.g. general freeways versus roads with bus lanes
Mode choice	Generalized cost difference between modes (time and money)
	Priority systems e.g. bus lanes, preferential traffic signals, turning movements
	Desire to experiment
	Quality aspects (comfort, cleanliness, privacy, sociability, security from crime)
	Safety
	Reliability, variability, punctuality, flexibility
	Possibilities of other activities (e.g. reading, working, sleeping, communications, entertainment)
Destination choice	Relative generalized cost (time and money) of access
	Number of options available
	Perception of attractiveness influenced by advertising and social fashion
	Differential property prices, wages, price of goods
	Life-style choices (e.g. occasional big shopping versus frequent small shopping; preference for suburban or inner city life styles)
	Availability of secondary facilities (e.g. interaction of work and school locations, or leisure facilities after work, etc.)
Number of trips	Usually assumed to be unaffected by any incentives. This is disputed. Some consider that it a stable part of human requirements, at about 3 trips per day; others say that, since it varies very substantially between individuals and for individuals over time, it cannot be stable. Evidence unclear but logically likely that it is affected by generalized cost and life-style choices at least.

Source: Goodwin, 2008.

(i.e. pleasantness of scenery, landmarks and iconic sculptures for route choice and perception of attractiveness influenced by advertising and social fashion for destination choice). Others are related to specific characteristics of the citizens (as the desire to experiment in mode choice and life-style choices for destination choice). In most of the cases, though, local authorities and transport mobility managers can adopt policies that can influence each stage of the travel decision process. In this context, one of the key elements to take into account in order to optimize urban passenger transport is surely the degree of security and safety that characterizes the alternative modalities such as, for example, the bicycle. In recent decades, various hypotheses have been suggested to improve bike transport safety. We must remember, in this respect, the dedicated bicycle paths and areas closed to motorized transport. A limit to these interventions has historically, and in many cases, been represented by the fact that there is a need of a continuous and integrated network, which has only seldom been put in place due to a whole series of reasons related to urban development. A policy that seems to be ever more diffused in order to encourage the transport by bike is the reduction to 30 km/h speed limit for cars and motorcycles in the city centres. This allows avoiding the need to provide bike lanes and substantially reduces the number of accidents involving cyclists, often with serious consequences. It is estimated that this speed is fatal in 15% of the accidents while, in case the speed is 50 km/h or more, the rate of fatality exceeds 50%. Another element to be considered to improve the city mobility is represented by the greater frequency and density of public transport. In this context, policies should be aimed at allowing modal integration and thus at enabling a larger use of public transport. Moreover, they should improve the accessibility and quality of public transport options, which must meet the users' demand to the greatest possible extent. In this context, origin/destination matrices among the various neighbourhoods of the city should be estimated in order to optimize the implementation of public transport services. Lastly, the connections between local public transport and other efficient ways, such as transportation by bike or on foot, and the nodes of the national and international networks involving the city of reference (the ports, airports and so on) should be optimized. Taking into consideration the fact that a large share of local transport will still be represented by private motorized vehicles, policies of smart mobility must also foster the use of cars and motorbikes that have as little environmental impact as possible. Therefore, the use of small-sized and of new generation cars must be endorsed by also penalizing those with higher consumption and that emit larger amounts of particulate pollutants. In the context of private transport, policies that have tended to minimize the time needed for transport through the construction of ever larger road infrastructures collided with the empirical observations according to which a major road infrastructure often leads to an increase in the rate of motorization with the consequent deterioration of mobility (Goodwin, 2008). This is due to increased congestion, longer average transport time, higher rates of accidents, higher fuel consumption and a more marked impact on the environment.

3.1 The role of behavioural economics strategies to modify urban travel patterns

One of the branches of transport economic research that has been gaining importance in the last few decades is the one that considers the behavioural motives that determine travel patterns of individuals and of firms. Travel behaviour has thus been associated with choices related to route, destination, time and mode of travel (Avineri, 2012). In this context, travel (in the case of passenger transport) and shipping (in the case of freight transport) decisions are taken more on the basis of attitudes and beliefs rather than following the traditional concept of utility maximization (Bamberg et al., 2010). The use of strategies based on the behavioural economics principles is particularly important for smart development. This is due to the fact that the change of attitudes and motivations is related to the medium term. Consequently, it has long-lasting effects on the patterns of mobility and of logistics activities of citizens and of firms.

A description of the most important principles that guide the behaviour of economic agents has been proposed by Dawnay and Shah (2005). The first principle is that other people's behaviour matters. A possible example related to transport economics proposed by the authors is the willingness to wear a seatbelt while driving. They state that, in the short term, there is resistance to abide to the norm, but as it becomes a social norm, people tend to follow it without considering the probability of getting caught without it or the likelihood of having an accident. Urban authorities should then consider all possible tools to shift the preferences of citizens and firms in the medium term. The second principle states that habits are important and difficult to change when they are repeated often and there are strong and incipient rewards. With respect to urban mobility, this may explain why many citizens continue to use their private cars even in the cases in which preferable public alternatives are offered by local administrations. A strategy to change this pattern can be based on offering financial incentives to use environmentally friendly transport options while raising the time and monetary costs to use private cars or motorbikes. The third principle is that, in many cases, people are motivated to do the right thing even when there is no financial compensation for their acts. Experimental economists have outlined that fairness is an important driver of people's actions. In these cases, a monetary reward can crowd out intrinsic motivations, and thus it can be counter-productive. As an example in urban mobility, it is possible to consider (Avineri, 2012) low penalties on illegal parking that may be considered as a probabilistic shadow market price that may substitute a positive social norm of good parking practices in certain developed urban areas.

The fourth principle implies that people's self-expectations influence how they behave. In this context, commitments can be very important as people are reluctant to change subsequently their choices especially when the commitment emerges from a whole group with a high degree of social capital. This principle may be used by urban policy makers to drive the behaviour of citizens and, more importantly, to consider cost effective ways to obtain commitments by small transport firms that may modify their warehousing and distributing strategies for a more environmentally and socially effective urban freight transport mobility. The fifth principle is related to the fact that people are loss averse. This implies that it is more likely that they would alter their behaviour in order to avoid some loss rather than to gain something. An analytical and empirical study to prove this assumption has been provided by Rose and Masiero (2010) that considered a large sample of commuters in the Sydney metropolitan area and estimated their value of travel time savings. Their results imply the need for policy makers to adopt correct decisions in terms of pricing for the use of public infrastructure. The sixth principle states that people are bad at computation. This is normally the outcome of one of several internal biases (salience, discounting, framing, defaults, intuition among others). This principle can be used by local policy makers, for example, in the context of travel information systems and planning. The best option from a social viewpoint may be presented as the default one in order to raise its modal share. Another possible case may be related to the lack of information about the energy consumption of the various transport modes. Providing clear and specific information about the various options may increase the awareness of citizens and modify, at least partially, the modal split of urban mobility.

The last principle is related to the fact that people need to feel involved and effective to make a change. Consequently, people need to feel capable of doing something to change a possible suboptimal situation. In this respect, too much information may determine helplessness and lack of control, which normally lead to inaction. On the other hand, the timeliness and density of information can make people able to take confident decisions and feel in control of the situation (Batty et al., 2012). Moreover, being exposed to many different choices could either have people avoiding to decide or feel that they have not taken the best possible decision. Moreover, bottom-up approaches to changing travel behaviour are in general more effective than top-down policies. An example was proposed by Bartle et al. (2011) who considered the sharing or travel information among commuter cyclists. The use of an interactive, dedicated web-based service determined a group membership feeling that increased the positive view of cycling as an environmentally friendly transport mode.

4 Information and Communication Technologies for smart city mobility

An important driver of smart urban mobility is definitely represented by Information and Communication Technologies especially tackling the issues represented by increasing economic societal and environmental pressure. A report by the EU Commission (2012) has listed the possible dimensions in which ICTs can strategically be used to facilitate more efficient mobility patterns towards an overall smart development of cities: (1) new trends and policy changes in urban environments; (2) ensuring that transport systems are accessible to all; (3) improving the safety and security of the users of urban transport networks; (4) reducing energy consumption, greenhouse gas emissions and air and noise pollution; (5) improving the efficiency and cost-effectiveness of the transportation of persons and of goods; and (6) enhancing the attractiveness and quality of the urban environment.

In order to fulfil the objectives mentioned earlier of smart mobility, several aspects of urban mobility can benefit CTs. Some of them are related to the public management of transport while others attain the private dimension. With respect to the public dimension, the first instance is represented by the provision of urban network management services, or the methods and technologies to allocate transport infrastructure and services. Another set of issues where ICTs play an important role is the management of speed by network users. This implies dynamic information mechanisms to warn users about the fact that they are exceeding the recommended speed limit and so they may incur in a fine. As it was shown in the preceding section of this chapter, this may have important effects on the enhancement of safety of urban mobility, especially for those (pedestrian and cyclists) who use more eco-friendly transport modes. ICTs are also used for Intelligent Speed Adaptation systems, where GPS tools can force a vehicle to travel at the maximum allowed speed. Lastly, there are the speed enforcement cameras that may either give raise to ticketing non-complying users or penalizing improper speeds by forcing drivers to stop temporarily at a dedicated traffic light. More generally, traffic control has historically been the first dimension of mobility in which ICTs have been used, both for central traffic management decision making and for specific junctions, nodes and arcs of the urban transport network. Traffic control systems encompass fixed and responsive systems. Access control to limited traffic zones represents an example of a fixed system that is used to minimize the degree of congestion and the environmental impact of mobility in historic centres of cities. Dynamic lanes (i.e. lanes that may be used in one direction during the peak hours in the morning when there is a large inflow of transport means to the city and in the other direction in the peak hours in the evening that witness an outflow from the city) are a possible instance of a responsive system.

The previous paragraph has discussed the aspects of public management where ICT can induce smart mobility. This paragraph will discuss some dimensions in which ICTs can foster smarter options of private mobility. The first one is represented by virtual mobility services, or a set of technologies (i.e. teleworking, teleshopping and telecommuting) that can be employed to provide viable alternatives for activities that require urban movements. A possible instance in this respect is represented by coworking centres that are being developed near the most crowded neighbourhoods in Paris and in Amsterdam that are showing, as an important side effect that is related to smart people, the cross-fertilization of ideas and the connections among firms. Another important issue where ICTs may have momentous influence in promoting smarter mobility options is travel planning. Multimodal journey planners are becoming very popular, via specific websites or smartphone applications, both to plan movement from a determined origin to a specific destination. These tools can either be related to the route choice and to the mode choice. Lastly, social networks are widely used to share information on transportation services and networks.

5 Conclusions

Given that smart mobility represents one of the important pillars for the deployment of overall smart urban development, policies related to this dimension should carefully take into account the effects on the other aspects of smartness of a city (economy, environment, people, living and governance). When freight urban mobility is considered, it is important to remind that the various involved stakeholders have heterogeneous interests that need to be reconciled and whose trade-offs have to be carefully estimated. The development an urban strategy for effective and efficient freight transport operations needs to consider the minimization of hindrance to residents and visitors.

With respect to passenger transport within a city, the incentives to pursue virtuous paths of smart development are related to the specific characteristics of urban neighbourhoods and of citizens. Local authorities should then carefully consider the various stages of travel demand decisions (route choice, mode choice and destination choice) to provide the most appropriate measure. One of the streams of economic research that may provide a good framework for the evaluation of alternative policies to alter the preferences of urban mobility users in the medium term is behavioural economics and its related principles. Lastly, safety and security of transport should be of paramount importance when considering mobility policies, especially with respect to the environmentally friendly alternatives. An important tool to tackle the problems arising from increasing economic, societal and environmental pressure in the urban context is definitely represented by ICTs. They can fruitfully be used both for the public management of transport and for its private dimension.

Bibliography

Avineri, E. (2012), On the use and potential of behavioural economics from the perspective of transport and climate change, *Journal of Transport Geography*, 24, 512–521.

Bamberg, S., Fujii, S., Friman, M. and Gärling, T. (2010), Behaviour theory and soft transport policy measures, *Transport Policy*, 18, 228–235.

Bartle, C., Avineri, E. and Chatterjee, K. (2011), *Information-sharing and community building: A case-study amongst commuter cyclists*, in The 43rd Annual UTSG (The Universities' Transport Study Group) Conference, Milton Keynes, UK.

Batty, M., Axhausen, K.W., Giannotti, F., Pozdnoukhov, A., Bazzani, A., Wachowicz, M., Ouzounis, G. and Portugali, Y. (2012), Smart cities of the future, *The European Physical Journal. Special topics*, 214, 481–518.

Browne, M., Allen, J., Toshinori, N., Patier, D. and Visser, J. (2012), Reducing social and environmental impacts from urban freight transport: A review of some major cities, *Procedia – Social and Behavioral Sciences*, 39, 19–33.

Caltrans. (2010), *Smart mobility 2010: A call to action for the New Decade*, Los Angeles, CA, Caltrans.

Dawnay, E. and Shah, H. (2005), *Behavioural economics: Seven principles for policymakers*, London, UK, New Economics Foundation.

EU Commission. (2012), *ICT concepts for optimization of mobility in smart cities*, Brussels, EU Commission.

Goodwin, P. (2008), Policy incentives to change behaviour in passenger transport, in *OECD/International Transport Forum on "Transport and Energy: The Challenge of Climate Change"*, Leipzig, Germany, pp. 28–30 May 2008.

Marcucci, E., Gatta, V., Valeri, E. and Stathopoulos, A. (2013), *Urban freight Transport modelling: An agent-specific approach*, Milano, FrancoAngeli.

Neirotti, P., De Marco, A., Cagliano, A.C., Mangano, G. and Scorrano, F. (2014), Current trends in Samrt City initiatives: Some stylised facts, *Cities*, 38, 25–36.

Rose, J.M. and Masiero, L. (2010), A comparison of the impacts of aspects of prospect theory on WTP/WTA estimated in preference and WTP/WTA space, *European Journal of Transport and Infrastructure Research*, 10 (4), 330–346.

Conclusion

Stefano Venier

1 Premise

Designing new opportunities of a smart rebound for the European economy became an exceedingly important concern in the last few years.

European Union institutions, together with all levels of governments, trade associations as well as scientific and technical bodies, have been involved in this crucial planning. In this framework, while the EU has put forward different valuable landscapes in this direction, the lack of an effective industrial policy risks maintaining design efforts far from real impacts.

In the meantime, different European industrial working groups tried to make concrete steps forward,[1] and the Hera Group with the initiatives taken by HerAcademy tried to contribute to this discussion along the lines suggested in this volume.

A scenario matching our action has been provided, according to which

> a circular economy, enabled by the technology revolution, allows Europe to grow resource productivity by up to 3 percent annually. This would generate a primary resource benefit of as much as euros0.6 trillion per year by 2030 to Europe's economies. In addition, it would generate euros1.2 trillion in non-resource and externality benefits, bringing the annual total benefits to around euros1.8 trillion versus today. This would translate into a GDP increase of as much as 7 percentage points relative to the current development scenario, with additional positive impacts on employment. Looking at the systems for three human needs (mobility, food, built environment) the study concludes that rapid technology adoption is necessary but not sufficient to capture the circular opportunity. Instead, circular principles must guide the transition differently from those that govern today's economy.
>
> (Ellen Macarthur Foundation, SUN and McKinsey Center for Business and Environment, 2015, p. 12)

This forecast is based on the idea that, while the European economy has generated unprecedented growth over the last century, we cannot just take it for granted that this growth will continue in the future, and even less so after the global crisis.

On the other hand, we are not necessarily headed toward the end of growth for technological and ecological reasons.[2]

The problem is to find solutions that involve answers to the issues raised by the social, environmental and economic sustainability. In this volume, we suggest that part of these solutions can be found investing in strategies combining the efforts for attaining "smart development" together with "smart community". This approach is similar to that recommending an "inclusive growth"[3] or "growth within".[4] The common emphasis on the need to exploit the existing potential for growth in local and global communities does not amount, however, to implying that easy way outs, based on the usual practices and customs, are on hand or that the reproduction of standard local patterns is enough. Instead, investments in new knowledge and infrastructures are needed and systemic changes to Europe's economic governance and government at the different levels are required.

In a knowledge-driven society, the concept of smartness embodies innovative elements in a by-now conventional scheme. Its evocative capacity relies on its intrinsic multi-dimensionality (social, economic, institutional) and the innovative element that underlies it. Its wideness and complexity, however, raises many issues. This book addresses them by approaching the concept of smart development across its different dimensions from both a theoretical and applied perspective. The notion of smartness is viewed as a fruitful combination of place-based development paths that combine the specificities of each area in terms of industrial sector, human capital and social capital. In particular, it emphasizes the endogenous elements and the bottom-up logic, stressing the involvement of the local "smart communities" as the subjects of strategies for taking advantage of the "opportunities to improve people's lives both by modernizing key infrastructures (such as for energy, water, or transportation) and by using information technology (often with open data) to enhance city operations and services" (PCAST, 2016, p. v).[5]

Within the framework of Europe 2020 strategy for smart sustainable and inclusive growth, all the contributions draw useful insights on the managerial and institutional tools that can promote the vocation of each local context, with particular attention to metropolitan areas.

In the first part of the volume, each essay dealt with critical issues related to the main single components of smart development: smart specialization on the supply side, the smart city on the demand side and the synergy between the two sides. A relevant reconsideration of traditional visions of local development *vis-à-vis* this new notion has been carried out because it is deemed an essential driver for change.

The second part of the book focused on the construction of appropriate sets of indicators and on the application of smart development policies in various Italian regions by highlighting both weaknesses and opportunities that characterize Italy in a comparative European perspective.

The third part of the volume investigated how smart development can be governed through smart communities combining the available tools of government and governance together.

This final chapter synthesizes the main achievements of the book and derives some tentative insight with regard to the potential contributions of multi-utilities to place-based policy enlightened by a smart development approach.

2 How to address smart specialization issues in the Italian framework?

With reference to smart specialization, the different essays consider the relationship between smart specialization and regional policies after the shift of the smart specialization strategy from a sort of neutral sectoral policy, based on an evolutionary theoretical model, to a regional cohesion policy founded on a place-based approach that differentiates the innovative potential of each region according to its technological specialization and learning capacity. Smart specialization takes into account the specificities of each area in terms of industrial sector, human capital and social capital, by promoting the vocation of each local context, urban or not. However, especially in the European context and under the Monetary Union, this approach can further emphasize gaps and differences between regions. While some regions can obtain higher competitiveness and economic performances, others risk progressive marginalization. This positive approach must indeed be accompanied by a strategy of interregional integration to be carried out at the European level. Accordingly a crucial issue related to smart specialization strategy deals with institutional innovation and, in particular, with the process of institutional building as a corollary of the policies of smart development on the supply side. On the basis of the possible methods of interaction between the different institutional sub-systems (coherence, hierarchy, complementarity), we can identify some properties of institutions qualifying for the smart development in accordance with the categories of embeddedness, relatedness and connectivity. Taken together, these properties can be understood as an attempt to address the problems of inconsistency, lack of coordination and poor complementarity underlying the inter-institutional relations, which are likely to inhibit the processes of smart development if they uniquely rely on the endogenous element and the bottom-up logic. Smart specialization thus requires a participative approach involving the actors of the innovative system, including firms. This means that research and innovation policies must consider local contexts in which they are implemented. However, this approach cannot be in itself a final solution to orient all regions to positive and successful trajectories. It can lead to internally coherent policies that create synergy and multiplier effects, or at the opposite side, it can generate widespread effects on several objectives, not coherent each other and not adequate to the context.

The diversity of smart specialization strategies at the regional level and their potential for original development paths based on innovation is well described with regard to two major Italian regions: Lombardia and Emilia-Romagna. In Emilia-Romagna, new forms of collaboration between private communities and public institutions have been built while bottom-up processes concerning innovative start-ups in creative and digital industries are taking place all around the region. On the other hand, in Lombardia, the smart specialization model is grounded on a "quadruple helix" perspective that adds innovation users to the classical "triple helix"-based network centred on the relationship between industry, university and government.[6]

3 Multi-dimensionality of the smart city concept and implications for Italian urban areas

In this book the concept of smart city embraces different dimensions and is associated with a plurality of benchmarks for the wide scope of participating actors. The smartness of an urban area is achieved through the concurrent combination of single aspects that range from innovation to education and quality of life, each of them differing from time to time. The distinguishing feature of a smart city is therefore its capability to combine together the pursuit of social, technological, environmental and cultural development. Accordingly, a crucial issue related to smart city strategy concerns the achievement of sustainability requirements and reorientation in behaviours in the market for social goods and services as corollaries of the policies of smart development on the demand side.

In this perspective, a wide set of related issues has been debated. First, a holistic and multi-dimensional approach to the concept of smart city innovation in each dimension constitutes the pillar on which policies aimed at transforming cities ought to be based. In turn, innovation is related to a plurality of dimensions too, so that actual policies will result from complex interactions involving institutions, society, the knowledge base and the economic constraints and opportunities. Different skills and types of knowledge are involved both in the analysis of the concept and in the prediction of the relevant applications. Second, the multi-dimensionality of the concept together with the pervasive effects of the policies implies the existence of complementary aspects for the improvement of the quality, efficiency and competitiveness of an urban or metropolitan area. This raises the need for coordination between different actors through the valorization of smart community mechanisms. Urban development is a complex process involving different dimensions, and the direction of the related policies mainly rests on local actors, on their preferences and individual objectives. Third, the smart city is grounded on the crucial role of people as conscious actors in the processes of transformation of the urban economic structure, which interacts with the critical role of innovation. This calls for a better understanding of the links between human capital, skills' portfolios and job creation/destruction processes in modern urban areas. Fourth, mobility is one of the important dimensions that allow a city to foster smart development paths. Although ICTs are an important tool to support smart mobility and to tackle the problems arising from increasing economic, societal and environmental pressure in the urban context, it can be accompanied by a wide set of policies that takes into account the heterogeneous interests of the involved stakeholders. Finally, the governance system, which is based on the interaction between communities, is required to promote accessibility to information, transparency, public involvement in the decisions making process, citizens' participation and social inclusion. Moreover, there should be no restriction on information flows, but there should be sufficient coordination between different levels of government. Indeed, the smart city perspective does not eliminate the risk of a lack of coordination. For instance, many environmental issues cannot be resolved locally but require policies on a larger scale, primarily to internalize, at least partially, the negative externalities that characterize them.

A common substrate is that modern urban areas rely on the quality of services provided to citizens – many of them with a social nature – and on good governance requirements concerning their production and provision. The construction of the smart city thus underpins a set of coordinated interventions able to interpret and revise the needs of users, consumers and citizens. Urban development is a complex process involving different dimensions, and the direction of the related policies mainly rests on local actors, on their preferences and individual objectives. By keeping in mind this, it is important that the policy maker takes into account the expectations of local actors when engaging in smart urban planning. Before engaging themselves in every type of technology-based project, cities should find a balance among conflicting and sometimes contradictory objectives, while moving towards holistic models of sustainable development. Moreover, in the elaboration and application of smart city projects, each single urban area should differentiate projects and interventions according to its strengths and weaknesses. This would allow them to develop projects in a close inter-relation between the competitiveness of its economic structure, the division of labour, the degree of inequality, the environmental issues and the drivers of urban areas attractiveness. In this respect, the different essays emphasize the need of including "soft" factors when assessing the degree of smartness of a urban area in presence of dimensions of the smart city concept that are not directly related to environmental and social dimensions, such as those variables associated with culture and tourism, on the one hand, and skills and human capital, on the other.

This role is particularly relevant in Italy, where the cultural dimension is strengthened by the historical and artistic content that distinguish most of the cities. Italian cities are part of an urban continental framework characterized by the restoration of the existing stock in terms of housing, infrastructures, transports and energy and cultural sites and by hard budget constraints that make large investments in infrastructure projects not affordable. In most of Italian cities, technological innovation and social cohesion must cope with outdated infrastructures, while natural, historic and cultural heritage needs to be valued in accordance with the major potential of our cities. A peculiarity of the Italian context refers to small cities, where 19% of the Italian population is concentrated. Accordingly, not only can the adoption of smart policies help small urban centres increase the range and efficiency of their services,[7] but also the whole economic system can benefit from the sustainable development of small urban communities. By taking into account such specificities, many Italian cities are making their way towards smart development, despite the economic scenario characterized by the shortage of resources and the lack of concrete models to be taken as benchmarks. However, the weaknesses of Italian cities, which are largely structural, cannot be addressed only at a local level. On the contrary, they require support and coordination of the upper levels of government, through the adoption of coordinated efforts able to provide strategic opportunities and solutions in the overall process of urban agglomeration.

4 Smart learning in smart communities

The main actor of the smart-oriented processes is the "smart community", which can be viewed as a social or economic network that successfully addresses the challenges of change and innovation through cooperation between its members. The smart community is a virtual place of application of new technological solutions and more generally a source of sustainable development paths. It is grounded on collective learning processes that improve network capabilities thanks to the interaction among their members. The different essays emphasize the learning process arising from the interplay between technology availability and emerging collective behaviours. The term community also put value on the local dimension and emphasizes the trust and relationship components that constitute social capital.[8] The local communities are thus considered as subjects of smart development strategies. However, the effects of smart communities on social sustainability are ambiguous. They can be either an opportunity for enhancing fairness or a threat that may lead to an undesirable growth of inequality, even within a city that can be otherwise considered as smart. In the second hypothesis, the boundary line depends on the long-term sustainability of urban areas at both individual and aggregate level. A typical risk in this respect is represented by progress/technical change associated with smart city projects. Indeed, it may accelerate the obsolescence of knowledge and skills to an extent that penalizes low-qualified workers.[9] This is likely to create social inequalities that may be hardly compatible with the other attributes of growth and development evoked by the concept of smartness as it has been outlined in the European context. However, modern groups and communities are not necessarily held together by tradition, interpersonal relations and non-rational bonds (Storper, 2005). In a smart community, active participation and internal cohesion help in building new ties that can eventually lead to original models for managing knowledge, either within the organizations or in the regional systems, based on the linkage between individuals and groups that have complementary skills or technologies.

When we refer to smart communities, it thus becomes increasingly clear that the "smart" label covers many domains; most of them are correlated and sometimes overlapping. The first domain deals with the creation and the use of different types of knowledge in order to generate smart development. This requires that an appropriate organization of knowledge within and outside the firm should be made available. Such organization should facilitate acquisition of human capital and deployment of new technologies through intra-group solidarity and activate collective action that trigger knowledge spillovers and generate increasing returns to knowledge investments (Easterly et al., 2006). The second domain deals with the technological dimension, with particular emphasis on ICTs. The pre-condition to possess the "right" knowledge is more and more based on our ability to gather, store and process data. The "internet of things" is gaining more and more ground and will help a better management of many aspects, providing better services where and when they are needed. However, predictive models, particularly when human behaviour is part of prediction, must be taken cautiously while fallback arrangements should be planned together with satisfactory solutions. An increasing number of decisions crucially depend on data availability and information must be reliable.[10]

The relationship between knowledge and technology in the construction of smart communities leads to the cross-cutting question about the effectiveness of learning processes in a smart development perspective. The contributions on these topics raise two main critical aspects. The first relates to the obsolescence of skills, associated with the dynamics of skill-biased technical change, that a boost to sector specialization may determine. The second is the polarization of the demand for human capital determined by innovative processes. This implies an inclusion of this issue in the policy agenda for smart development in order to drive the growth of human capital and the access to education and training in accordance with the specialization paths. In particular, this requires the rethinking of the role of the external organization of knowledge in upgrading human capital of the workforce in the local labour markets in order to cope with the new "knowledge needs". Adequate policies for training and advanced education are essential to contribute to smart development processes. For instance, while in strongest regions the education and training system is an essential component of the virtuous circle, in other regions, such activities must be highly tailored and supported with other policies in order to effectively contribute to growth and competitiveness. However, the objectives identified by smart development policies, although aimed at local development, are not always addressable with interventions on a limited scale, with the consequent recognition of the need for some form of top-down action and coordination among various local actors in order to comply with investments required.

5 Multi-utilities as strategic enablers of smart development in smart communities

In a smart development perspective, multi-utilities can become strategic enablers for the local systems in which they operate. Within a smart specialization strategy, they can facilitate new innovative processes by driving the potential of the new technological infrastructure towards the delivery of new and/or more effective services by providing incentives for citizens' involvement and in assessing their needs.

If cities have to support sustainable development it is essential to understand how individuals and networks are actually behaving and working in each location. At the same time, data derived directly or indirectly from human activities that refer to all aspects of daily life are increasingly collected from administrative sources. Among the numerous examples, we can include data generated by city governments and utilities on the supply and demand of urban services (e.g. energy, water, public transportation, zoning, public spaces).

Starting from this premise, the *Report to the President: Technology and the Future of Cities* of President's Council of Advisors on Science and Technology gives concrete suggestions of how multi-utilities can bring in crucial inputs for smart development in smart communities:

> [U]niversities and national laboratories have powerful modeling tools and access to data about city buildings, demographics, employment, and transportation – but not utility usage or utility reliability data. In isolation, these data sources yield some insight into issues such as the interdependencies between access to transportation and opportunities for employment or education. Combined, such data could provide guidance for more effective programs aimed at energy costs, allowing for investment in addressing root causes (e.g. insulating walls) rather than ongoing symptoms (e.g. assistance with heating bills).
>
> (PCAST, 2016, pp. 48–49)

Moreover,

> the danger of viewing cities as collections of independent, vertically integrated systems (buildings, transportation, utilities, etc.) is that innovation at the intersection of sectors, where often the most promising solutions lie, is crippled by the discontinuities between these separate systems. This is true even if within each vertical there are open standards for (internal) interoperability.
>
> (PCAST, 2016, pp. 51–52)

However, the idiosyncratic interactions between users, agents and institutions are sources of variance that can also become relevant for the innovation outcome in terms of value creation. Users or citizens are users and appliers of knowledge. Thereby they are thought to contribute with a region-specific habits and experiences. In line with this model, new innovative services and solutions can be developed with the involvement of users in their role of co-developers and co-creators as long as they agree to cooperate and share the resulting benefits.[11] The proximity between producers and consumers that can characterize public utilities could be able to favour social interaction and may induce direct and indirect networks effects.[12] Furthermore, in a smart city framework, multi-utilities are key actors in supporting and orienting the collective learning with a multi focal and integrated approach, thanks to their nature of highly structured networks with a visible and tangible role in the urban space. In a direct way, they propose and enable new forms and opportunities of behaviour on the demand side. In an indirect way, they contribute to reinforce the place-based knowledge systems. Indeed a large part of the ongoing transformation of urban areas stems from the collaboration between public and private agents, in particular between local governments and utilities.

Overall, the peculiar nature of the multi-utilities as corporate, shared value-oriented organizations controlled by a balanced mix of public and private shareholders can favour the cognitive interactions between the different actors at local level. On the other hand, multi-utilities can share information, knowledge and skills both within and outside the organization and get results that would be unattainable by less co-operative firms. Thanks to the commitment to corporate social responsibility each stakeholder will have an interest in cooperating because she/he is expecting to get tangible returns from the others' efforts. If multi-utilities accomplish in doing so and build up a proper reputation across the community they can eventually contribute to positive and innovative agreements between demand-side and supply-side interests. Multi-utilities can then create value through stakeholders' cooperation by establishing complementarities between networks and markets in which they operate. To conclude, multi-utilities can contribute to the development of learning communities by leveraging on original combinations of knowledge, innovation and ethics. This role would eventually enhance the capability of the city, metropolitan area and region to generate smart communities.

Notes

1 Among the others, we can mention the contributions by the Ellen Macarthur Foundation et al. (2015) and the project in the high-tech strategy known as "Industrie 4.0".
2 This suggestion comes among the others from Piketty (2014).
3 See for instance the report prepared for the World Economic Forum by Samans et al. (2015).
4 See again Ellen Macarthur Foundation et al. (2015).
5 The report on *Technology and the Future of Cities*, prepared by the President's Council of Advisors on Science and Technology of the United States, seems to take the same direction trying to complement and go beyond the ideas captured by the label "smart city". It reminds us how:

> These opportunities illuminate new directions for place-based policy – investments to renew infrastructures will have greater payoff when they incorporate innovations rather than merely replace old and failing systems. Combined, the innovations that are increasingly within reach provide an opportunity to revamp how cities operate at all levels and for all stakeholders. Transforming cities around the world in this way is already a race – one that the United States cannot afford to lose. It is generating demand for new products, new companies, and new skilled jobs in the effort to produce the best urban environments.
>
> (PCAST, 2016, p. v)

6 See for instance Leydesdorff and Etzkowitz (2003).
7 And the consequent improvement in quality of life.
8 Reference should be made to Bourdieu (1985), Coleman (1988), Putnam et al. (1993) and Putnam (2000).
9 The so-called skill-biased technical change.
10 Redundancy and resilience should be considered relevant side by side with efficiency.

11 As shown in the literature, mutual monitoring and high levels of co-operation can work even in communities of substantial size (Bowles and Gintis, 2002).
12 For instance, by involving public and private economic actors operating in the innovation system multi-utilities can contribute to the sharing of results in case of public consultations.

Bibliography

Bourdieu, P. (1985), The forms of capital, in J. Richardson (ed.), *Handbook of theory and research for the sociology of education*, New York, Greenwood, pp. 241–258.

Bowles, S. and Gintis, H. (2002), Social capital and community governance, *The Economic Journal*, 112, F419–F436.

Coleman, J.S. (1988), Social capital in the creation of human capital, *American Journal of Sociology*, 94, 909–930.

Easterly, W., Ritzen, J. and Woolcock, M. (2006), Social cohesion, institutions, and growth, *Economics & Politics*, 18, 103–120.

Ellen Macarthur Foundation, SUN and McKinsey Center for Business and Environment. (2015), Growth within: A circular economy vision for a competitive Europe, Ellen Macarthur Foundation, SUN and McKinsey Center for Business and Environment, June.

Leydesdorff, L. and Etzkowitz, H. (2003), Can "the public" be considered as a fourth helix in university–industry–government relations? Report of the fourth Triple Helix conference. *Science and Public Policy*, 30, 55–61.

Piketty, T. (2014), *Capital in the twenty-first century*, Cambridge, MA, The Belknap Press of Harvard University Press.

President's Council of Advisors on Science and Technology (PCAST) (2016), *Report to the President. Technology and the future of cities*, February, Washington, DC, Executive Office of the President of the United States (www.whitehouse.gov/ostp/pcast).

Putnam, R.D. (2000), *Bowling alone: The collapse and revival of American community*, New York, Simon and Schuster.

Putnam, R.D., Leonardi, R. and Nanetti, R.Y. (1993), *Making democracy work: Civic traditions in modern Italy*, Princeton, NJ, Princeton University Press.

Samans, R., Blanke, J., Corrigan, G. and Drzeniek, M. (2015), *The Inclusive growth and development report 2015*, Geneva, World Economic Forum.

Storper, M. (2005), Society, community, and economic development, *Studies in Comparative International Development*, 39, 30–57.

Author index

Subject index

Note: Italicized page numbers indicate a figure on the corresponding page. Page numbers in bold indicate a table on the corresponding page.

For Product Safety Concerns and Information please contact our EU
representative GPSR@taylorandfrancis.com Taylor & Francis Verlag GmbH,
Kaufingerstraße 24, 80331 München, Germany

Printed and bound by CPI Group (UK) Ltd, Croydon, CR0 4YY

01/05/2025

01858459-0004